TSUBASA

15

CLAMP

TRANSLATED AND ADAPTED BY
William Flanagan

LETTERED BY
Dana Hayward

BALLANTINE BOOKS · NEW YORK

Tsubasa, vol. 15 is a work of fiction. Names, characters, places, and incidents are the products of the author's imagination or are used fictitiously. Any resemblance to actual events, locales, or persons, living or dead, is entirely coincidental.

A Del Rey Manga/Kodansha Trade Paperback Original

Published in the United States by Del Rey Books, an imprint of The Random House Publishing Group, a division of Random House, Inc., New York.

DEL REY is a registered trademark and the Del Rey colophon is a trademark of Random House, Inc.

Publication rights arranged through Kodansha, Ltd.

First published in Japan in 2006 by Kodansha, Ltd., Tokyo.

ISBN 978-0-345-49831-1

Printed in the United States of America

www.delreymanga.com

9 8 7 6 5 4 3 2 1

Translation and adaptation—William Flanagan
Lettering—Dana Hayward

Contents

Tsubasa crosses over with *xxxHOLiC*. Although it isn't necessary to read *xxxHOLiC* to understand the events in *Tsubasa*, you'll get to see the same events from different perspectives if you read both series!

Honorifics Explained

Throughout the Del Rey Manga books, you will find Japanese honorifics left intact in the translations. For those not familiar with how the Japanese use honorifics and, more important, how they differ from American honorifics, we present this brief overview.

Politeness has always been a critical facet of Japanese culture. Ever since the feudal era, when Japan was a highly stratified society, use of honorifics—which can be defined as polite speech that indicates relationship or status—has played an essential role in the Japanese language. When addressing someone in Japanese, an honorific usually takes the form of a suffix attached to one's name (example: "Asuna-san"), is used as a title at the end of one's name, or appears in place of the name itself (example: "Negi-sensei," or simply "Sensei!").

Honorifics can be expressions of respect or endearment. In the context of manga and anime, honorifics give insight into the nature of the relationship between characters. Many English translations leave out these important honorifics, and therefore distort the feel of the original Japanese. Because Japanese honorifics contain nuances that English honorifics lack, it is our policy at Del Rey not to translate them. Here, instead, is a guide to some of the honorifics you may encounter in Del Rey Manga.

-san: This is the most common honorific, and is equivalent to Mr., Miss, Ms., or Mrs. It is the all-purpose honorific and can be used in any situation where politeness is required.

-sama: This is one level higher than "-san." It is used to confer great respect.

-dono: This comes from the word "tono," which means "lord." It is an even higher level than "-sama" and confers utmost respect.

-kun: This suffix is used at the end of boys' names to express familiarity or endearment. It is also sometimes used by men among friends, or when addressing someone younger or of a lower station.

-chan: This is used to express endearment, mostly toward girls. It is also used for little boys, pets, and even among lovers. It gives a sense of childish cuteness.

Bozu: This is an informal way to refer to a boy, similar to the English terms "kid" and "squirt."

Sempai/Senpai: This title suggests that the addressee is one's senior in a group or organization. It is most often used in a school setting, where underclassmen refer to their upperclassmen as "sempai." It can also be used in the workplace, such as when a newer employee addresses an employee who has seniority in the company.

Kohai: This is the opposite of "sempai," and is used toward underclassmen in school or newcomers in the workplace. It connotes that the addressee is of a lower station.

Sensei: Literally meaning "one who has come before," this title is used for teachers, doctors, or masters of any profession or art.

-[blank]: This is usually forgotten in these lists, but it is perhaps the most significant difference between Japanese and English. The lack of honorific means that the speaker has permission to address the person in a very intimate way. Usually, only family, spouses, or very close friends have this kind of permission. Known as *yobisute*, it can be gratifying when someone who has earned the intimacy starts to call one by one's name without an honorific. But when that intimacy hasn't been earned, it can be very insulting.

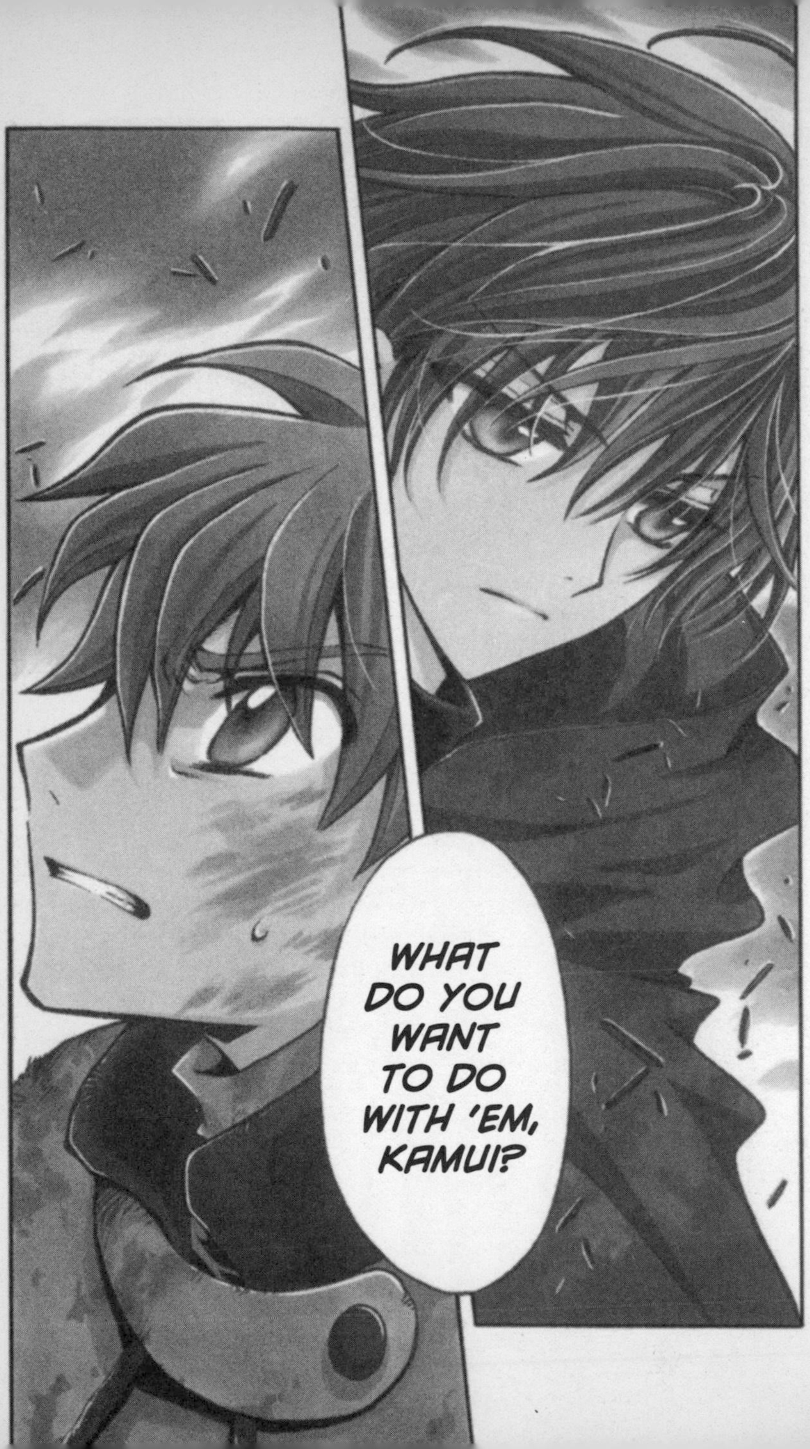
WHAT DO YOU WANT TO DO WITH 'EM, KAMUI?

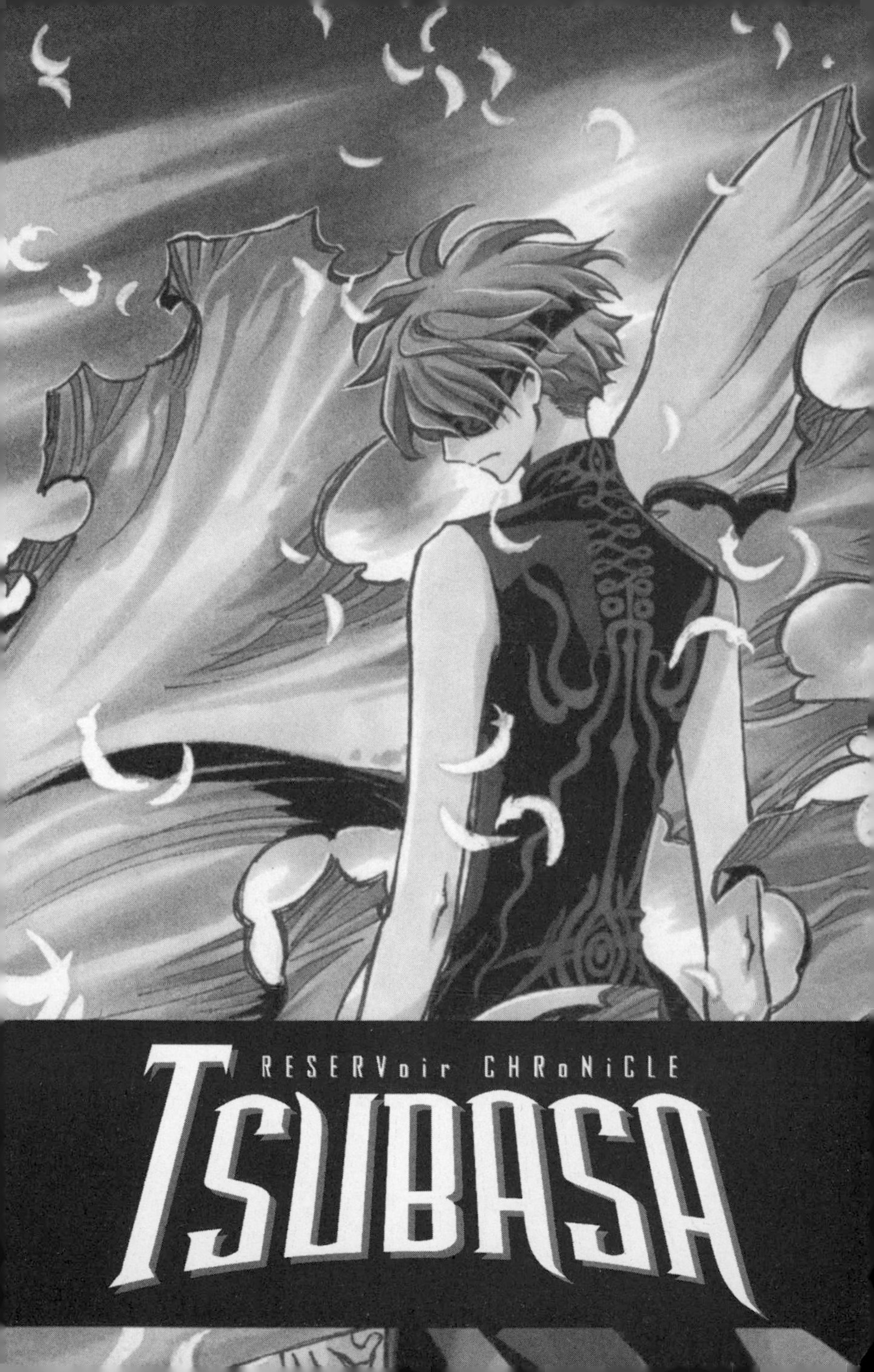
RESERVoir CHRoNiCLE
TSUBASA

Chapitre.109
Child of the Gods

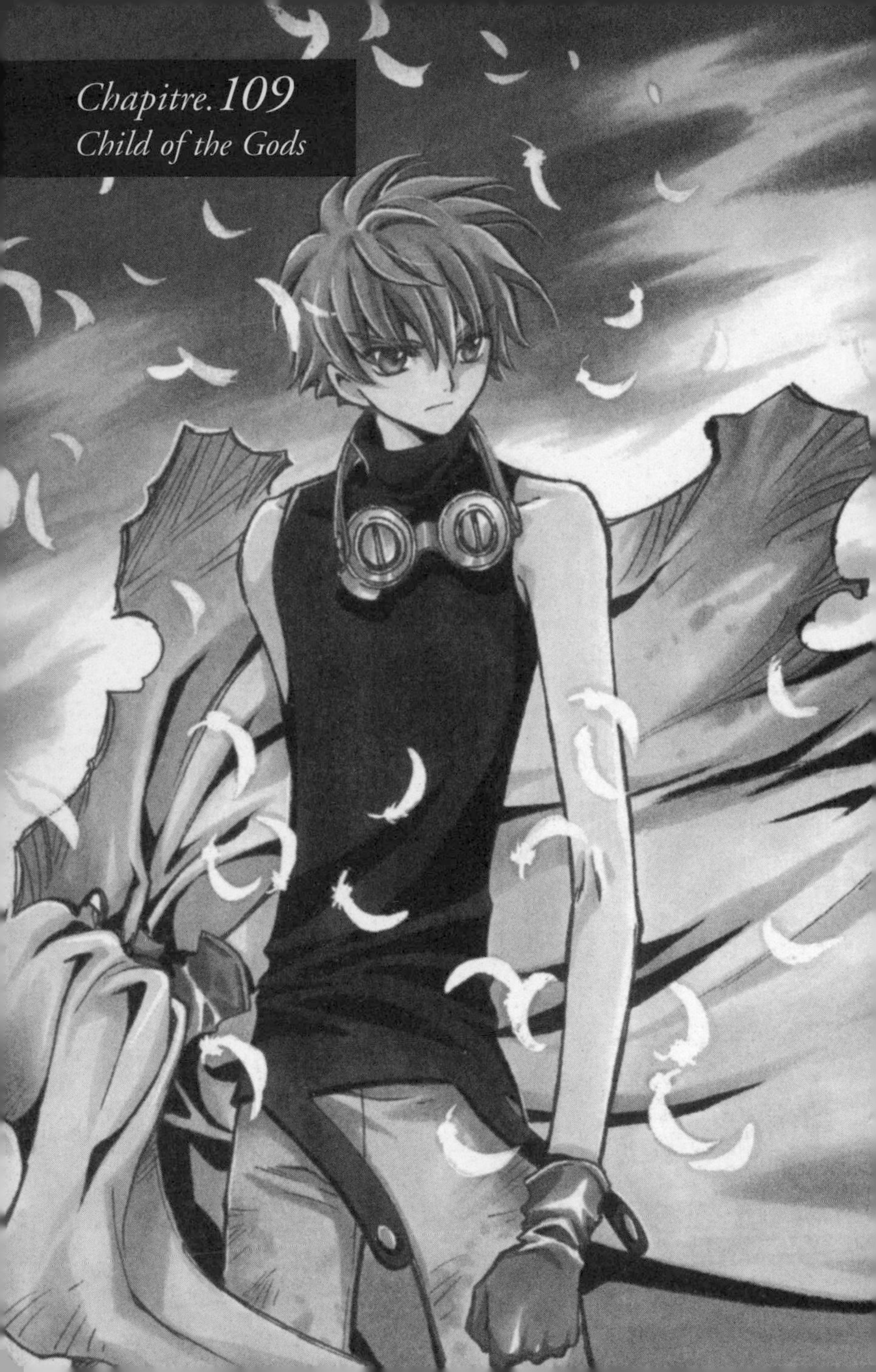

ツバサ
RESERVoir CHRoNiCLE

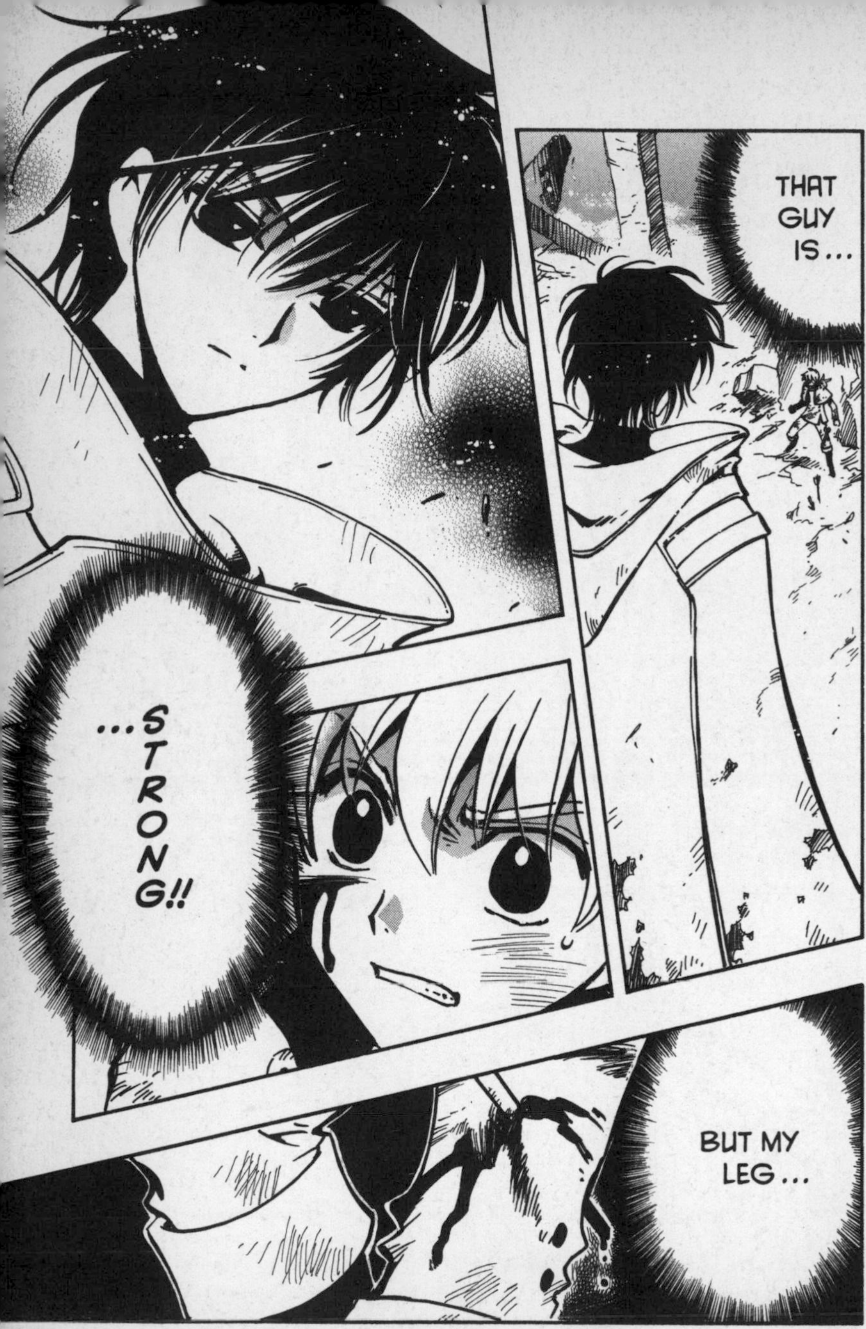
THAT GUY IS...
...STRONG!!
BUT MY LEG...

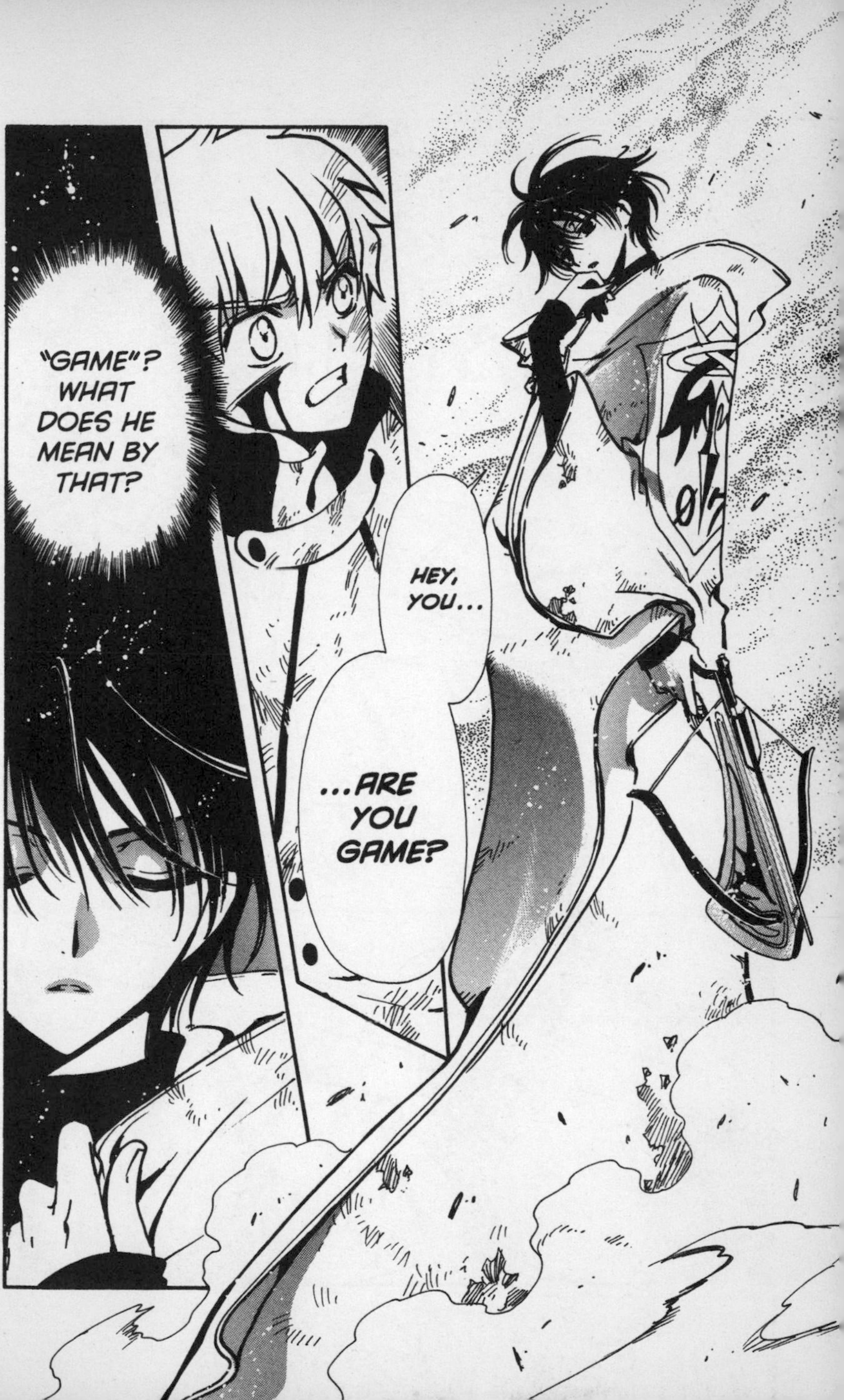
HEY, YOU...
...ARE YOU GAME?
"GAME"? WHAT DOES HE MEAN BY THAT?

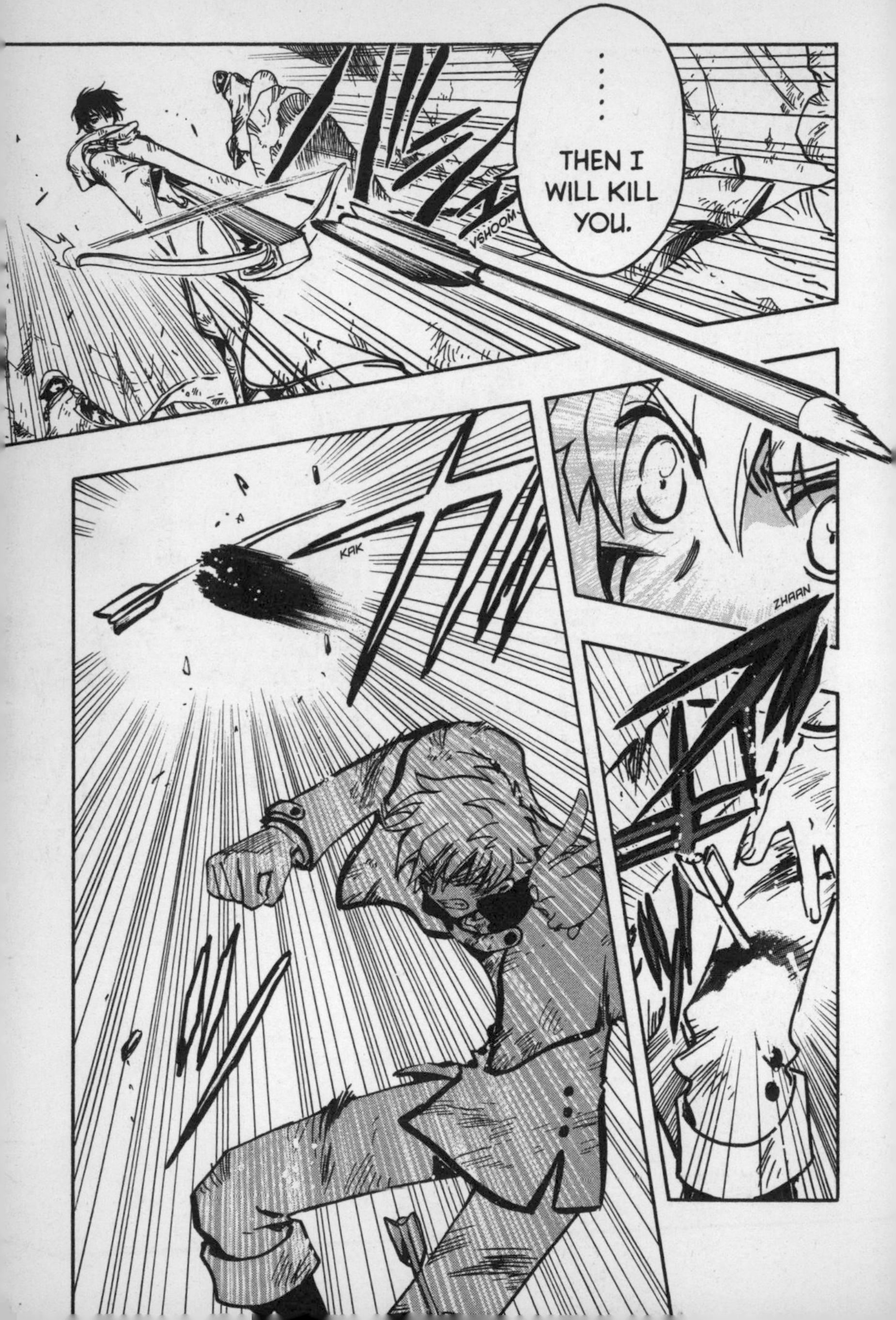
......
THEN I WILL KILL YOU.
VSHOOM
KAK
ZHAAN

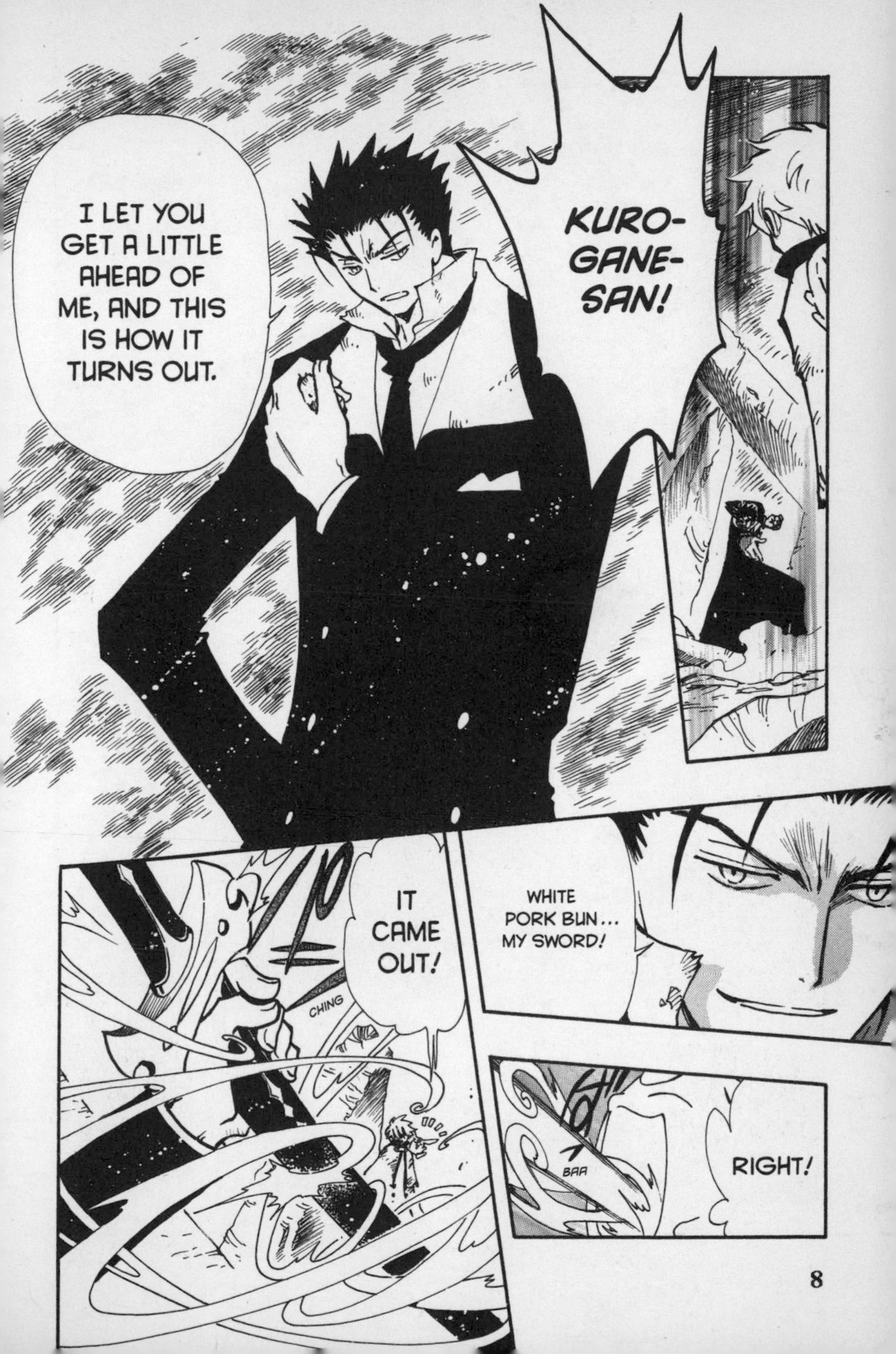
KURO-GANE-SAN!
I LET YOU GET A LITTLE AHEAD OF ME, AND THIS IS HOW IT TURNS OUT.
WHITE PORK BUN... MY SWORD!
RIGHT!
BAA
IT CAME OUT!
CHING

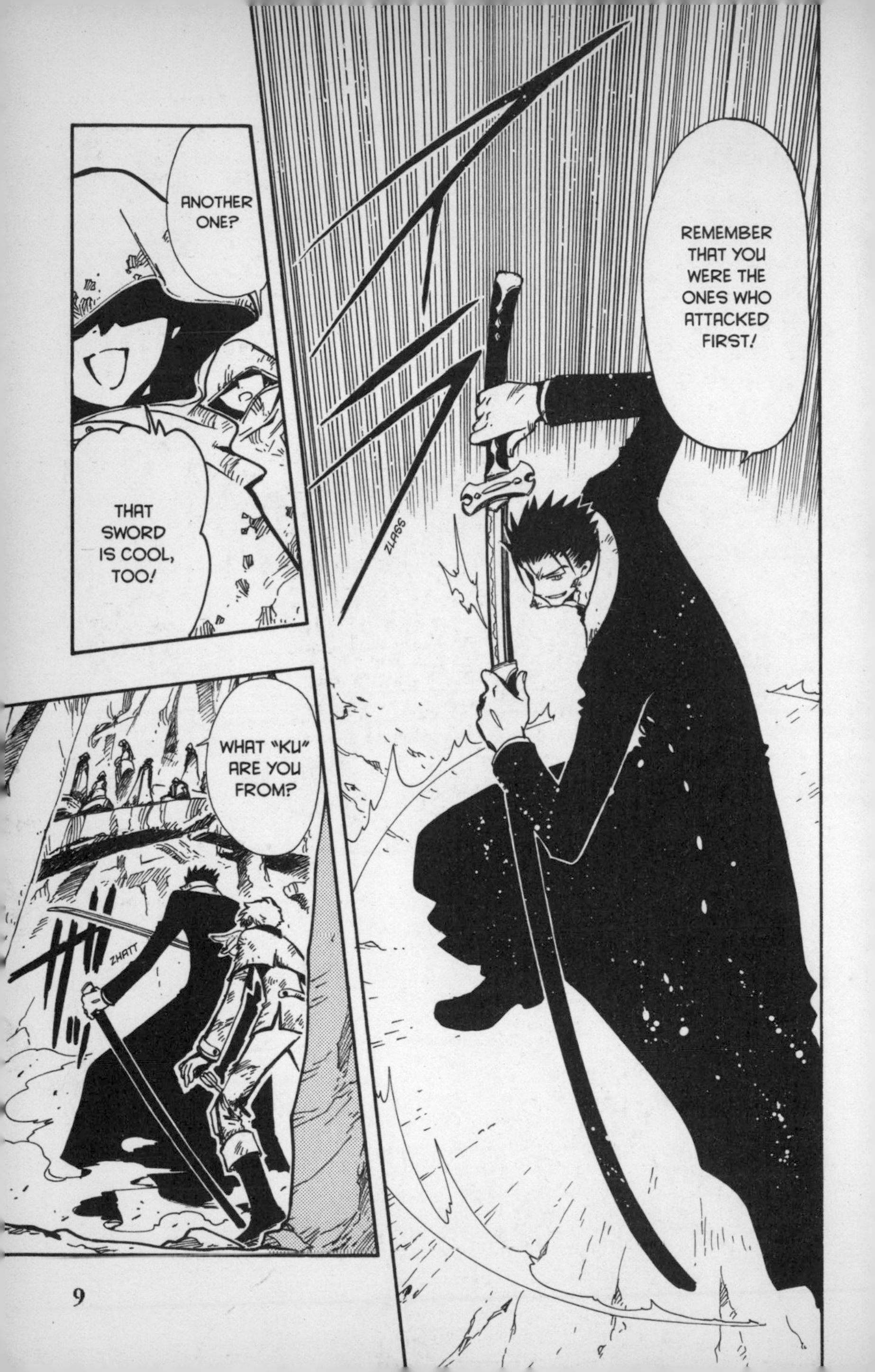
REMEMBER THAT YOU WERE THE ONES WHO ATTACKED FIRST!
ZLASS
ANOTHER ONE?
THAT SWORD IS COOL, TOO!
WHAT "KU" ARE YOU FROM?
ZHATT

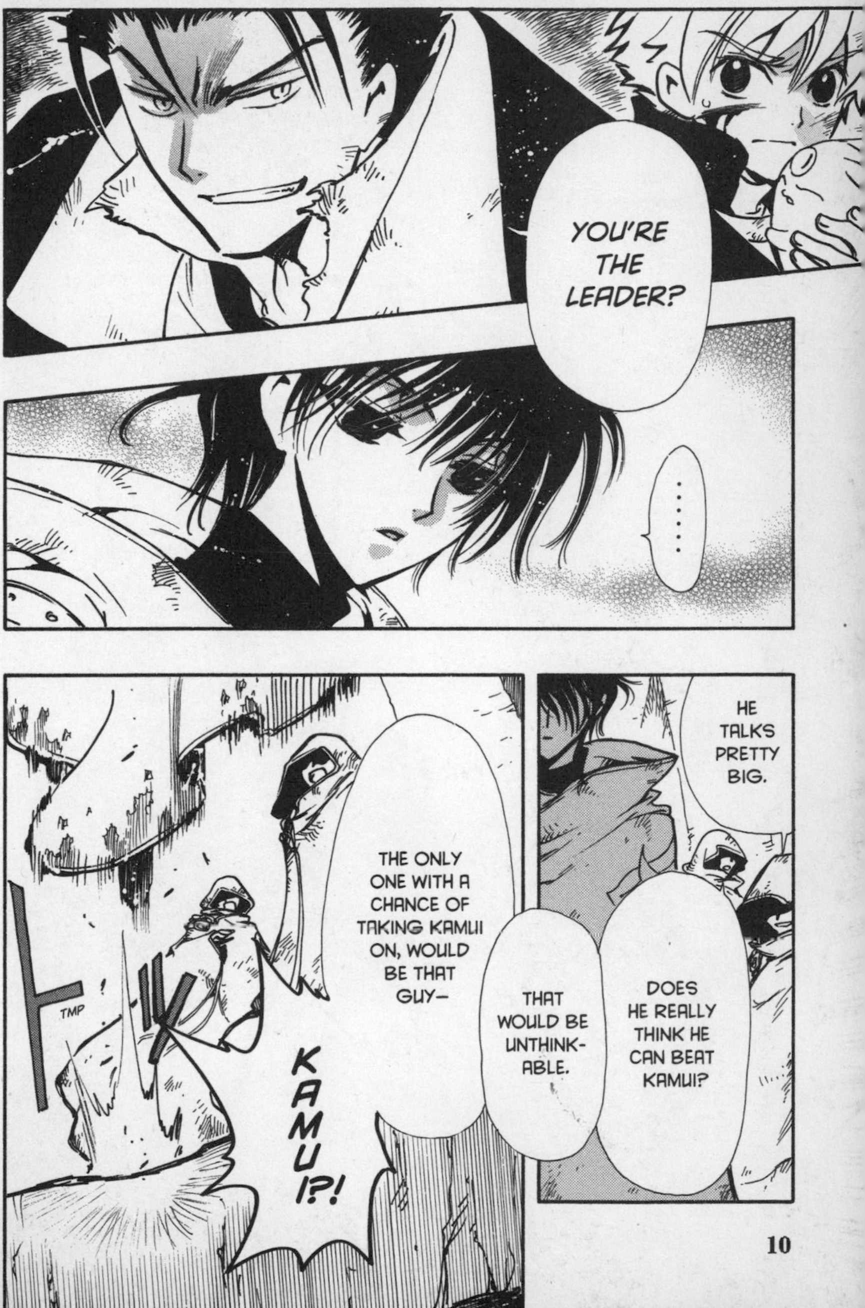
YOU'RE THE LEADER?
......
HE TALKS PRETTY BIG.
DOES HE REALLY THINK HE CAN BEAT KAMUI?
THAT WOULD BE UNTHINK-ABLE.
THE ONLY ONE WITH A CHANCE OF TAKING KAMUI ON, WOULD BE THAT GUY—
KAMUI!?!
TMP

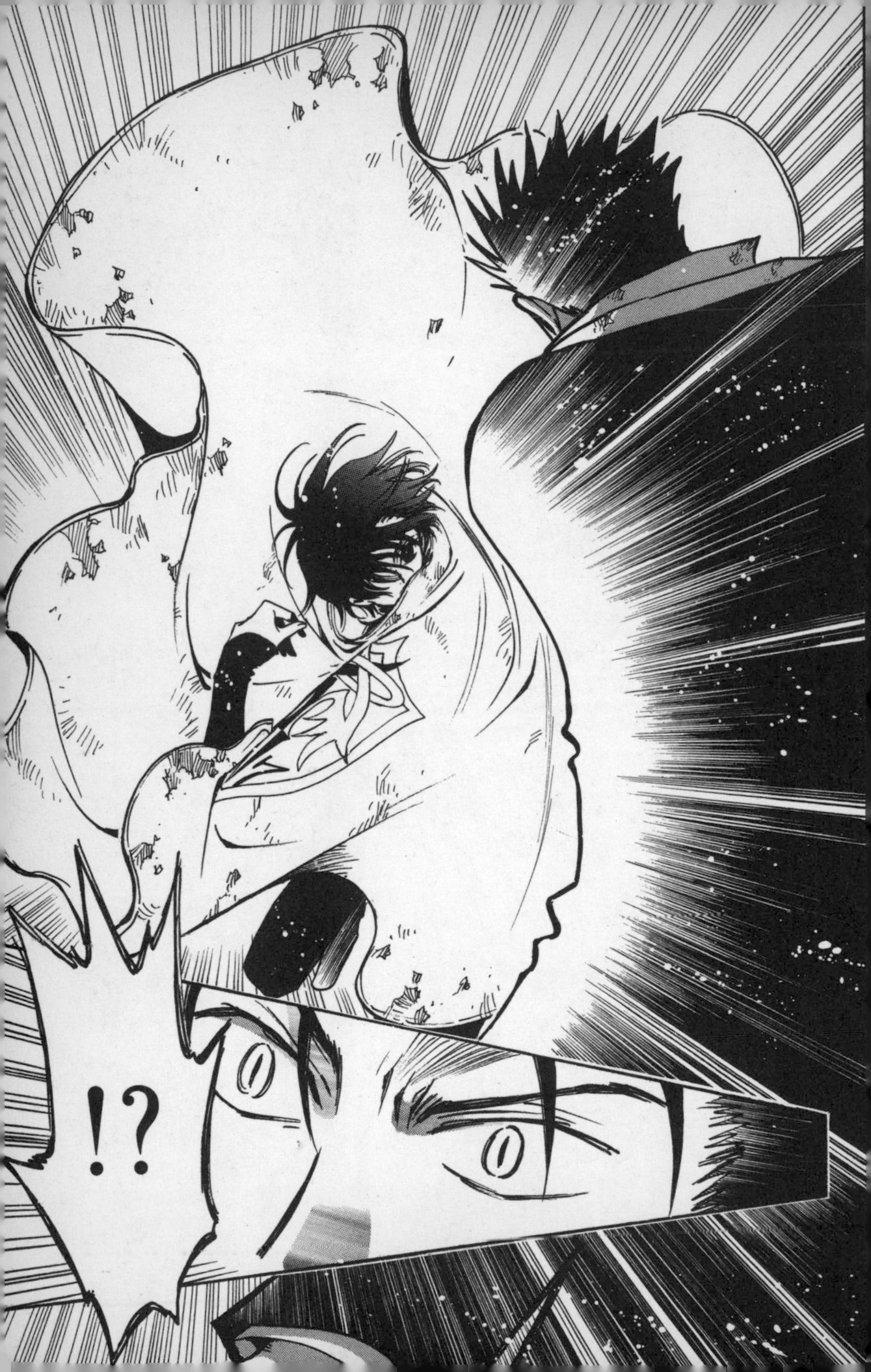
!?

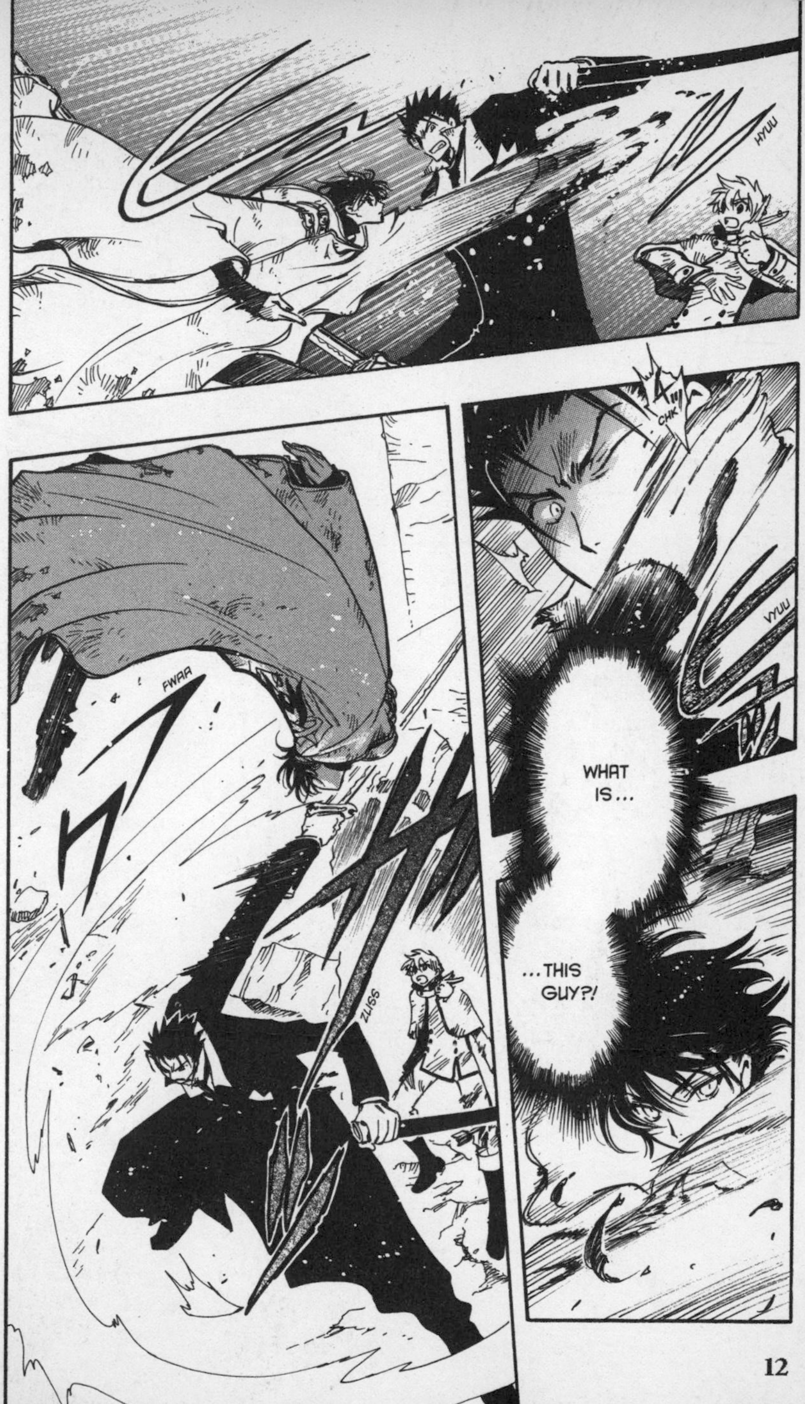
HYUU
CHK
VYUU
WHAT IS...
...THIS GUY?!
FWAA
ZLISS

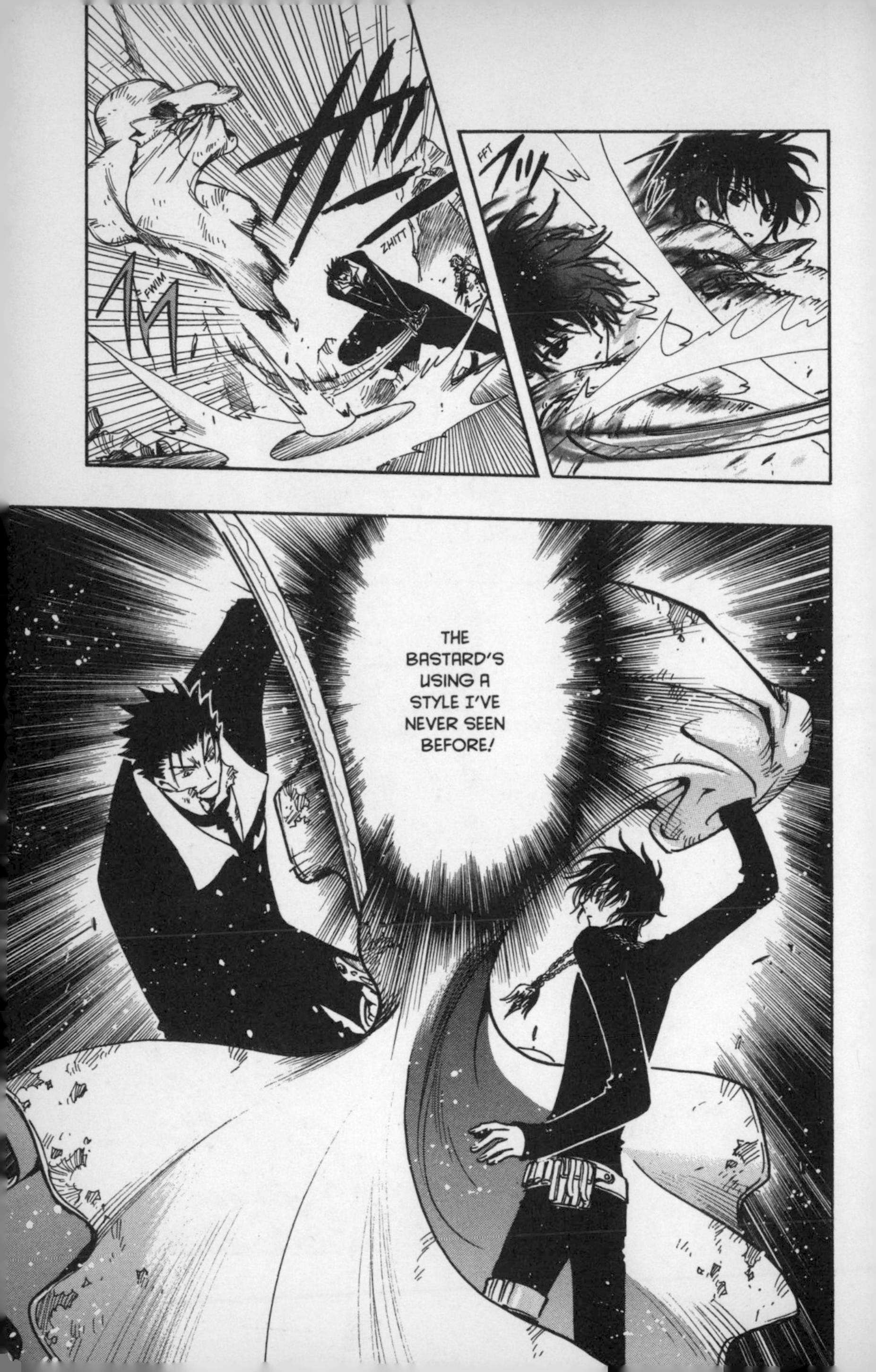
FFT
ZHITT
FWIM
THE BASTARD'S USING A STYLE I'VE NEVER SEEN BEFORE!

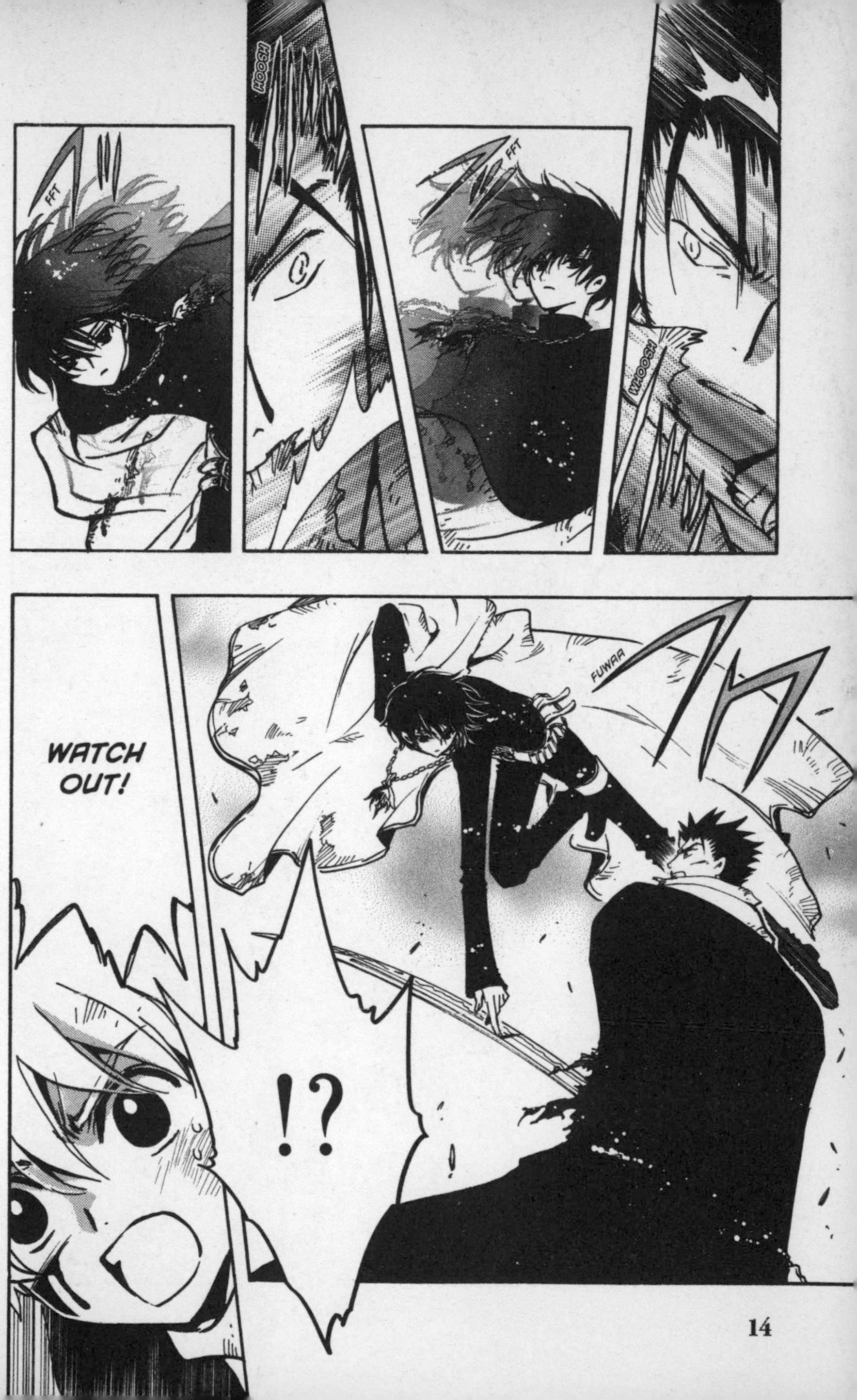
WHOOSH
FFT
WHOOSH
FFT
FUWAA
WATCH OUT!
!?

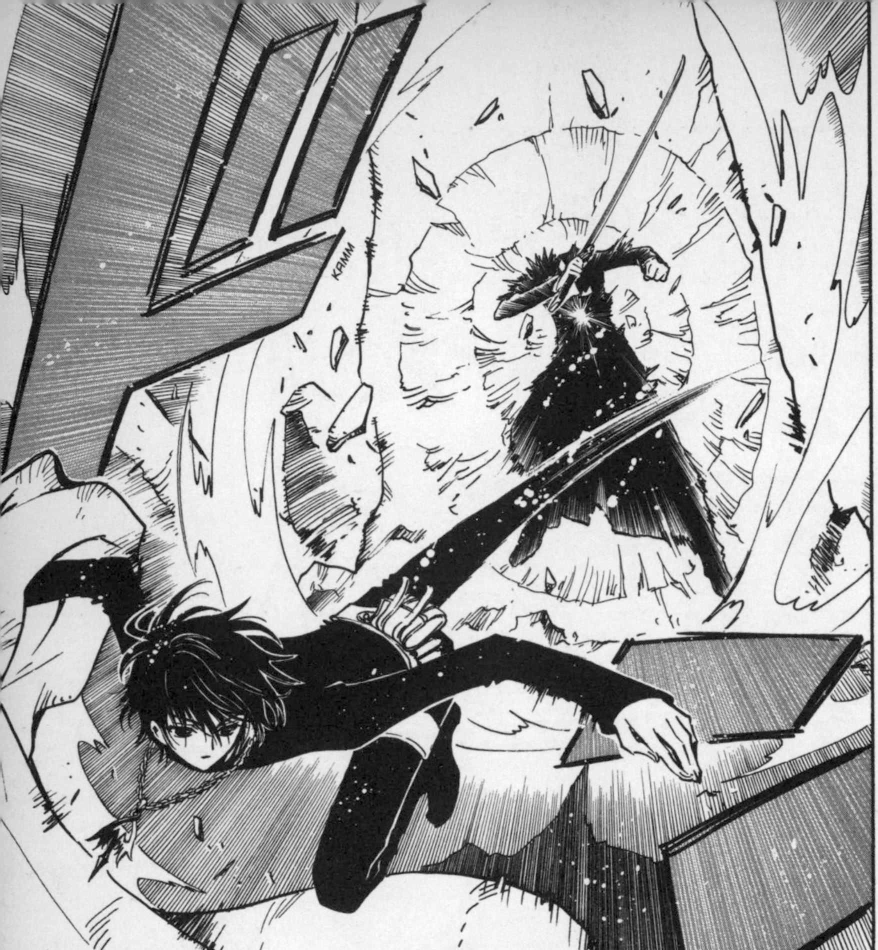
KAMM
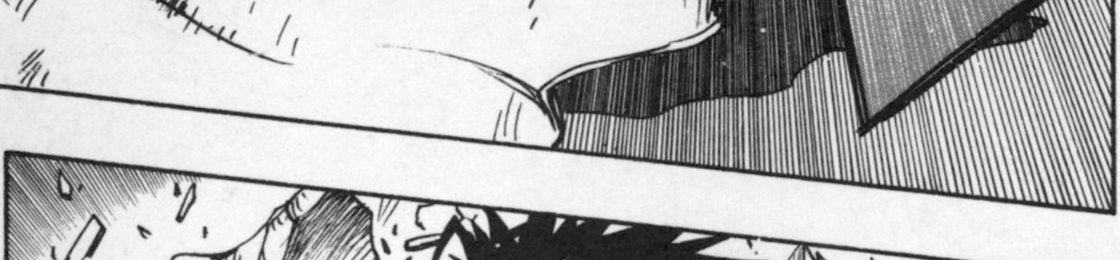
KRITCH

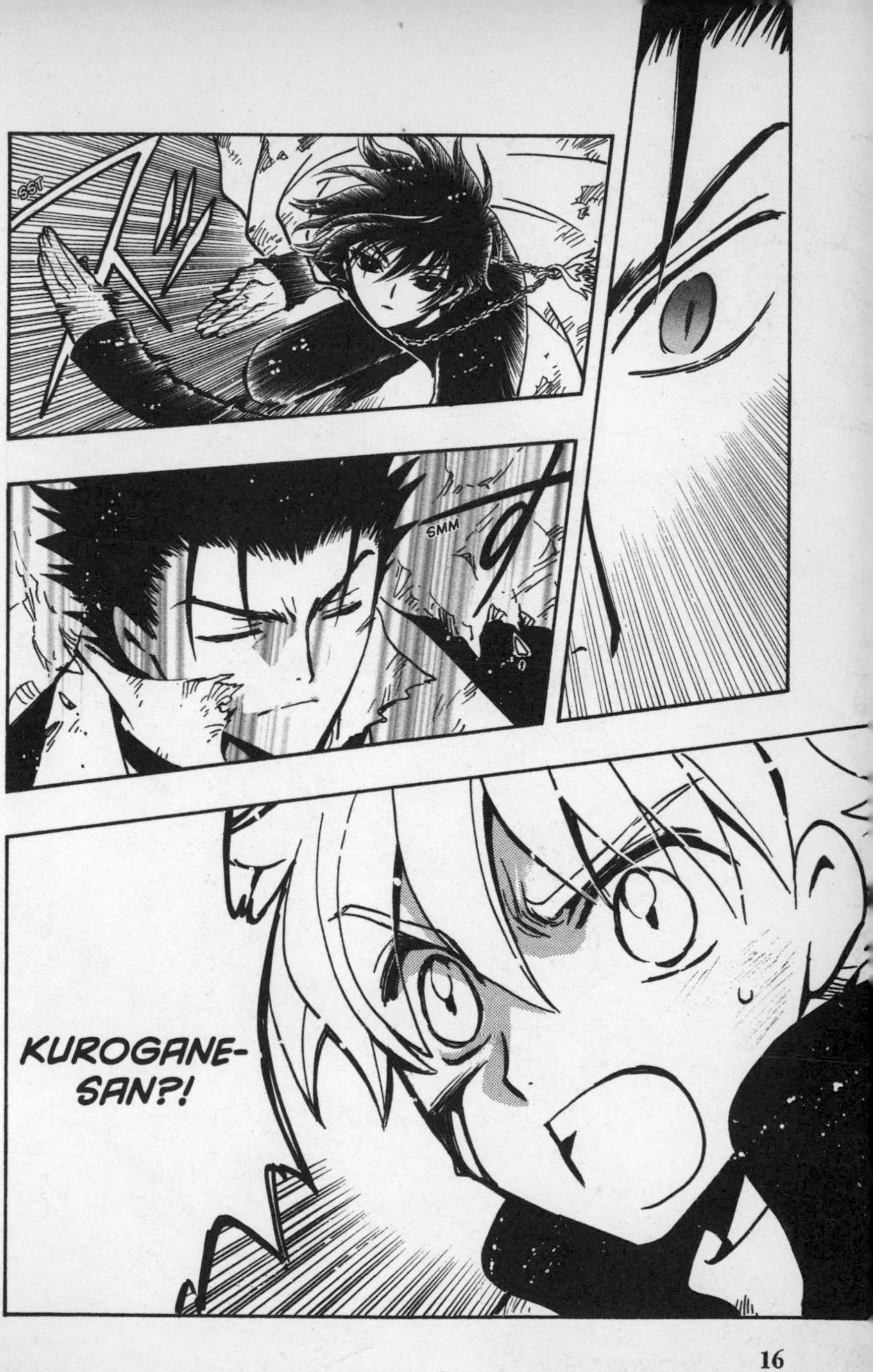
SST
SMM
KUROGANE-SAN?!

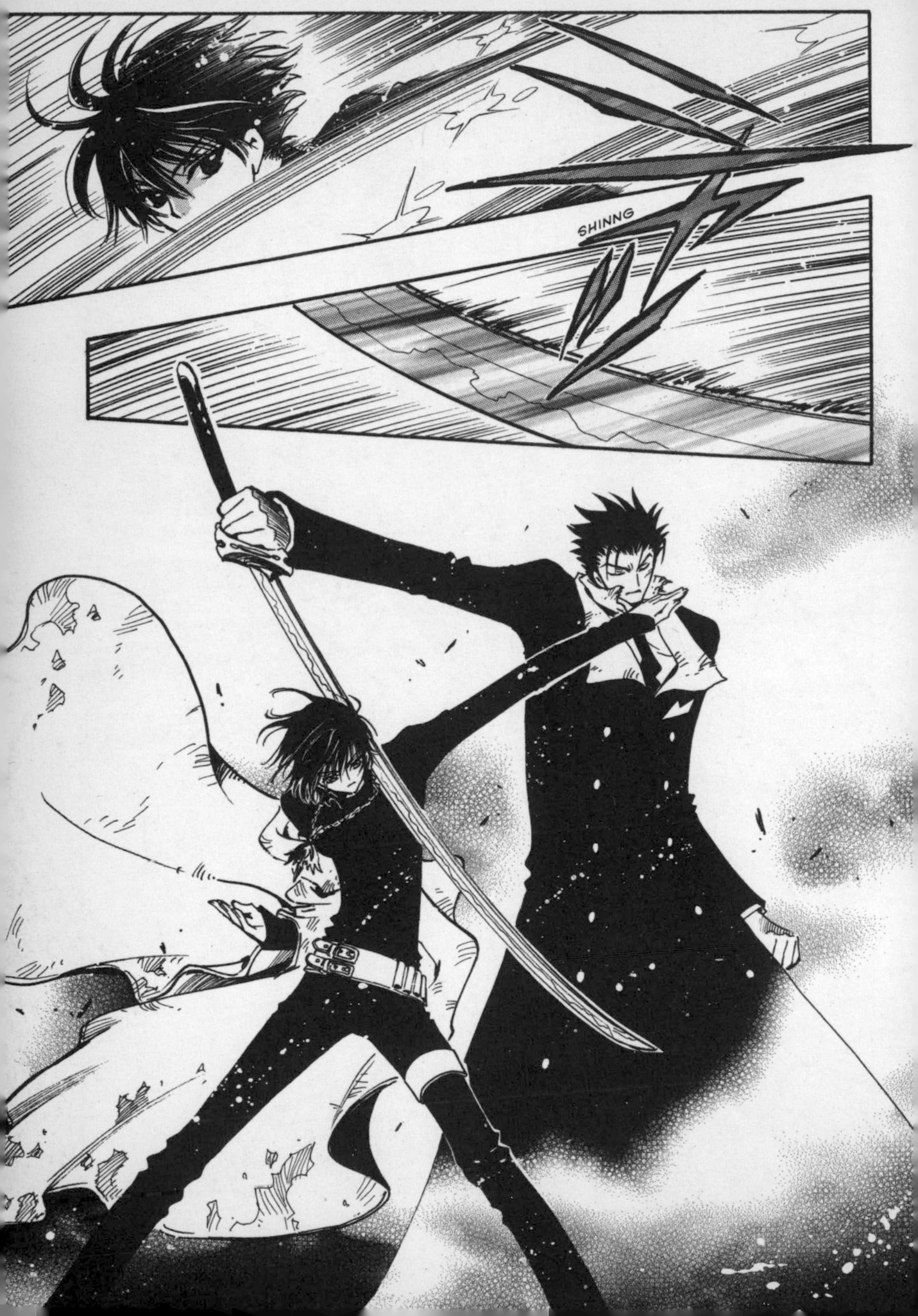
SHINNG

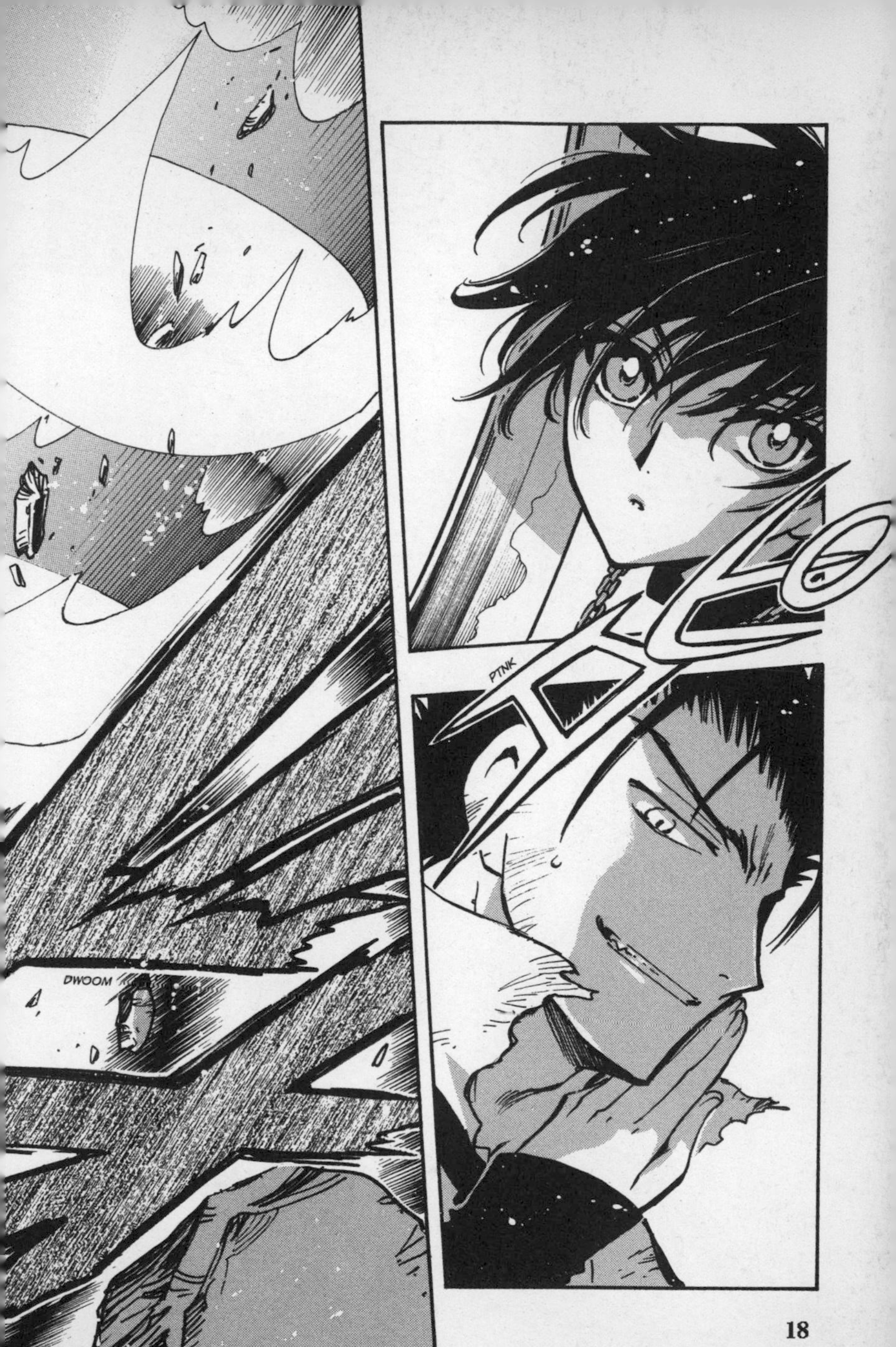
PTNK
DWOOM

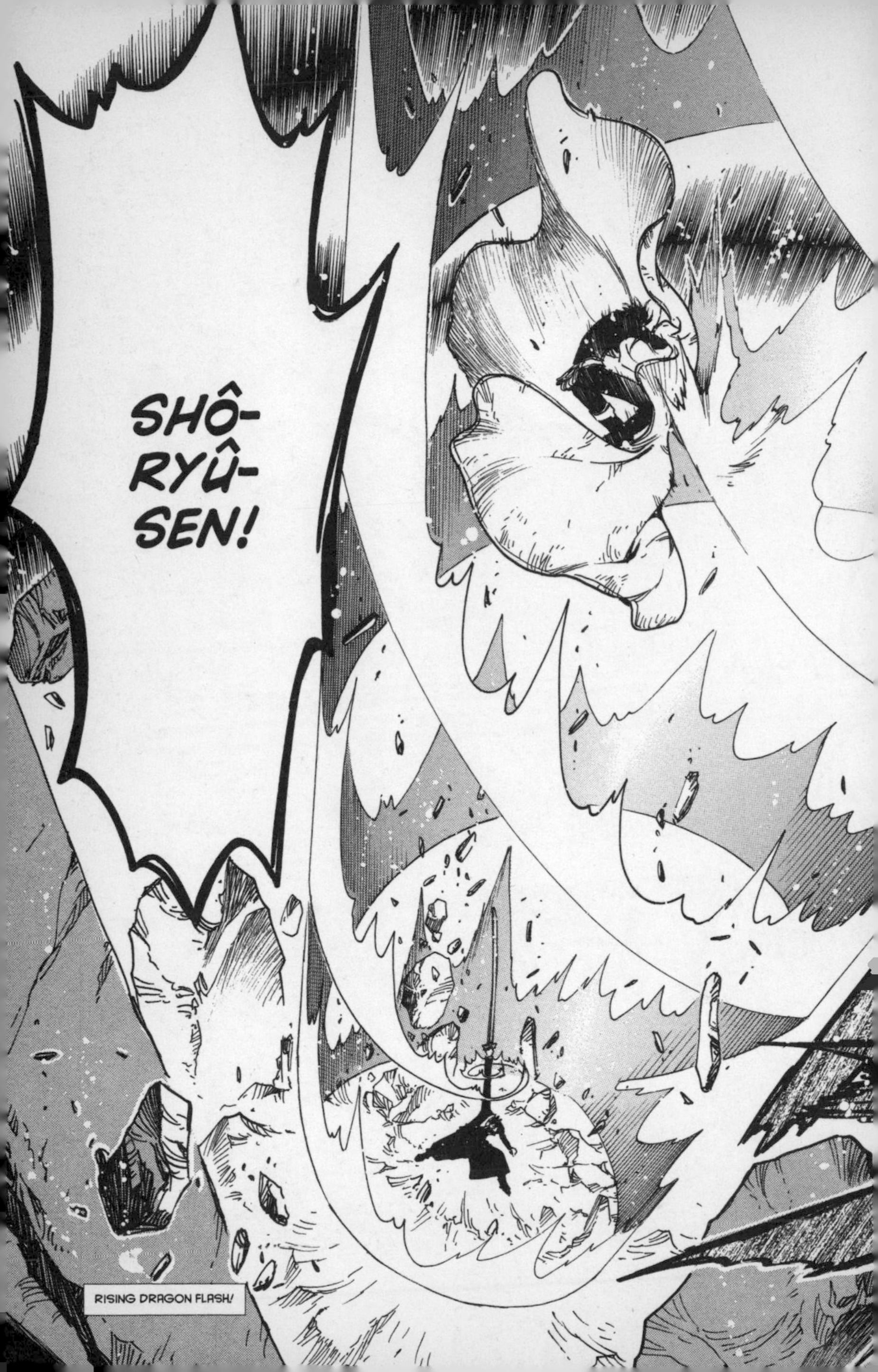
SHÔ-
RYÛ-
SEN!
RISING DRAGON FLASH!

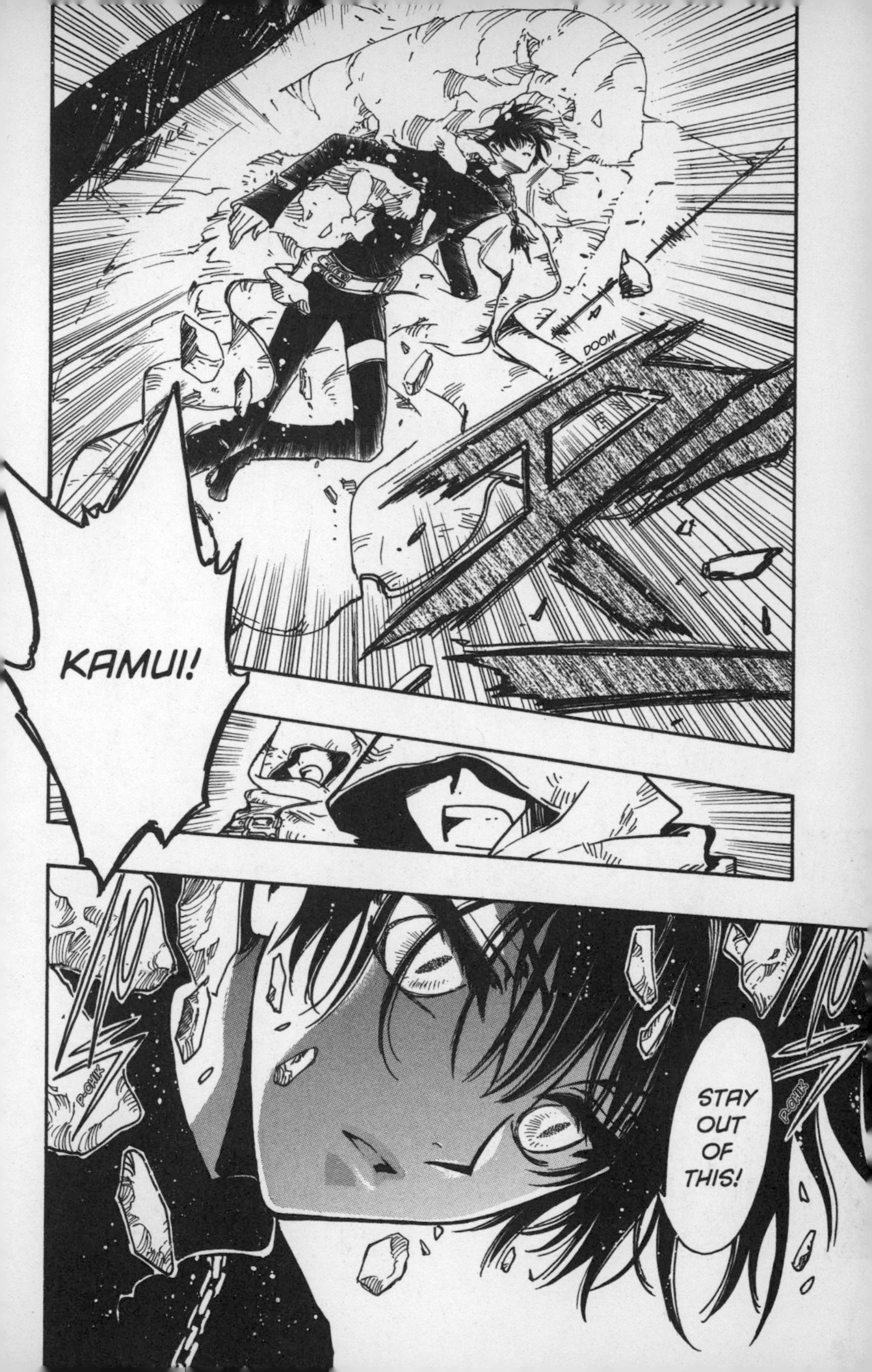
DOOM
KAMUI!
P-CHIK
STAY OUT OF THIS!
P-CHIK

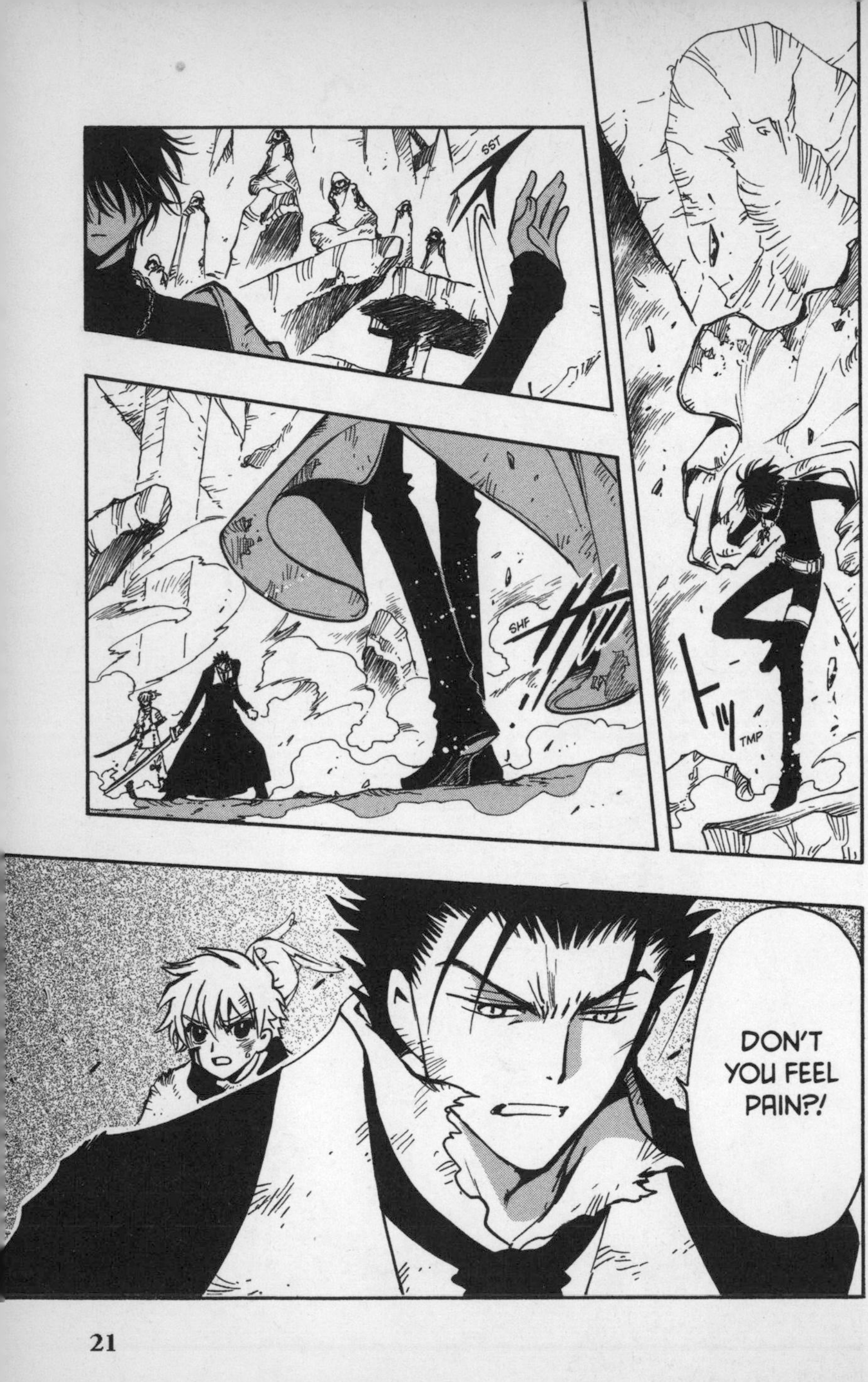
トッ
TMP
SST
SHF
DON'T YOU FEEL PAIN?!

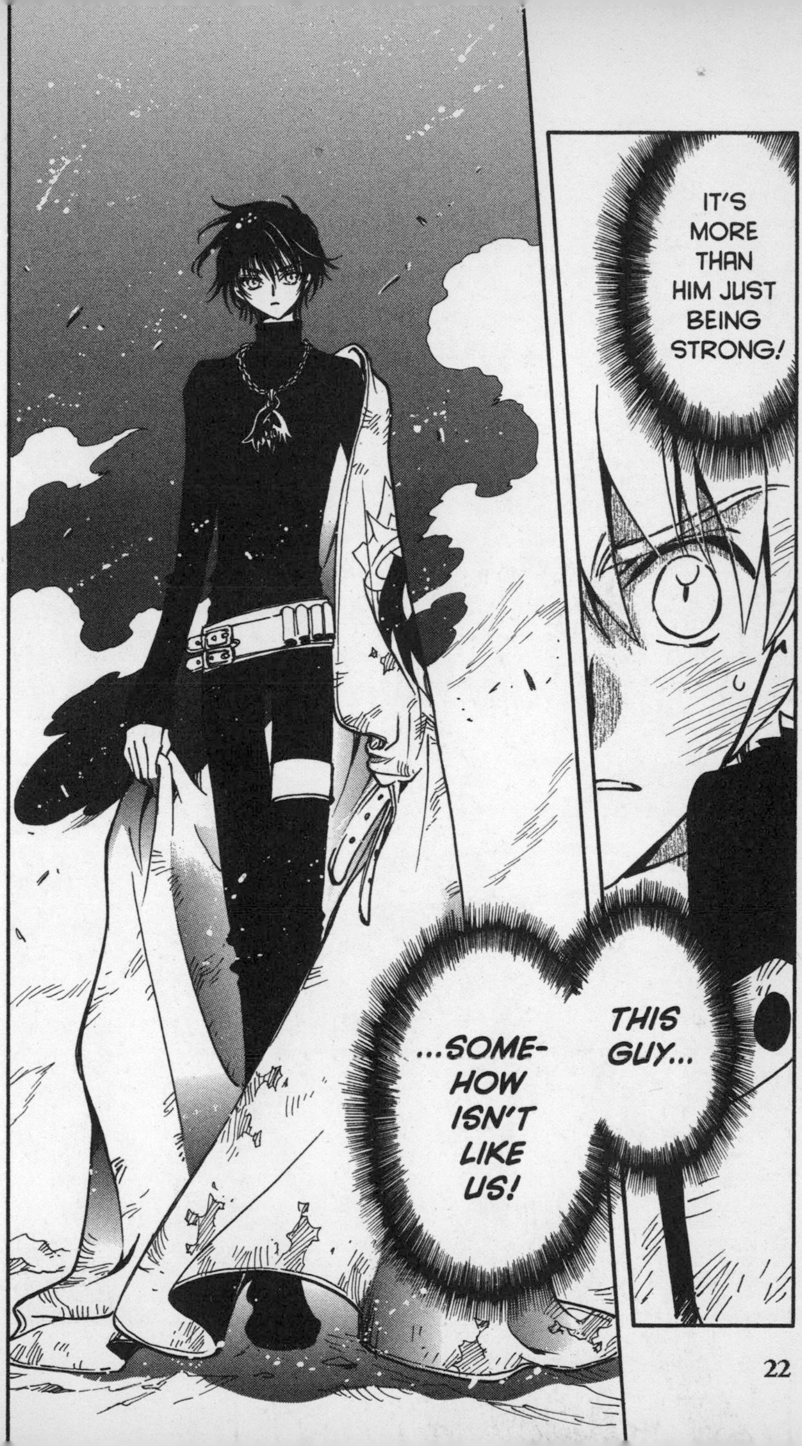
IT'S MORE THAN HIM JUST BEING STRONG!
THIS GUY...
...SOME-HOW ISN'T LIKE US!

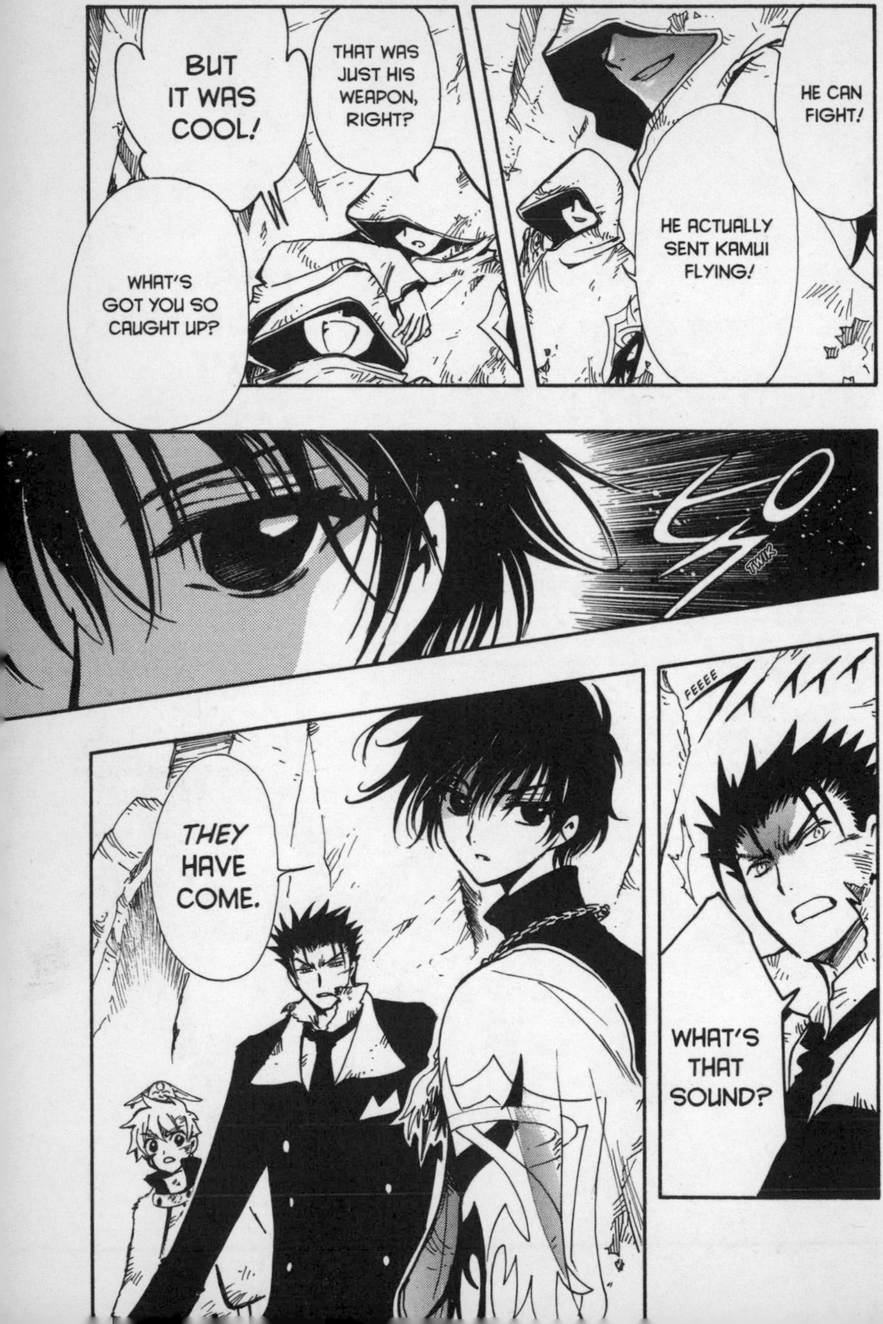
HE CAN FIGHT!
HE ACTUALLY SENT KAMUI FLYING!
THAT WAS JUST HIS WEAPON, RIGHT?
BUT IT WAS COOL!
WHAT'S GOT YOU SO CAUGHT UP?
TWIK
FEEEE
WHAT'S THAT SOUND?
THEY HAVE COME.

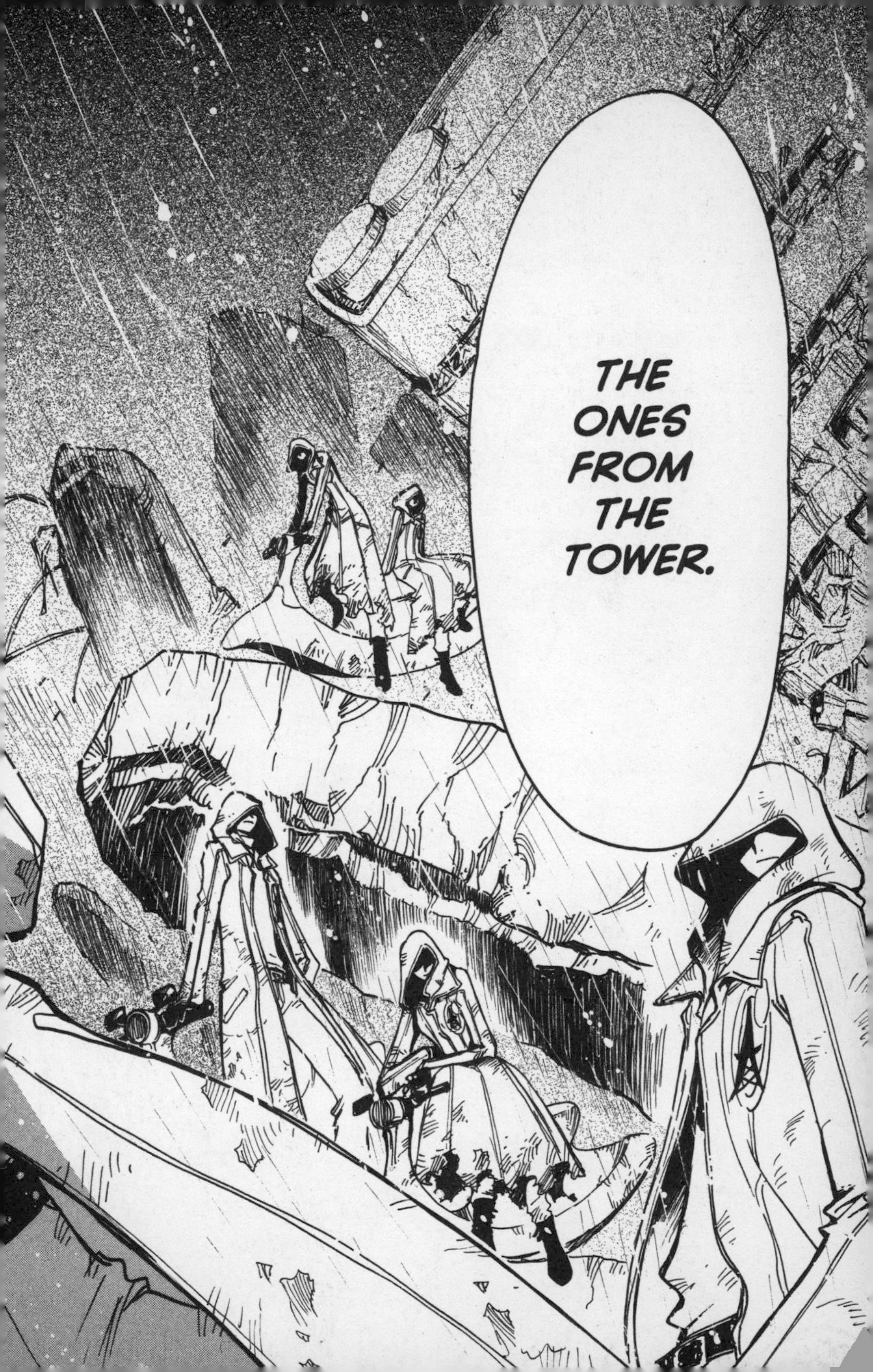
THE ONES FROM THE TOWER.

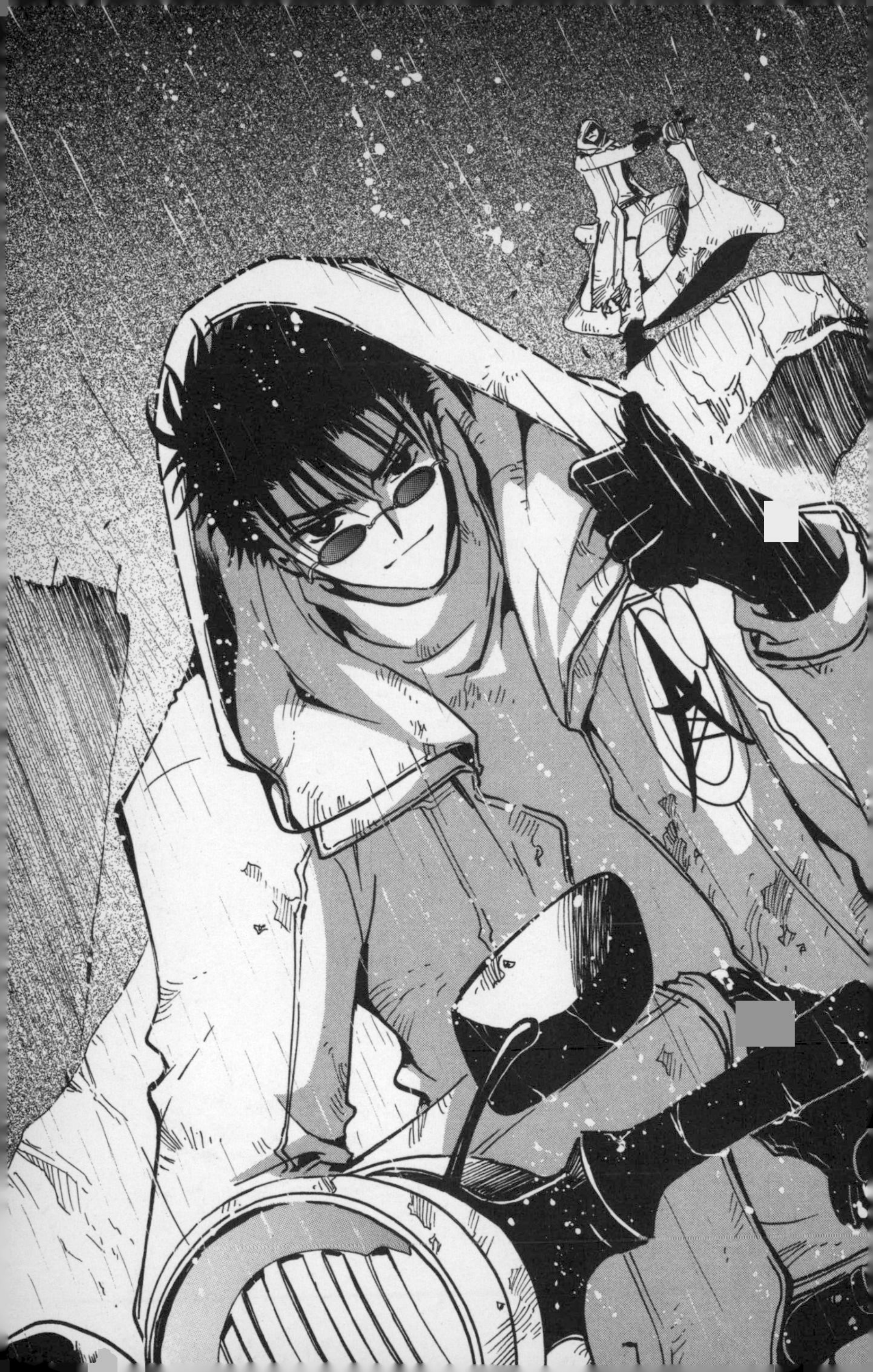

ツバサ
RESERVoir CHRoNiCLE

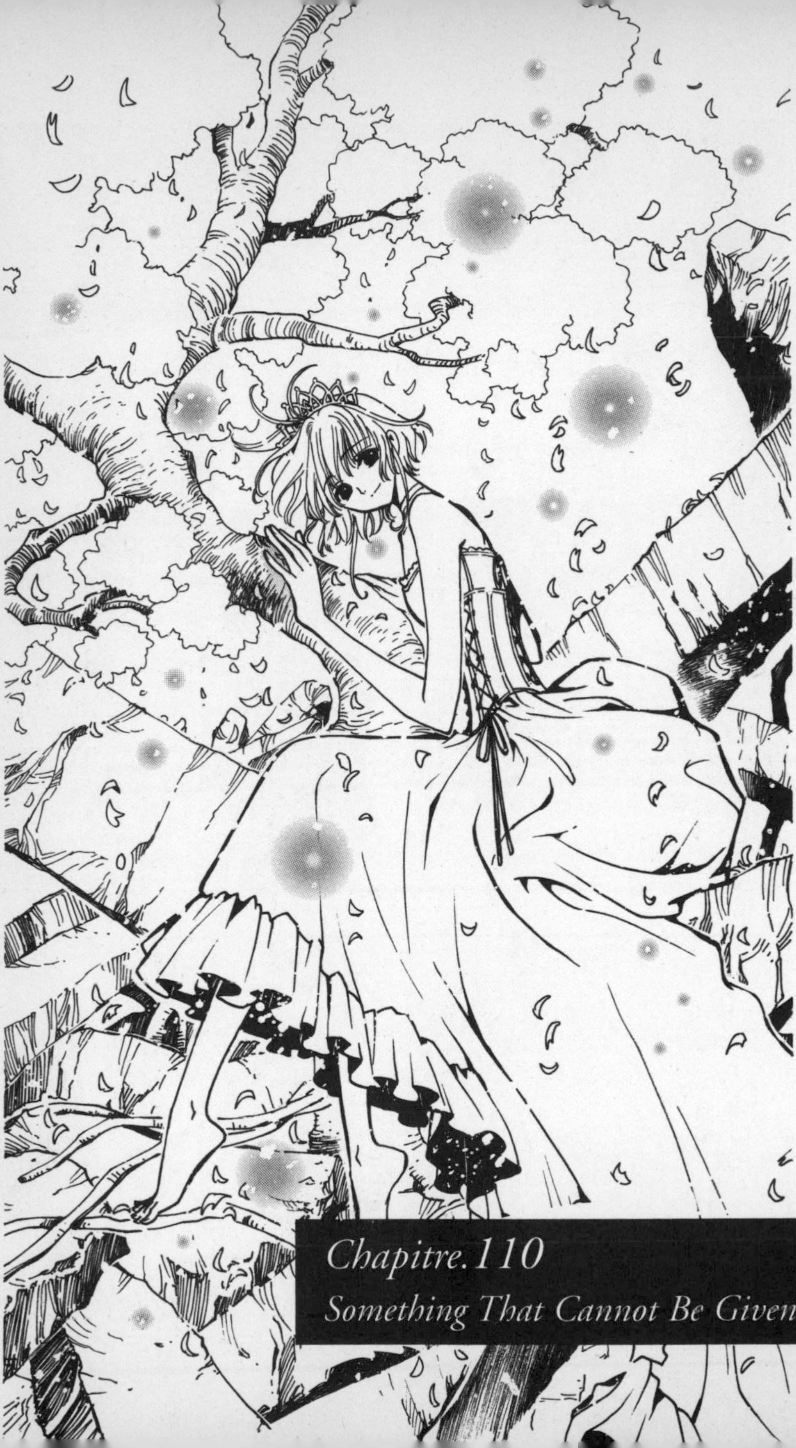

Chapitre.110
Something That Cannot Be Given

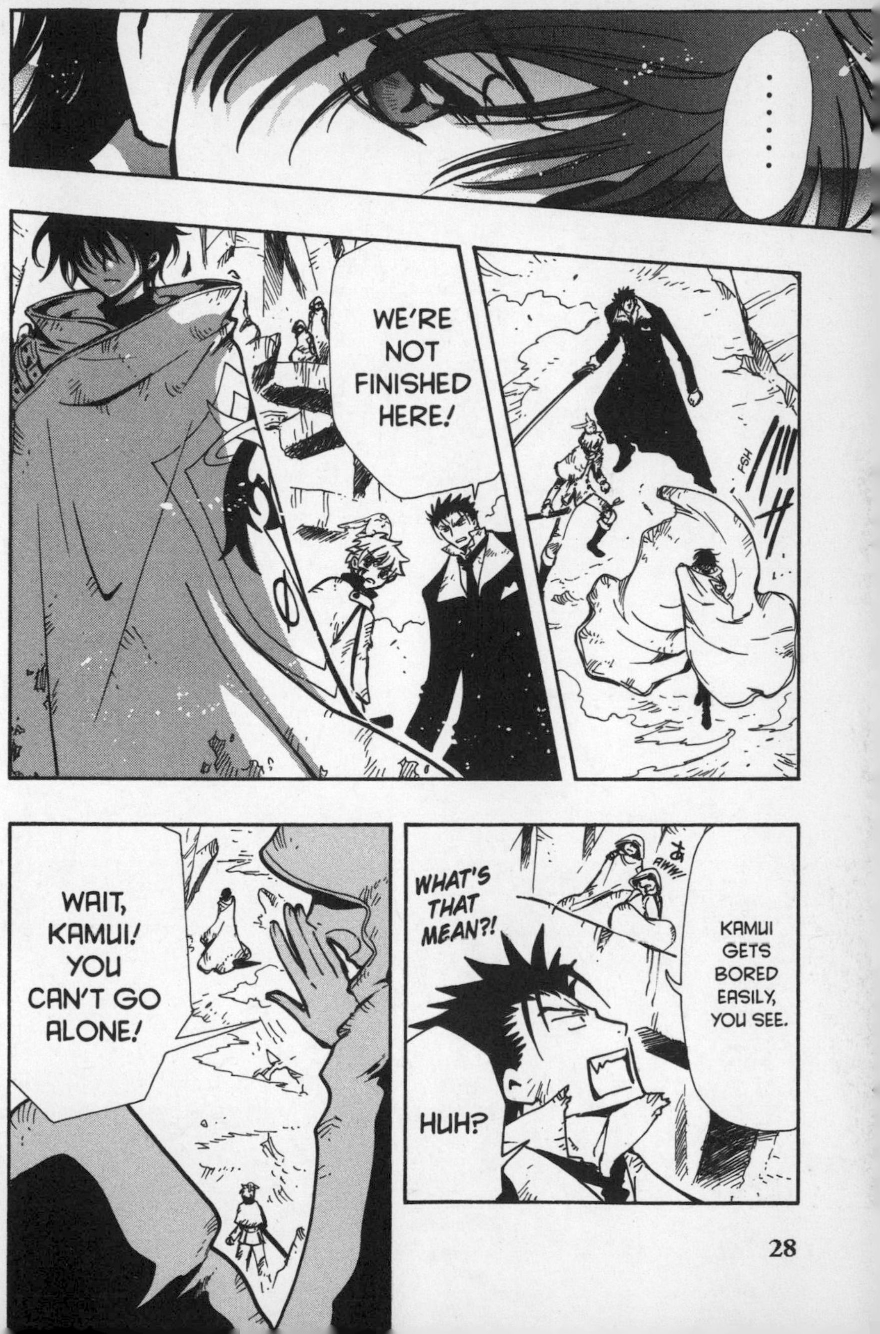
……
FSH
WE'RE NOT FINISHED HERE!
あ AWW!
KAMUI GETS BORED EASILY, YOU SEE.
WHAT'S THAT MEAN?!
HUH?
WAIT, KAMUI! YOU CAN'T GO ALONE!

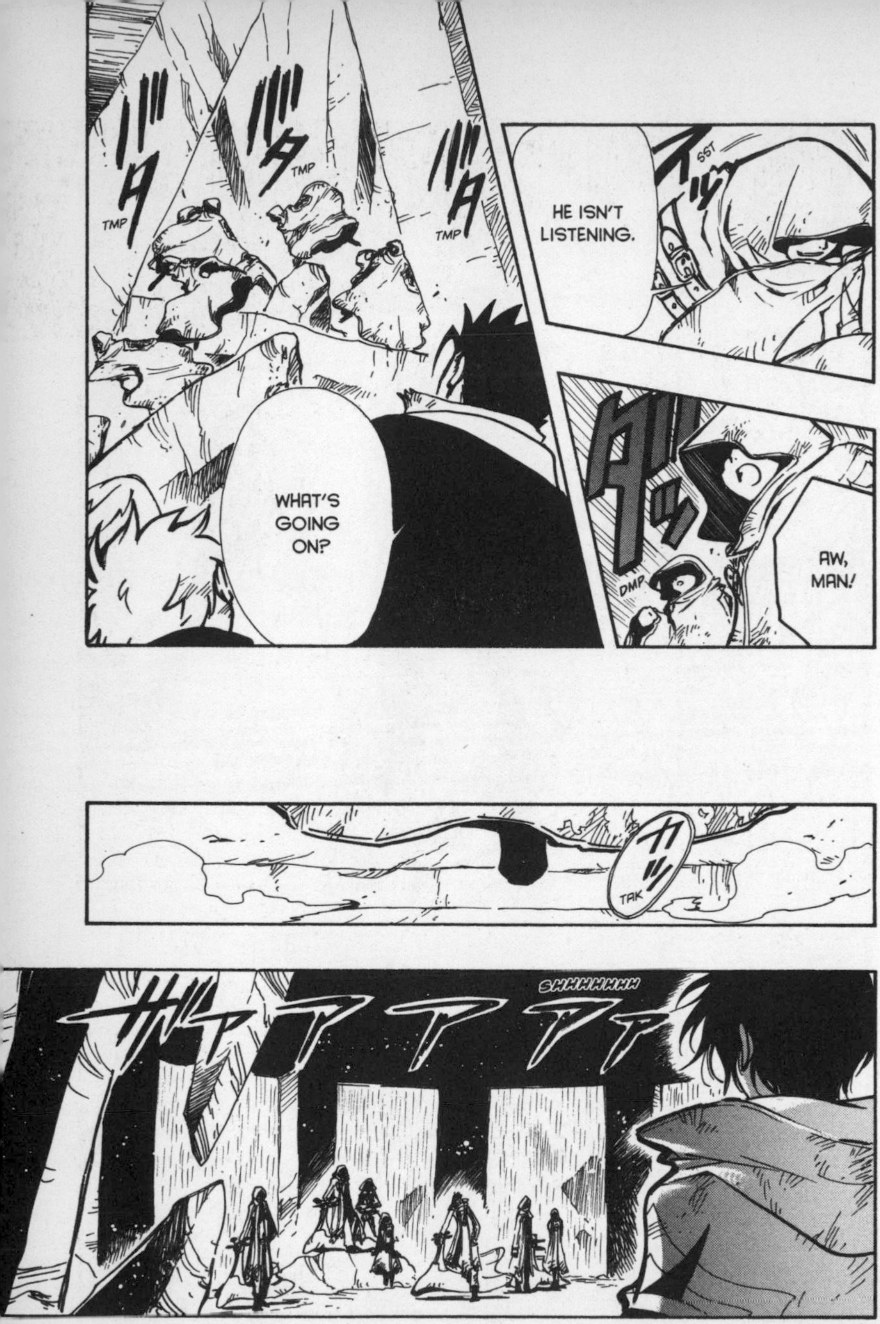
SST
HE ISN'T LISTENING.
DMP
AW, MAN!
TMP
TMP
TMP
WHAT'S GOING ON?
TAK
SHHHHHHH

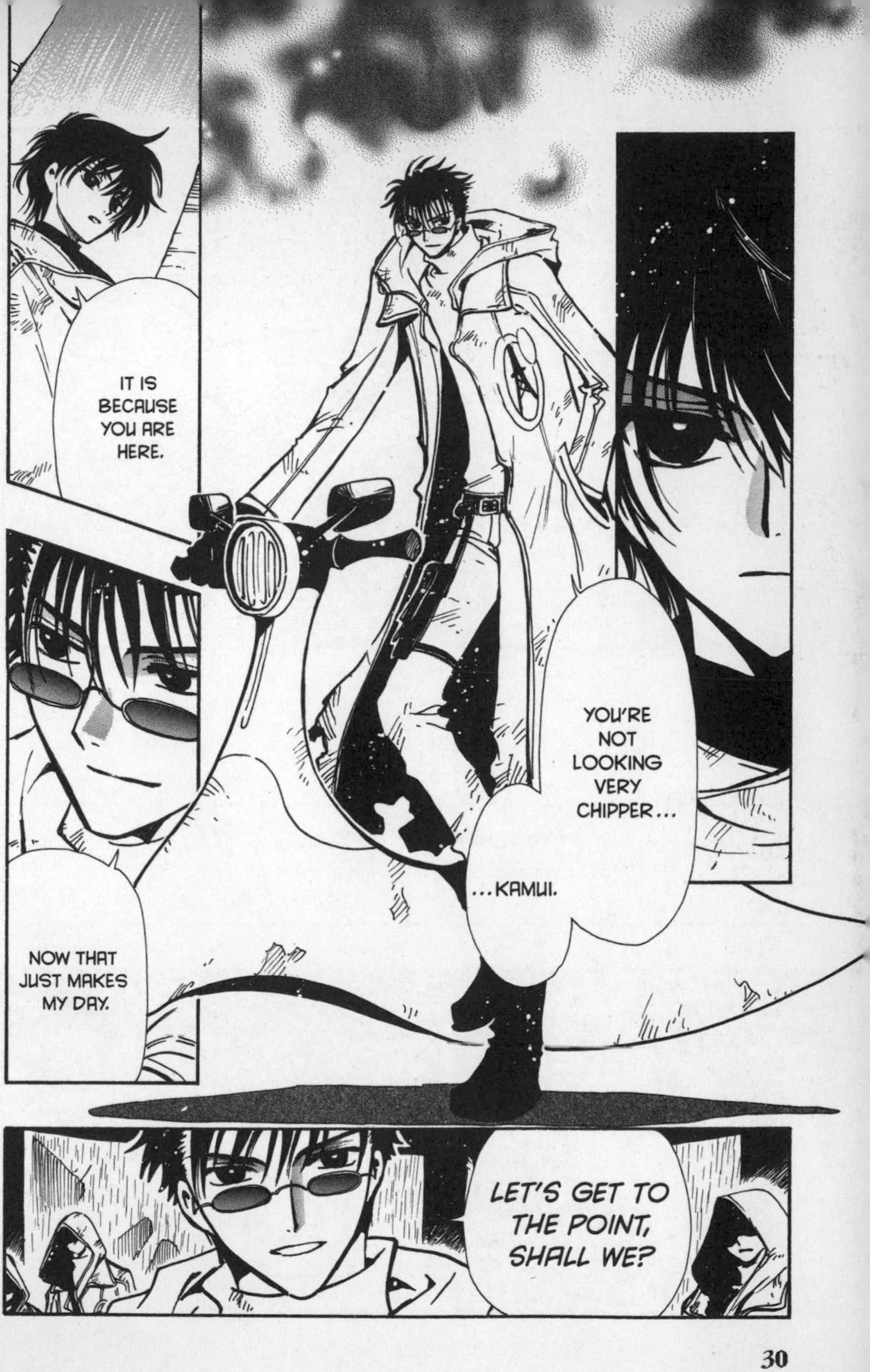
YOU'RE NOT LOOKING VERY CHIPPER...
...KAMUI.
IT IS BECAUSE YOU ARE HERE.
NOW THAT JUST MAKES MY DAY.
LET'S GET TO THE POINT, SHALL WE?

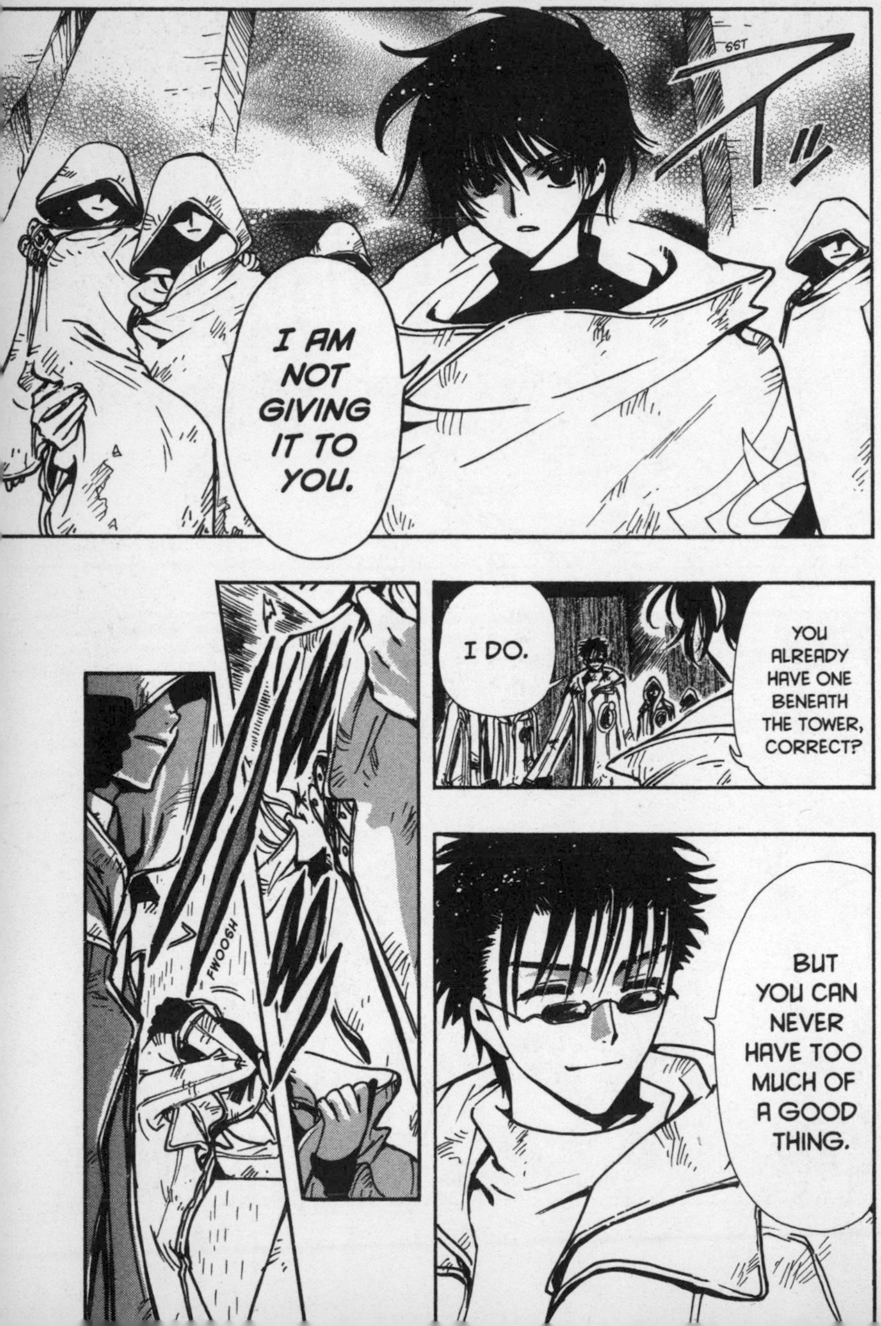
SST
I AM NOT GIVING IT TO YOU.
YOU ALREADY HAVE ONE BENEATH THE TOWER, CORRECT?
I DO.
BUT YOU CAN NEVER HAVE TOO MUCH OF A GOOD THING.
FWOOSH

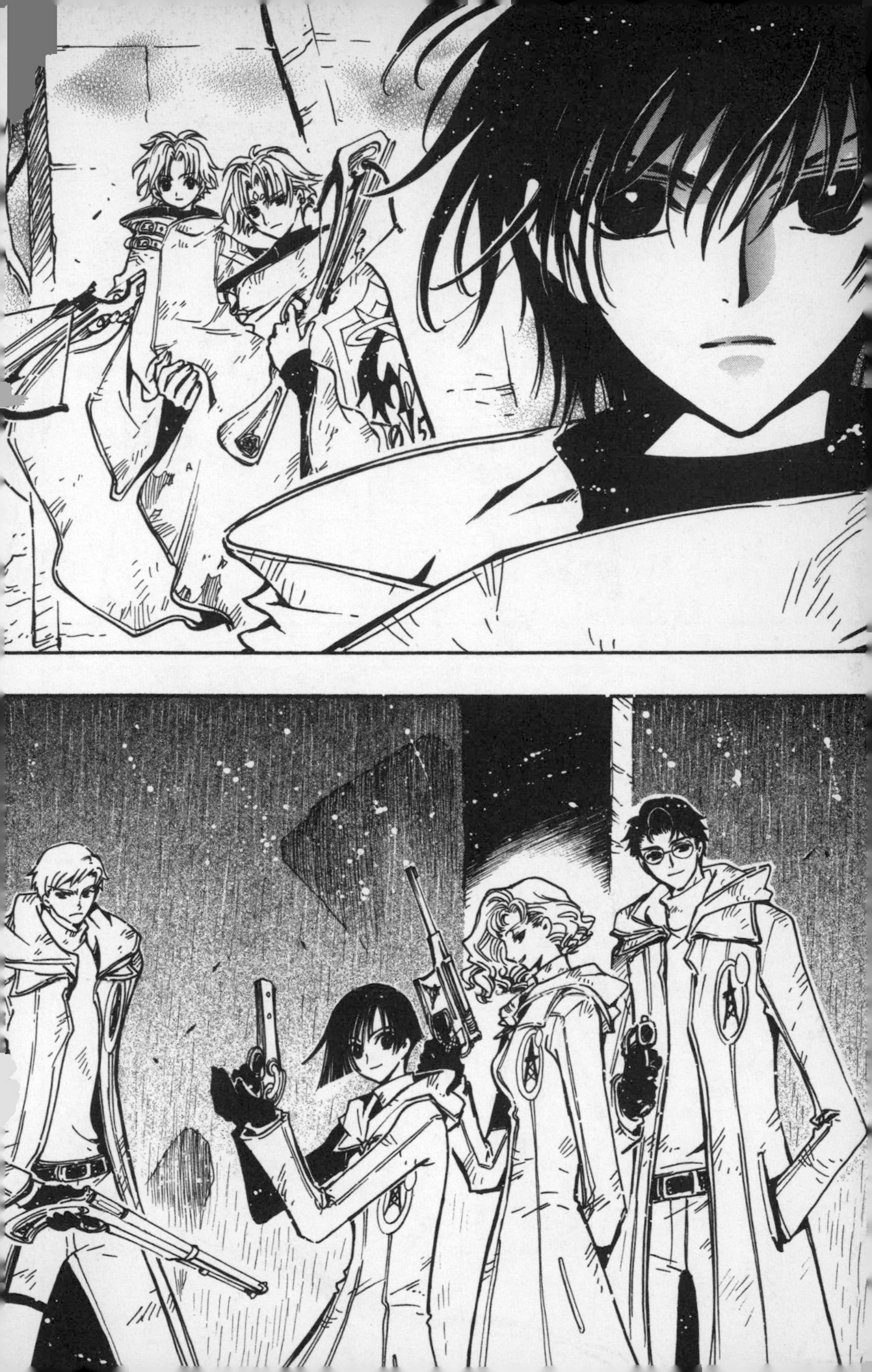

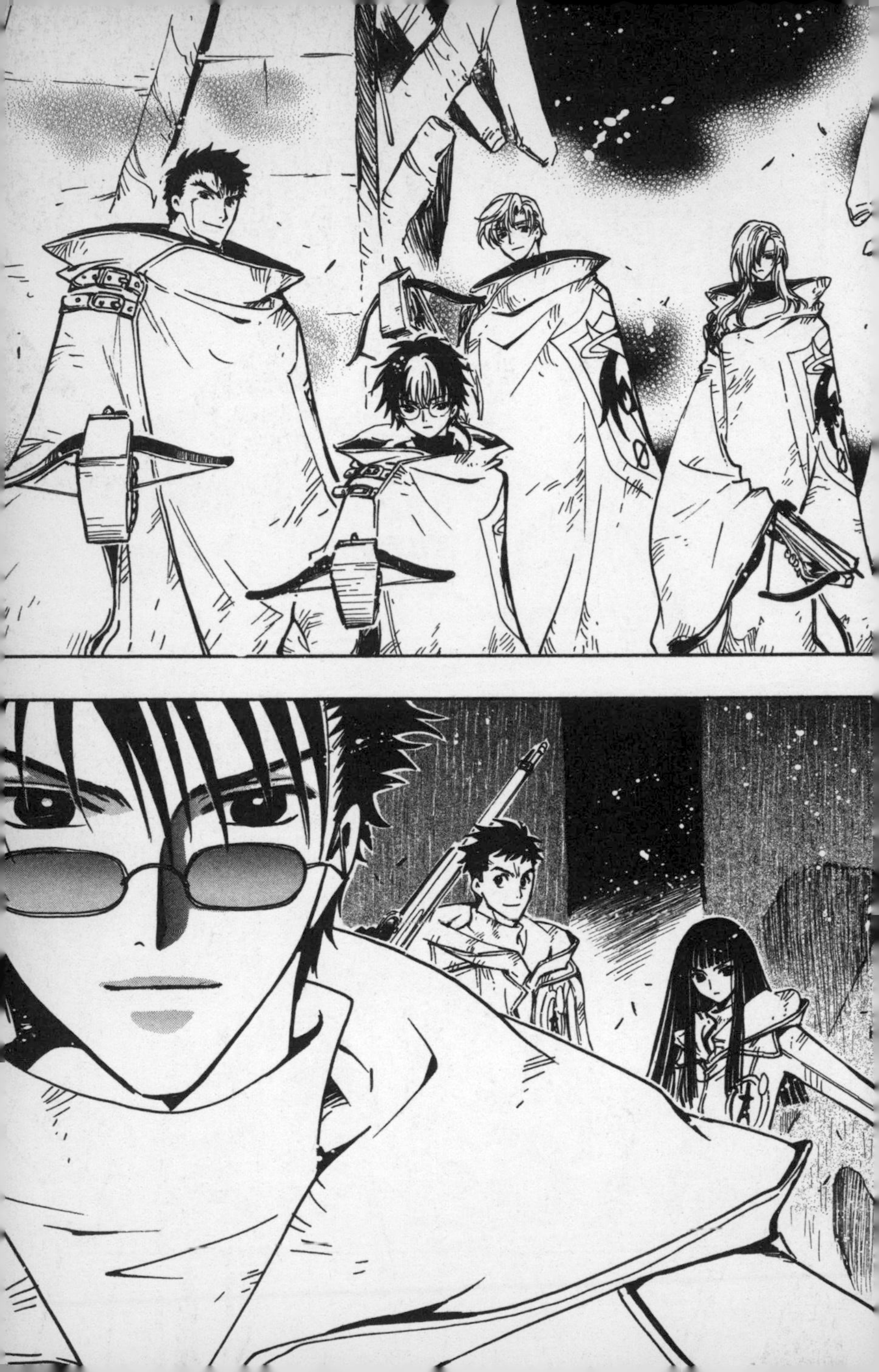

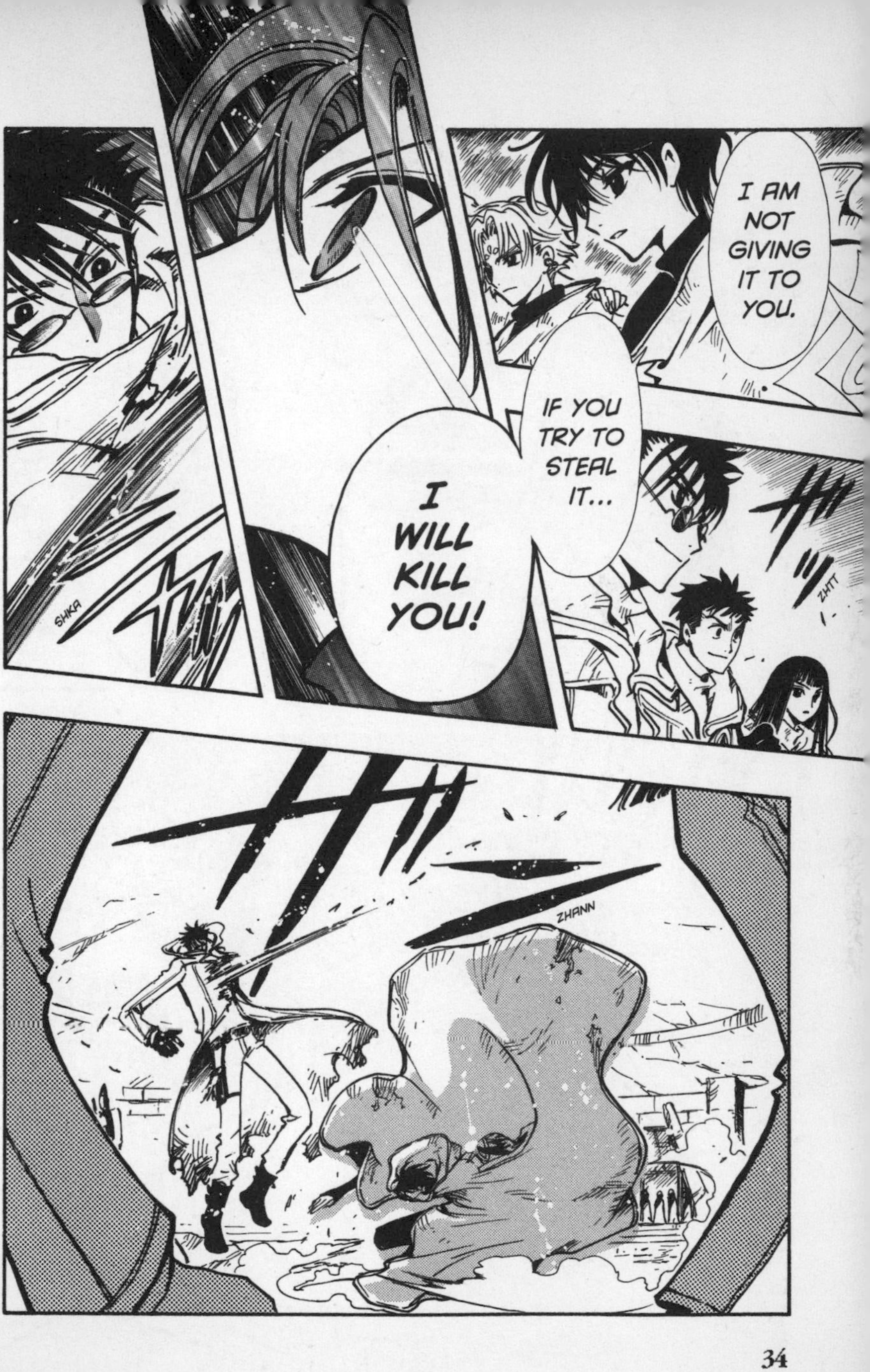
I AM NOT GIVING IT TO YOU.
ZHTT
IF YOU TRY TO STEAL IT...
I WILL KILL YOU!
SHKA
ZHANN

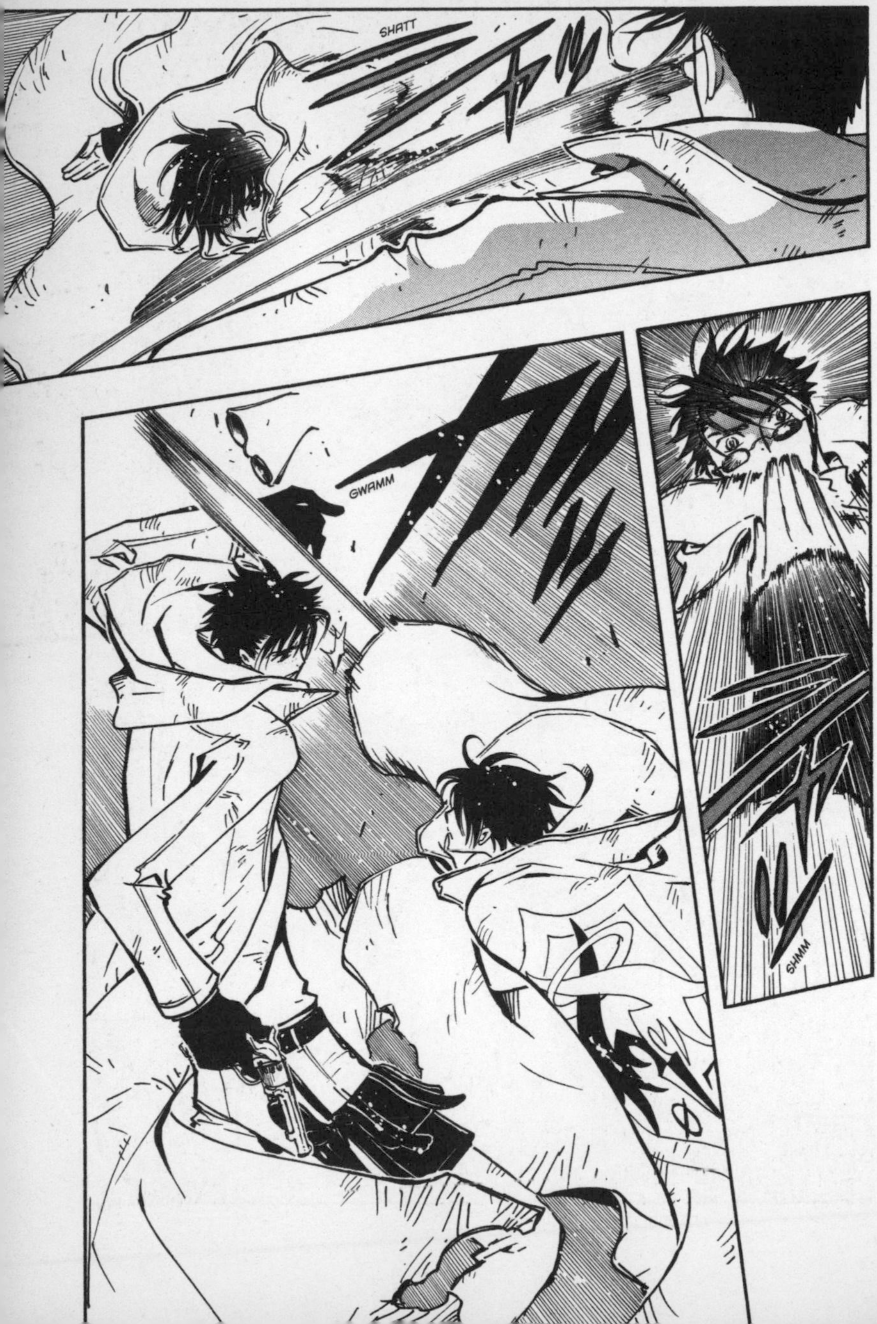
SHATT
SHMM
GWAMM

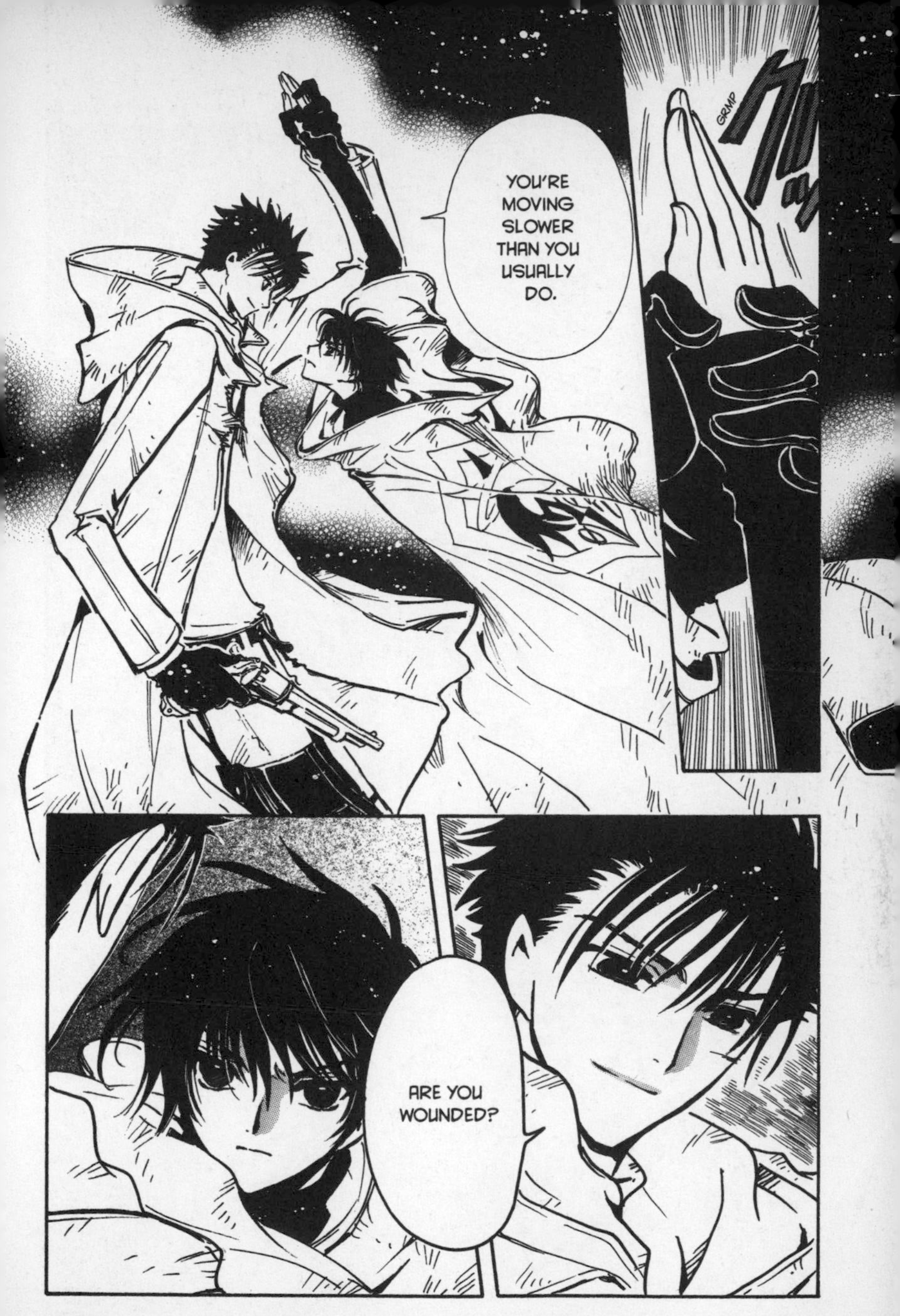
GRMP
YOU'RE MOVING SLOWER THAN YOU USUALLY DO.
ARE YOU WOUNDED?

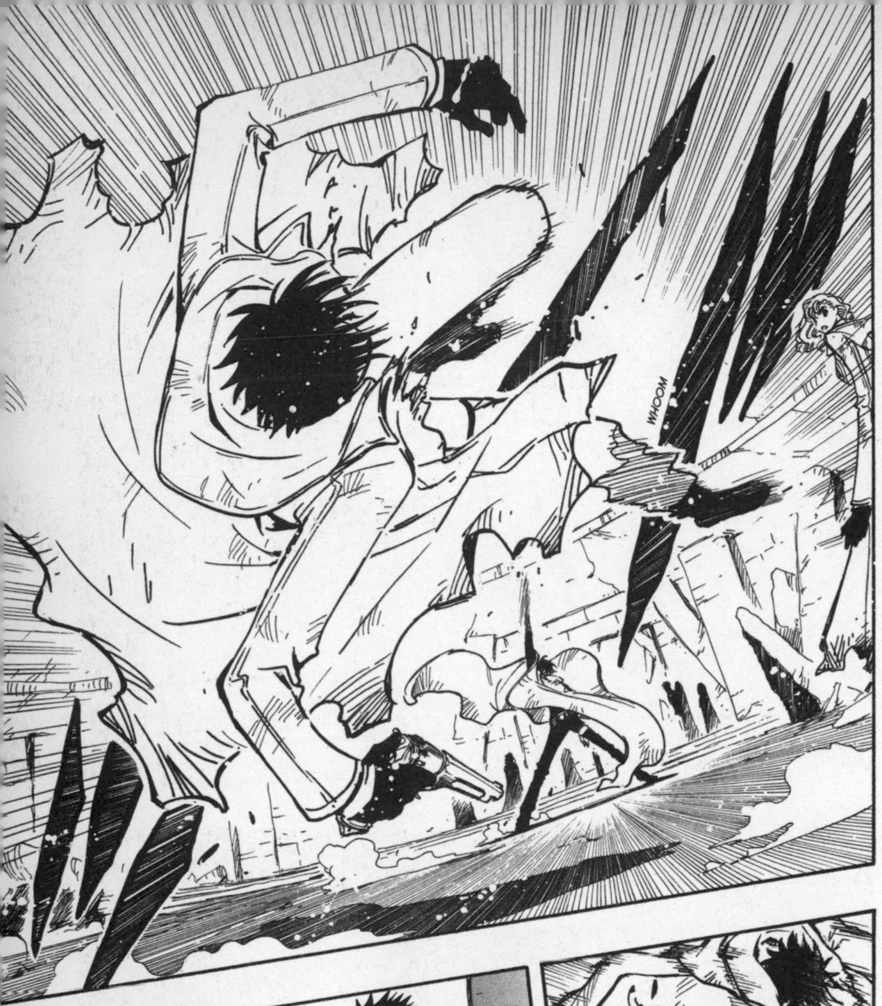
WHOOM

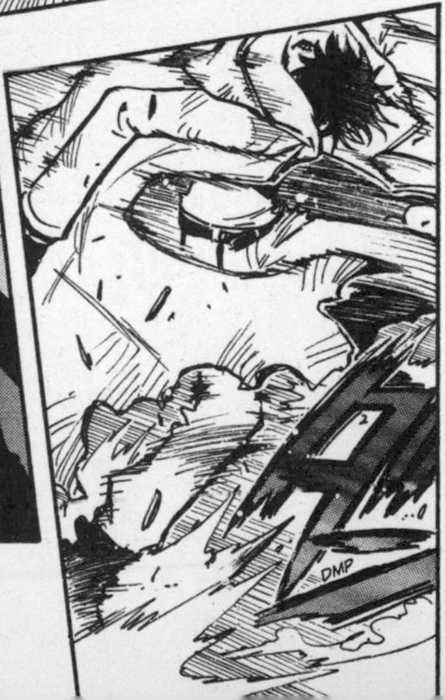
DMP

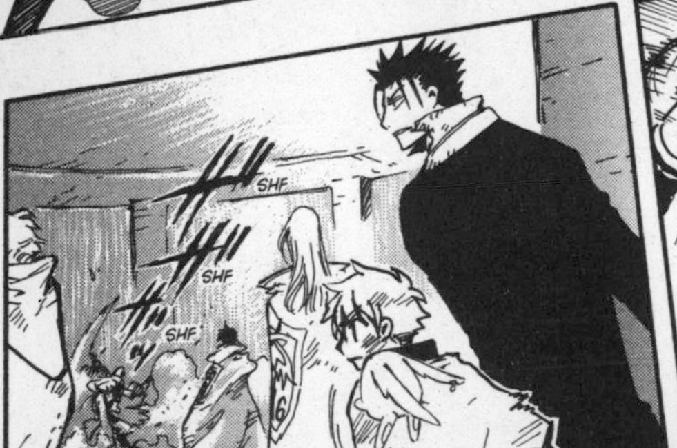
SHF
SHF
SHF

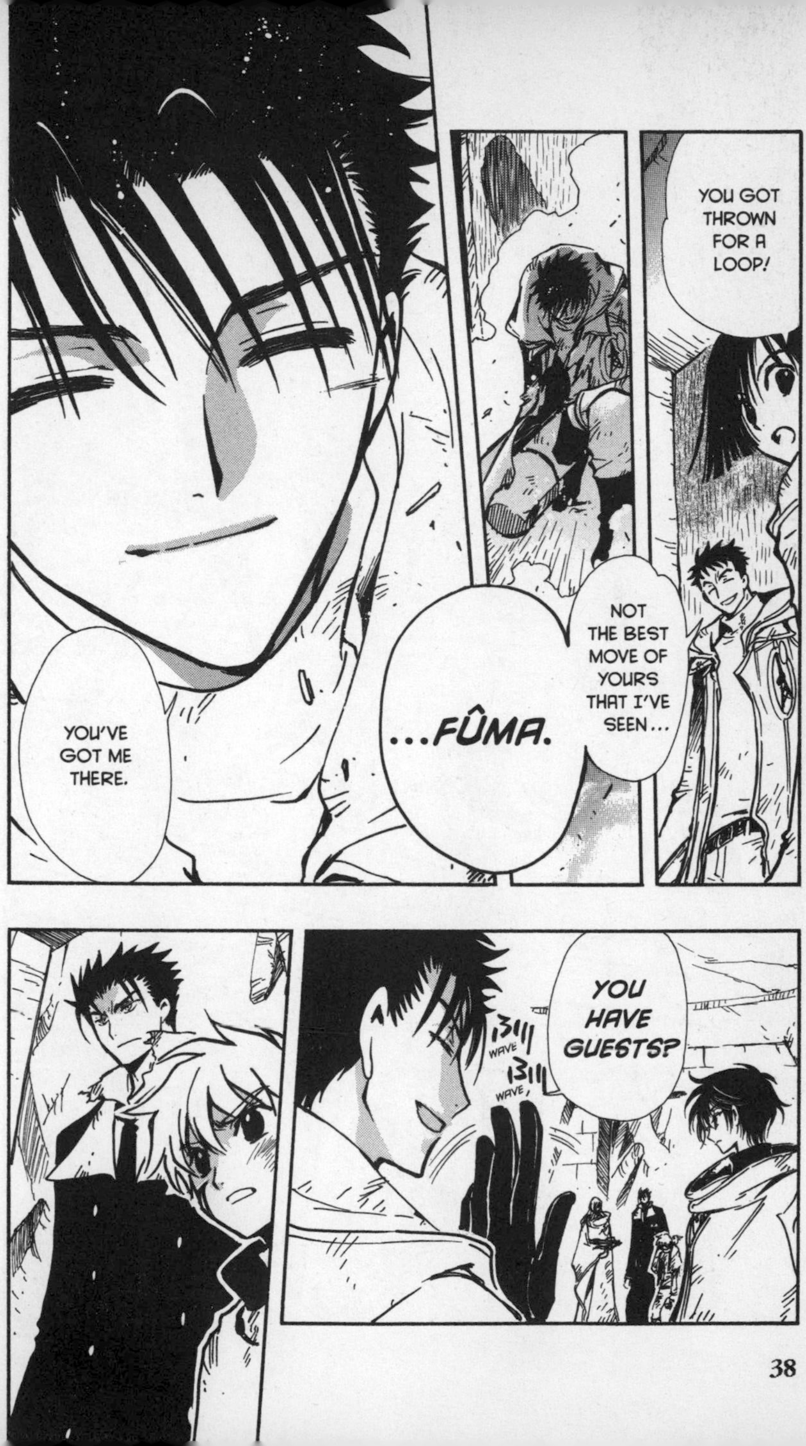
YOU GOT THROWN FOR A LOOP!
NOT THE BEST MOVE OF YOURS THAT I'VE SEEN...
...FÛMA.
YOU'VE GOT ME THERE.
YOU HAVE GUESTS?
WAVE
WAVE,

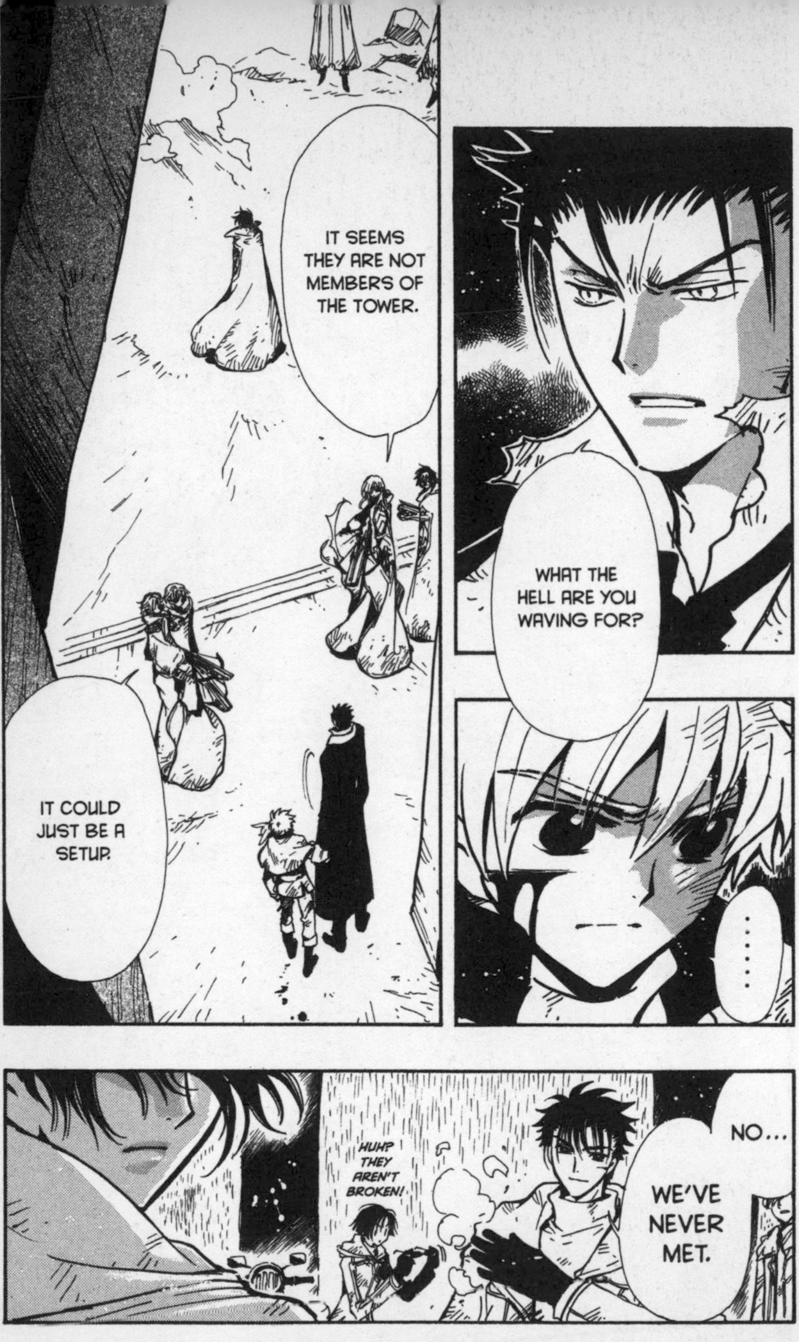
WHAT THE HELL ARE YOU WAVING FOR?
......
IT SEEMS THEY ARE NOT MEMBERS OF THE TOWER.
IT COULD JUST BE A SETUP.
NO...
WE'VE NEVER MET.
HUH? THEY AREN'T BROKEN!

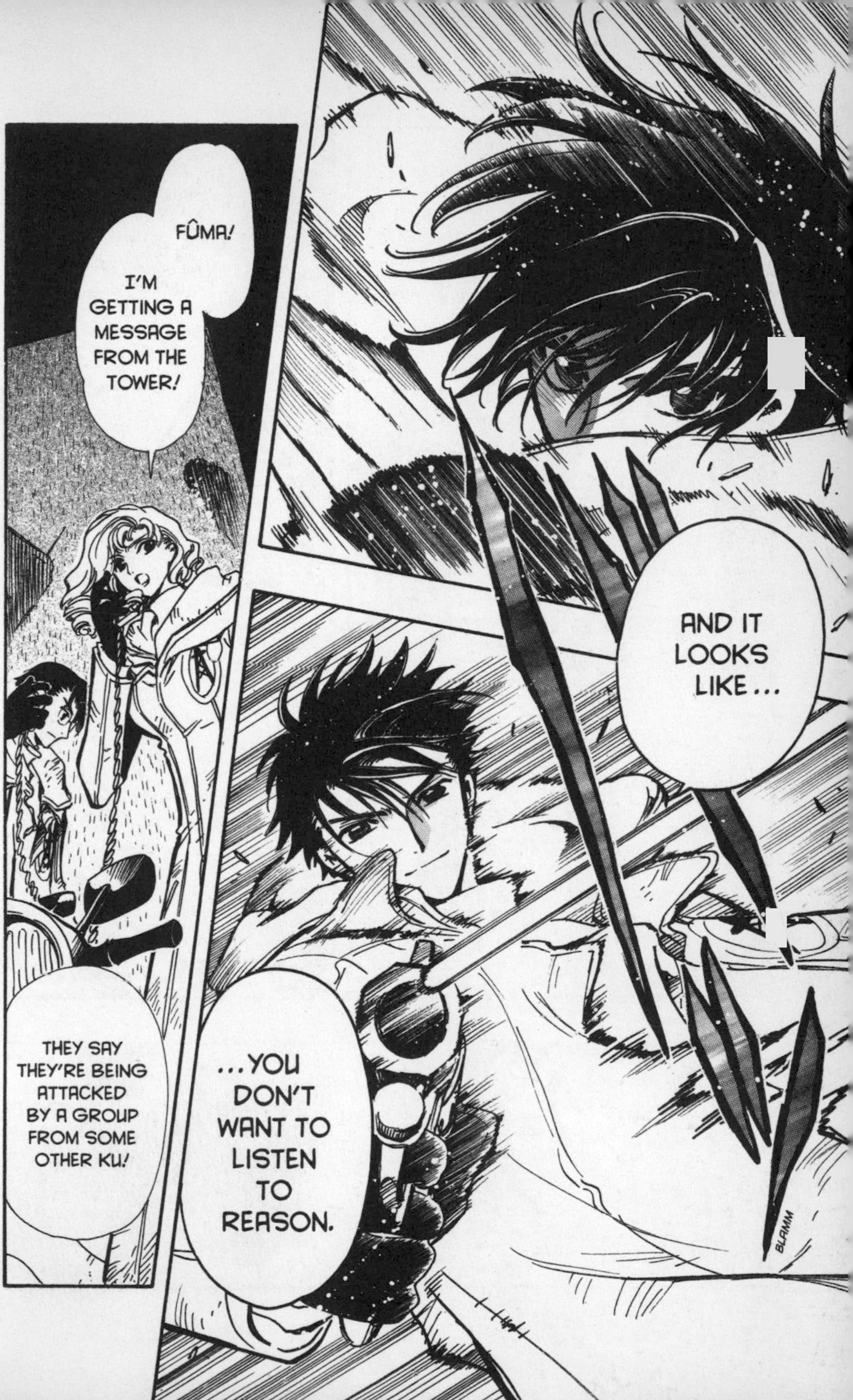
AND IT LOOKS LIKE...
...YOU DON'T WANT TO LISTEN TO REASON.
BLAMM
FÛMA!
I'M GETTING A MESSAGE FROM THE TOWER!
THEY SAY THEY'RE BEING ATTACKED BY A GROUP FROM SOME OTHER KU!

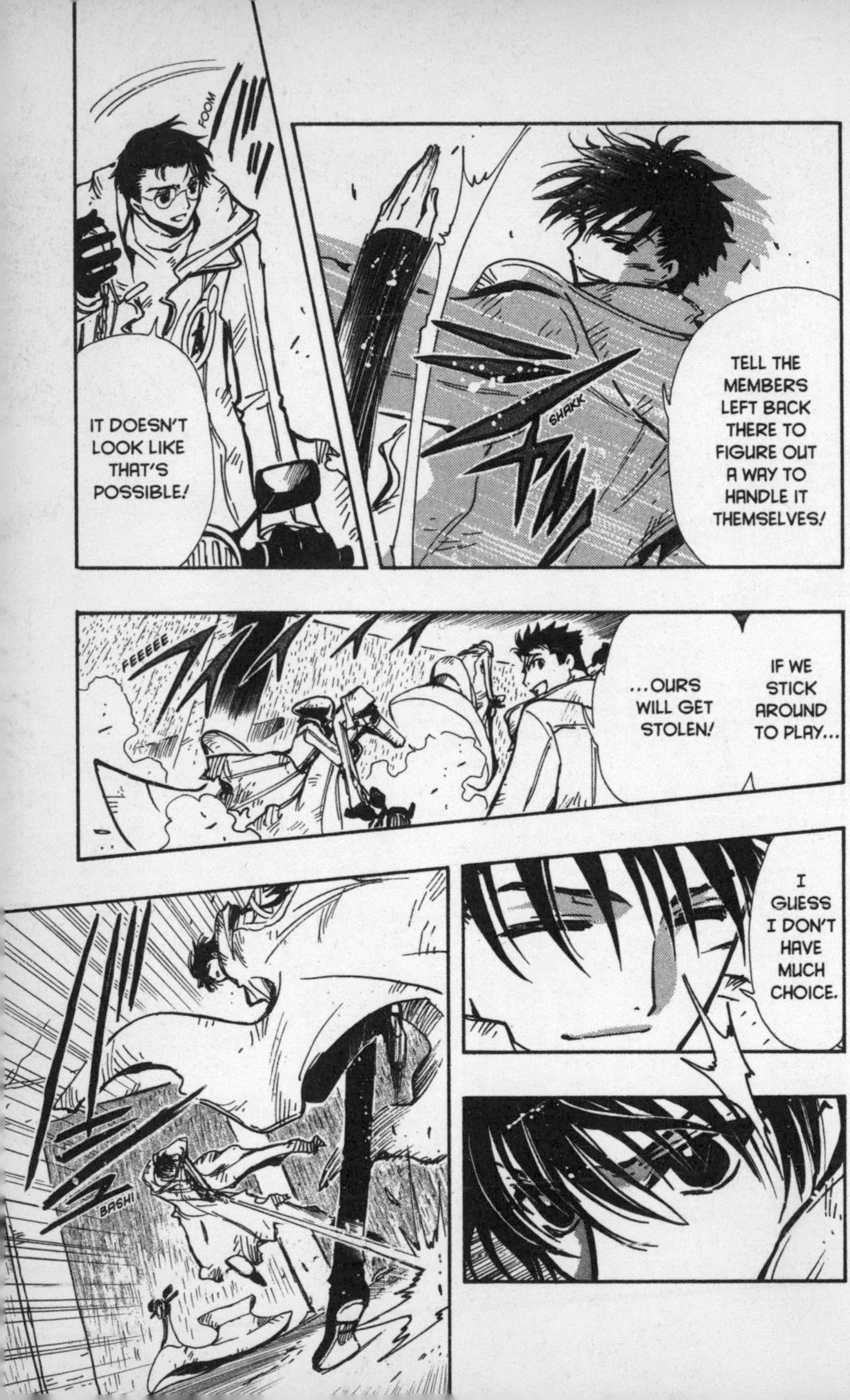
TELL THE MEMBERS LEFT BACK THERE TO FIGURE OUT A WAY TO HANDLE IT THEMSELVES!
SHAKK
FOOM
IT DOESN'T LOOK LIKE THAT'S POSSIBLE!
IF WE STICK AROUND TO PLAY...
...OURS WILL GET STOLEN!
FEEEEE
I GUESS I DON'T HAVE MUCH CHOICE.
BASHI

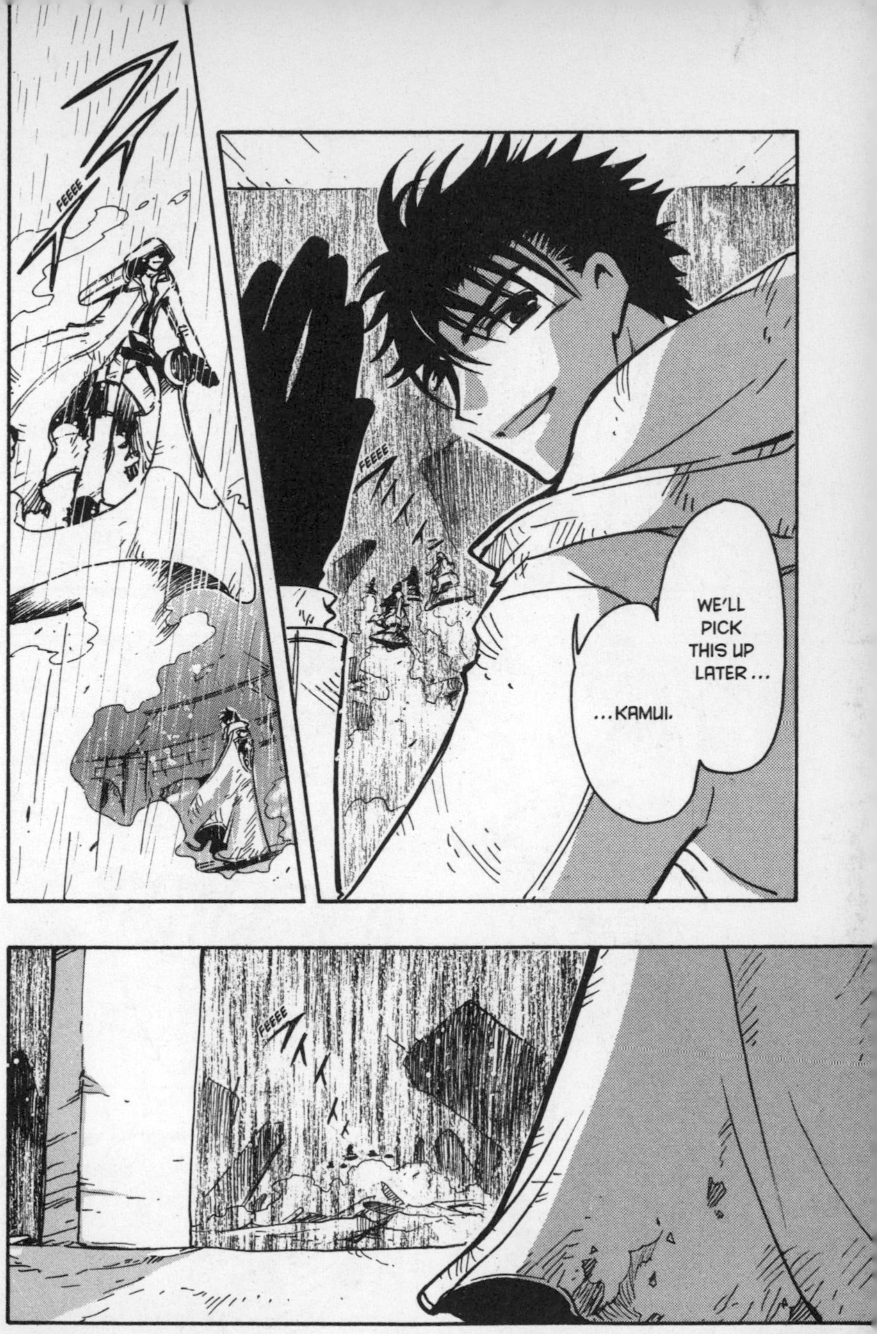
FEEEE
WE'LL PICK THIS UP LATER...
...KAMUI.
FEEEE
FEEEE

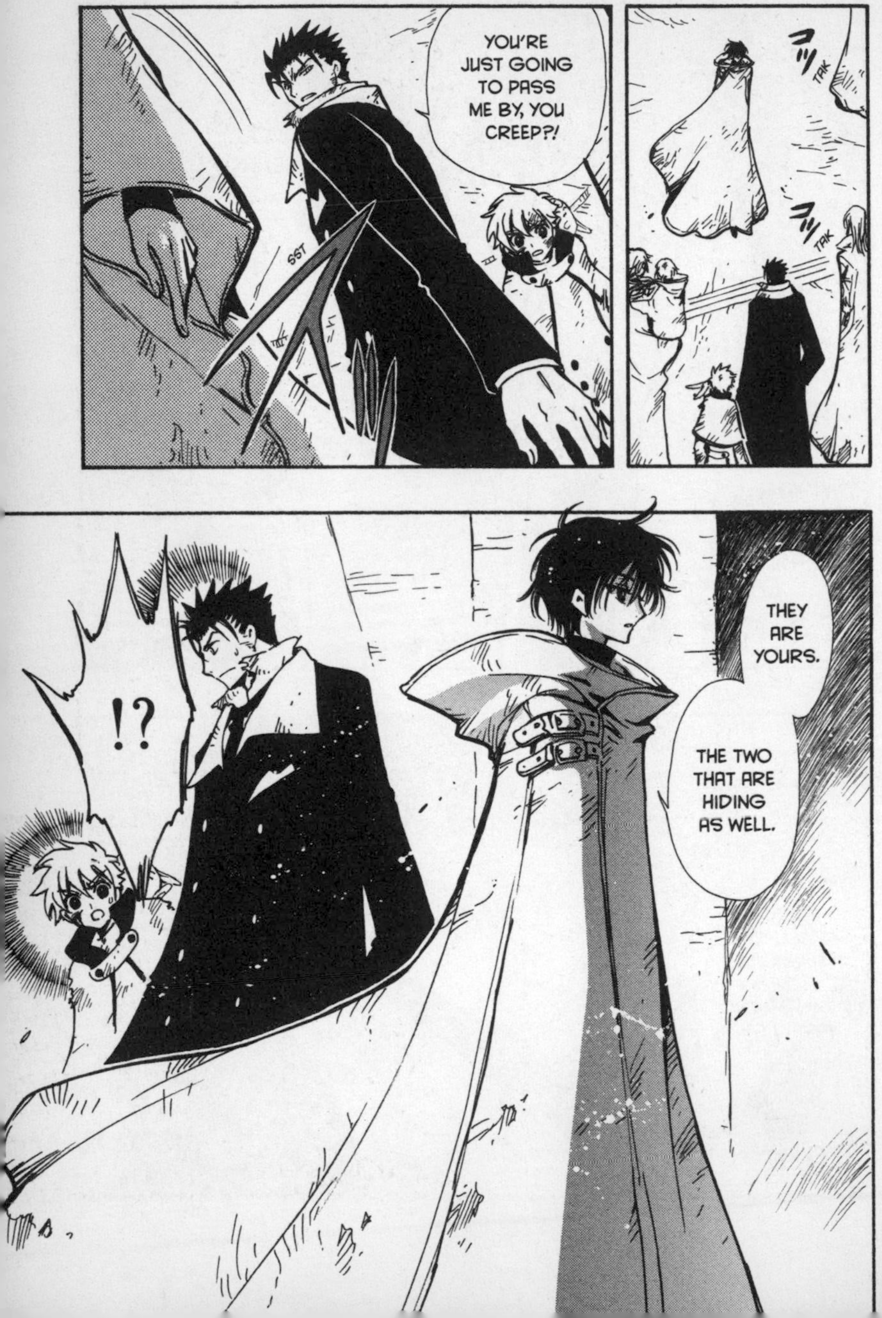
TAK
TAK
YOU'RE JUST GOING TO PASS ME BY, YOU CREEP?!
SST
THEY ARE YOURS.
THE TWO THAT ARE HIDING AS WELL.
!?

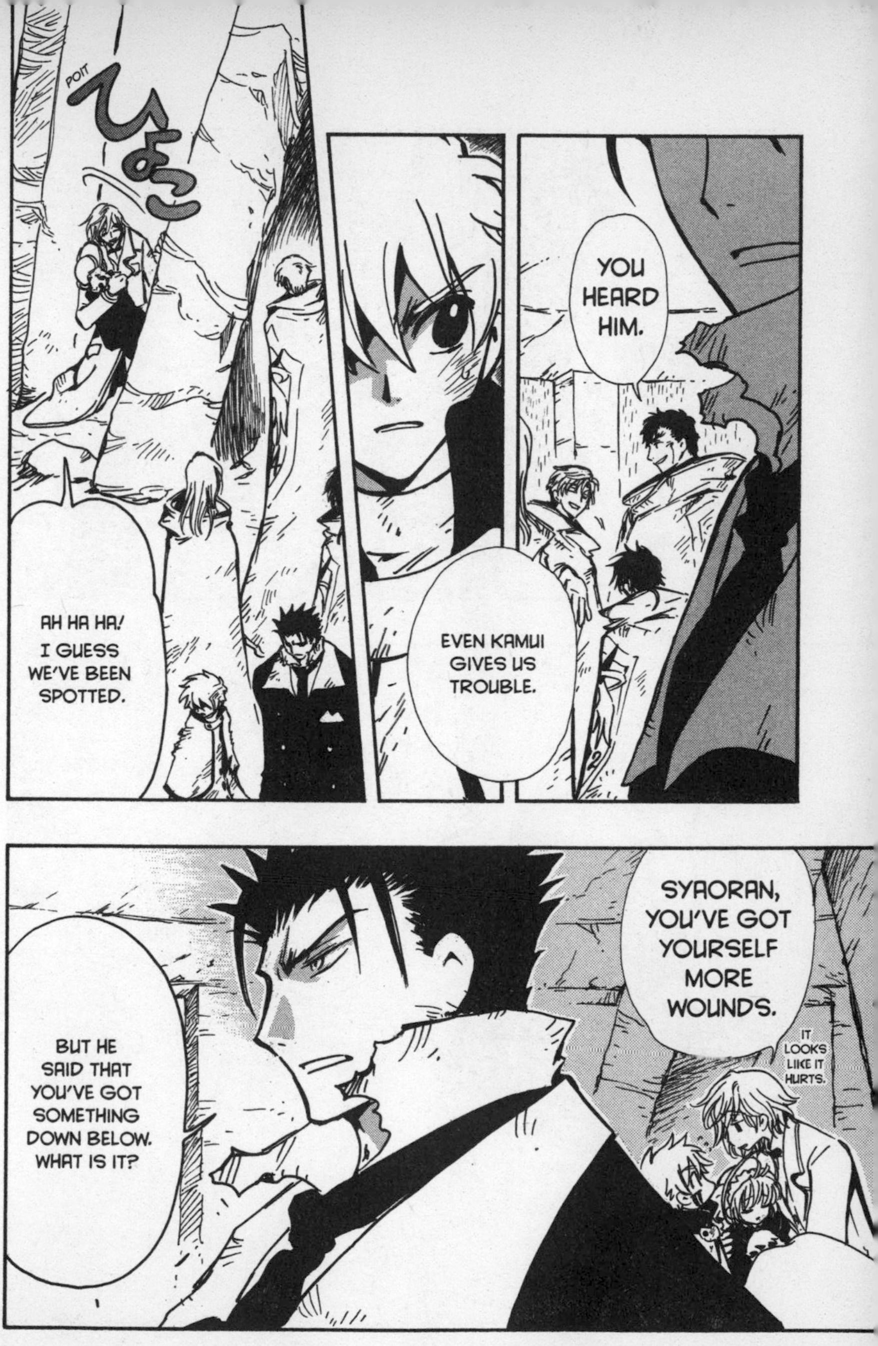
YOU HEARD HIM.
EVEN KAMUI GIVES US TROUBLE.
POIT
ひょこ
AH HA HA! I GUESS WE'VE BEEN SPOTTED.
SYAORAN, YOU'VE GOT YOURSELF MORE WOUNDS.
IT LOOKS LIKE IT HURTS.
BUT HE SAID THAT YOU'VE GOT SOMETHING DOWN BELOW. WHAT IS IT?

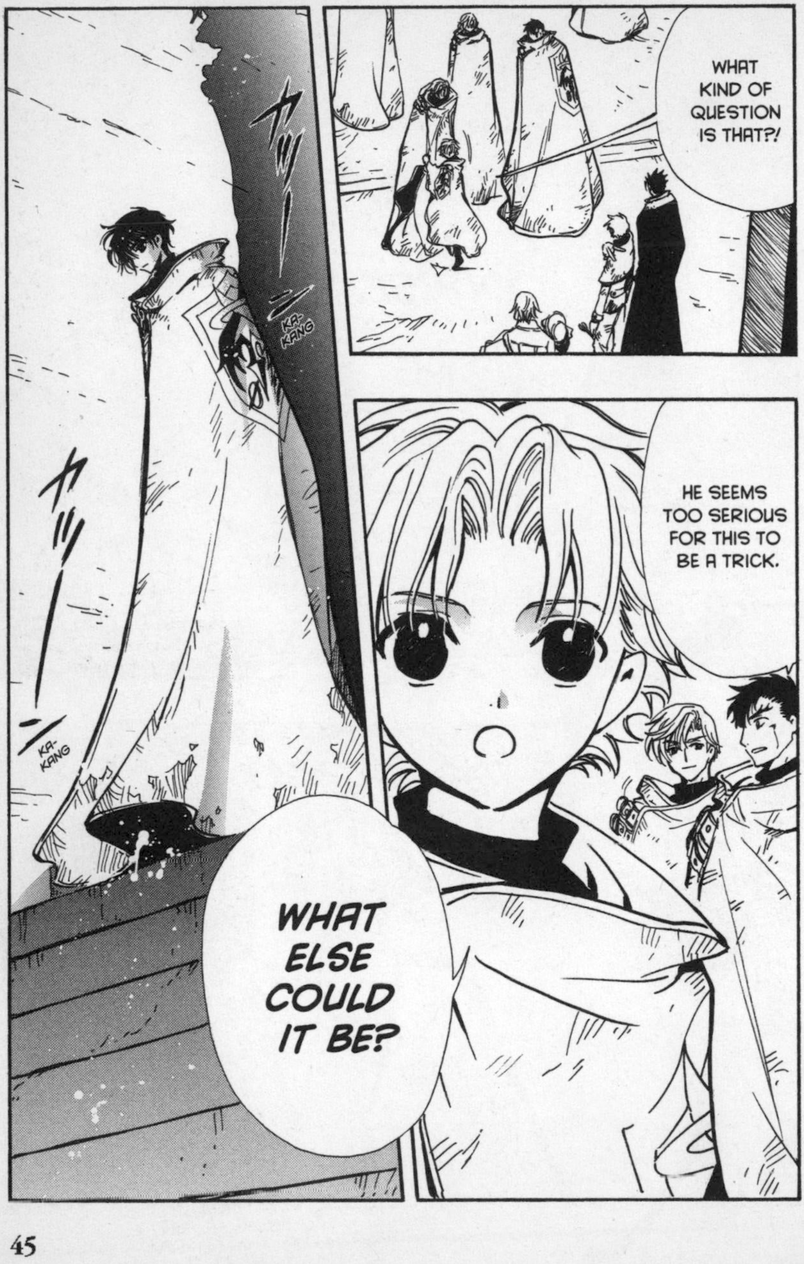
WHAT KIND OF QUESTION IS THAT?!
HE SEEMS TOO SERIOUS FOR THIS TO BE A TRICK.
WHAT ELSE COULD IT BE?
KA-KANG
KA-KANG

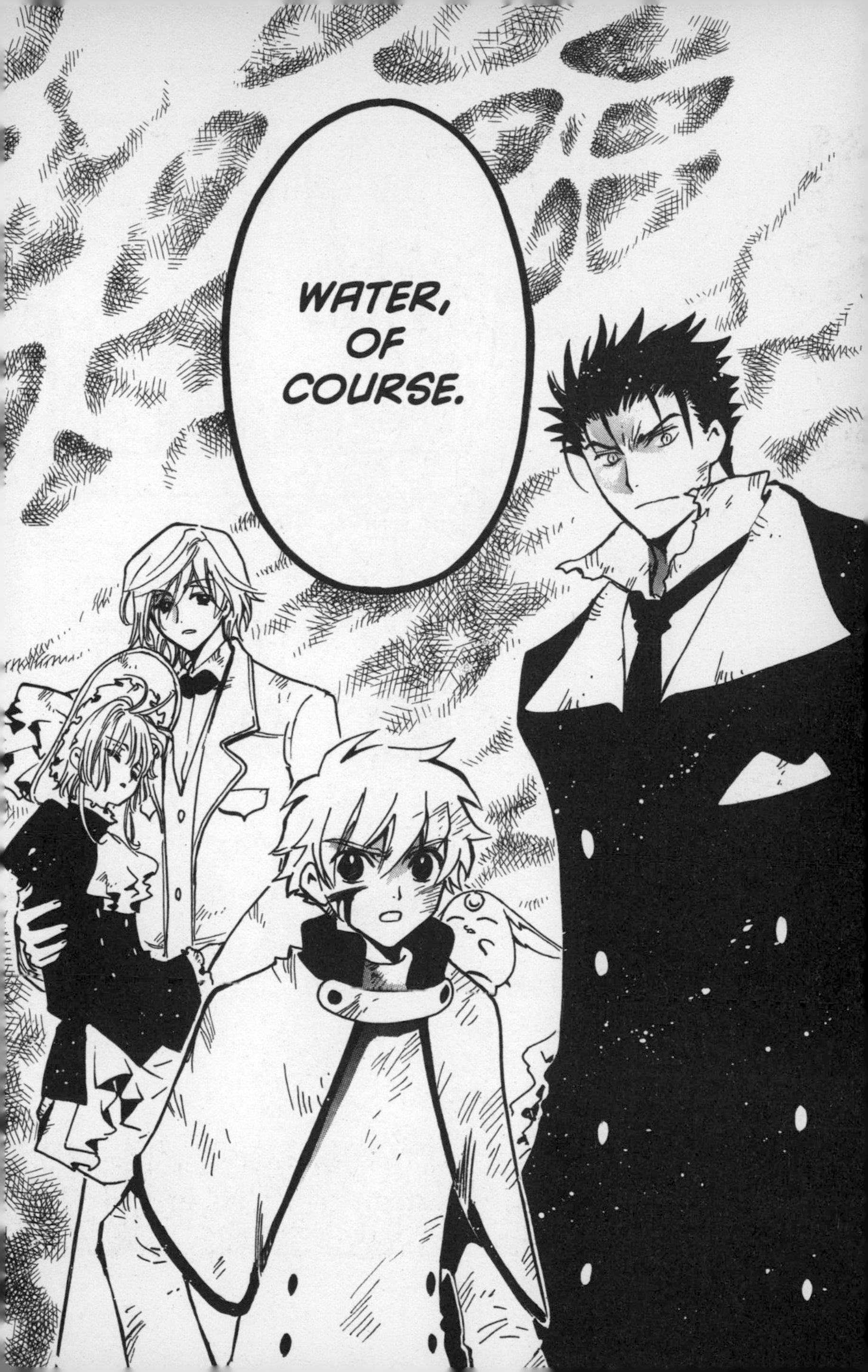
WATER, OF COURSE.

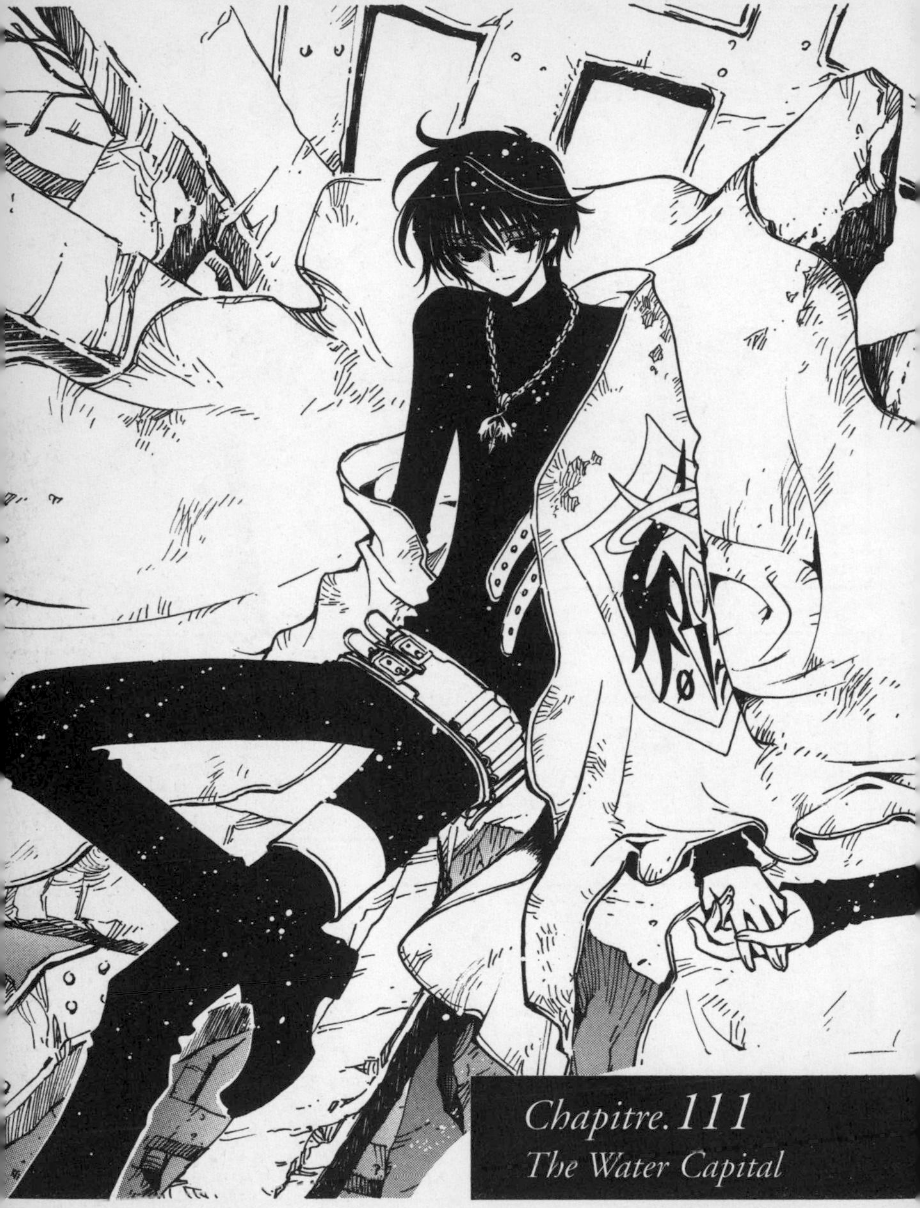

Chapitre. 111
The Water Capital

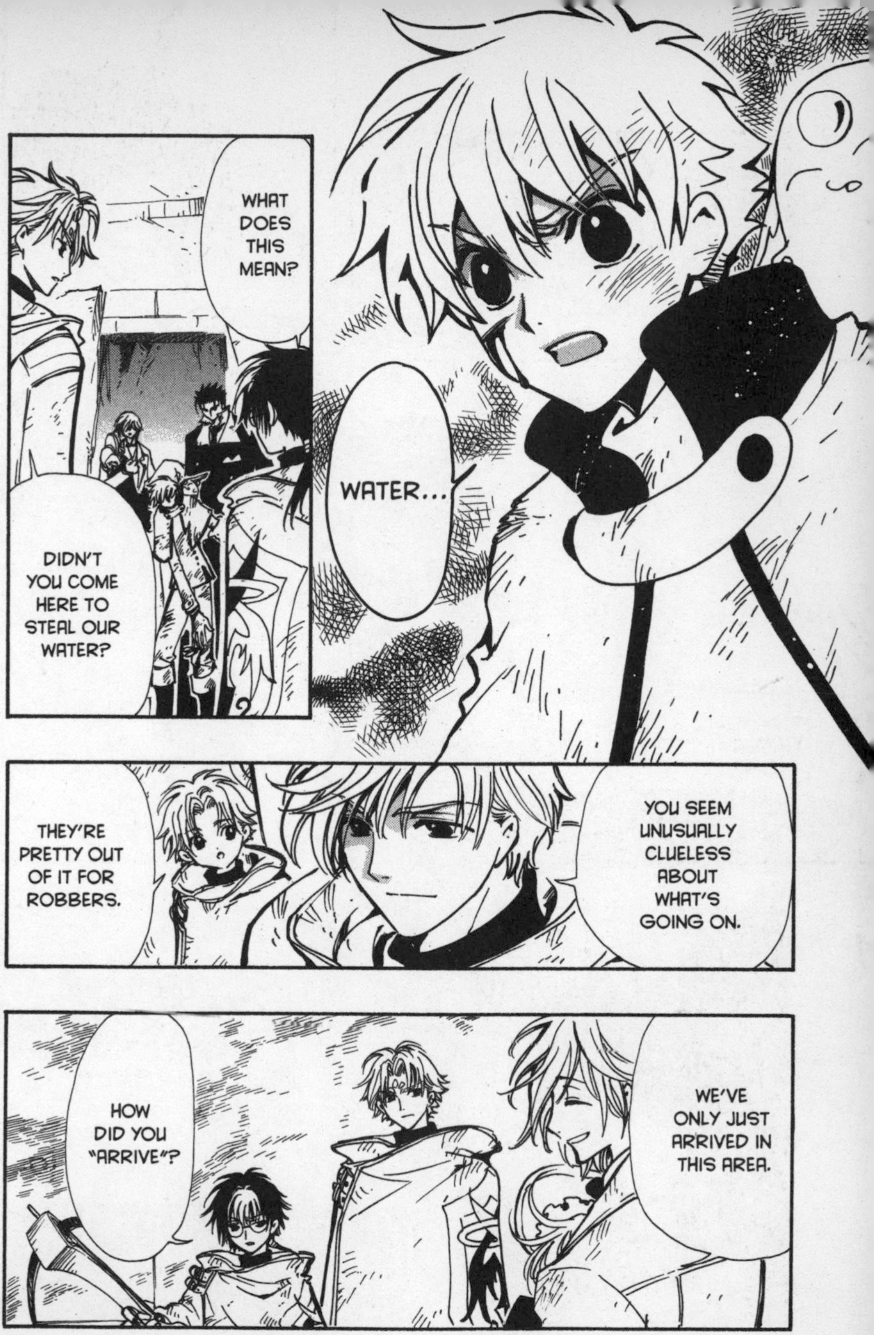
WATER...
WHAT DOES THIS MEAN?
DIDN'T YOU COME HERE TO STEAL OUR WATER?
YOU SEEM UNUSUALLY CLUELESS ABOUT WHAT'S GOING ON.
THEY'RE PRETTY OUT OF IT FOR ROBBERS.
WE'VE ONLY JUST ARRIVED IN THIS AREA.
HOW DID YOU "ARRIVE"?

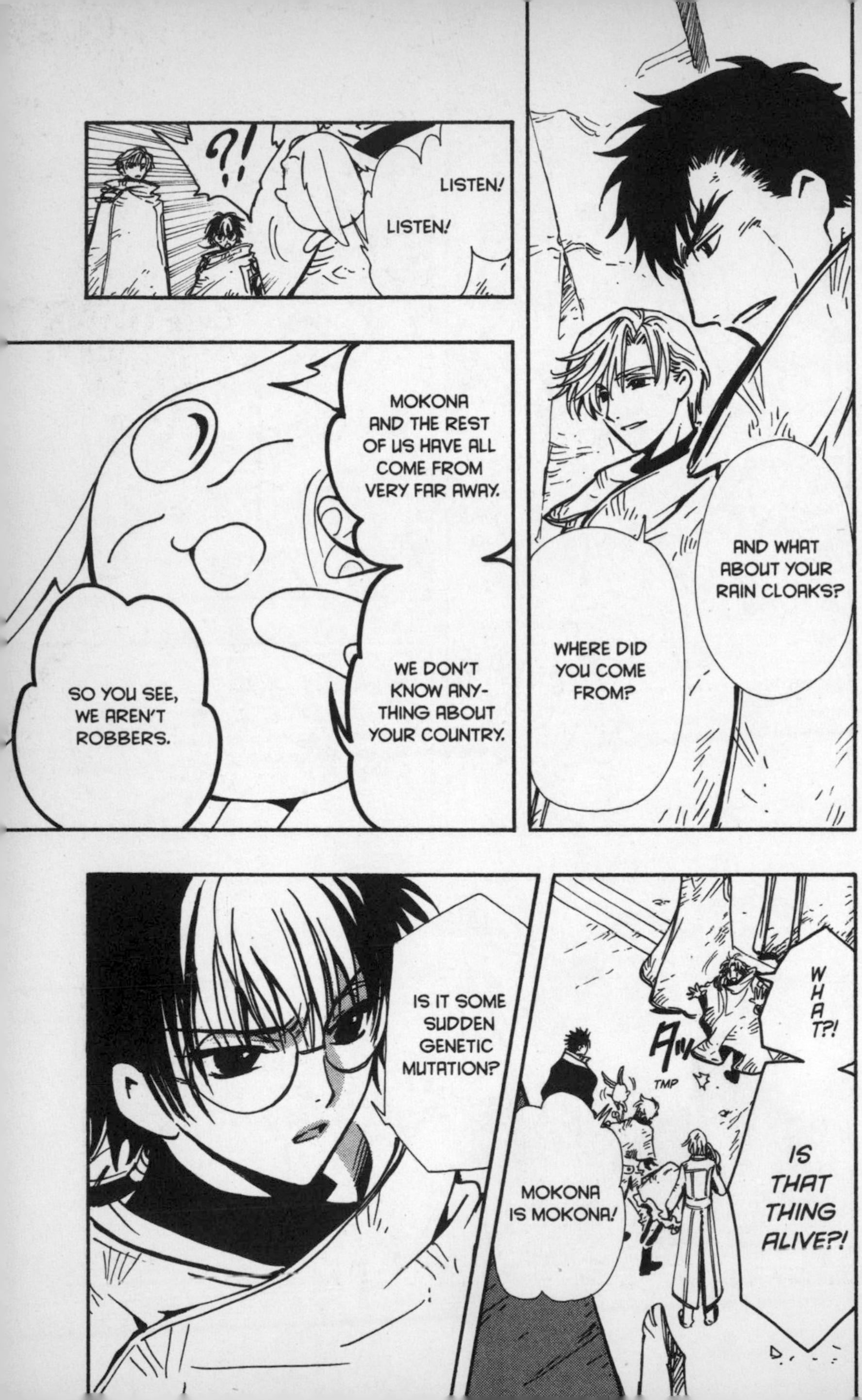
AND WHAT ABOUT YOUR RAIN CLOAKS?
WHERE DID YOU COME FROM?
?!
LISTEN!
LISTEN!
MOKONA AND THE REST OF US HAVE ALL COME FROM VERY FAR AWAY.
WE DON'T KNOW ANY-THING ABOUT YOUR COUNTRY.
SO YOU SEE, WE AREN'T ROBBERS.
WHAT?!
IS THAT THING ALIVE?!
TMP
MOKONA IS MOKONA!
IS IT SOME SUDDEN GENETIC MUTATION?

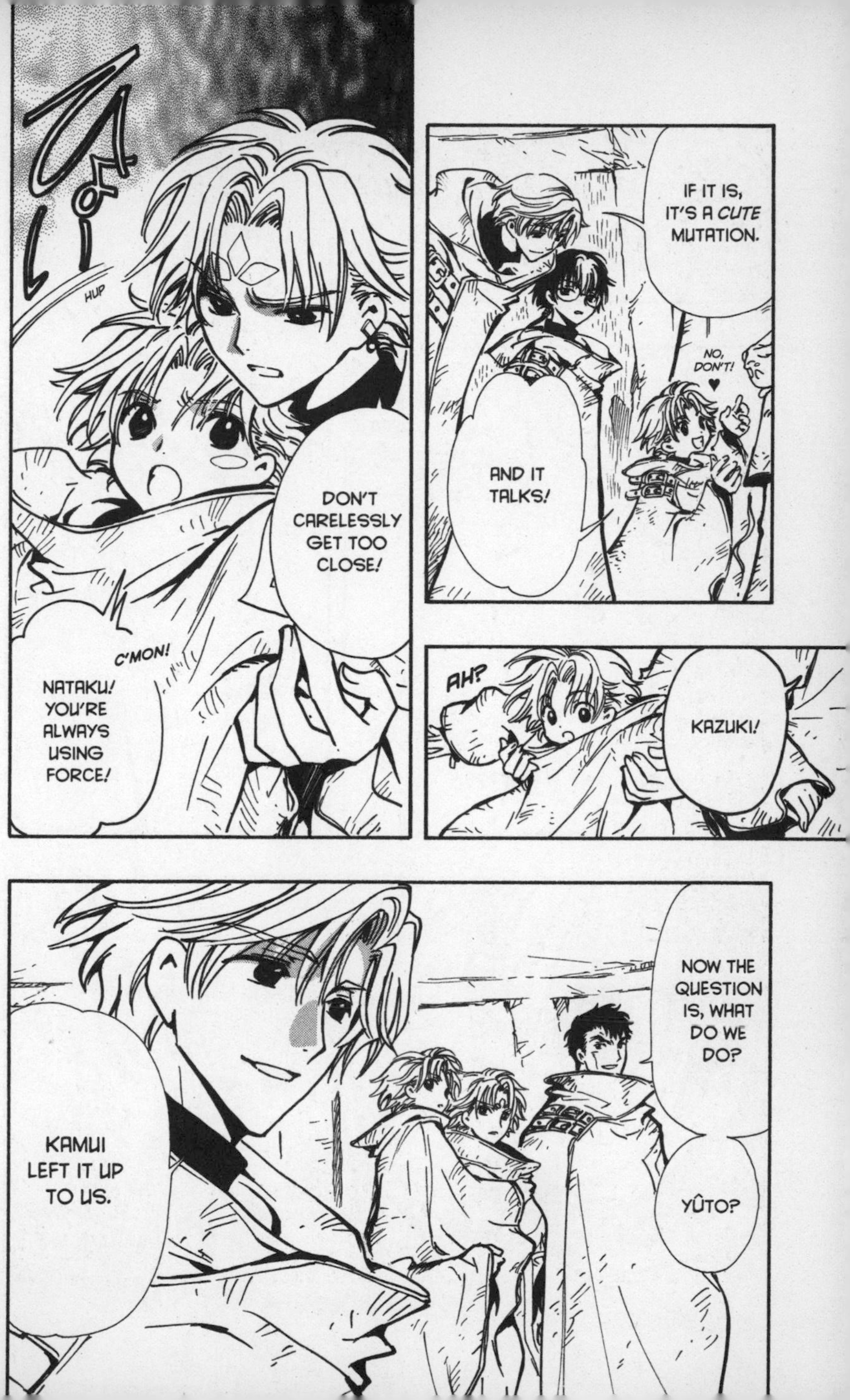
IF IT IS, IT'S A *CUTE* MUTATION.
NO, DON'T! ♥
AND IT TALKS!
KAZUKI!
AH?
HUP
DON'T CARELESSLY GET TOO CLOSE!
C'MON!
NATAKU! YOU'RE ALWAYS USING FORCE!
NOW THE QUESTION IS, WHAT DO WE DO?
YÛTO?
KAMUI LEFT IT UP TO US.

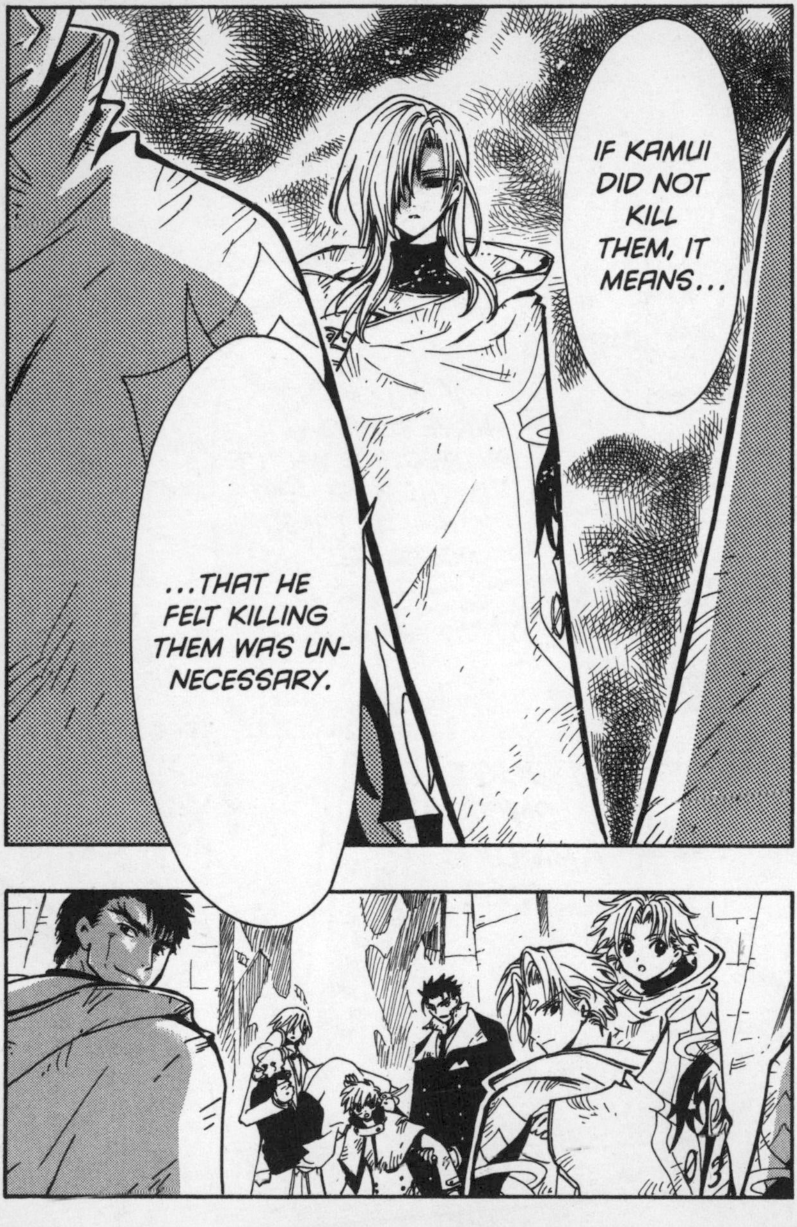
IF KAMUI DID NOT KILL THEM, IT MEANS...
...THAT HE FELT KILLING THEM WAS UN-NECESSARY.

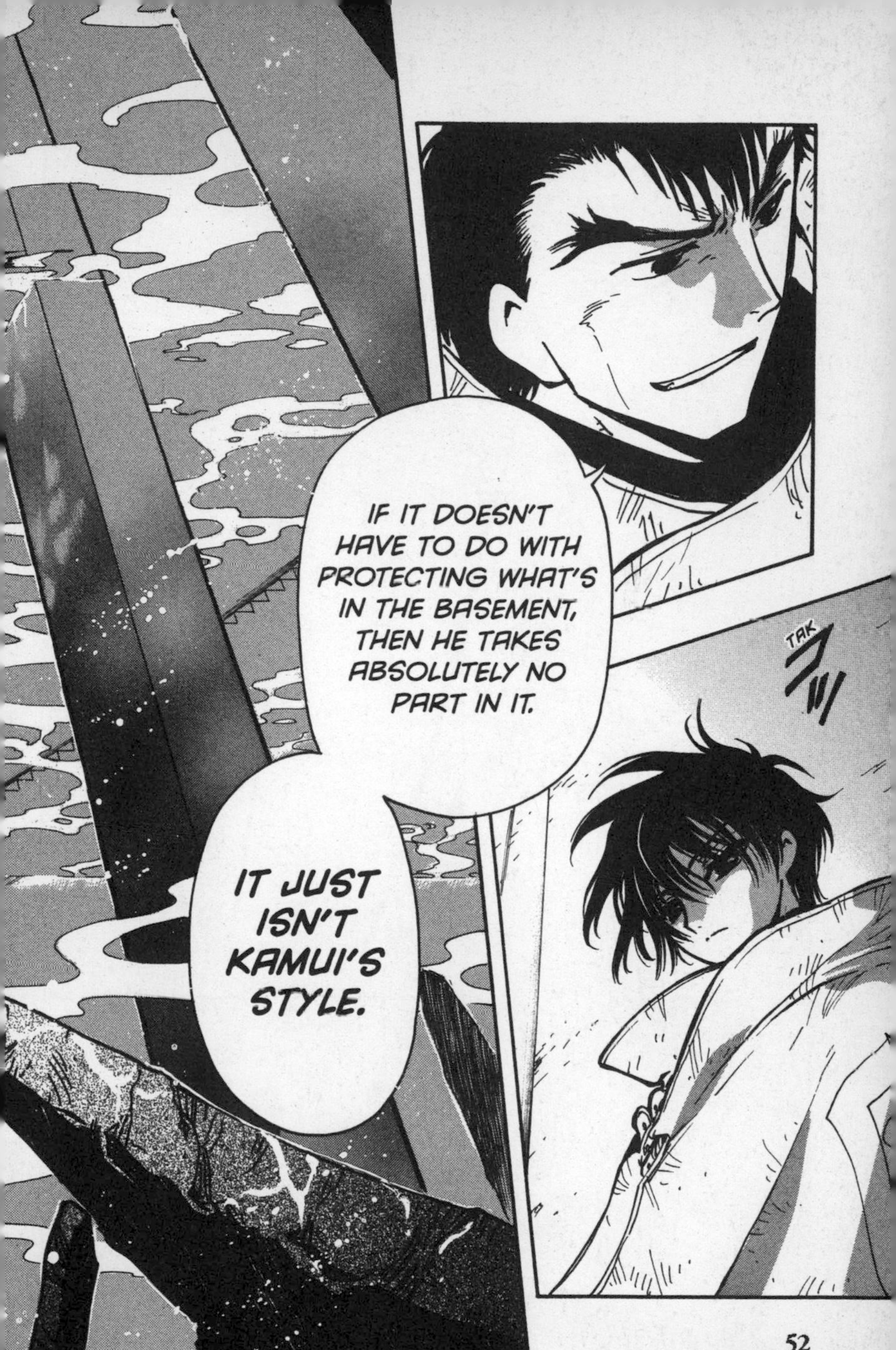
IF IT DOESN'T HAVE TO DO WITH PROTECTING WHAT'S IN THE BASEMENT, THEN HE TAKES ABSOLUTELY NO PART IN IT.
IT JUST ISN'T KAMUI'S STYLE.
TAK

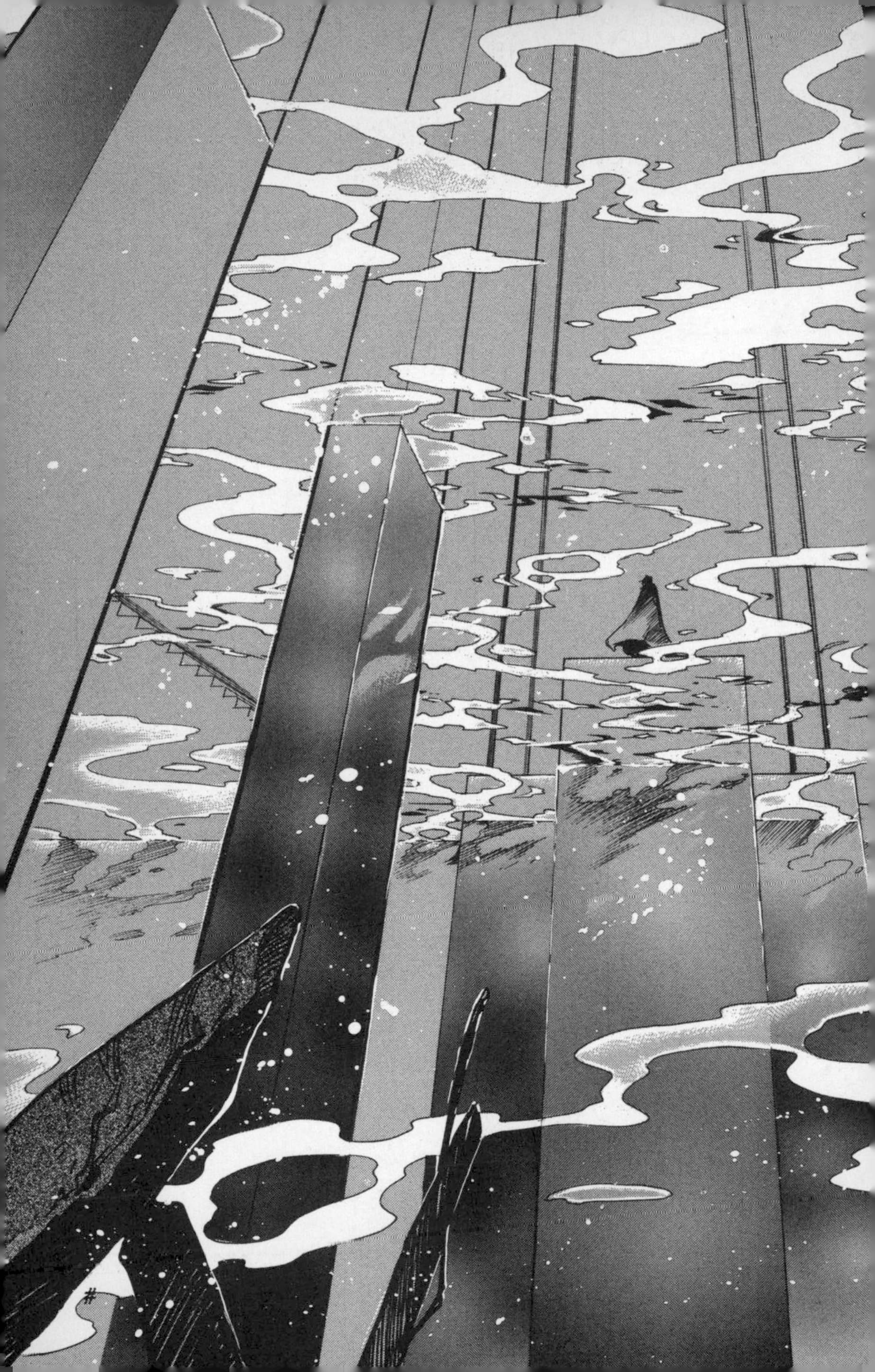

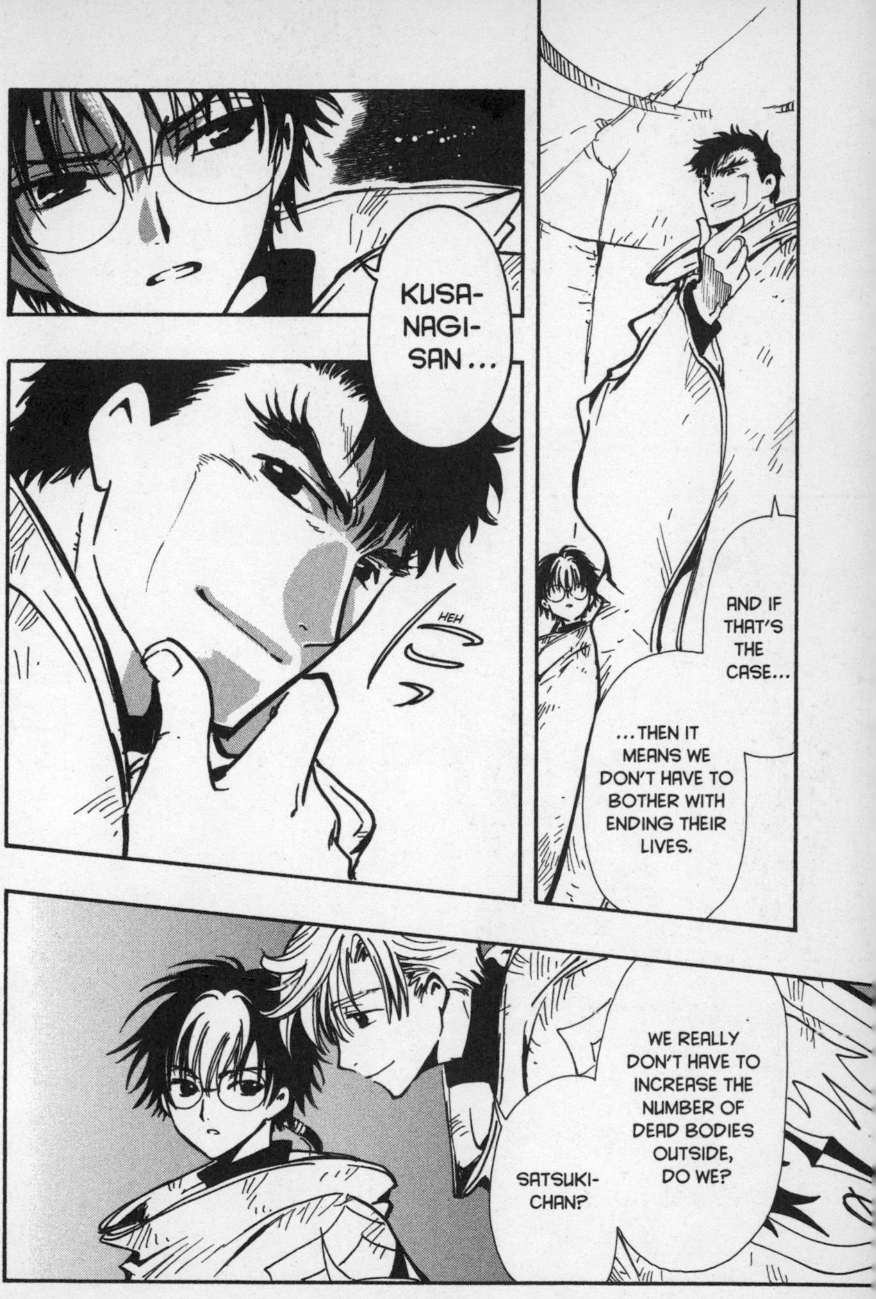
AND IF THAT'S THE CASE...
...THEN IT MEANS WE DON'T HAVE TO BOTHER WITH ENDING THEIR LIVES.
KUSA-NAGI-SAN...
HEH
WE REALLY DON'T HAVE TO INCREASE THE NUMBER OF DEAD BODIES OUTSIDE, DO WE?
SATSUKI-CHAN?

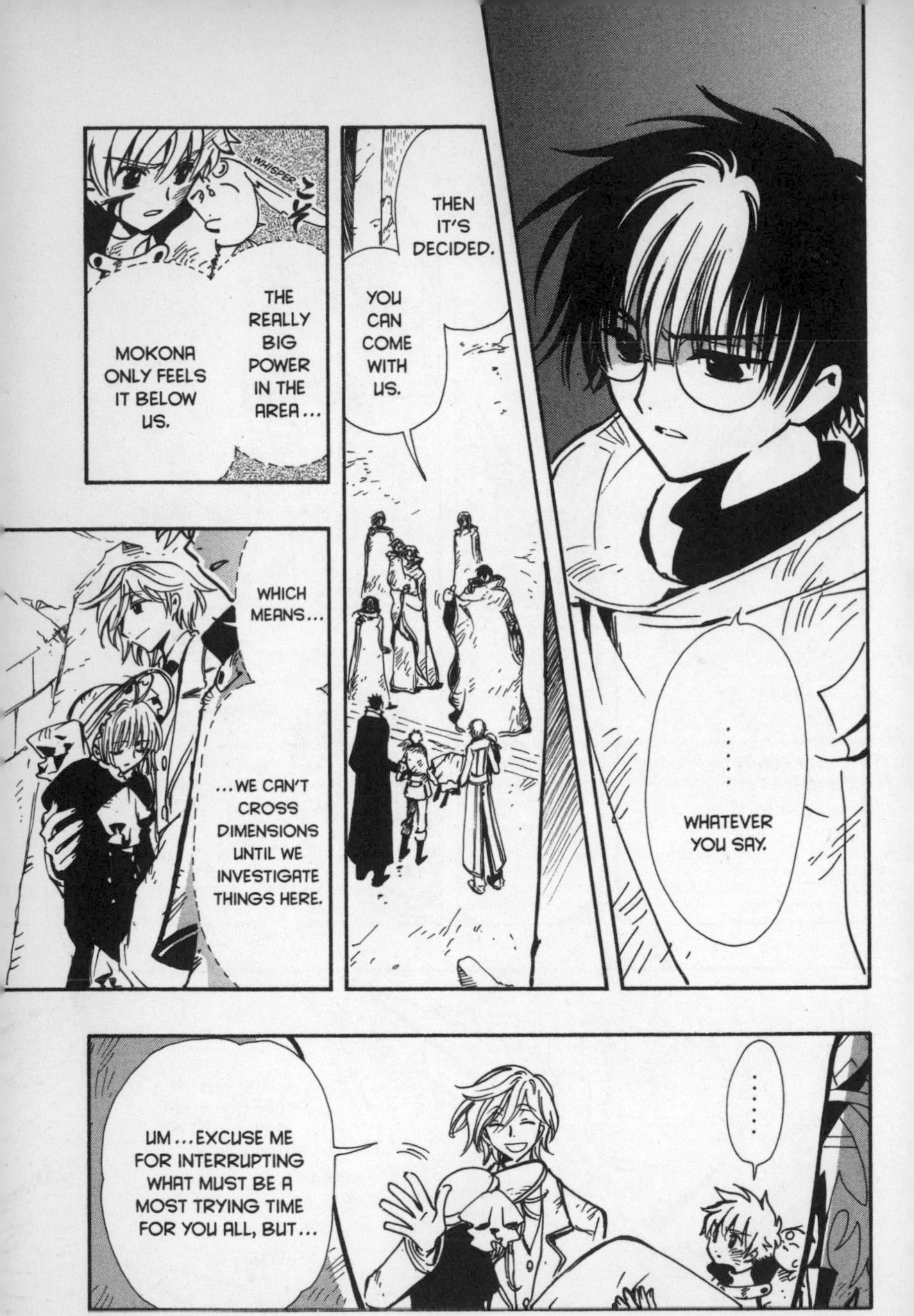
......
WHATEVER YOU SAY.
THEN IT'S DECIDED.
YOU CAN COME WITH US.
WHISPER
THE REALLY BIG POWER IN THE AREA...
MOKONA ONLY FEELS IT BELOW US.
WHICH MEANS...
...WE CAN'T CROSS DIMENSIONS UNTIL WE INVESTIGATE THINGS HERE.
......
UM...EXCUSE ME FOR INTERRUPTING WHAT MUST BE A MOST TRYING TIME FOR YOU ALL, BUT...

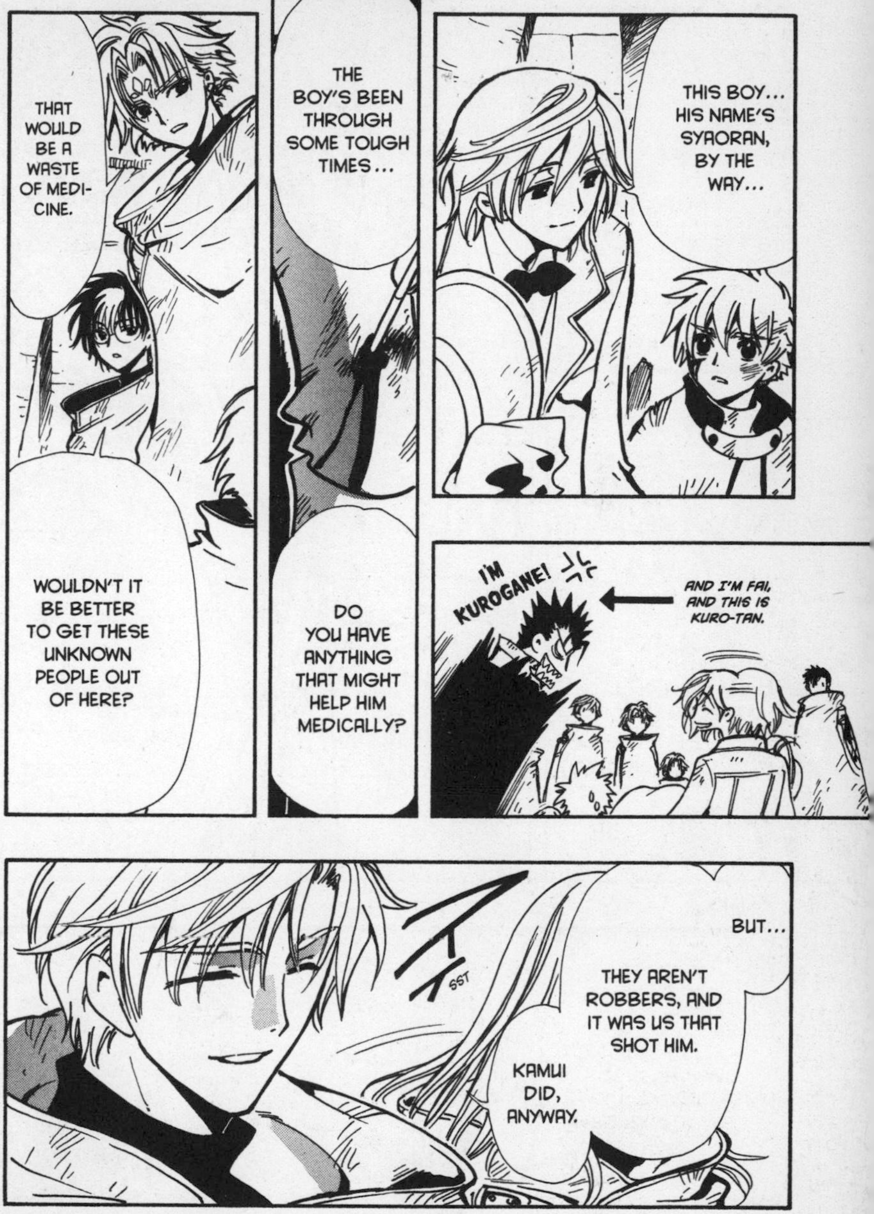
THIS BOY... HIS NAME'S SYAORAN, BY THE WAY...
AND I'M FAI, AND THIS IS KURO-TAN.
I'M KUROGANE!
THE BOY'S BEEN THROUGH SOME TOUGH TIMES...
DO YOU HAVE ANYTHING THAT MIGHT HELP HIM MEDICALLY?
THAT WOULD BE A WASTE OF MEDI-CINE.
WOULDN'T IT BE BETTER TO GET THESE UNKNOWN PEOPLE OUT OF HERE?
BUT...
THEY AREN'T ROBBERS, AND IT WAS US THAT SHOT HIM.
KAMUI DID, ANYWAY.
SST

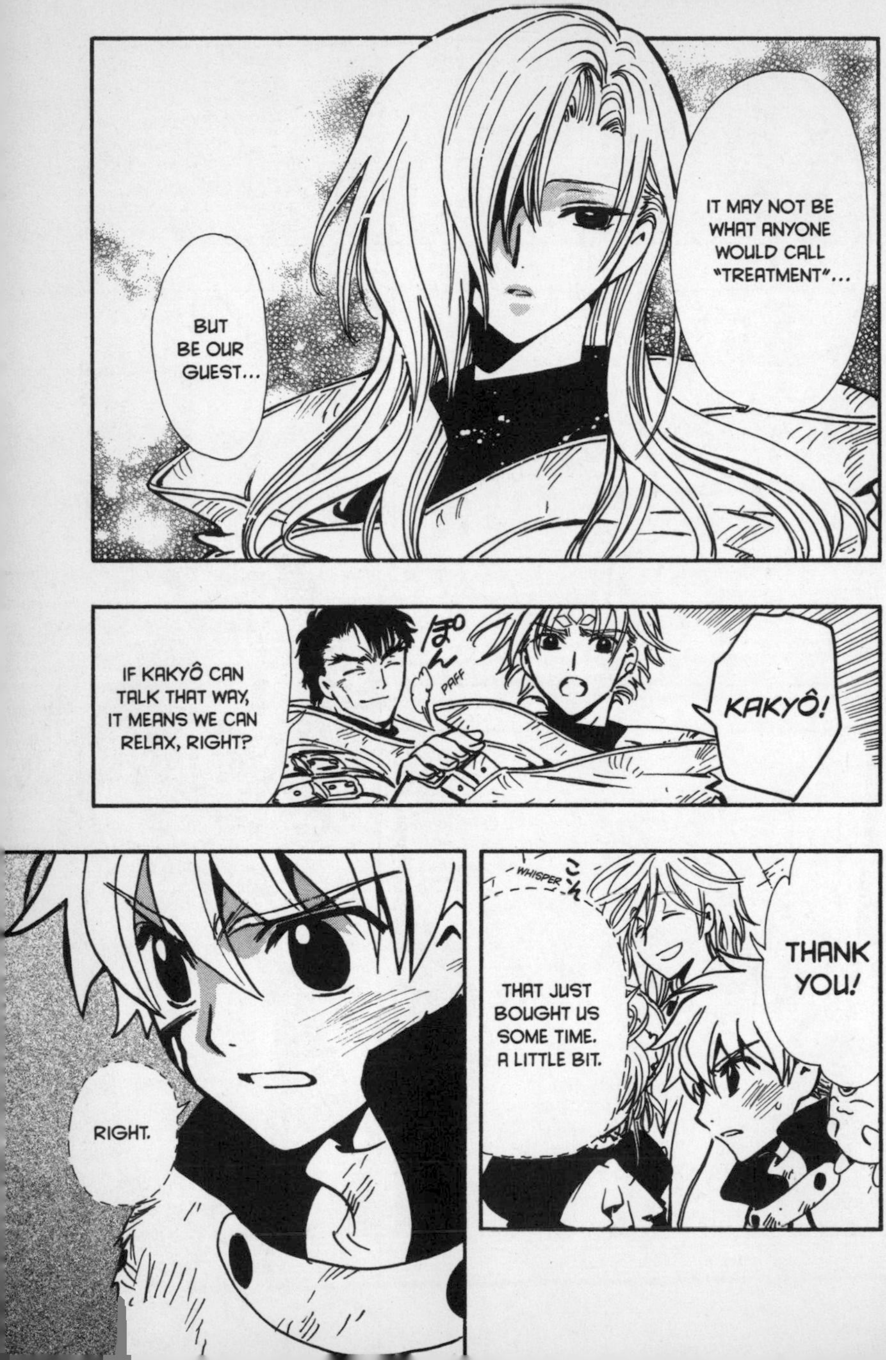
IT MAY NOT BE WHAT ANYONE WOULD CALL "TREATMENT"...
BUT BE OUR GUEST...
KAKYÔ!
ぽん
PAFF
IF KAKYÔ CAN TALK THAT WAY, IT MEANS WE CAN RELAX, RIGHT?
THANK YOU!
こそ
WHISPER
THAT JUST BOUGHT US SOME TIME. A LITTLE BIT.
RIGHT.

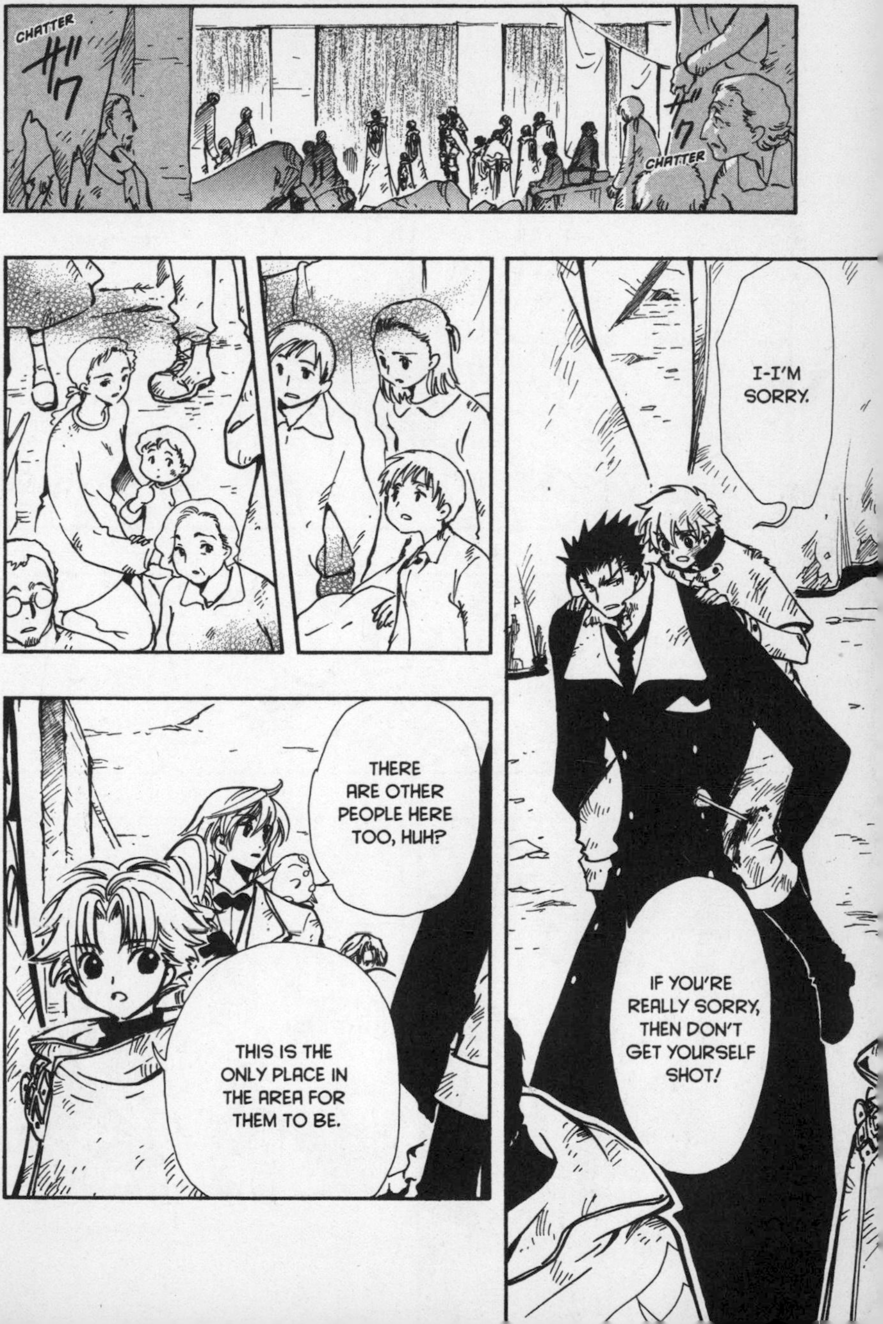
ザワ
CHATTER
ザワ
CHATTER
I-I'M SORRY.
IF YOU'RE REALLY SORRY, THEN DON'T GET YOURSELF SHOT!
THERE ARE OTHER PEOPLE HERE TOO, HUH?
THIS IS THE ONLY PLACE IN THE AREA FOR THEM TO BE.

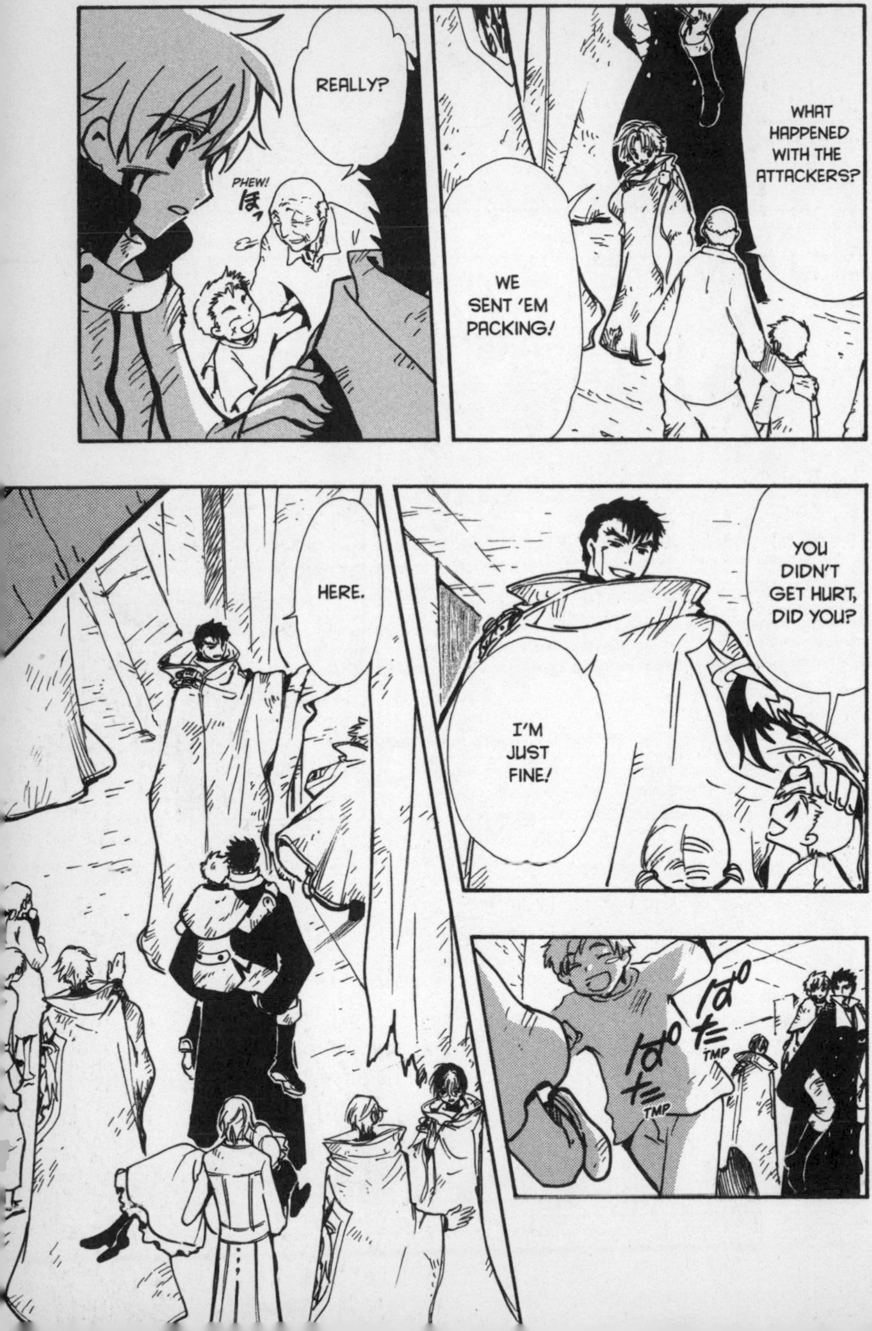
WHAT HAPPENED WITH THE ATTACKERS?
WE SENT 'EM PACKING!
REALLY?
PHEW!
ほっ
YOU DIDN'T GET HURT, DID YOU?
I'M JUST FINE!
ぱた
TMP
ぱた
TMP
HERE.

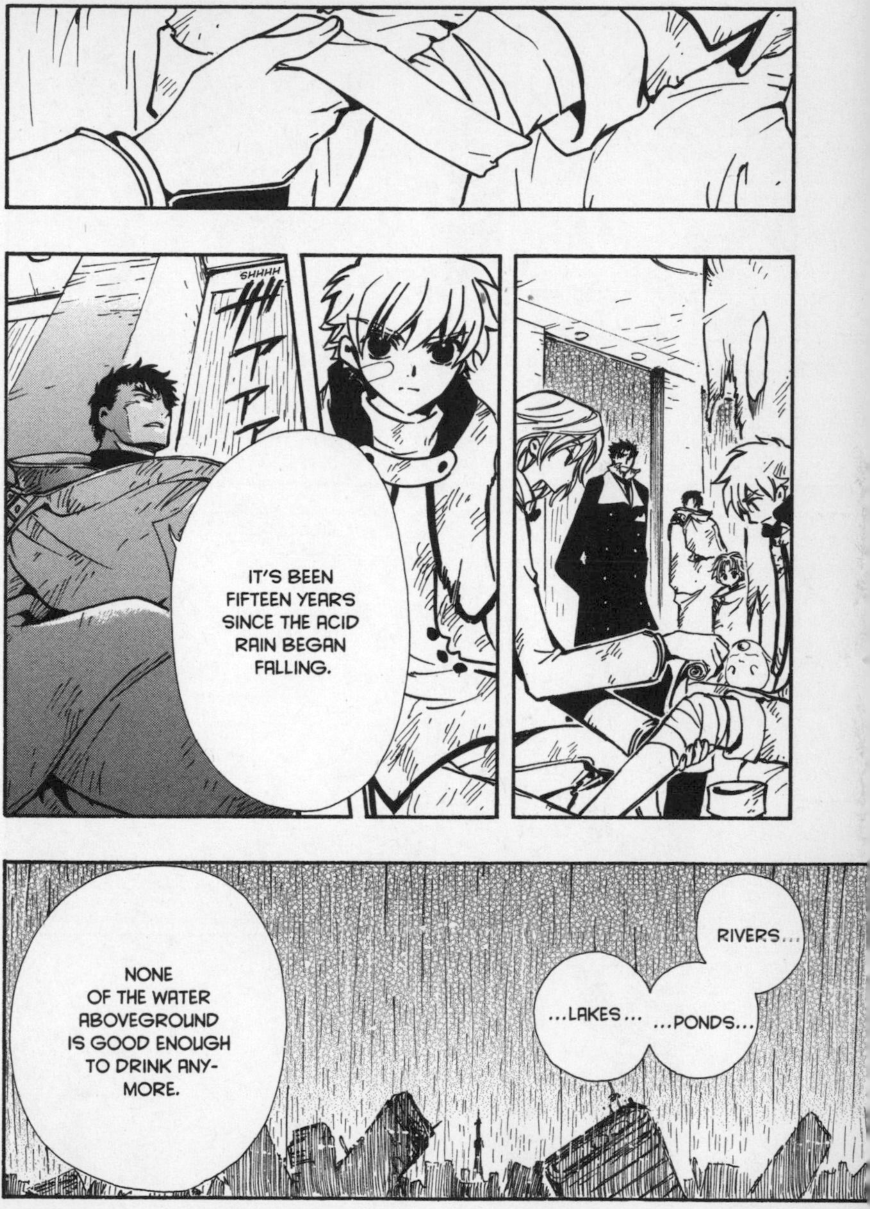
IT'S BEEN FIFTEEN YEARS SINCE THE ACID RAIN BEGAN FALLING.
SHHHH
RIVERS...
...LAKES...
...PONDS...
NONE OF THE WATER ABOVEGROUND IS GOOD ENOUGH TO DRINK ANY-MORE.

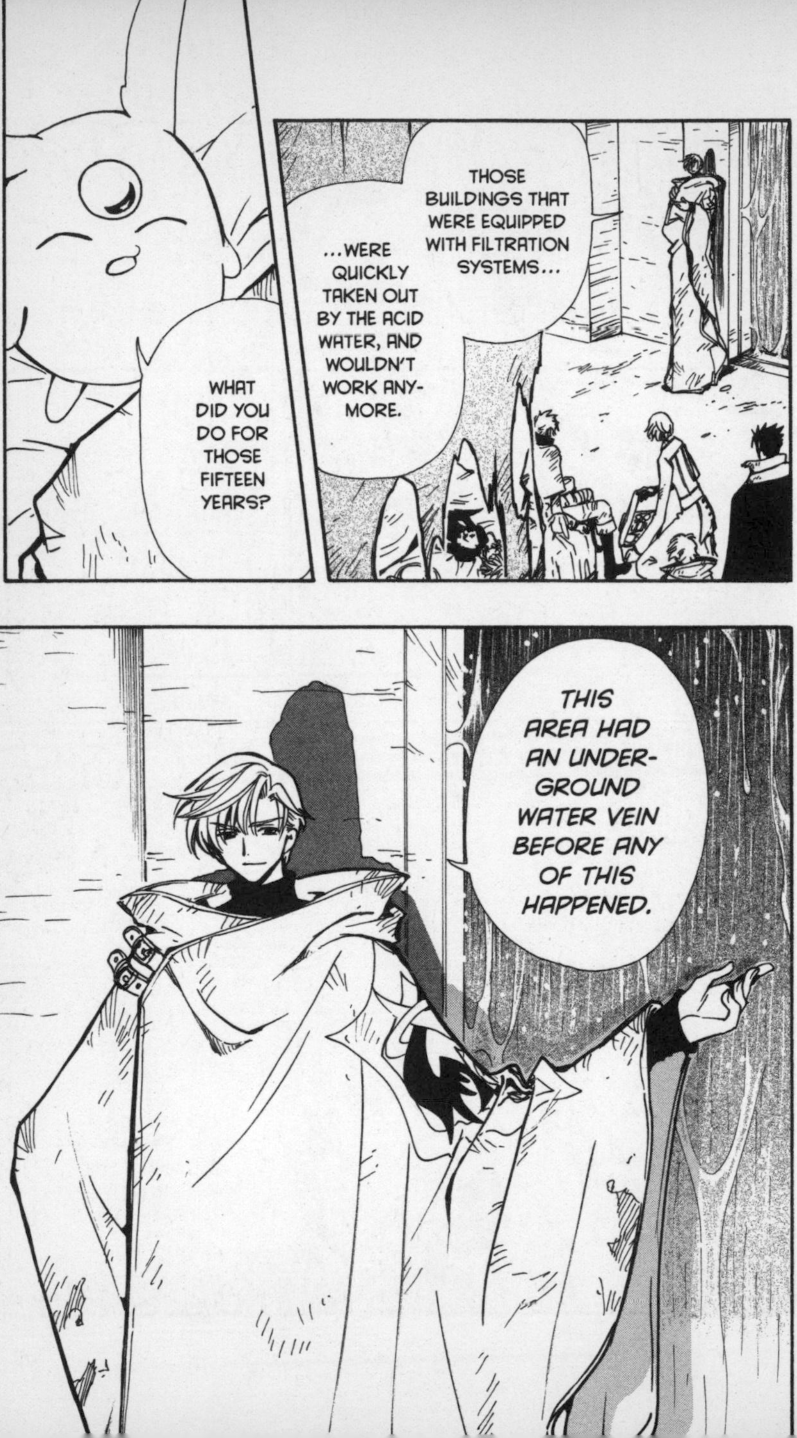
THOSE BUILDINGS THAT WERE EQUIPPED WITH FILTRATION SYSTEMS...
...WERE QUICKLY TAKEN OUT BY THE ACID WATER, AND WOULDN'T WORK ANY-MORE.
WHAT DID YOU DO FOR THOSE FIFTEEN YEARS?
THIS AREA HAD AN UNDER-GROUND WATER VEIN BEFORE ANY OF THIS HAPPENED.

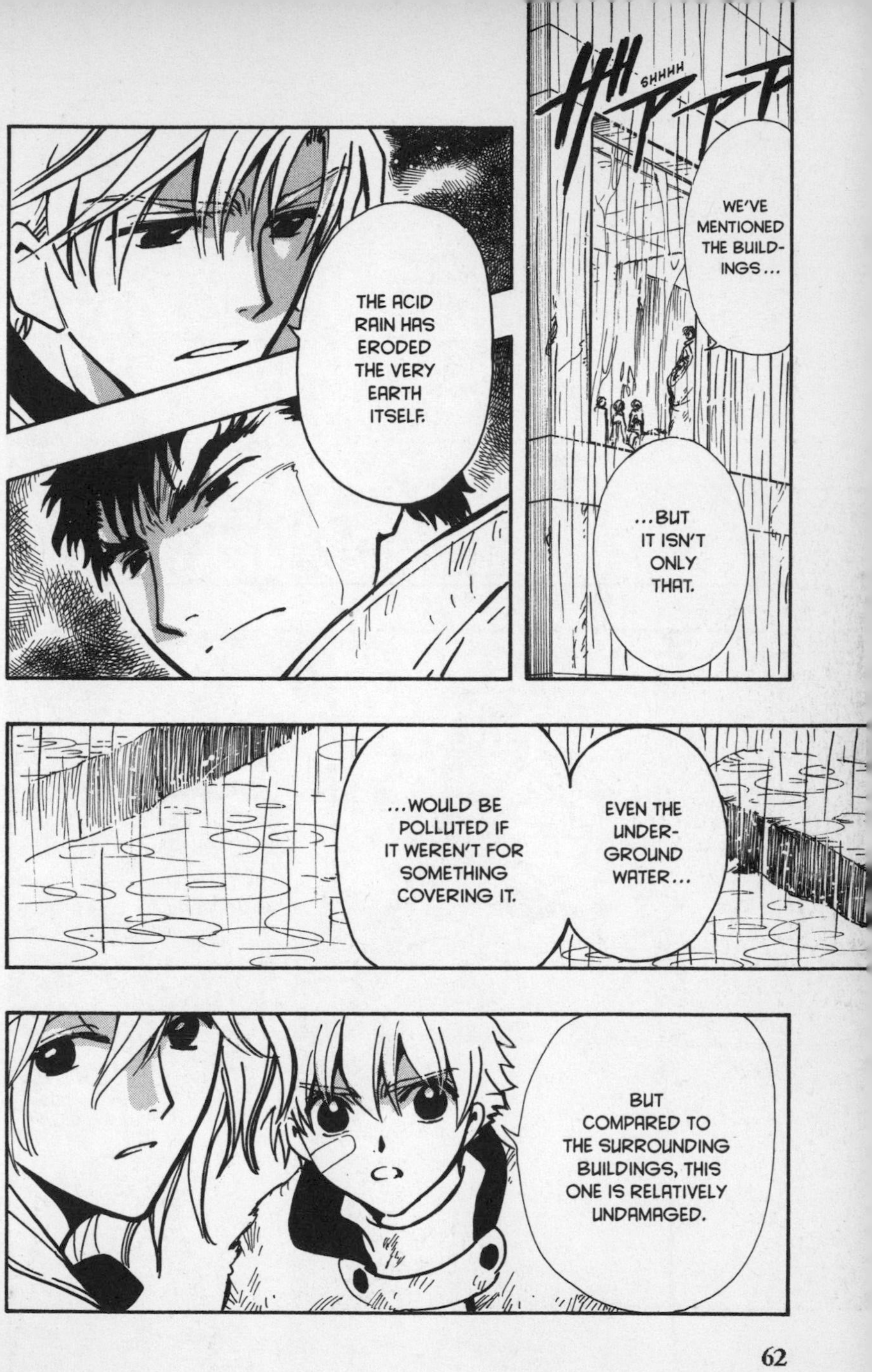
SHHHH
WE'VE MENTIONED THE BUILD-INGS...
...BUT IT ISN'T ONLY THAT.
THE ACID RAIN HAS ERODED THE VERY EARTH ITSELF.
EVEN THE UNDER-GROUND WATER...
...WOULD BE POLLUTED IF IT WEREN'T FOR SOMETHING COVERING IT.
BUT COMPARED TO THE SURROUNDING BUILDINGS, THIS ONE IS RELATIVELY UNDAMAGED.

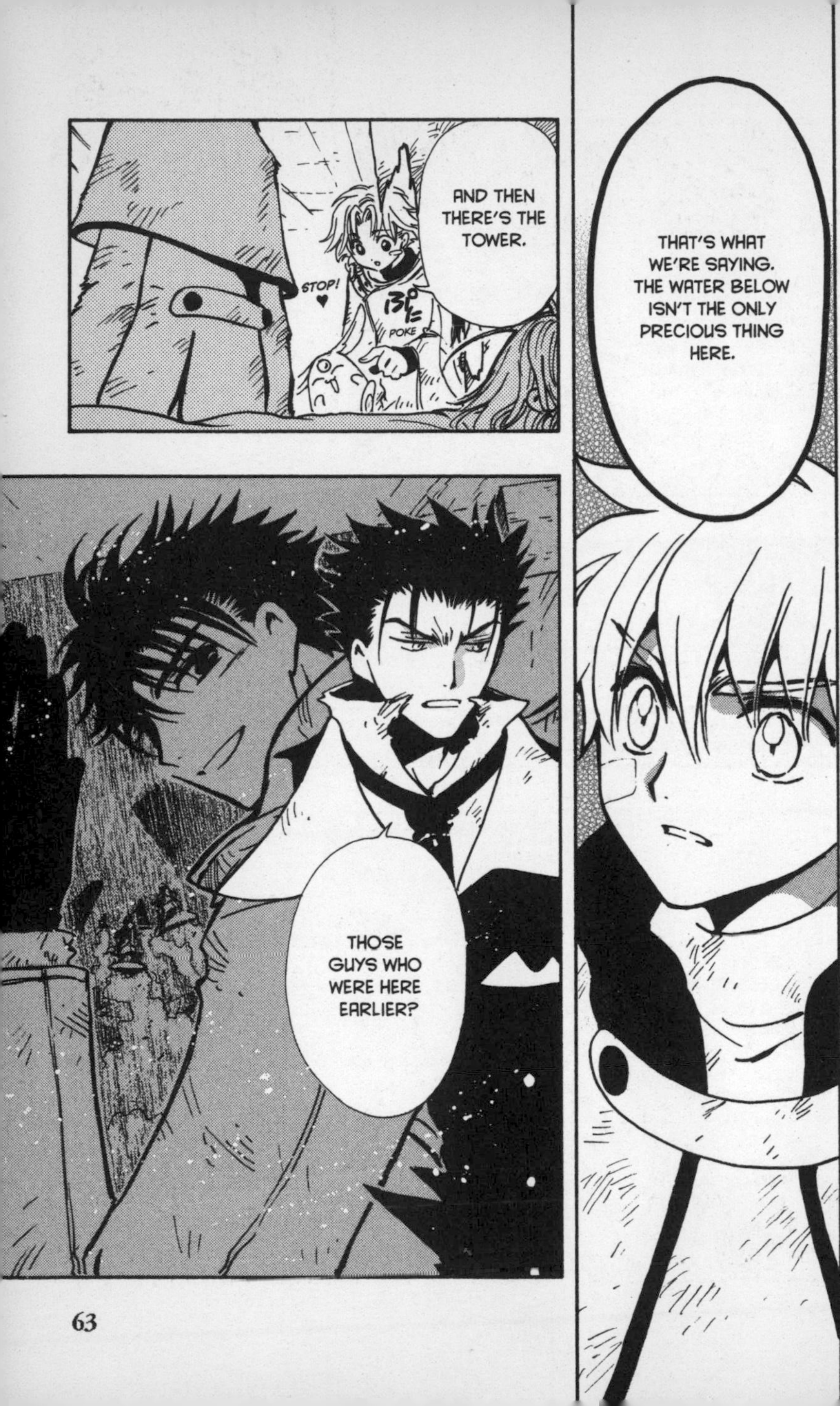
THAT'S WHAT WE'RE SAYING. THE WATER BELOW ISN'T THE ONLY PRECIOUS THING HERE.
AND THEN THERE'S THE TOWER.
STOP! ♥
POKE
THOSE GUYS WHO WERE HERE EARLIER?

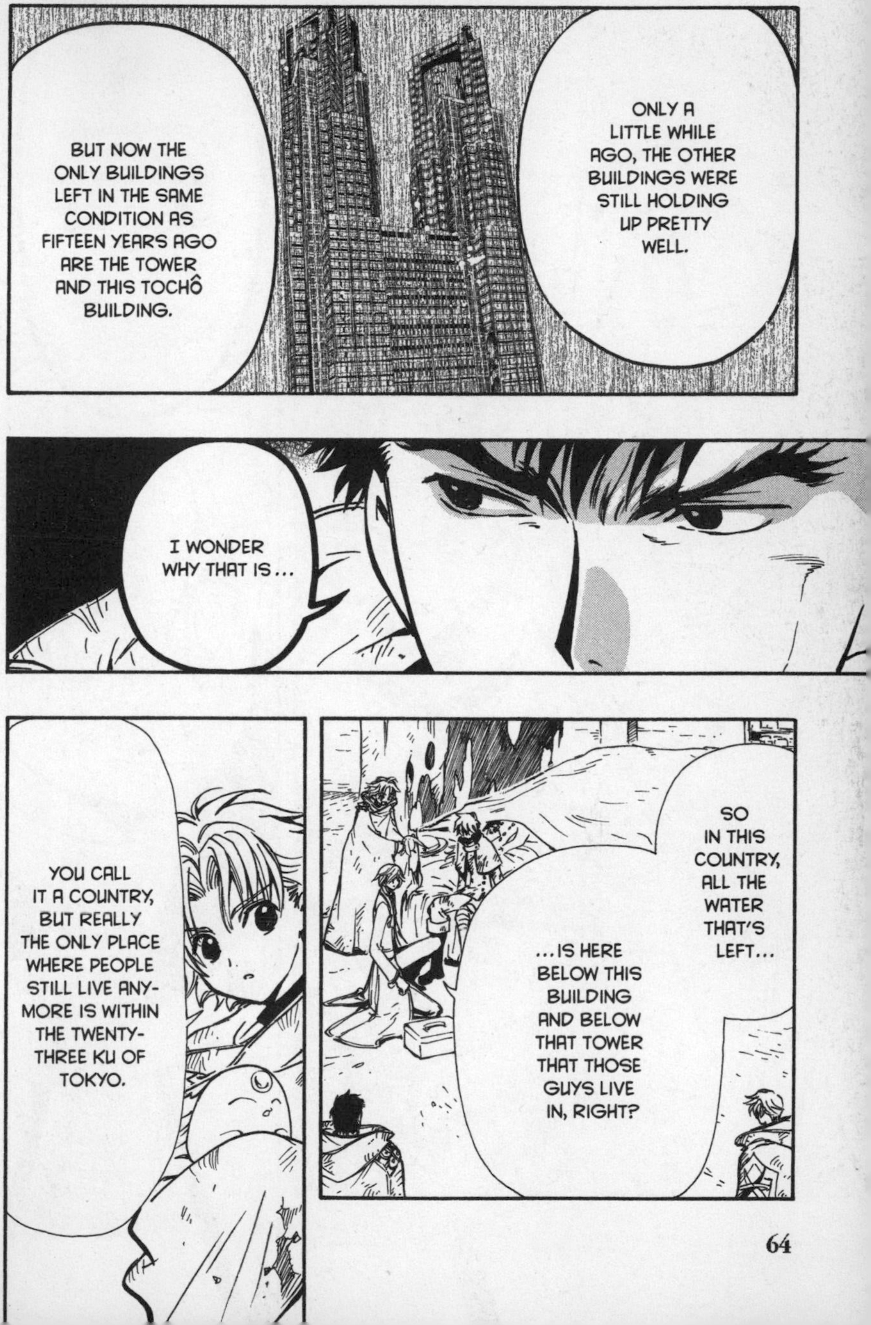
ONLY A LITTLE WHILE AGO, THE OTHER BUILDINGS WERE STILL HOLDING UP PRETTY WELL.
BUT NOW THE ONLY BUILDINGS LEFT IN THE SAME CONDITION AS FIFTEEN YEARS AGO ARE THE TOWER AND THIS TOCHÔ BUILDING.
I WONDER WHY THAT IS...
SO IN THIS COUNTRY, ALL THE WATER THAT'S LEFT...
...IS HERE BELOW THIS BUILDING AND BELOW THAT TOWER THAT THOSE GUYS LIVE IN, RIGHT?
YOU CALL IT A COUNTRY, BUT REALLY THE ONLY PLACE WHERE PEOPLE STILL LIVE ANYMORE IS WITHIN THE TWENTY-THREE KU OF TOKYO.

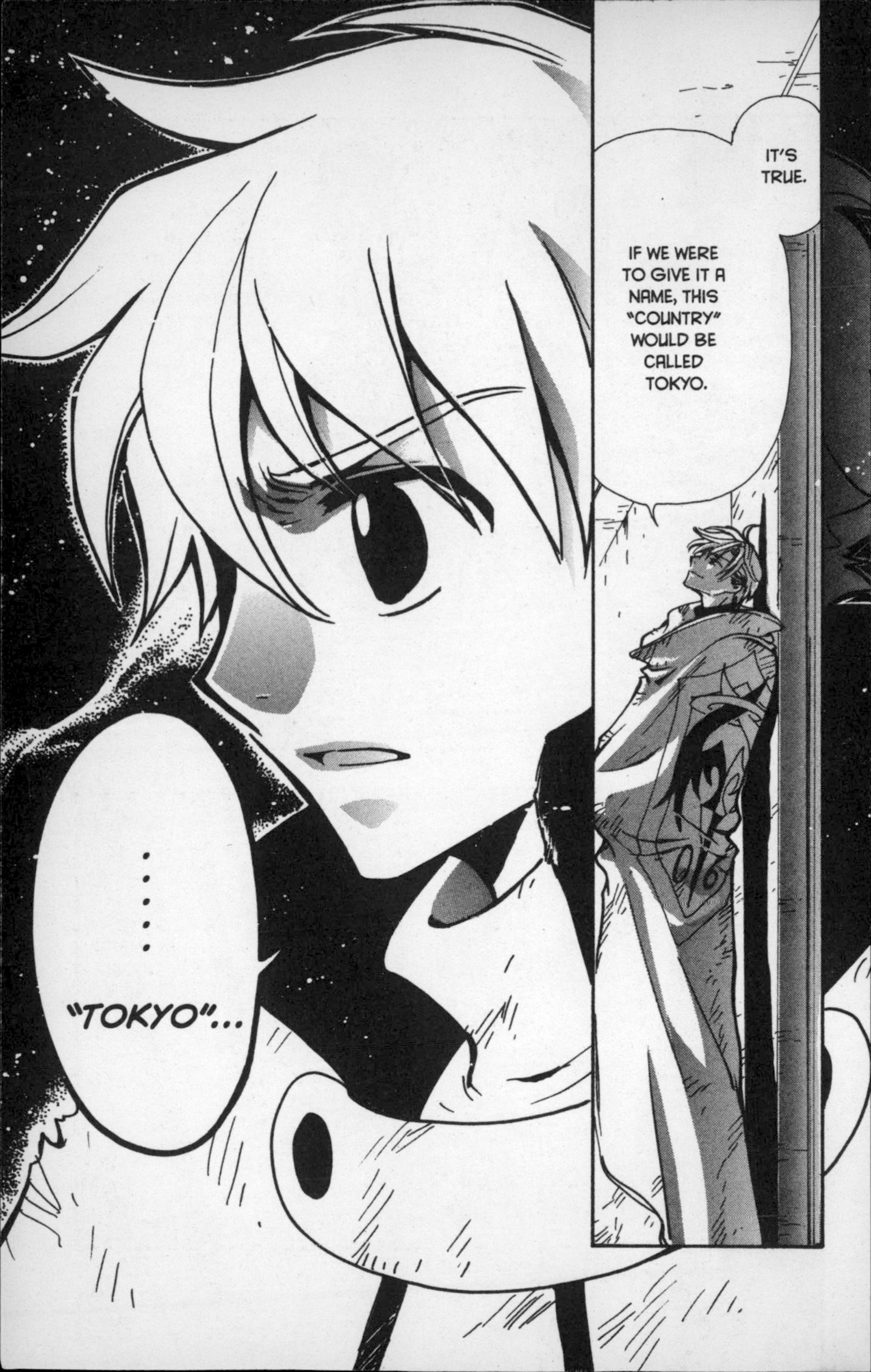
IT'S TRUE.
IF WE WERE TO GIVE IT A NAME, THIS "COUNTRY" WOULD BE CALLED TOKYO.
......
"TOKYO"...

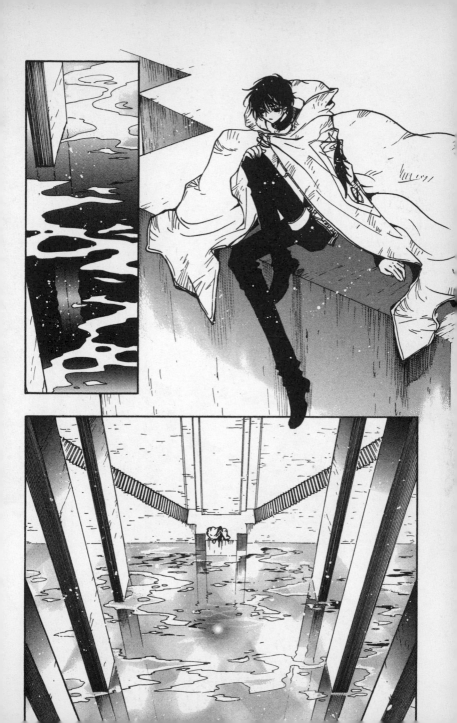

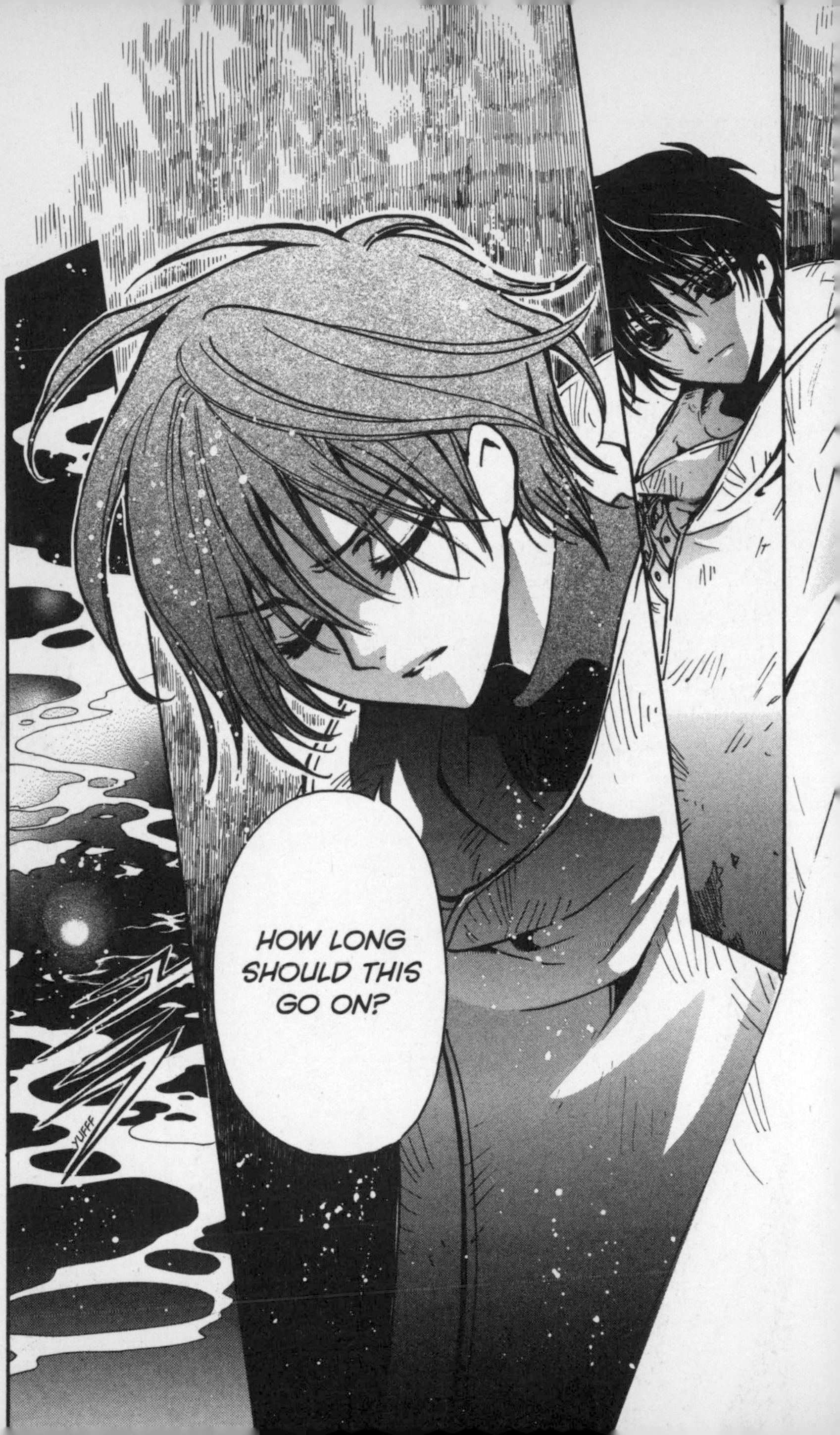
HOW LONG SHOULD THIS GO ON?
YUFFF

ツバサ

RESERVoir CHRoNiCLE

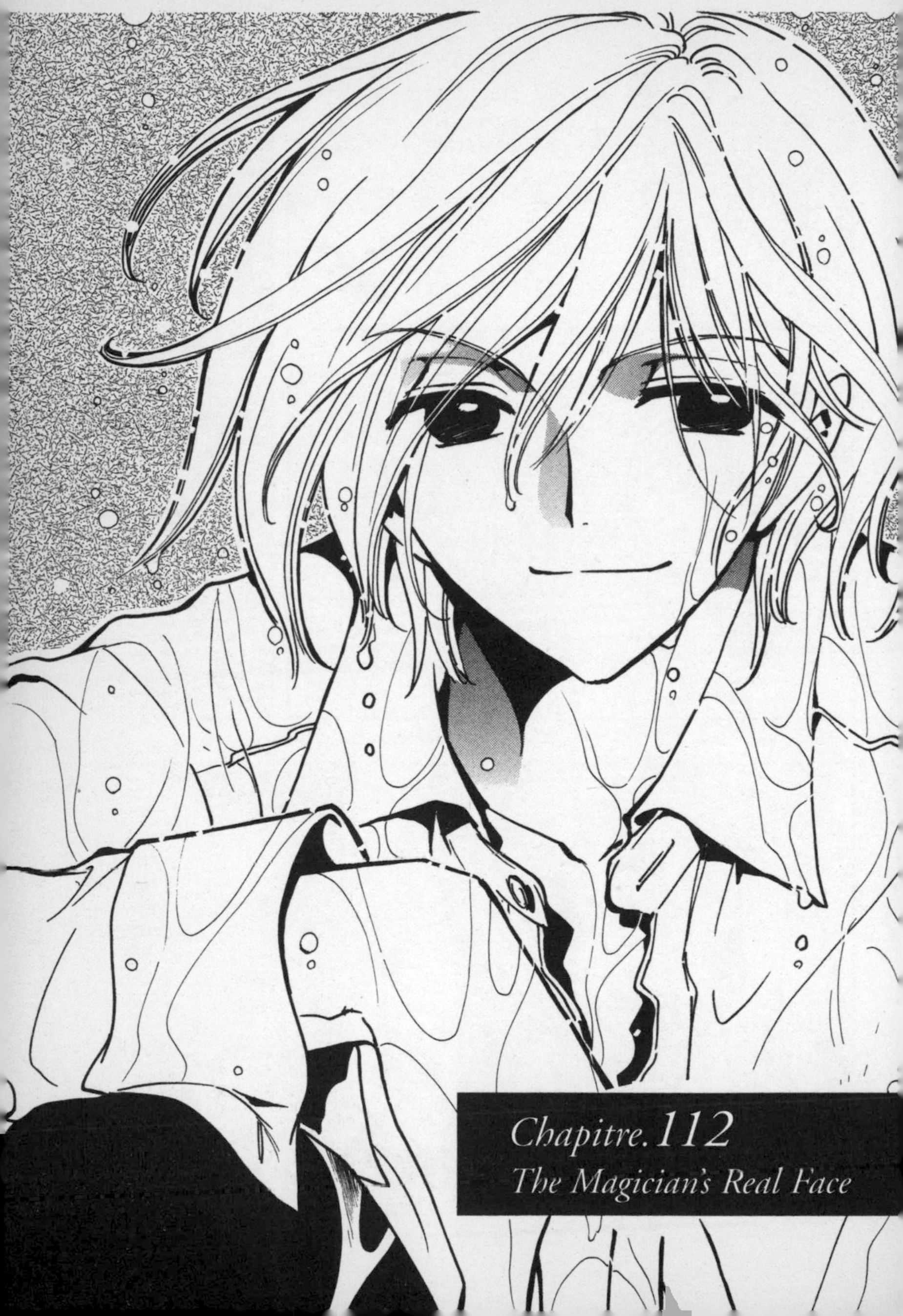
Chapitre. 112
The Magician's Real Face

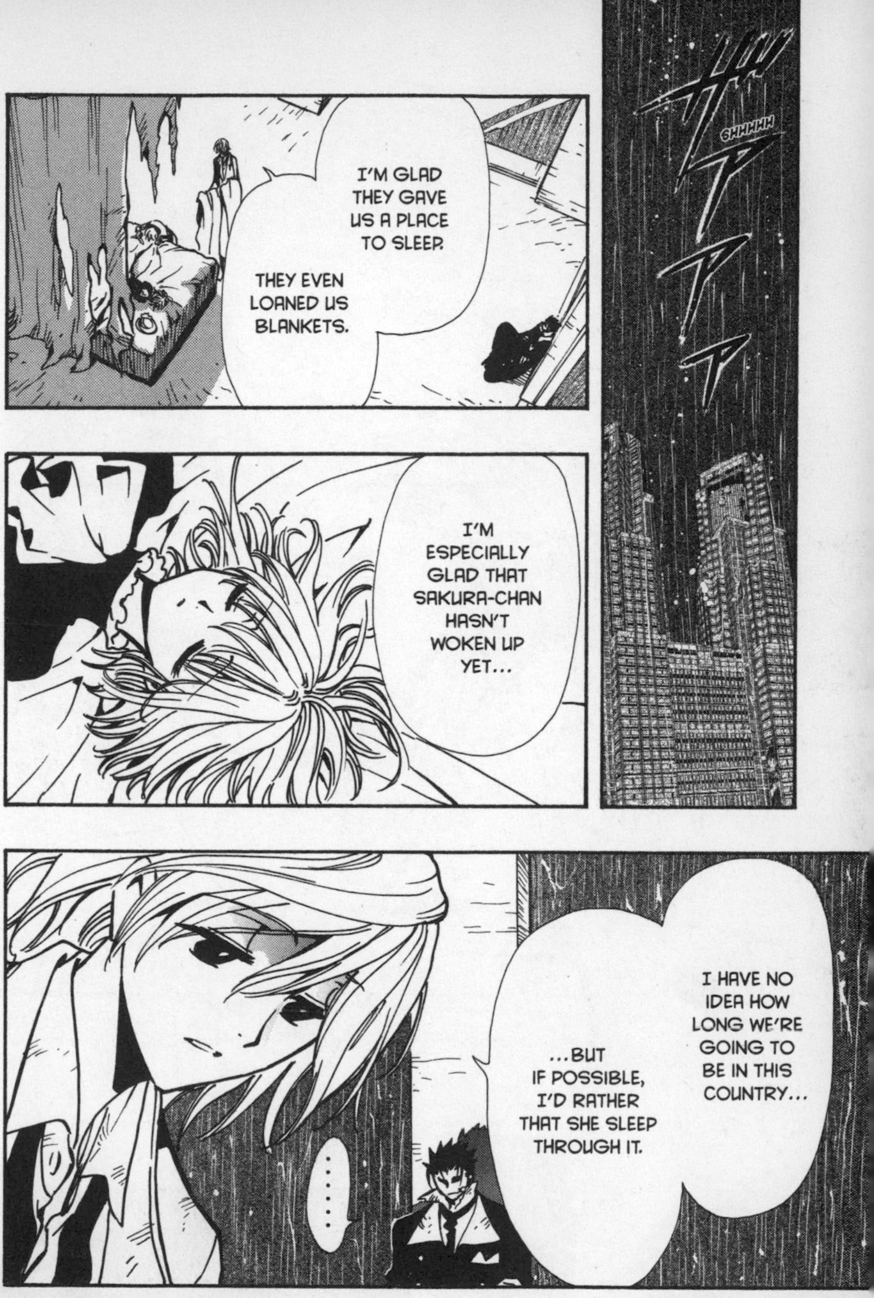
SHHHHH
I'M GLAD THEY GAVE US A PLACE TO SLEEP.
THEY EVEN LOANED US BLANKETS.
I'M ESPECIALLY GLAD THAT SAKURA-CHAN HASN'T WOKEN UP YET...
I HAVE NO IDEA HOW LONG WE'RE GOING TO BE IN THIS COUNTRY...
...BUT IF POSSIBLE, I'D RATHER THAT SHE SLEEP THROUGH IT.
......

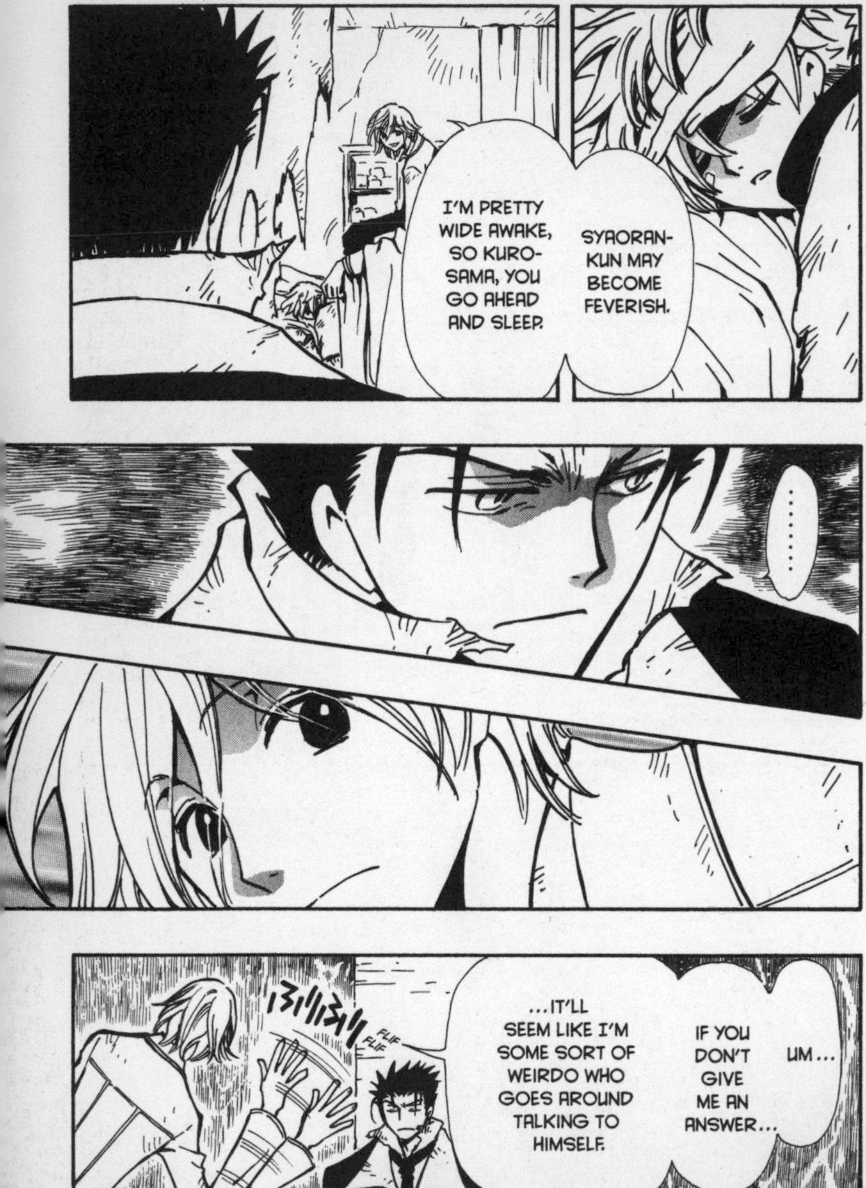
SYAORAN-KUN MAY BECOME FEVERISH.
I'M PRETTY WIDE AWAKE, SO KURO-SAMA, YOU GO AHEAD AND SLEEP.
……
UM…
IF YOU DON'T GIVE ME AN ANSWER…
…IT'LL SEEM LIKE I'M SOME SORT OF WEIRDO WHO GOES AROUND TALKING TO HIMSELF.
ふりふり
FLIF FLIF

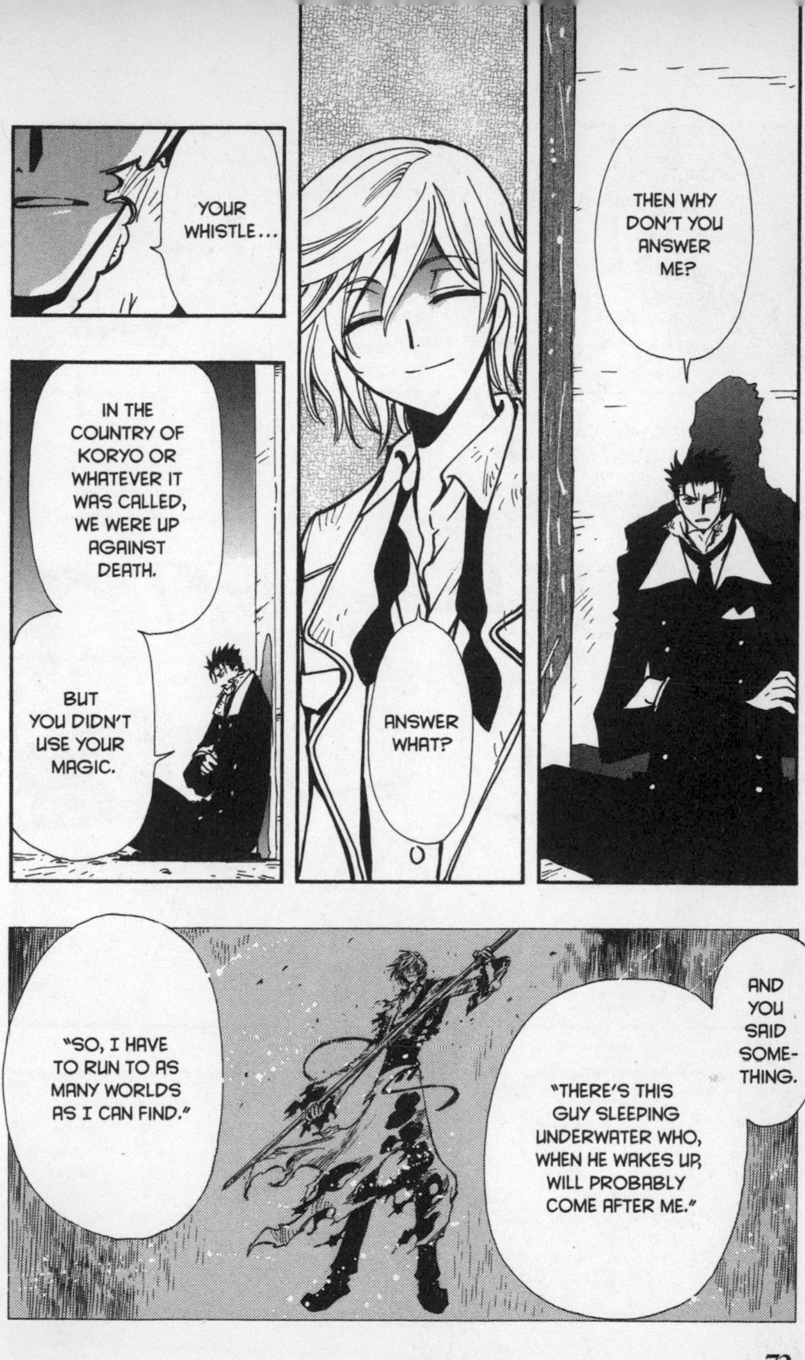
THEN WHY DON'T YOU ANSWER ME?
ANSWER WHAT?
YOUR WHISTLE...
IN THE COUNTRY OF KORYO OR WHATEVER IT WAS CALLED, WE WERE UP AGAINST DEATH.
BUT YOU DIDN'T USE YOUR MAGIC.
AND YOU SAID SOME-THING.
"THERE'S THIS GUY SLEEPING UNDERWATER WHO, WHEN HE WAKES UP, WILL PROBABLY COME AFTER ME."
"SO, I HAVE TO RUN TO AS MANY WORLDS AS I CAN FIND."

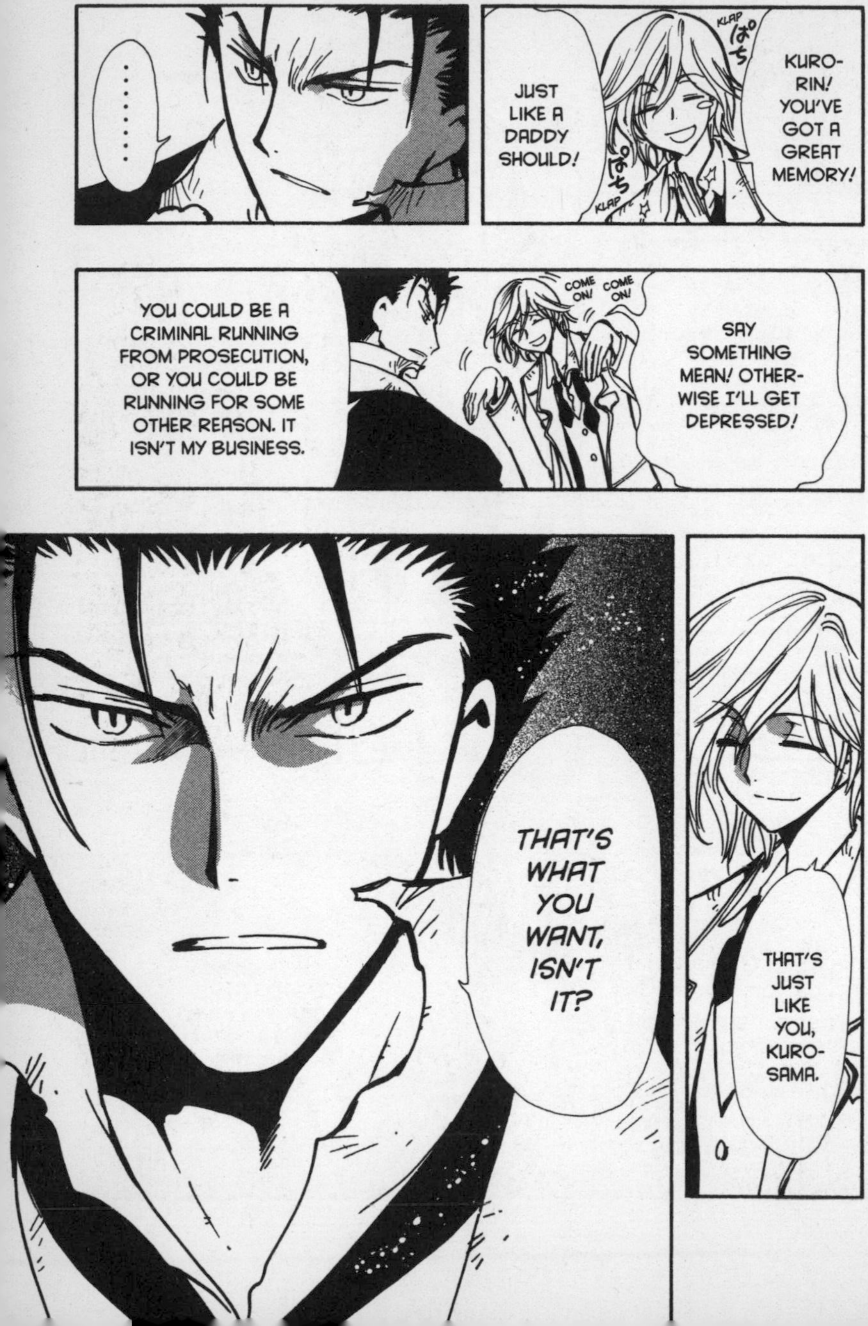
KLAP ぱち
KURO-RIN! YOU'VE GOT A GREAT MEMORY!
JUST LIKE A DADDY SHOULD!
ぱち KLAP
....
SAY SOMETHING MEAN! OTHER-WISE I'LL GET DEPRESSED!
COME ON! COME ON!
YOU COULD BE A CRIMINAL RUNNING FROM PROSECUTION, OR YOU COULD BE RUNNING FOR SOME OTHER REASON. IT ISN'T MY BUSINESS.
THAT'S JUST LIKE YOU, KURO-SAMA.
THAT'S WHAT YOU WANT, ISN'T IT?

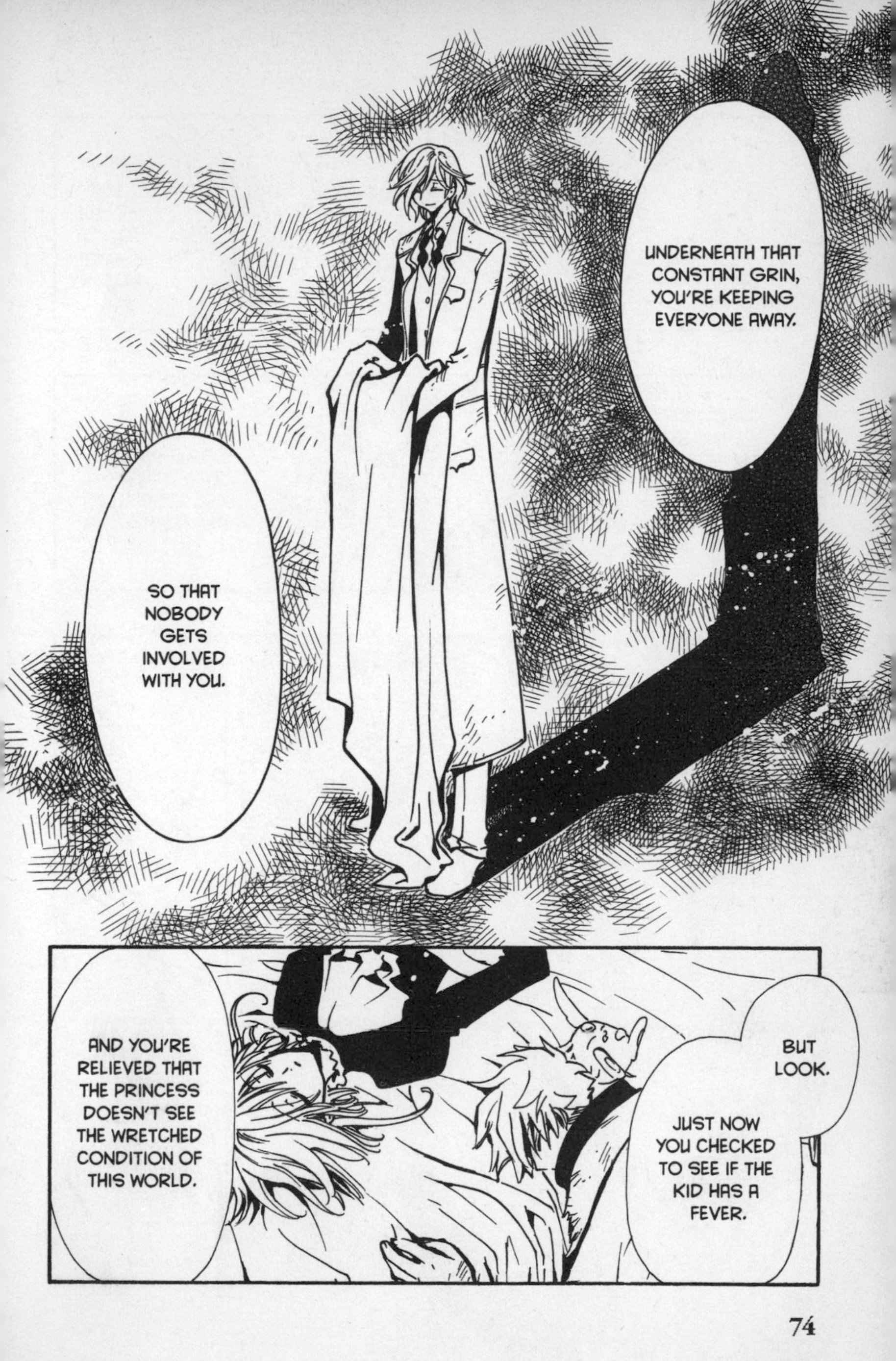
UNDERNEATH THAT CONSTANT GRIN, YOU'RE KEEPING EVERYONE AWAY.
SO THAT NOBODY GETS INVOLVED WITH YOU.
AND YOU'RE RELIEVED THAT THE PRINCESS DOESN'T SEE THE WRETCHED CONDITION OF THIS WORLD.
BUT LOOK.
JUST NOW YOU CHECKED TO SEE IF THE KID HAS A FEVER.

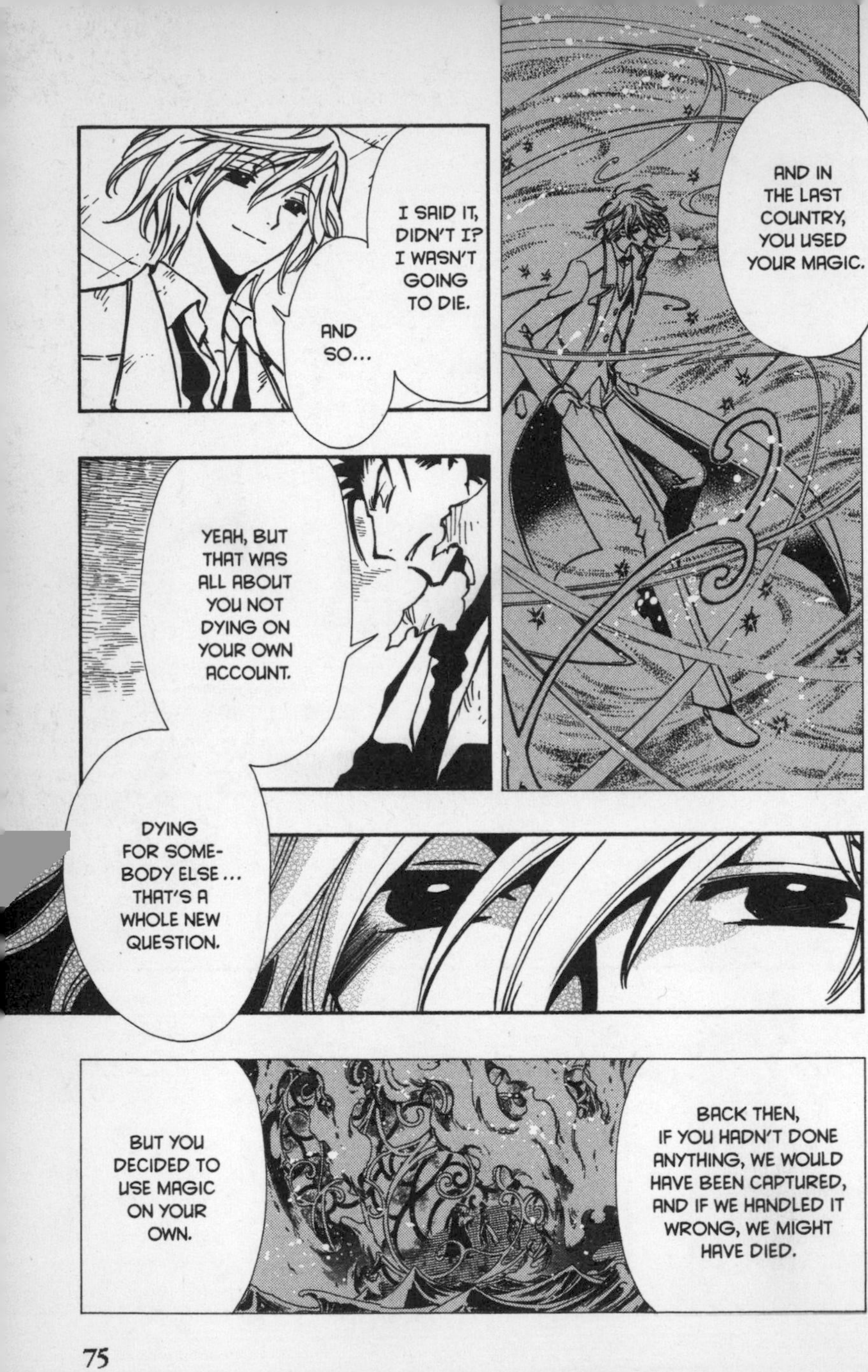
AND IN THE LAST COUNTRY, YOU USED YOUR MAGIC.
I SAID IT, DIDN'T I? I WASN'T GOING TO DIE.
AND SO...
YEAH, BUT THAT WAS ALL ABOUT YOU NOT DYING ON YOUR OWN ACCOUNT.
DYING FOR SOME-BODY ELSE... THAT'S A WHOLE NEW QUESTION.
BACK THEN, IF YOU HADN'T DONE ANYTHING, WE WOULD HAVE BEEN CAPTURED, AND IF WE HANDLED IT WRONG, WE MIGHT HAVE DIED.
BUT YOU DECIDED TO USE MAGIC ON YOUR OWN.

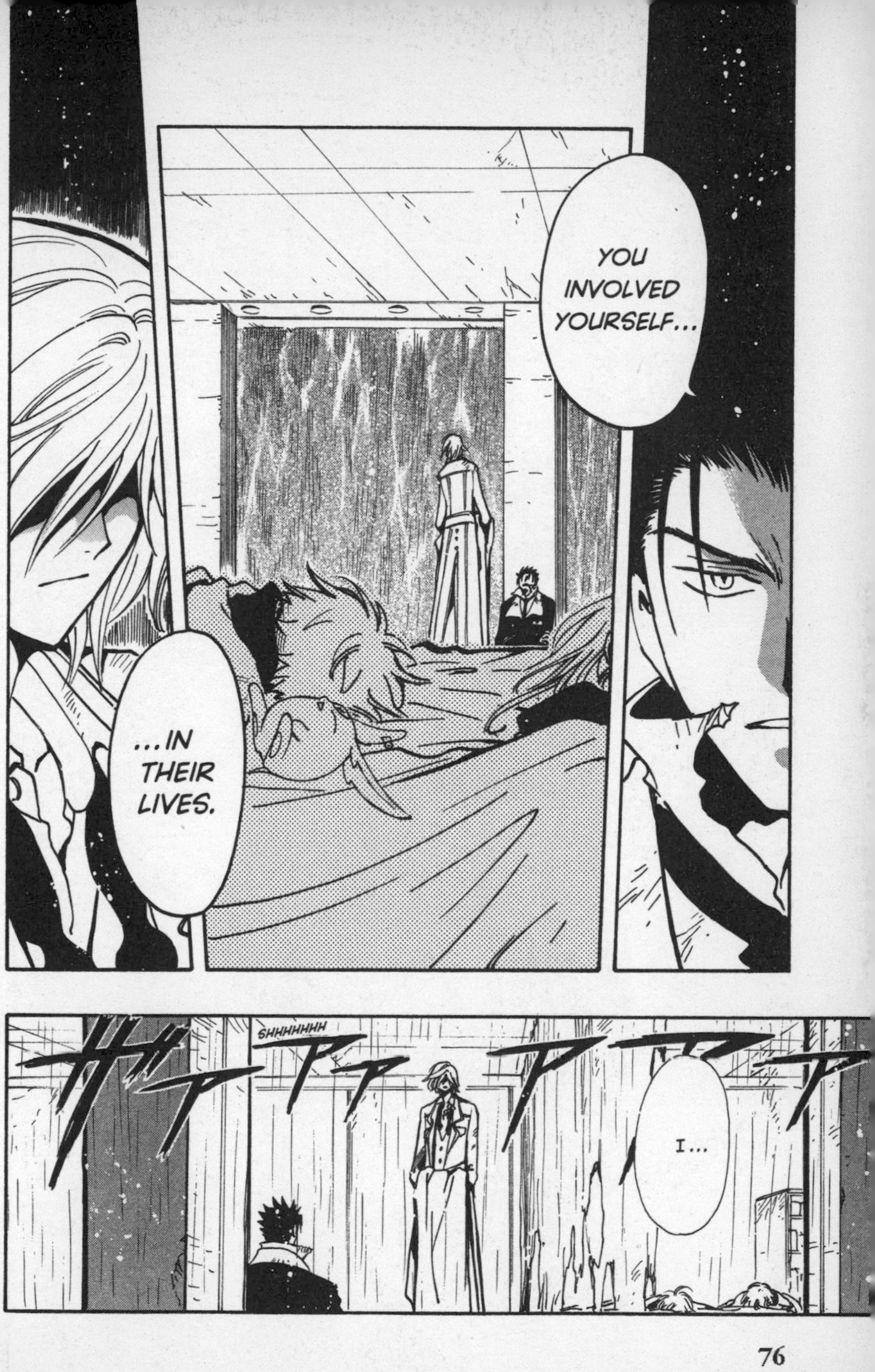
YOU INVOLVED YOURSELF...
...IN THEIR LIVES.
SHHHHHHH
I...

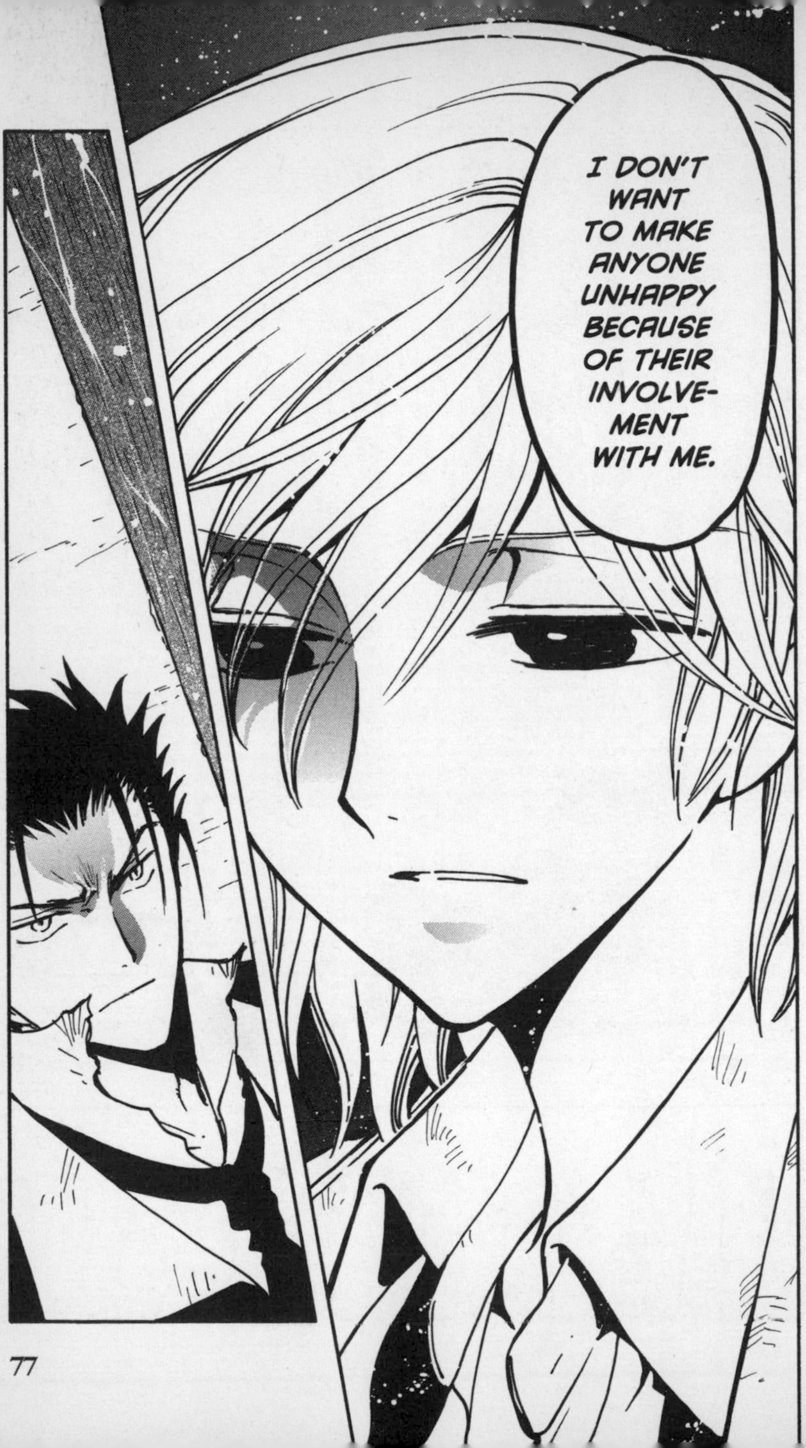
I DON'T WANT TO MAKE ANYONE UNHAPPY BECAUSE OF THEIR INVOLVEMENT WITH ME.

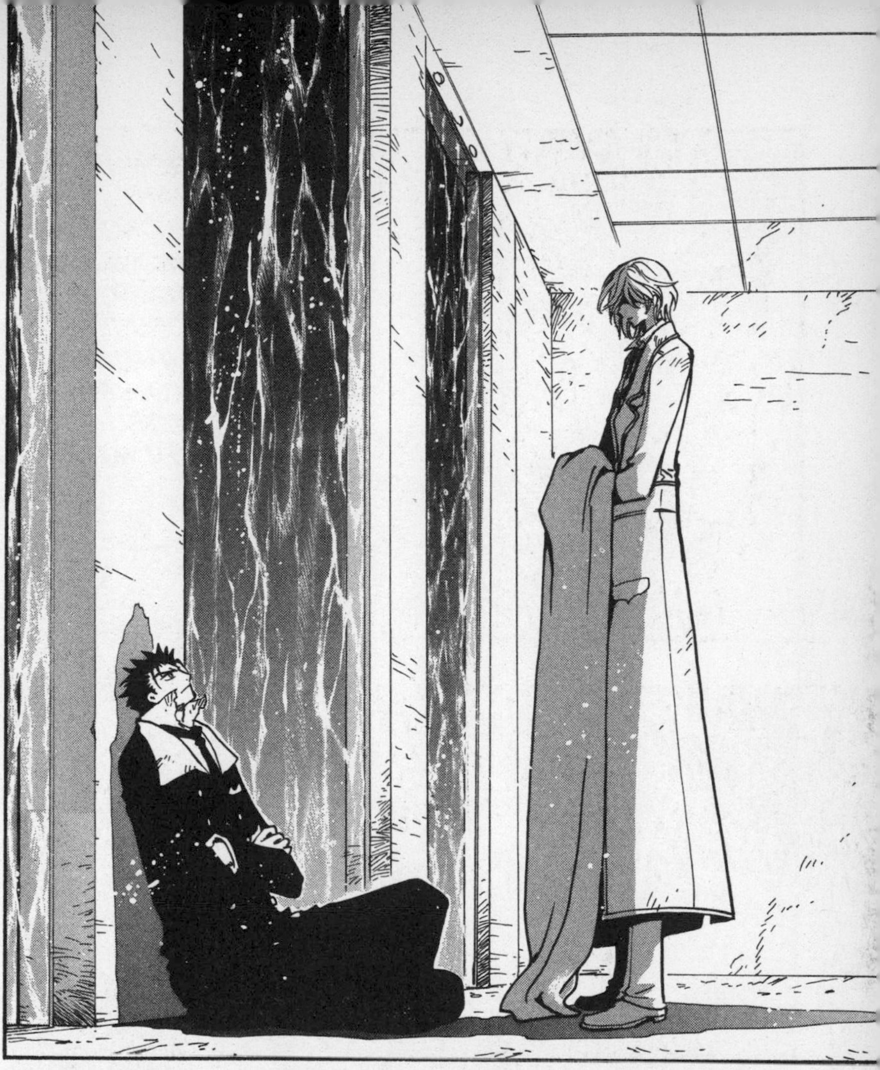
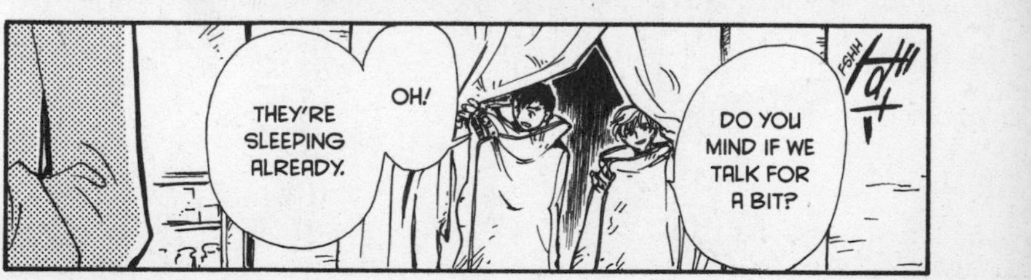
FSHH
DO YOU MIND IF WE TALK FOR A BIT?
OH!
THEY'RE SLEEPING ALREADY.

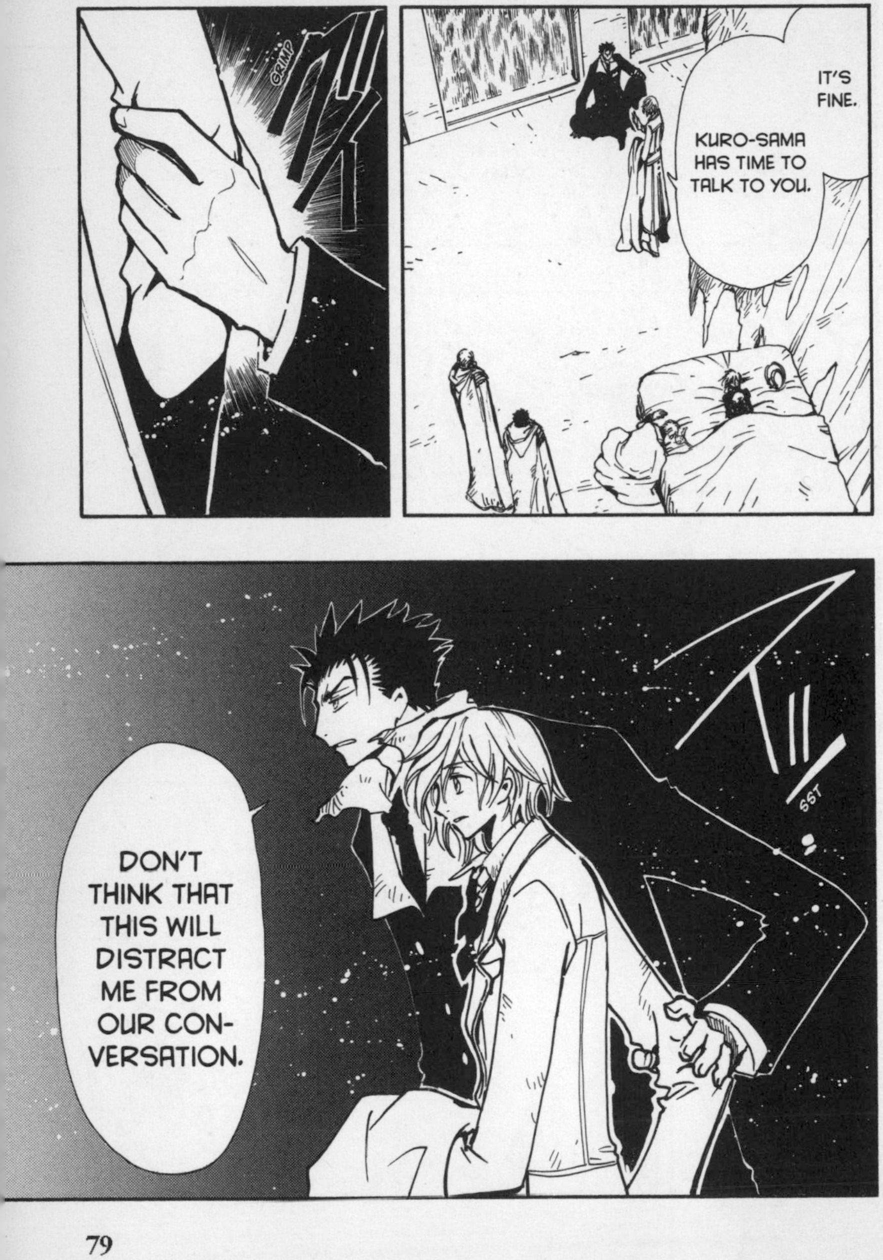
IT'S FINE.
KURO-SAMA HAS TIME TO TALK TO YOU.
CRIMP
DON'T THINK THAT THIS WILL DISTRACT ME FROM OUR CON-VERSATION.
SST

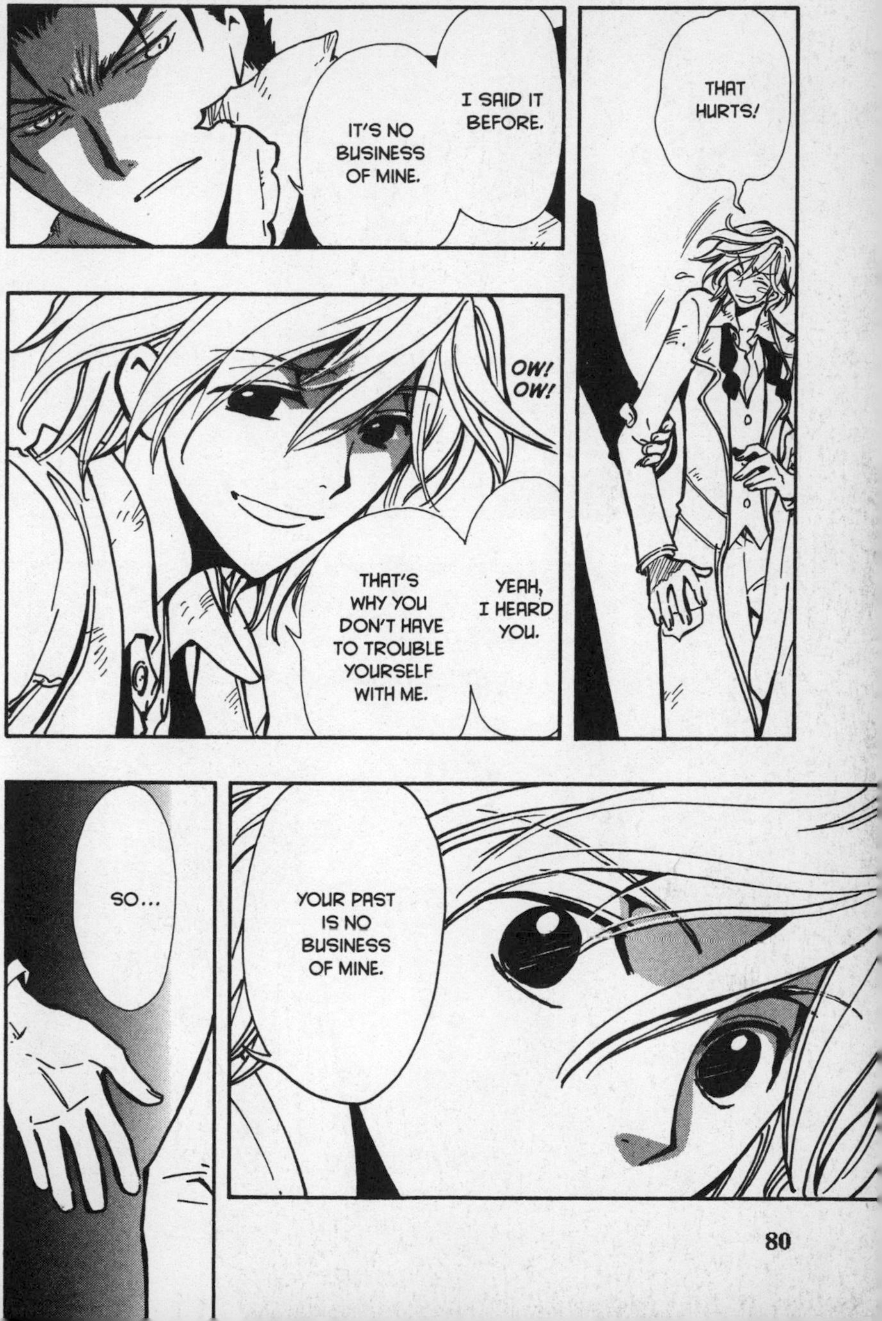
THAT HURTS!
I SAID IT BEFORE.
IT'S NO BUSINESS OF MINE.
OW! OW!
YEAH, I HEARD YOU.
THAT'S WHY YOU DON'T HAVE TO TROUBLE YOURSELF WITH ME.
YOUR PAST IS NO BUSINESS OF MINE.
SO...

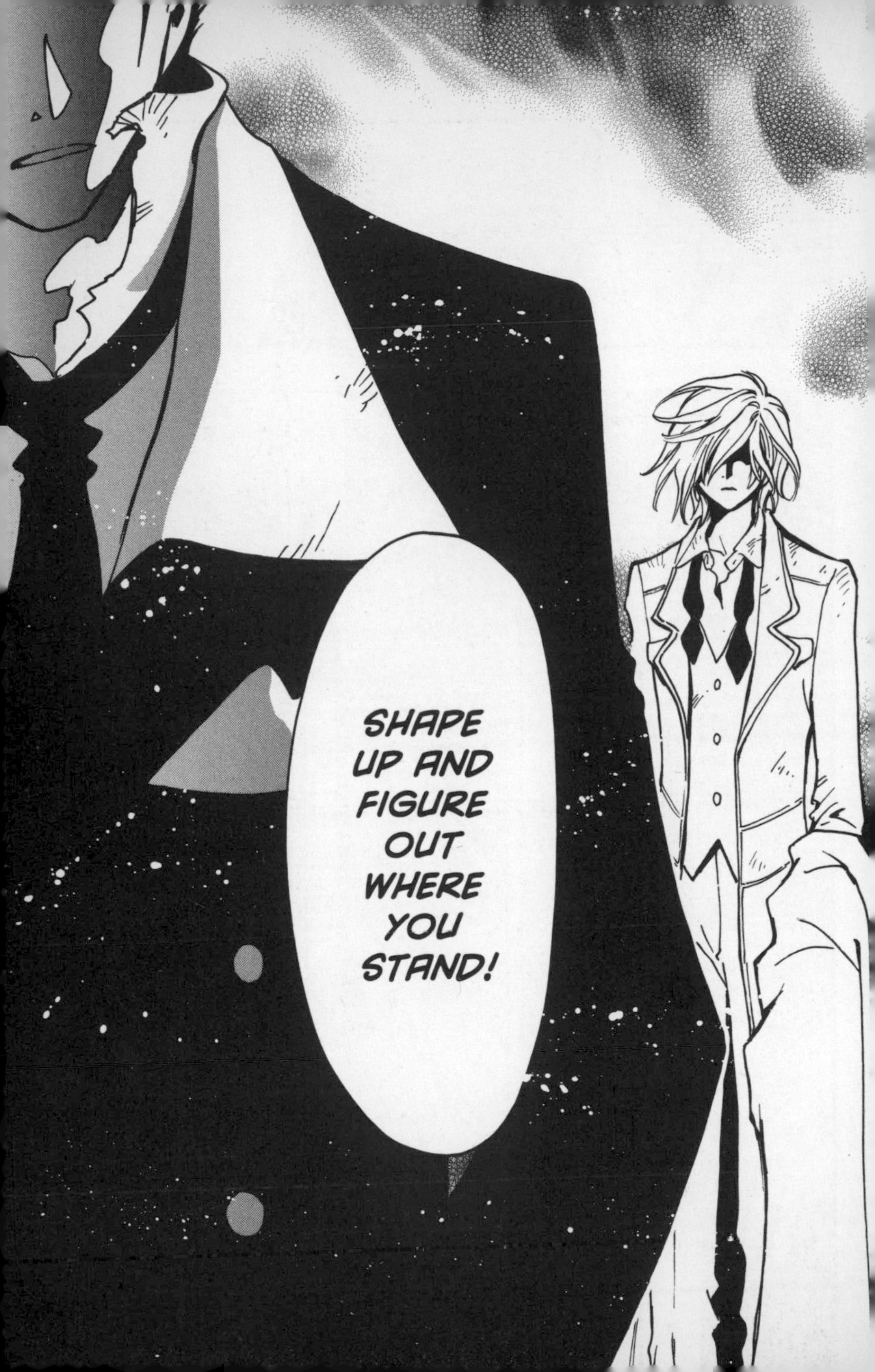
SHAPE UP AND FIGURE OUT WHERE YOU STAND!

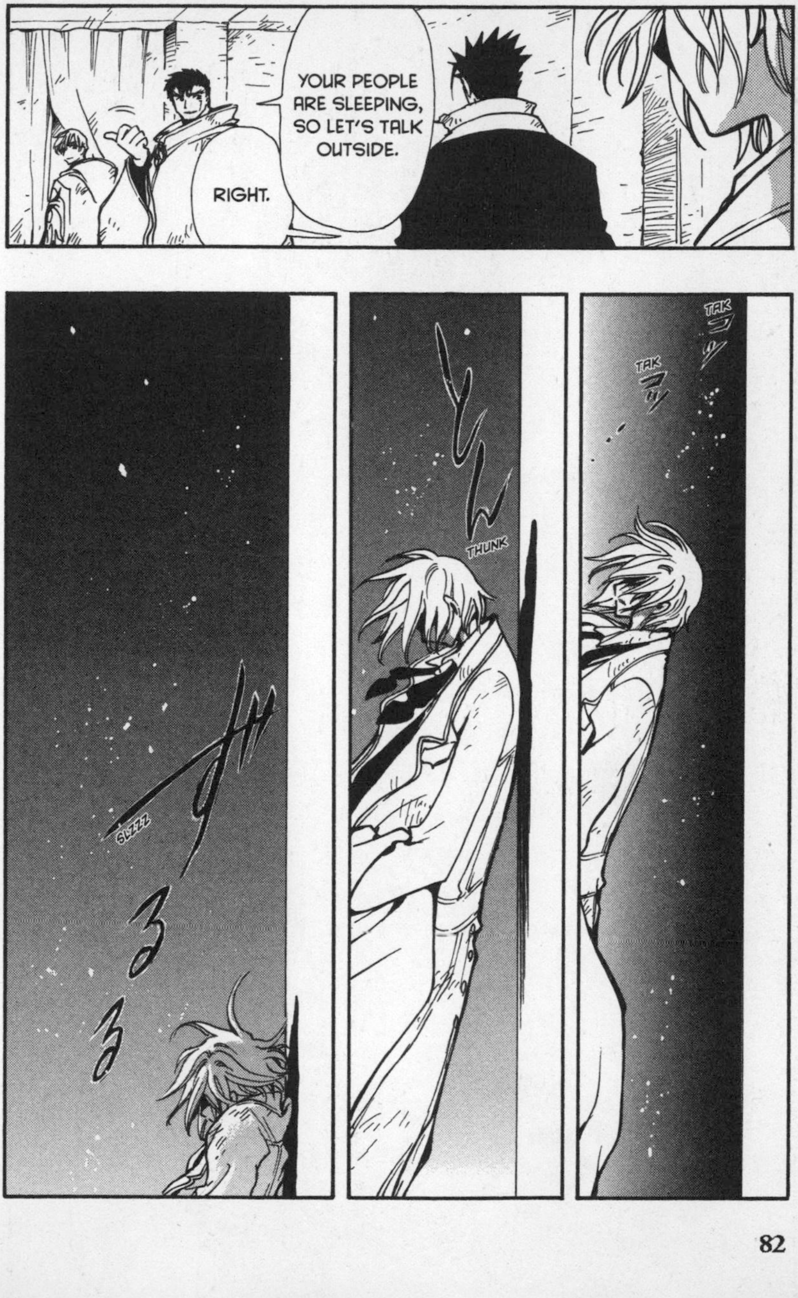
YOUR PEOPLE ARE SLEEPING, SO LET'S TALK OUTSIDE.
RIGHT.
TAK
TAK
THUNK
SLZZZ

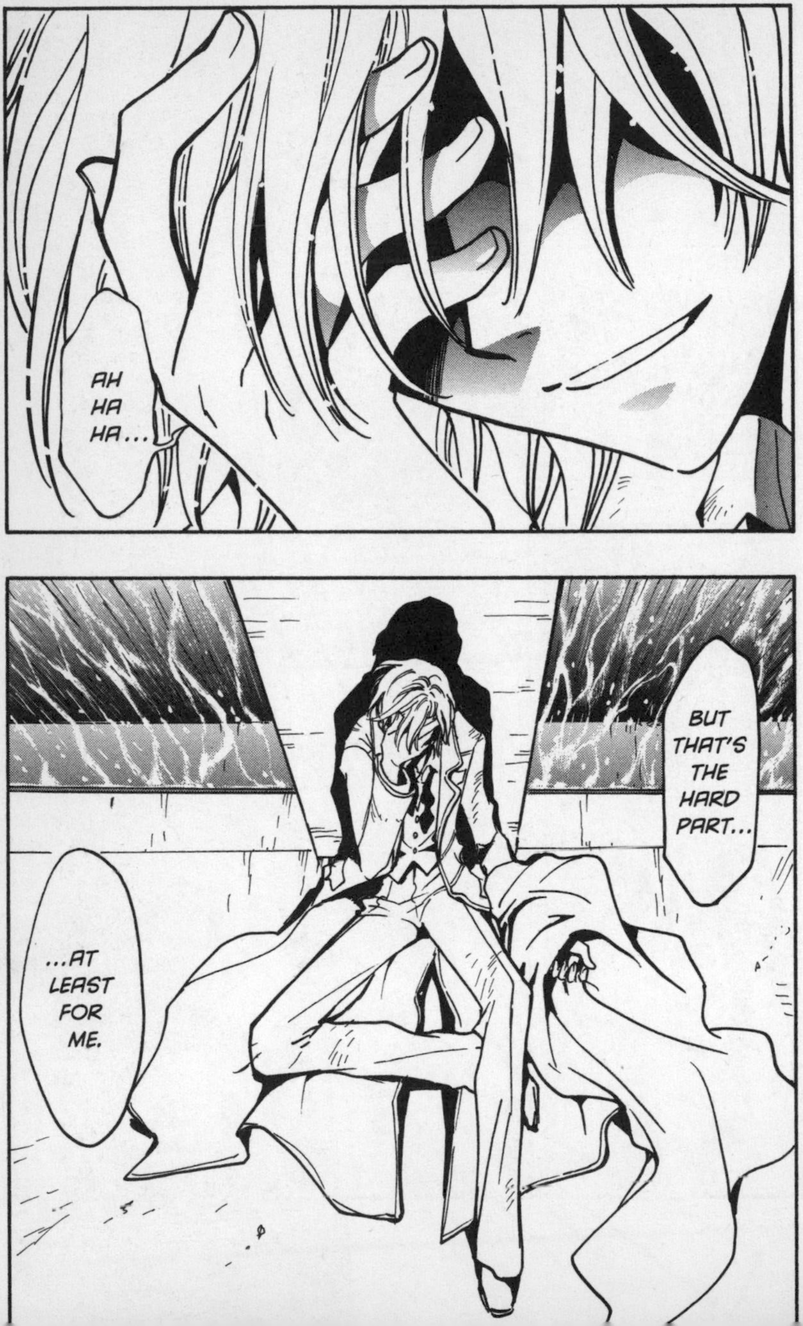
AH HA HA...
BUT THAT'S THE HARD PART...
...AT LEAST FOR ME.

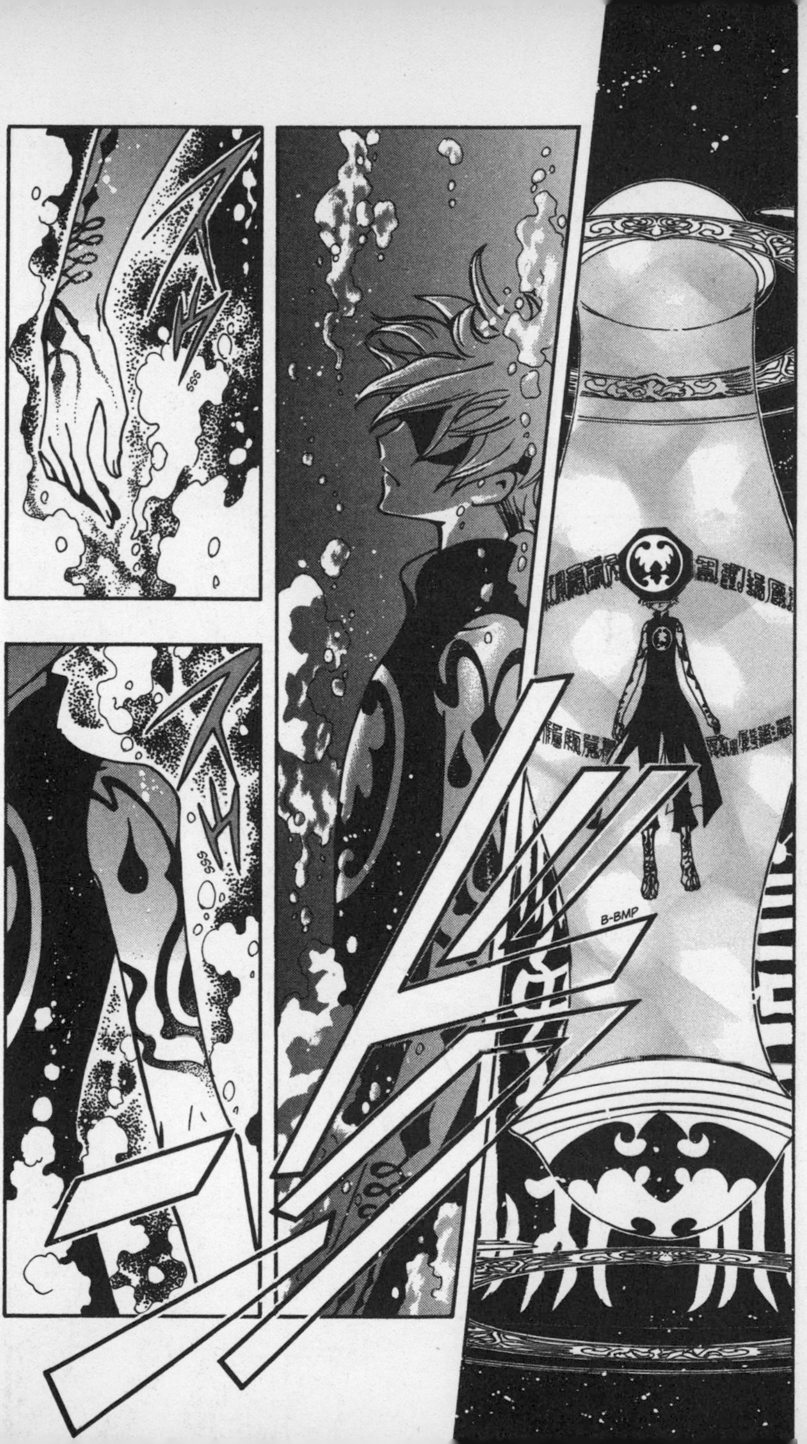
B-BMP
SSS
SSS

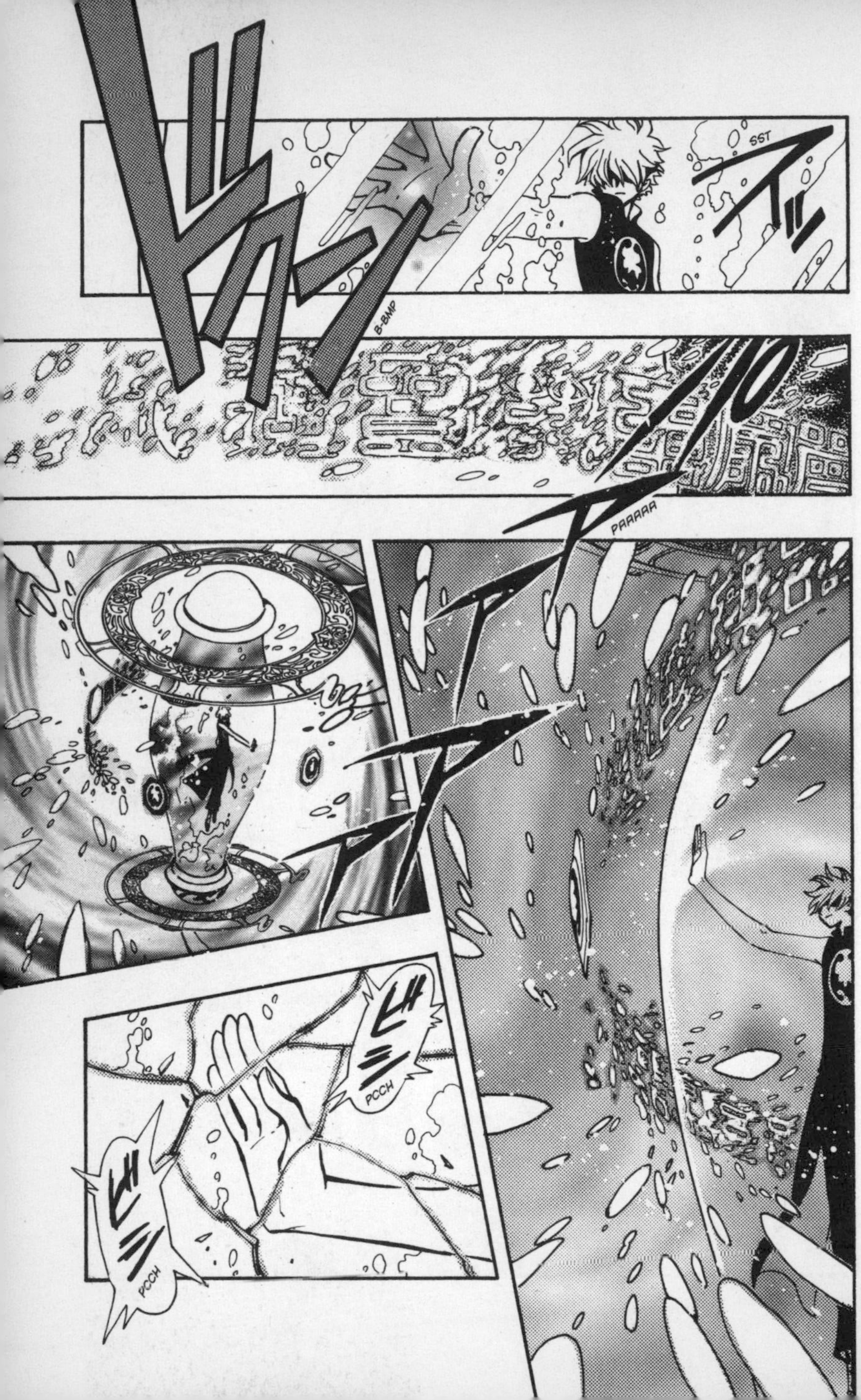
SST
B-BMP
PAAAAA
PCCH
PCCH

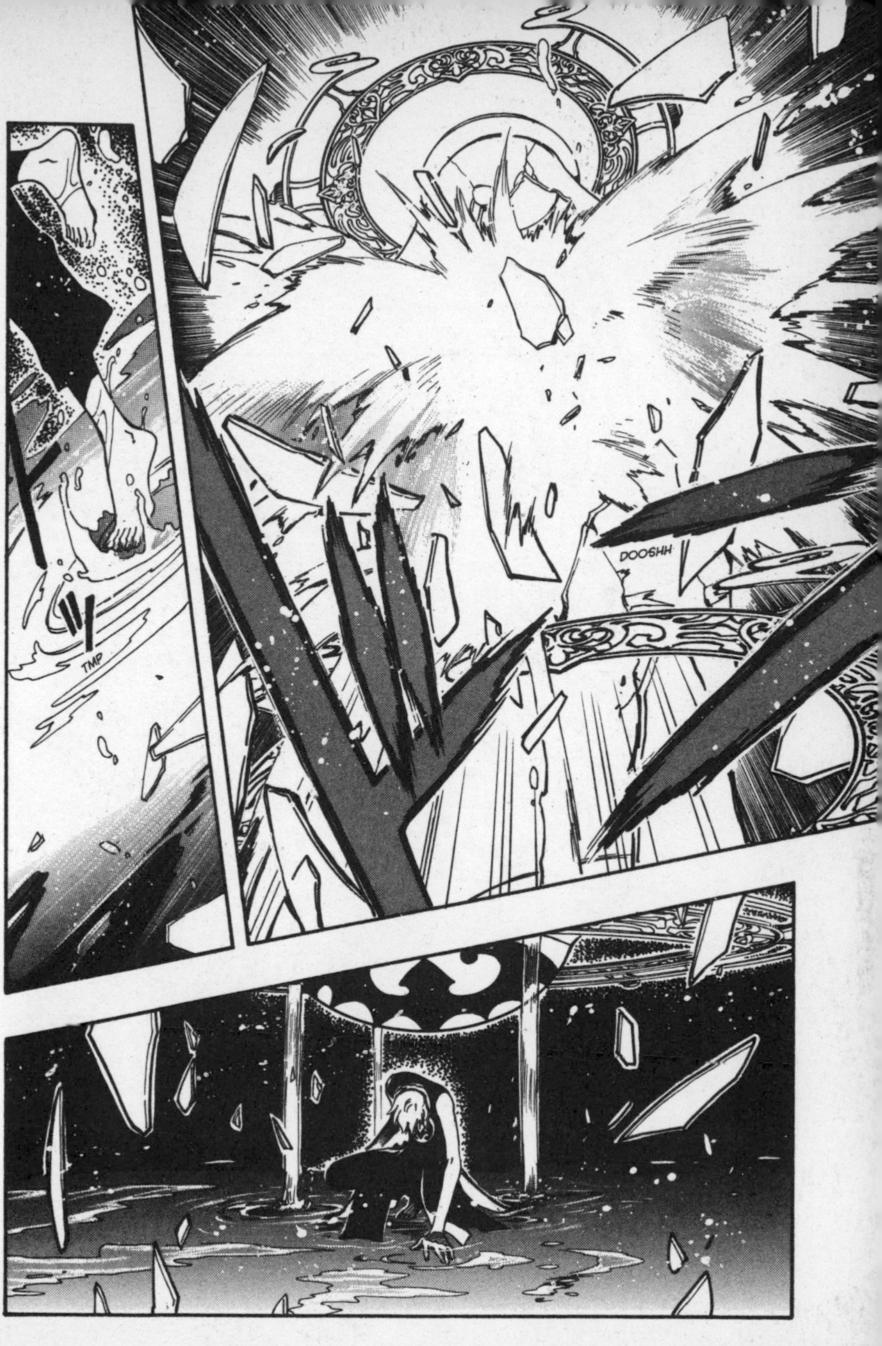
DOOSHH
TMP

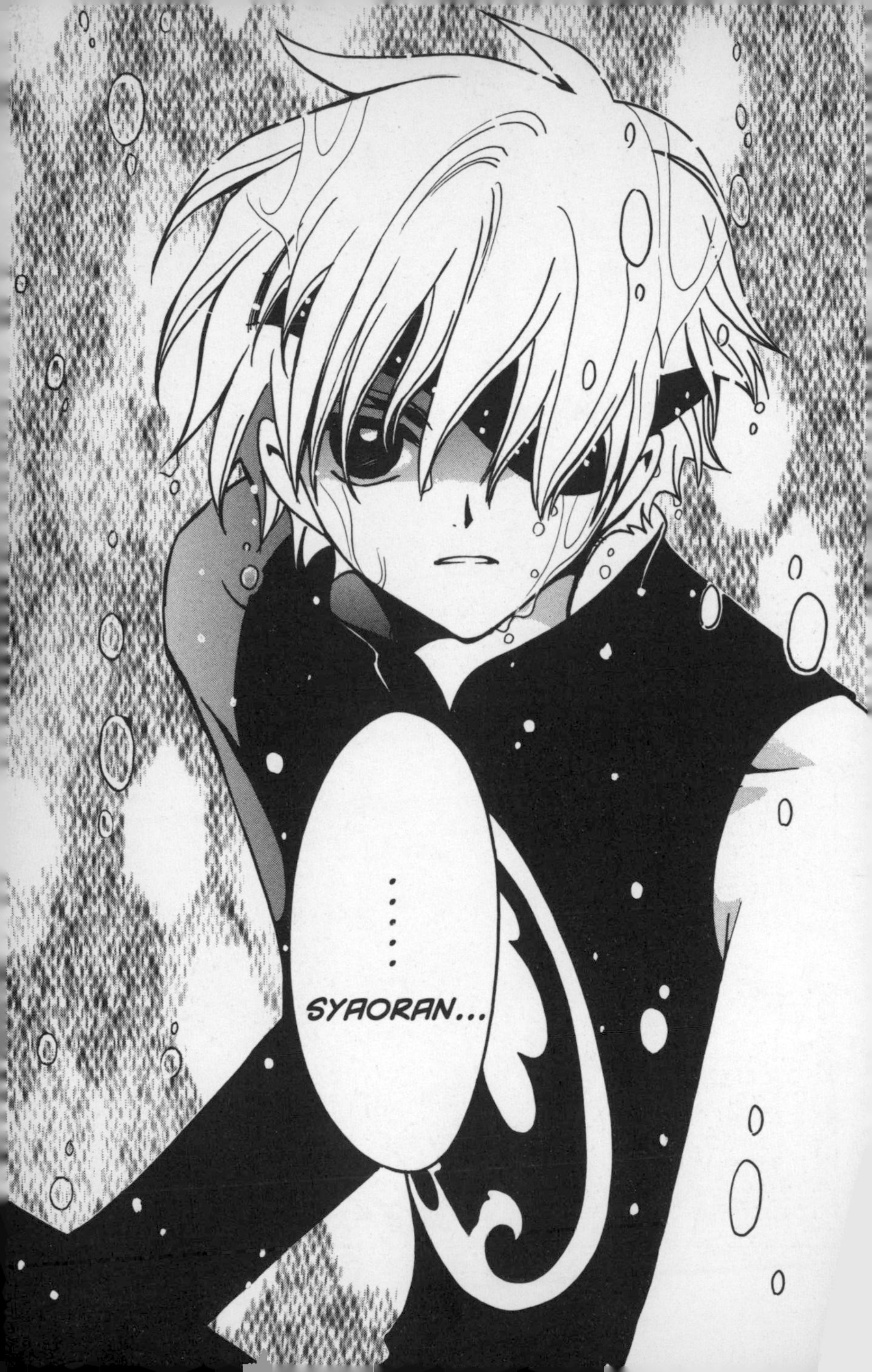

......
SYAORAN...

ツバサ

RESERVoir CHRoNiCLE

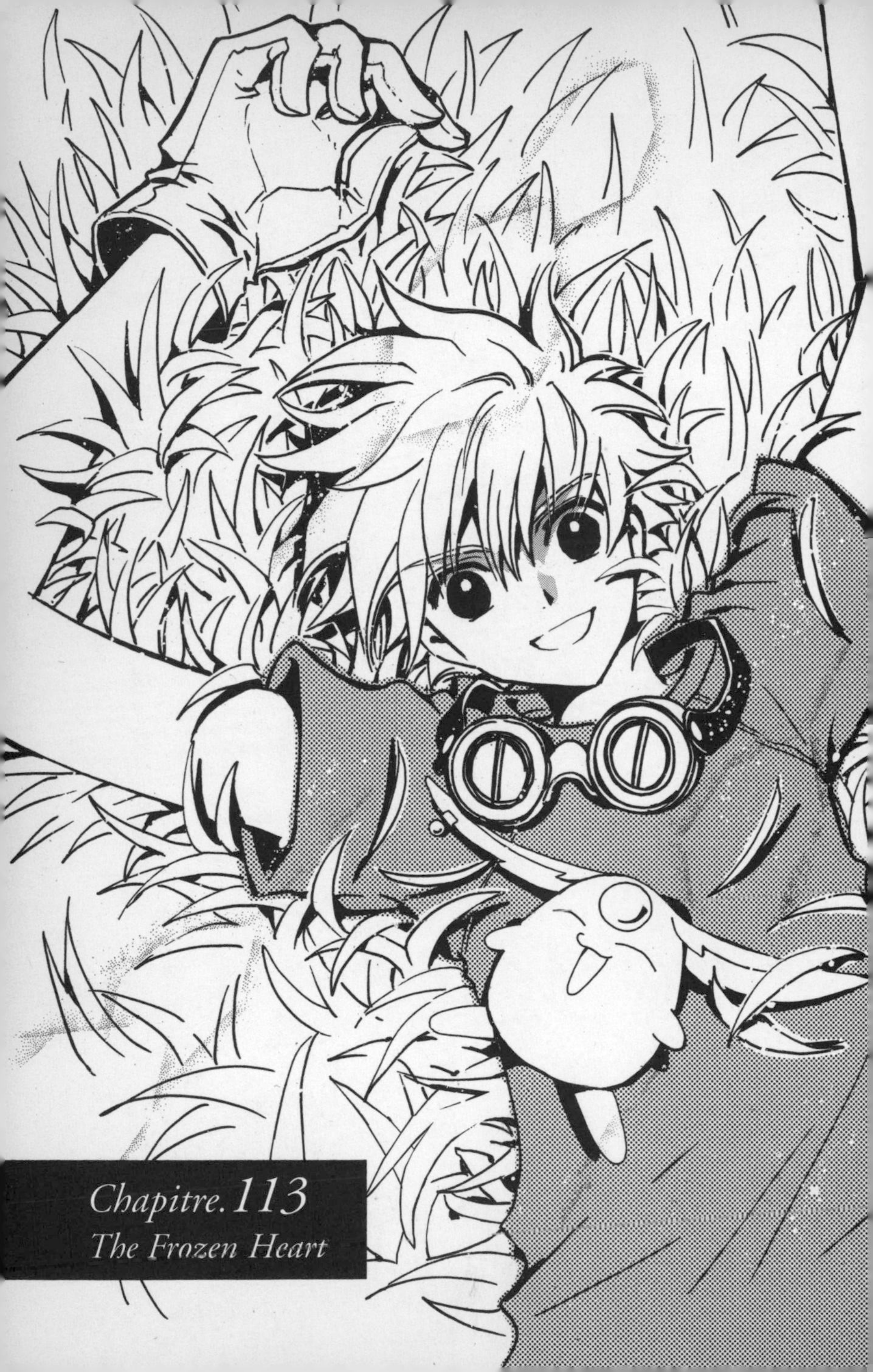
Chapitre.113
The Frozen Heart

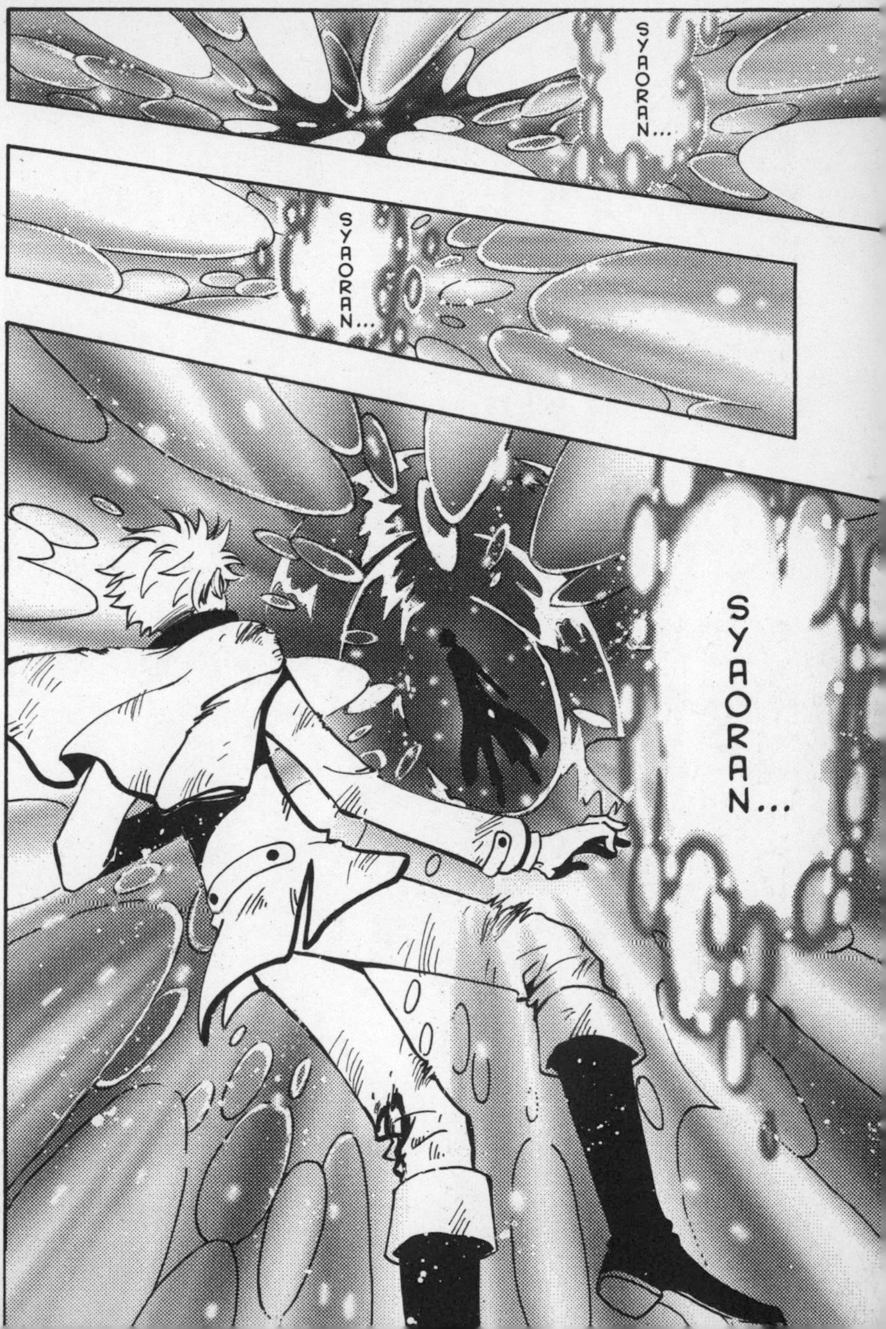
SYAORAN...
SYAORAN...
SYAORAN...

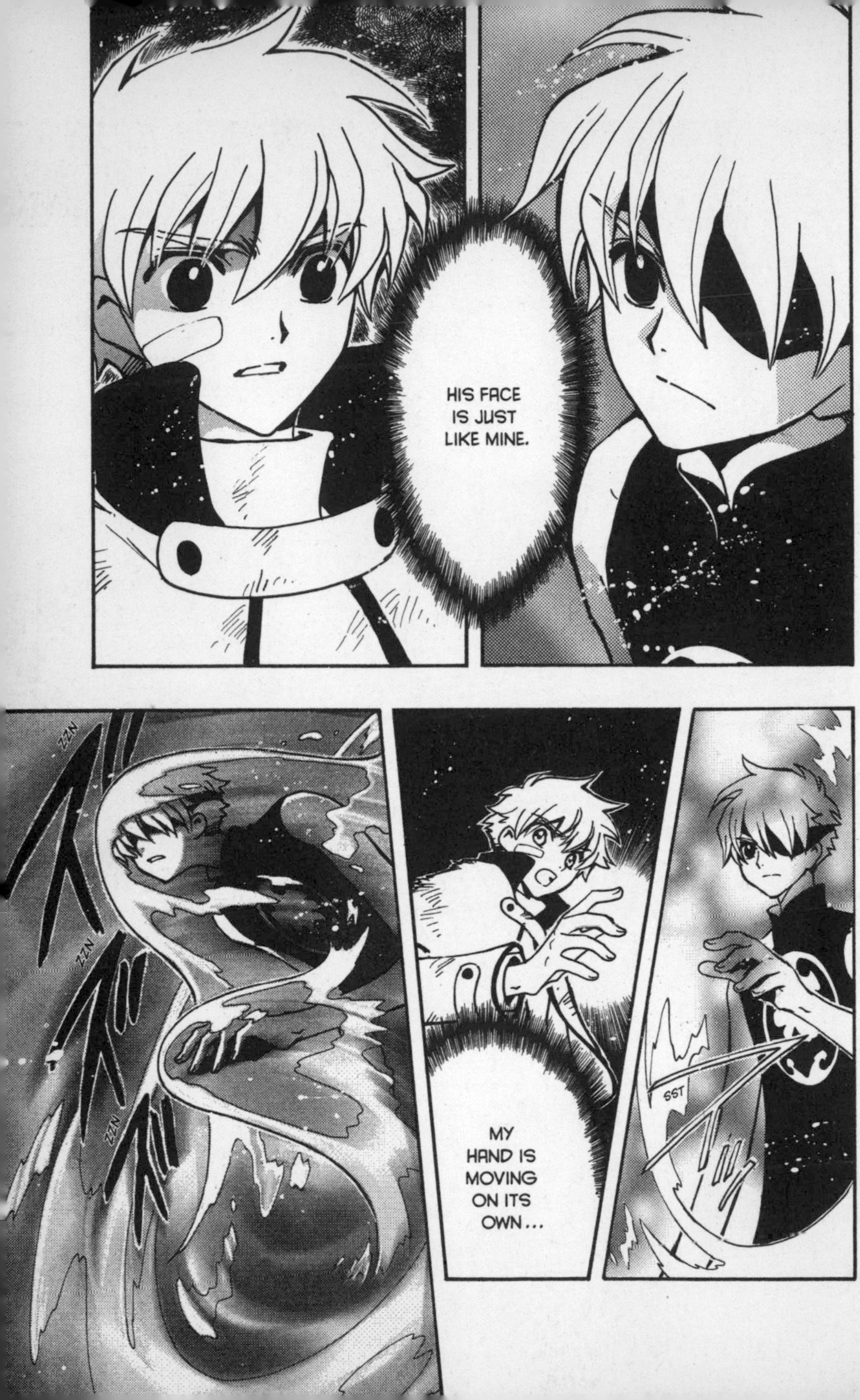
HIS FACE IS JUST LIKE MINE.
SST
MY HAND IS MOVING ON ITS OWN…
ZZN
ZZN
ZZN

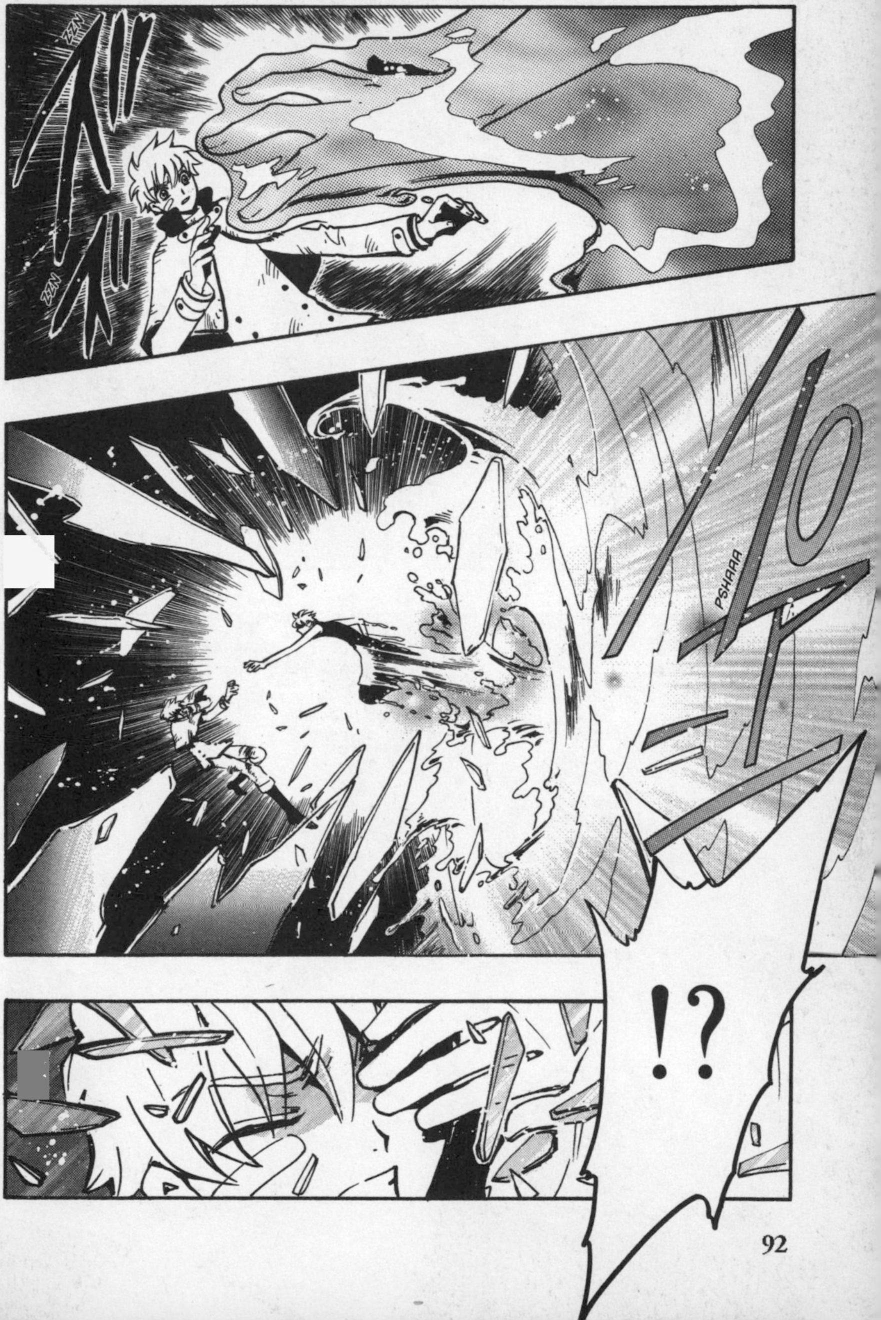
ZZN
ZZN
PSHAAA
!?

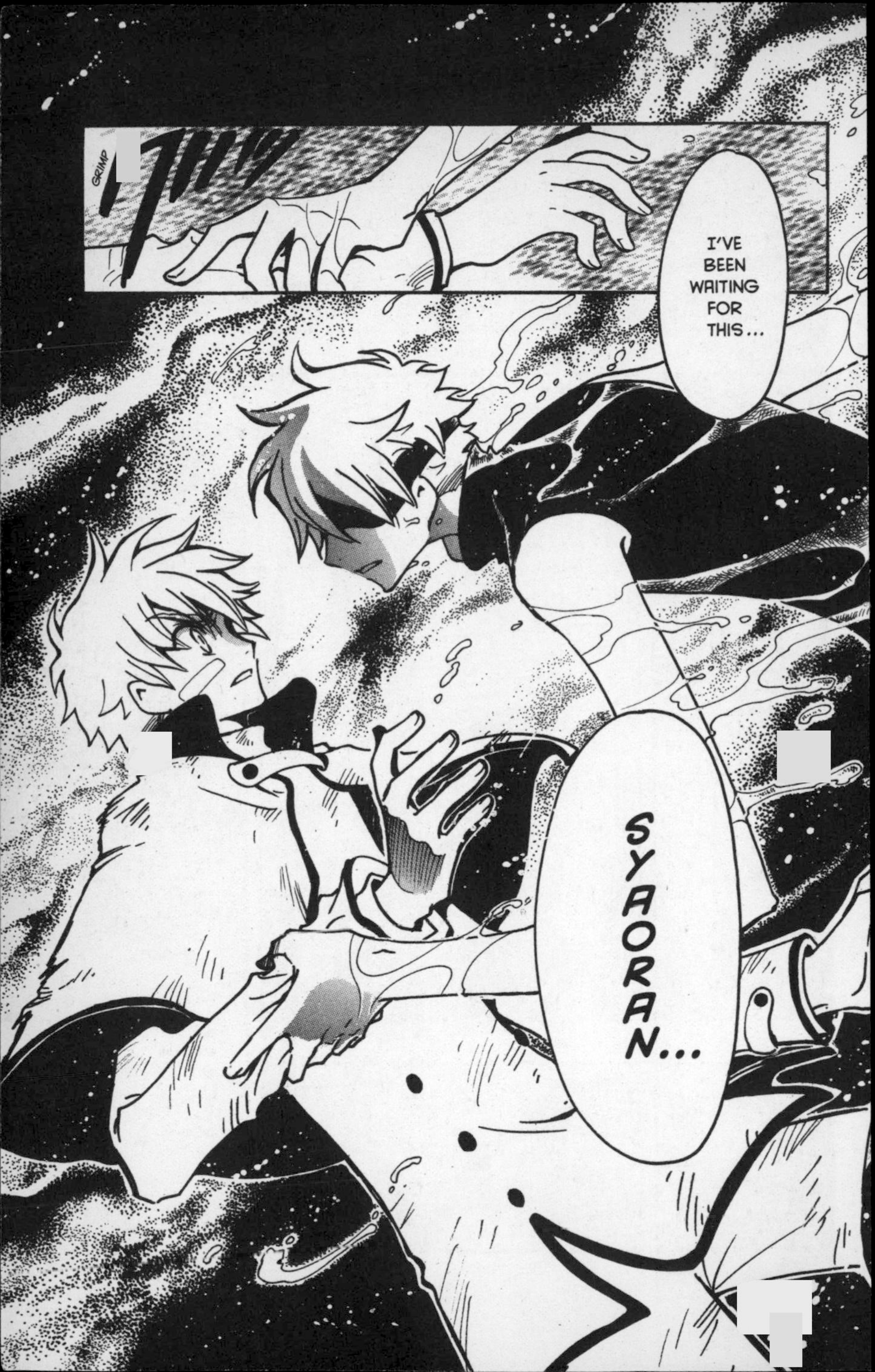
GRIMP
I'VE BEEN WAITING FOR THIS...
SYAORAN...

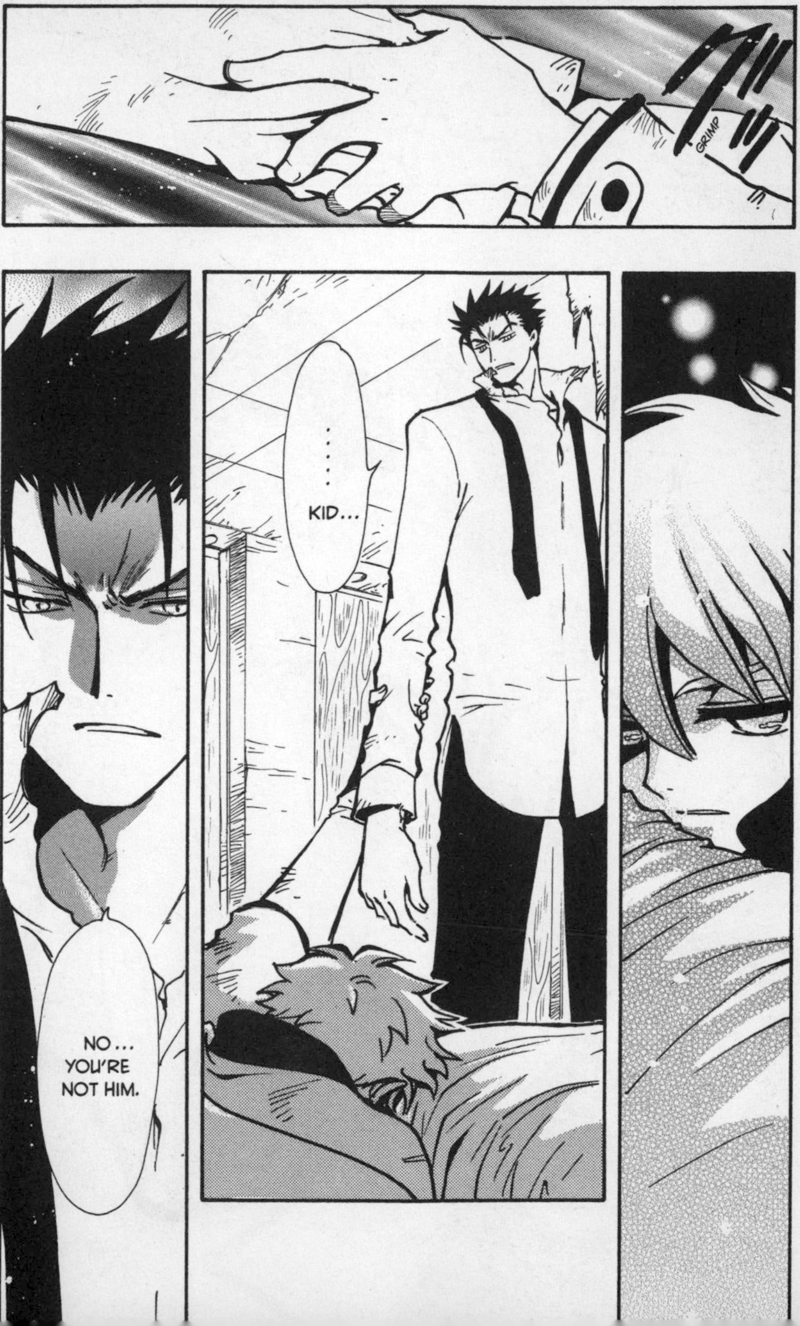
GRIMP
...... KID...
NO... YOU'RE NOT HIM.

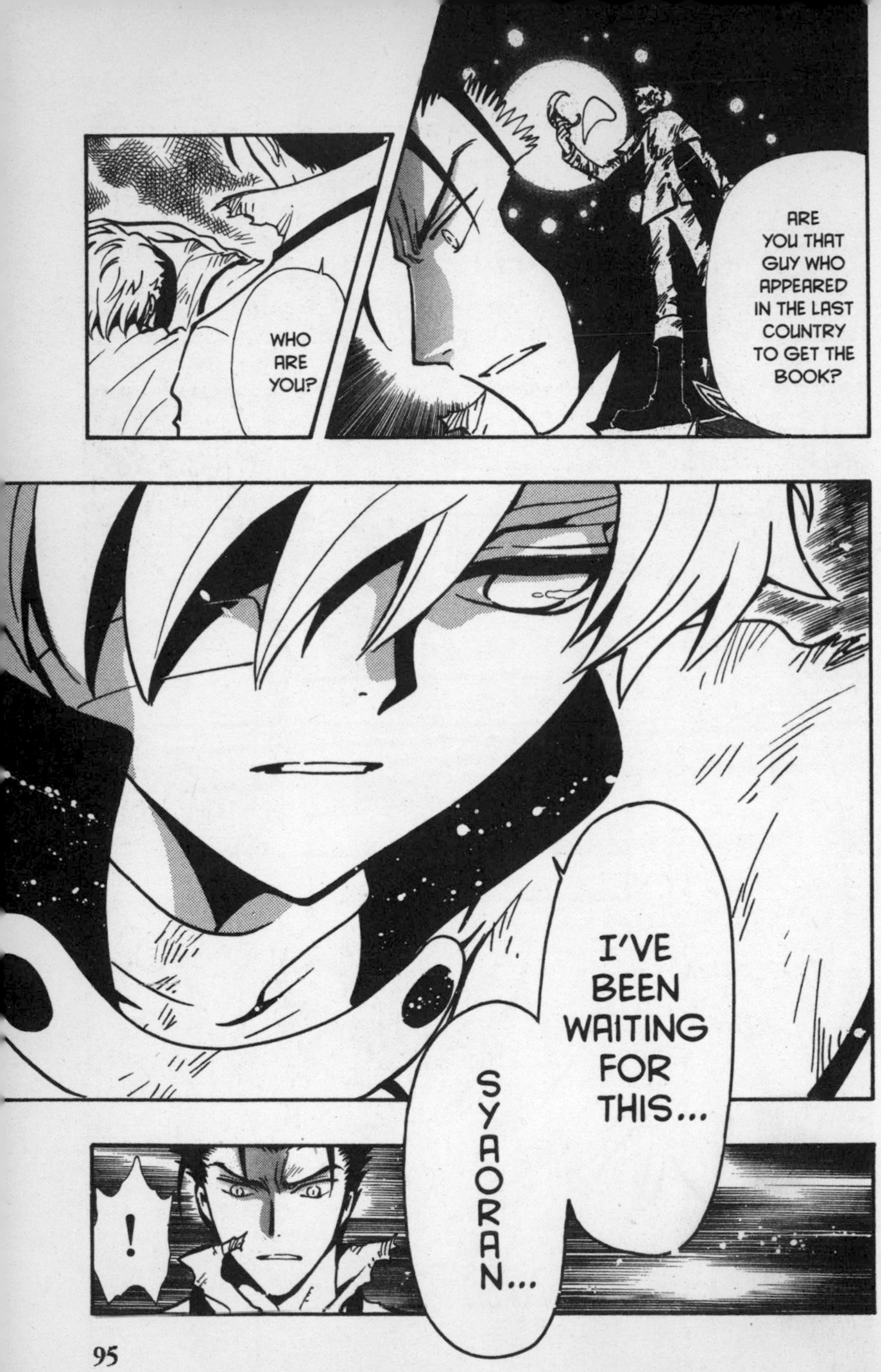
ARE YOU THAT GUY WHO APPEARED IN THE LAST COUNTRY TO GET THE BOOK?
WHO ARE YOU?
I'VE BEEN WAITING FOR THIS...
SYAORAN...
!

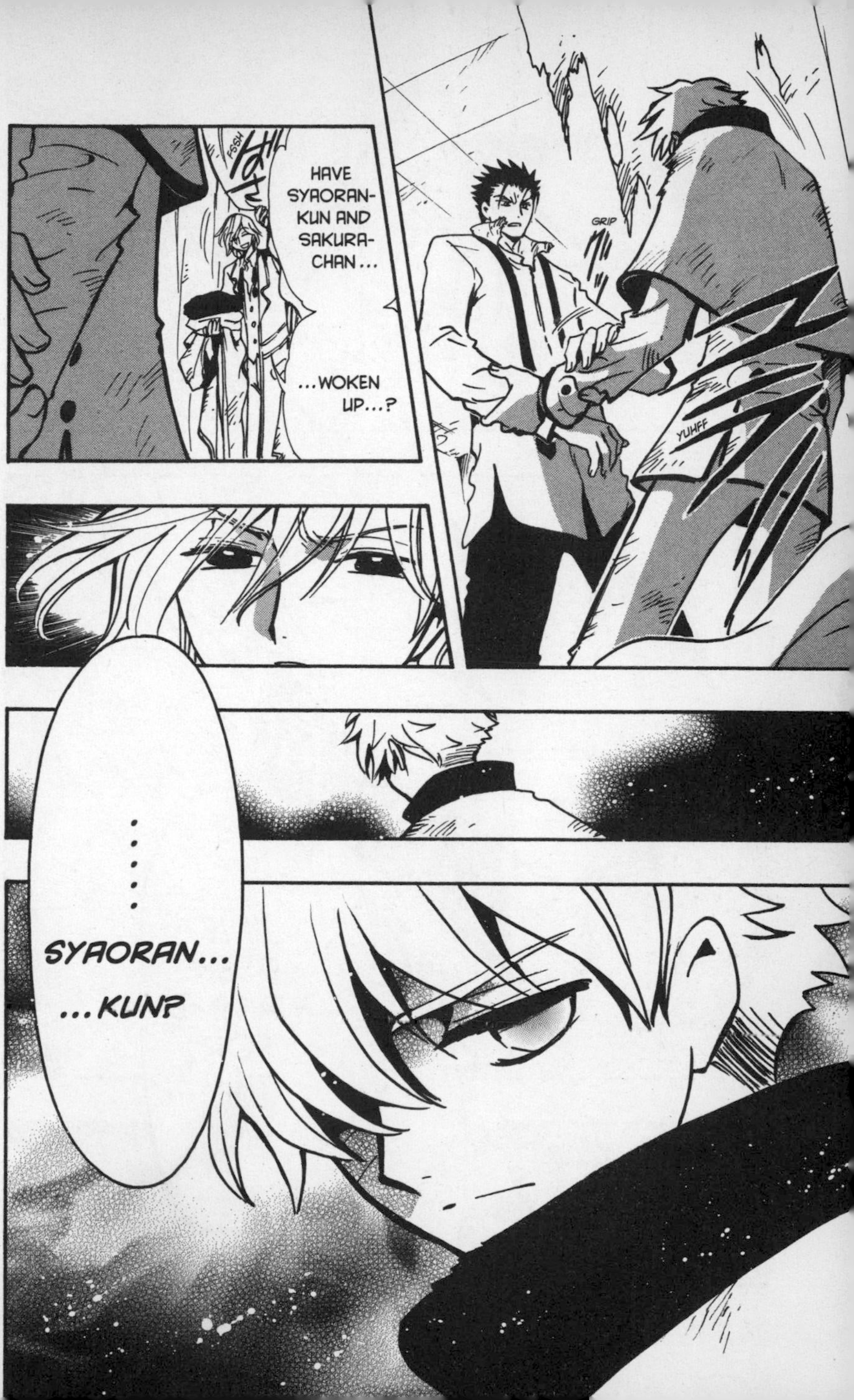
GRIP
YUHFF
FSSH
HAVE SYAORAN-KUN AND SAKURA-CHAN...
...WOKEN UP...?
.....
SYAORAN...
...KUN?

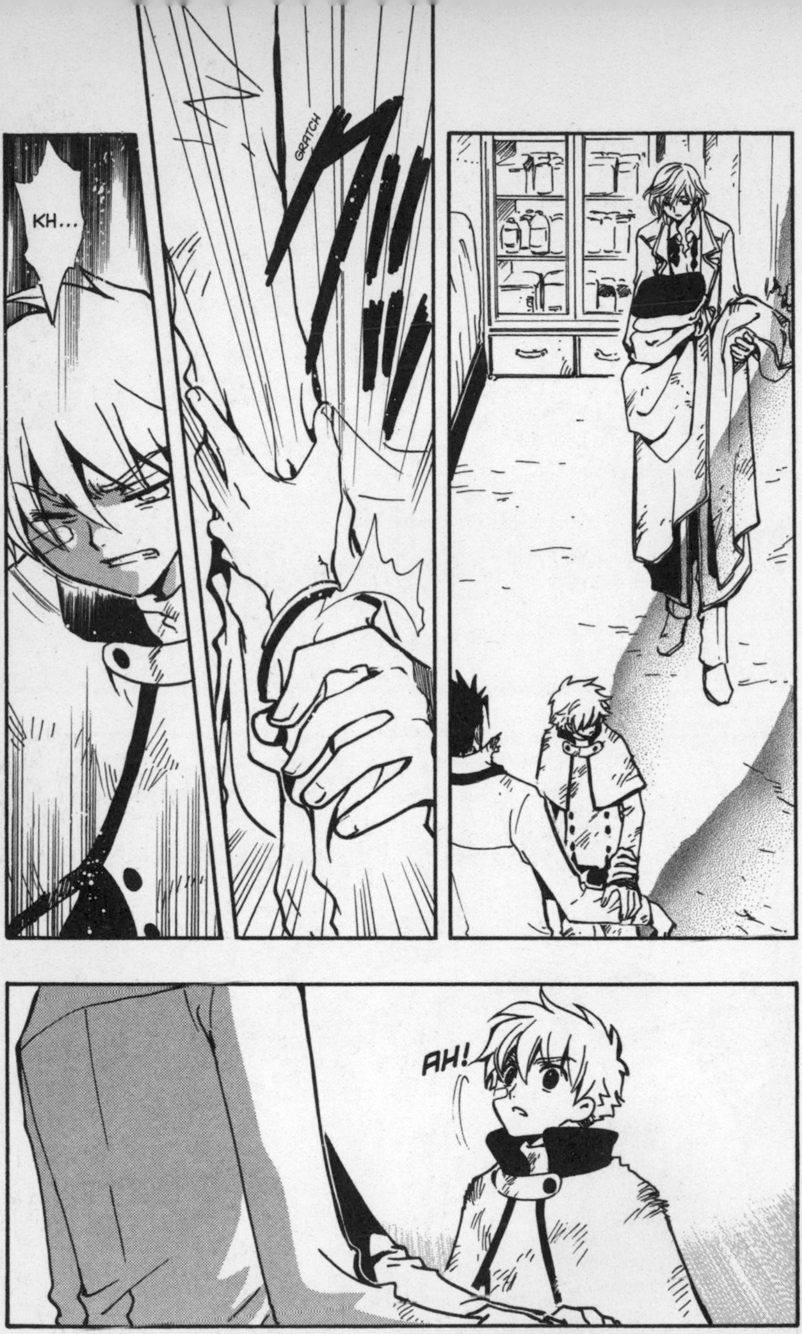
GRATCH
KH...
AH!

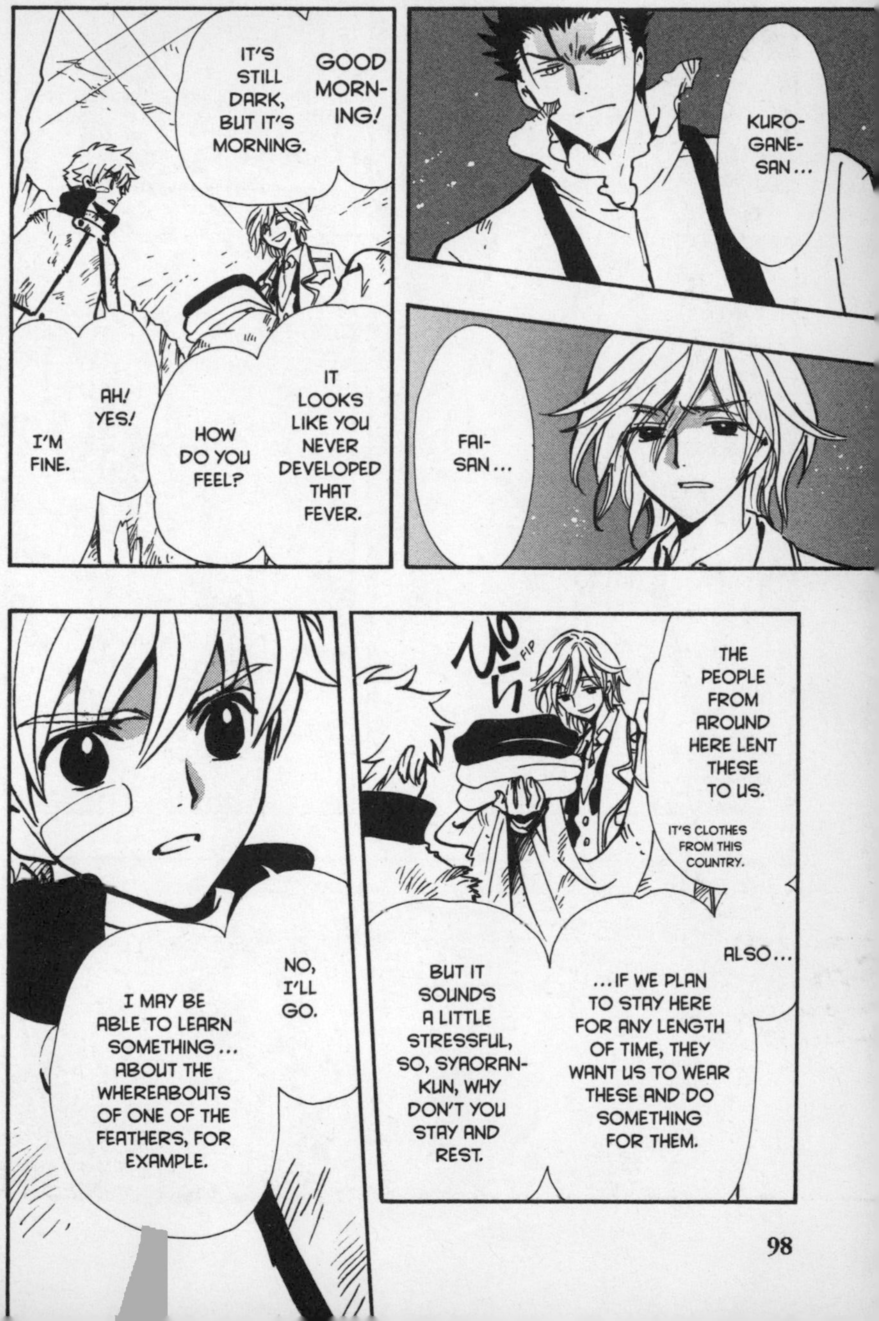
KURO-GANE-SAN...
FAI-SAN...
GOOD MORN-ING!
IT'S STILL DARK, BUT IT'S MORNING.
IT LOOKS LIKE YOU NEVER DEVELOPED THAT FEVER.
HOW DO YOU FEEL?
AH! YES!
I'M FINE.
FIP
THE PEOPLE FROM AROUND HERE LENT THESE TO US.
IT'S CLOTHES FROM THIS COUNTRY.
ALSO...
...IF WE PLAN TO STAY HERE FOR ANY LENGTH OF TIME, THEY WANT US TO WEAR THESE AND DO SOMETHING FOR THEM.
BUT IT SOUNDS A LITTLE STRESSFUL, SO, SYAORAN-KUN, WHY DON'T YOU STAY AND REST.
NO, I'LL GO.
I MAY BE ABLE TO LEARN SOMETHING... ABOUT THE WHEREABOUTS OF ONE OF THE FEATHERS, FOR EXAMPLE.

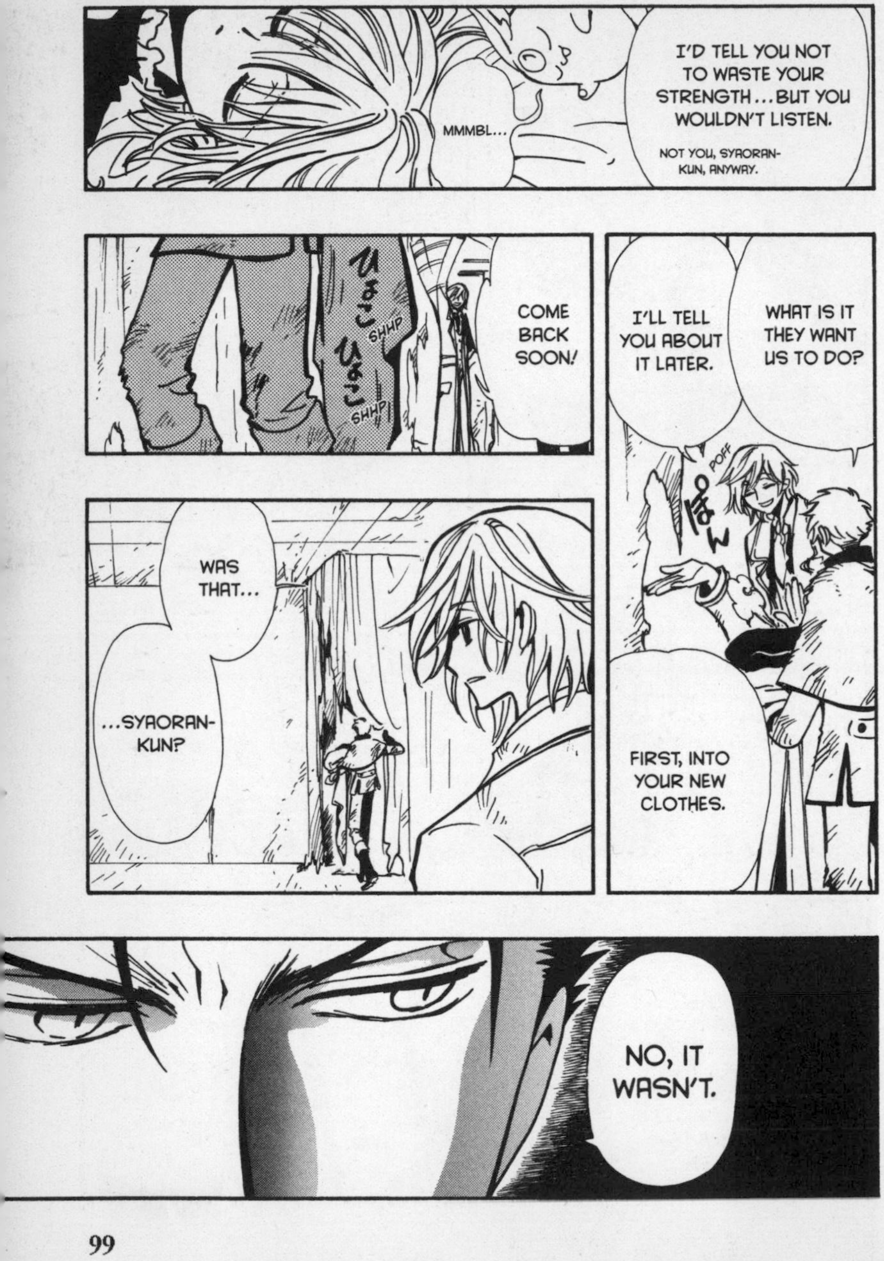
I'D TELL YOU NOT TO WASTE YOUR STRENGTH... BUT YOU WOULDN'T LISTEN.
NOT YOU, SYAORAN-KUN, ANYWAY.
MMMBL...
WHAT IS IT THEY WANT US TO DO?
I'LL TELL YOU ABOUT IT LATER.
POFF
FIRST, INTO YOUR NEW CLOTHES.
COME BACK SOON!
SHHP
SHHP
WAS THAT...
...SYAORAN-KUN?
NO, IT WASN'T.

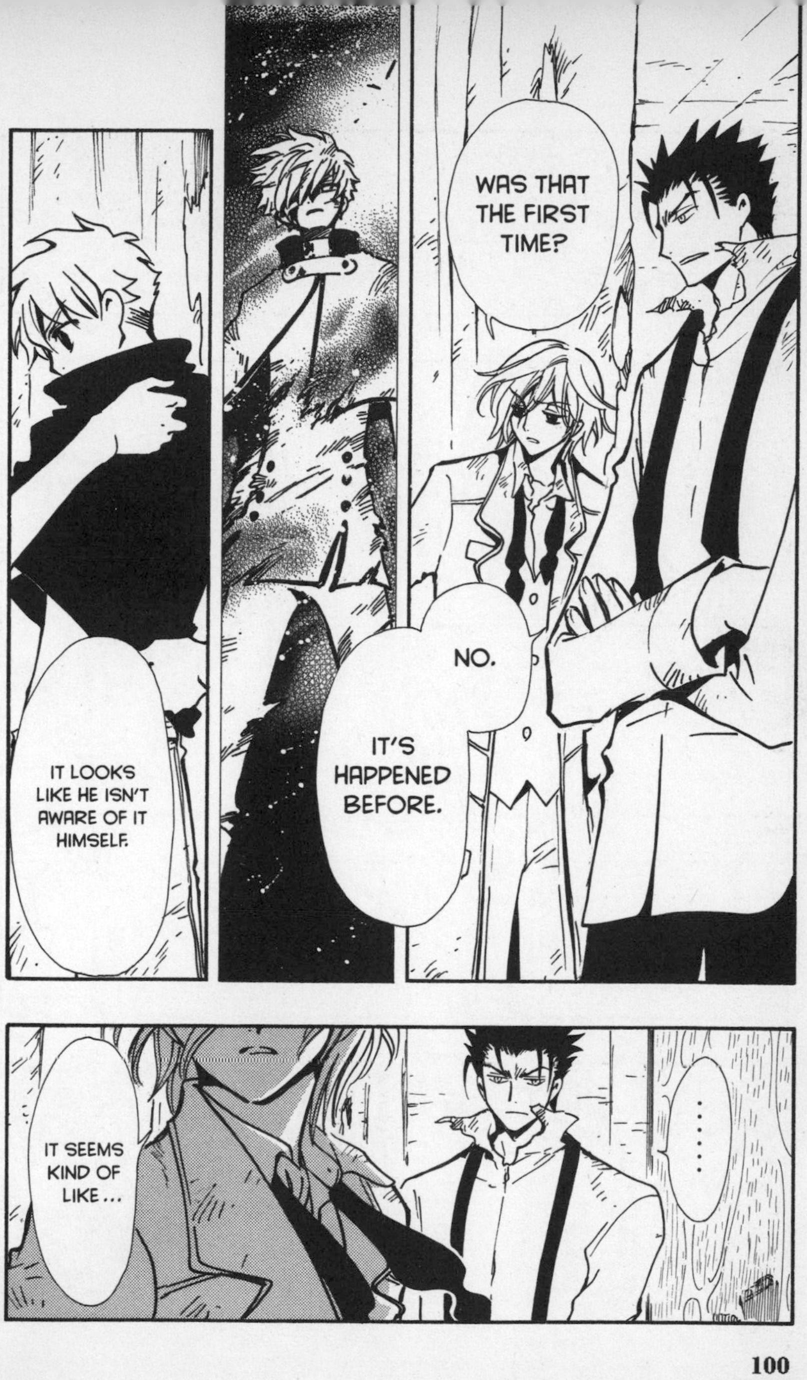
WAS THAT THE FIRST TIME?
NO.
IT'S HAPPENED BEFORE.
IT LOOKS LIKE HE ISN'T AWARE OF IT HIMSELF.
......
IT SEEMS KIND OF LIKE...

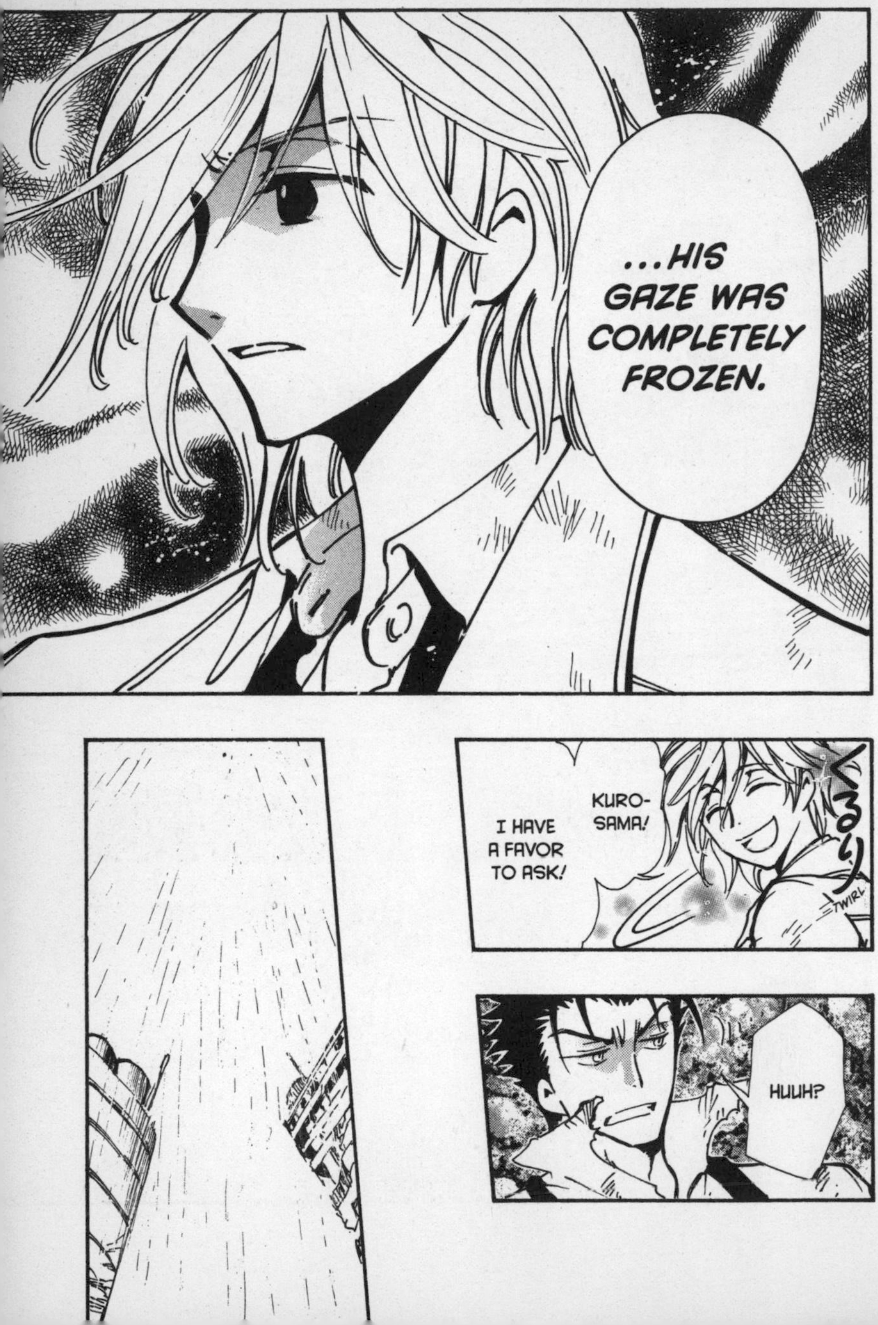
...HIS GAZE WAS COMPLETELY FROZEN.
KURO-SAMA!
I HAVE A FAVOR TO ASK!
TWIRL
HUUH?

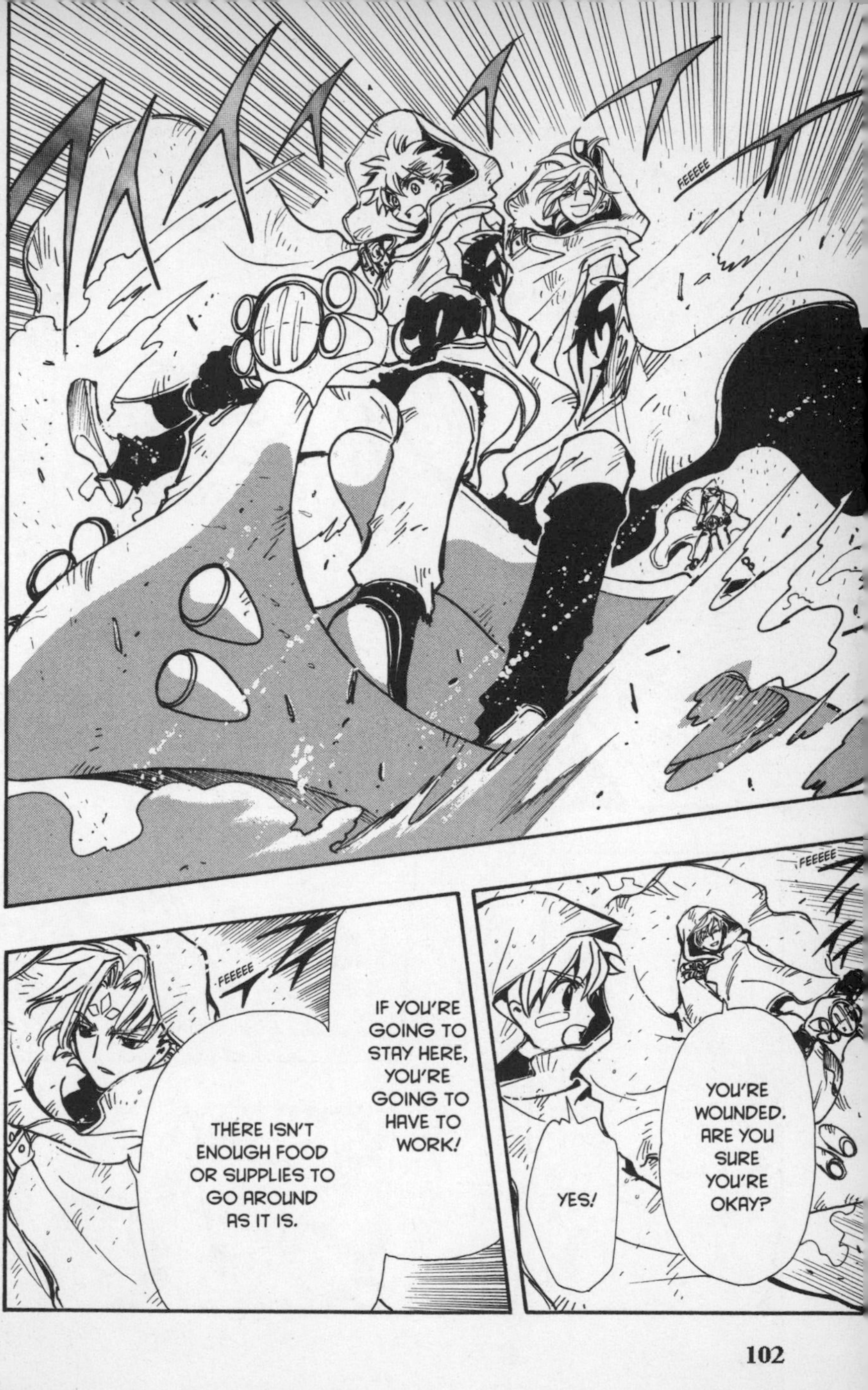
FEEEEE
FEEEEE
YOU'RE WOUNDED. ARE YOU SURE YOU'RE OKAY?
YES!
FEEEEE
IF YOU'RE GOING TO STAY HERE, YOU'RE GOING TO HAVE TO WORK!
THERE ISN'T ENOUGH FOOD OR SUPPLIES TO GO AROUND AS IT IS.

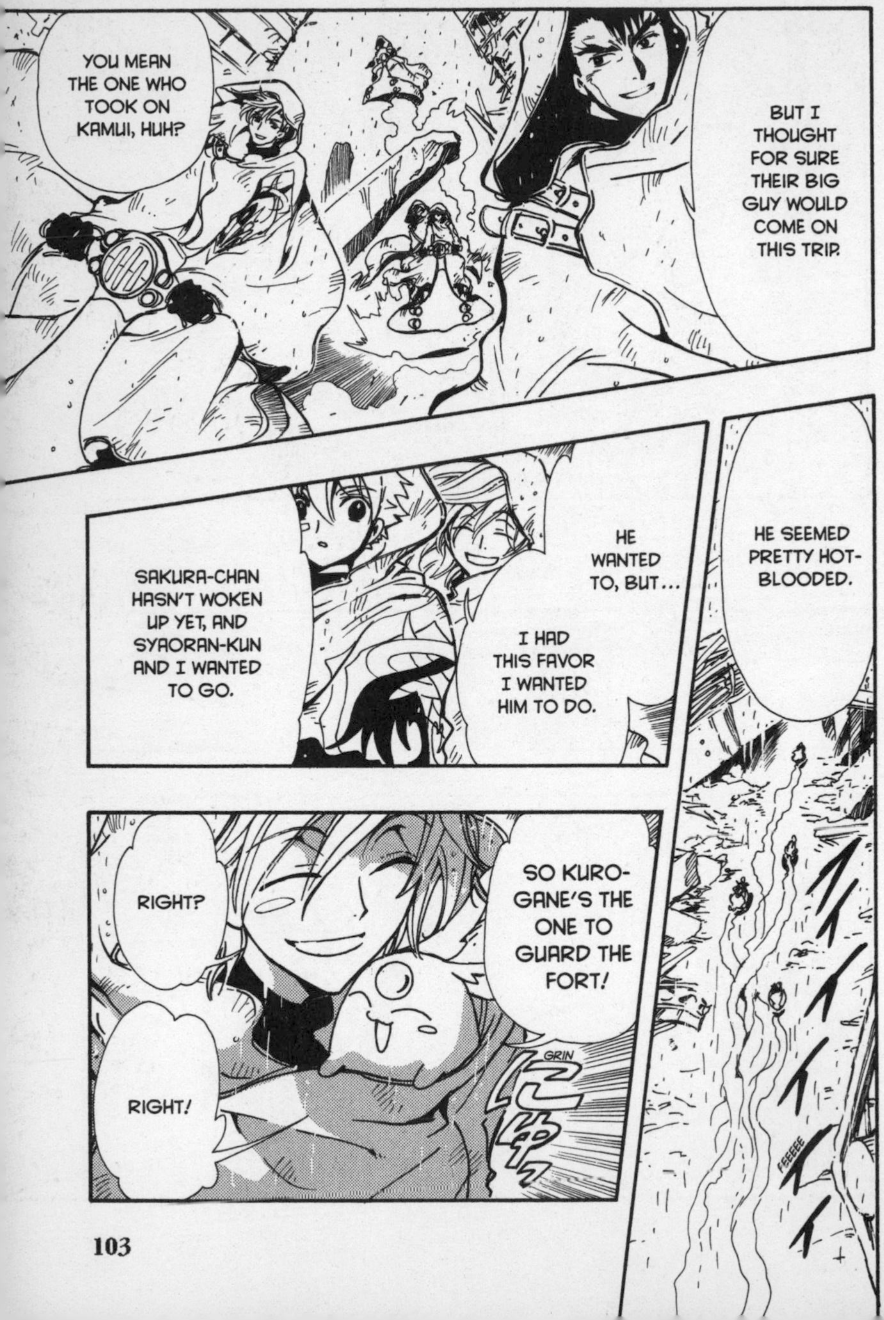
BUT I THOUGHT FOR SURE THEIR BIG GUY WOULD COME ON THIS TRIP.
YOU MEAN THE ONE WHO TOOK ON KAMUI, HUH?
HE SEEMED PRETTY HOT-BLOODED.
FEEEEE
HE WANTED TO, BUT...
I HAD THIS FAVOR I WANTED HIM TO DO.
SAKURA-CHAN HASN'T WOKEN UP YET, AND SYAORAN-KUN AND I WANTED TO GO.
SO KURO-GANE'S THE ONE TO GUARD THE FORT!
GRIN
RIGHT?
RIGHT!

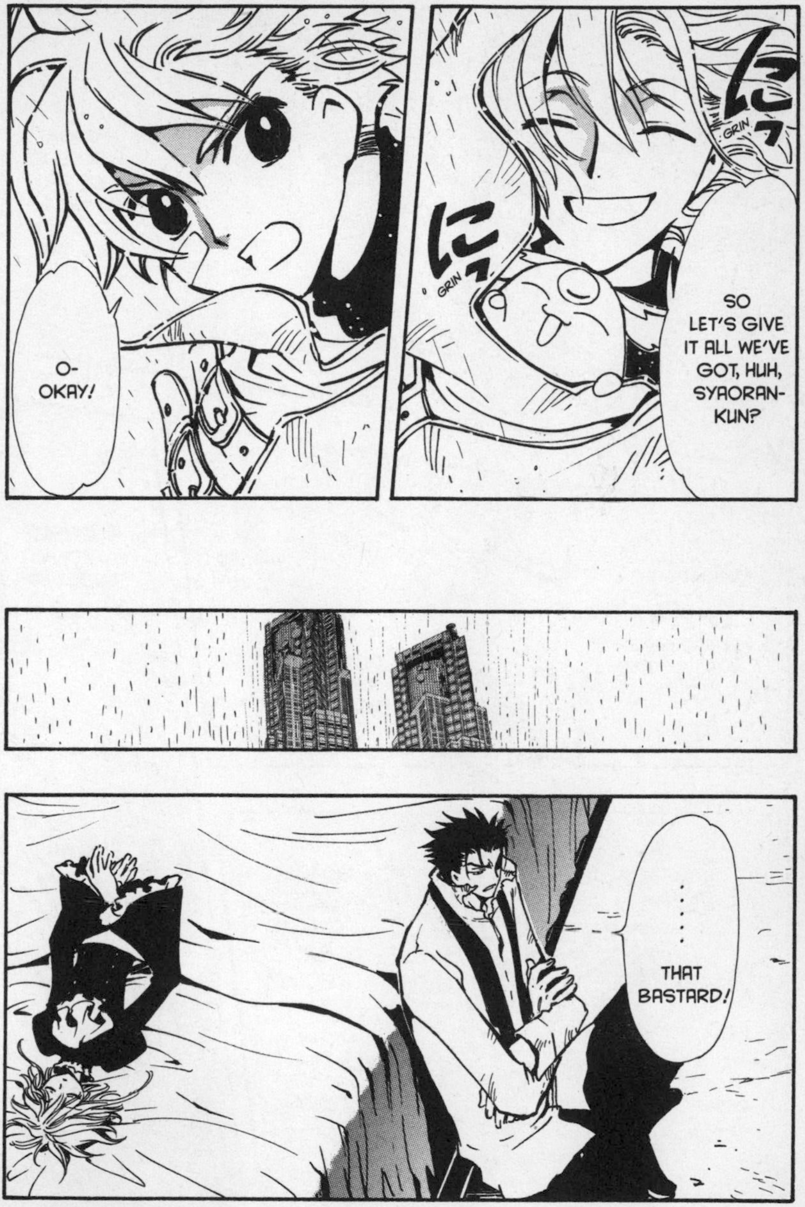

GRIN
GRIN
SO LET'S GIVE IT ALL WE'VE GOT, HUH, SYAORAN-KUN?
O-OKAY!
......
THAT BASTARD!

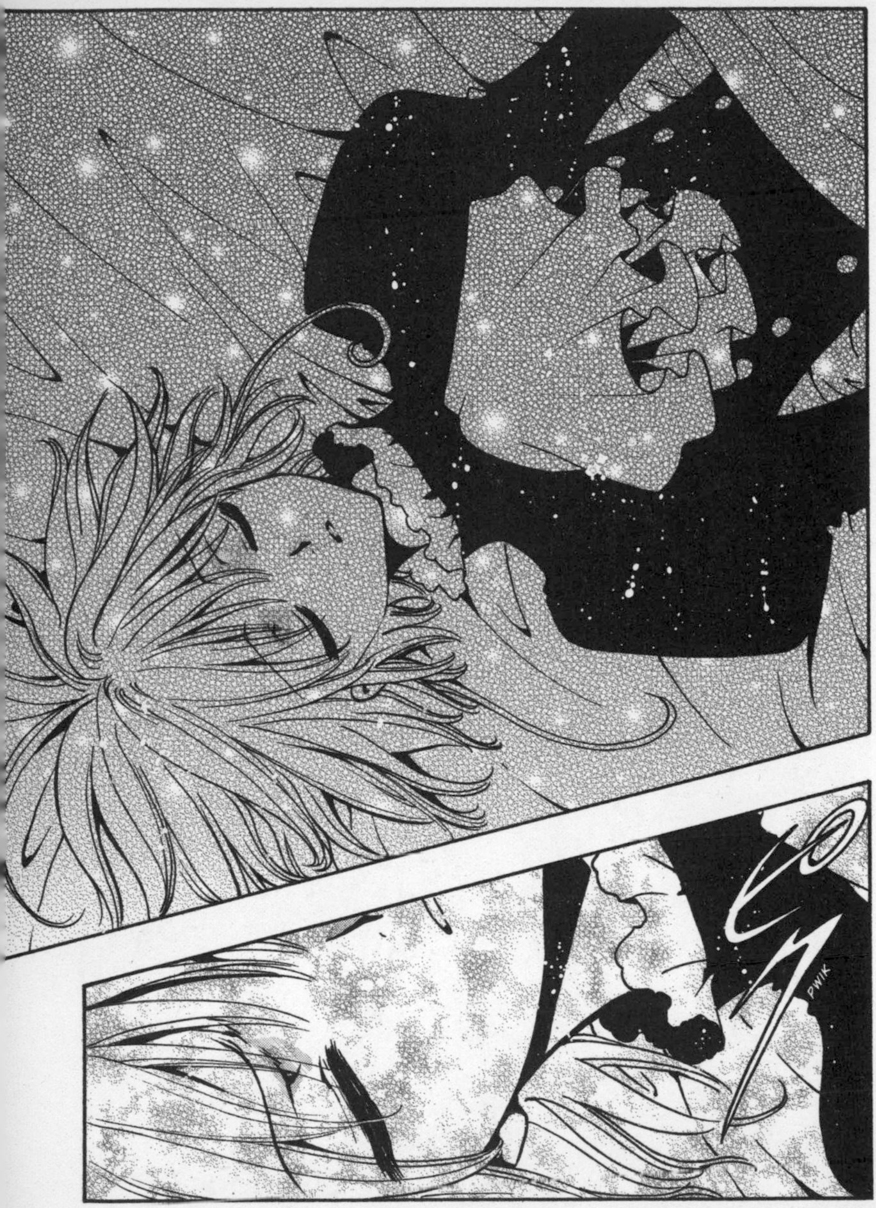
PWIK

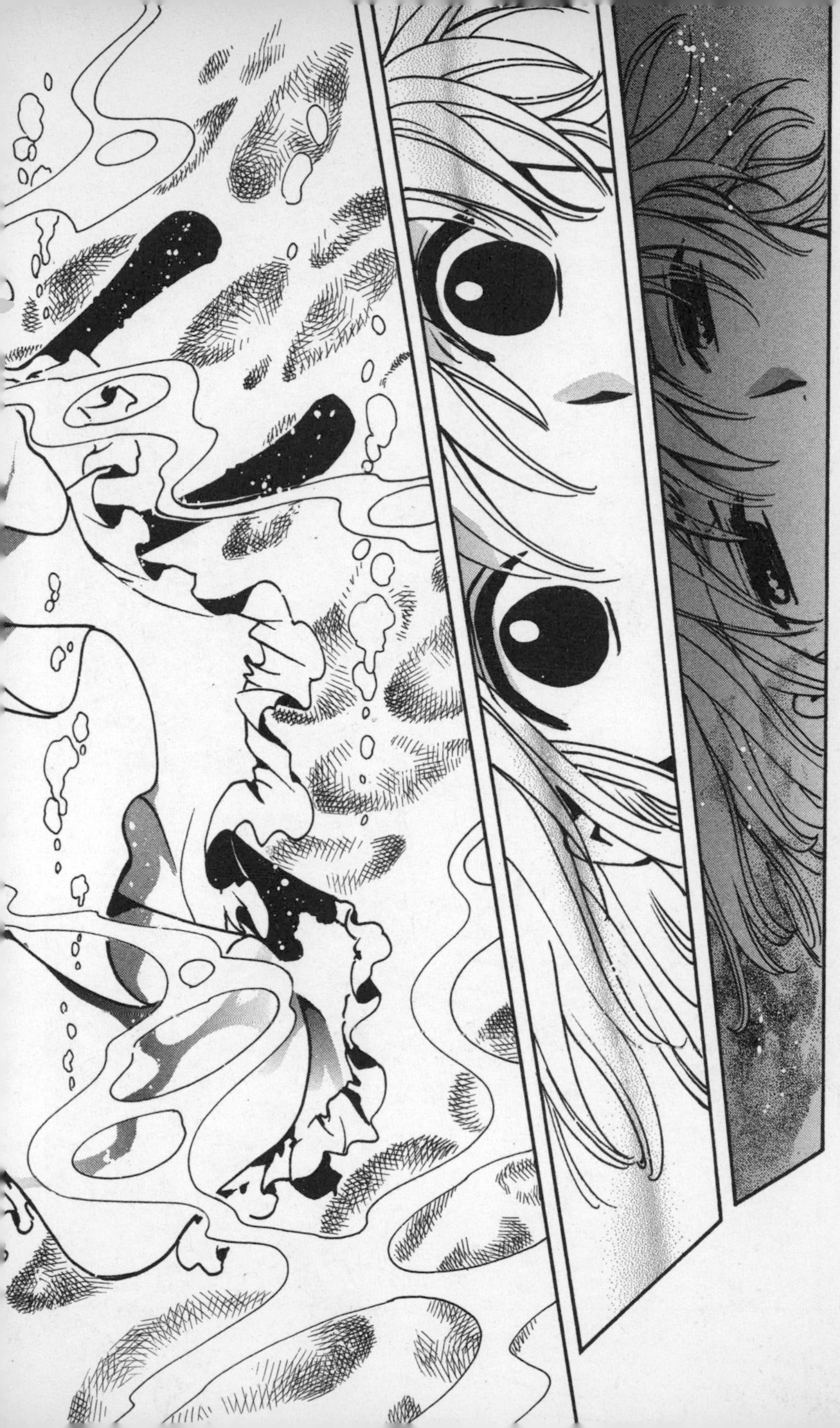

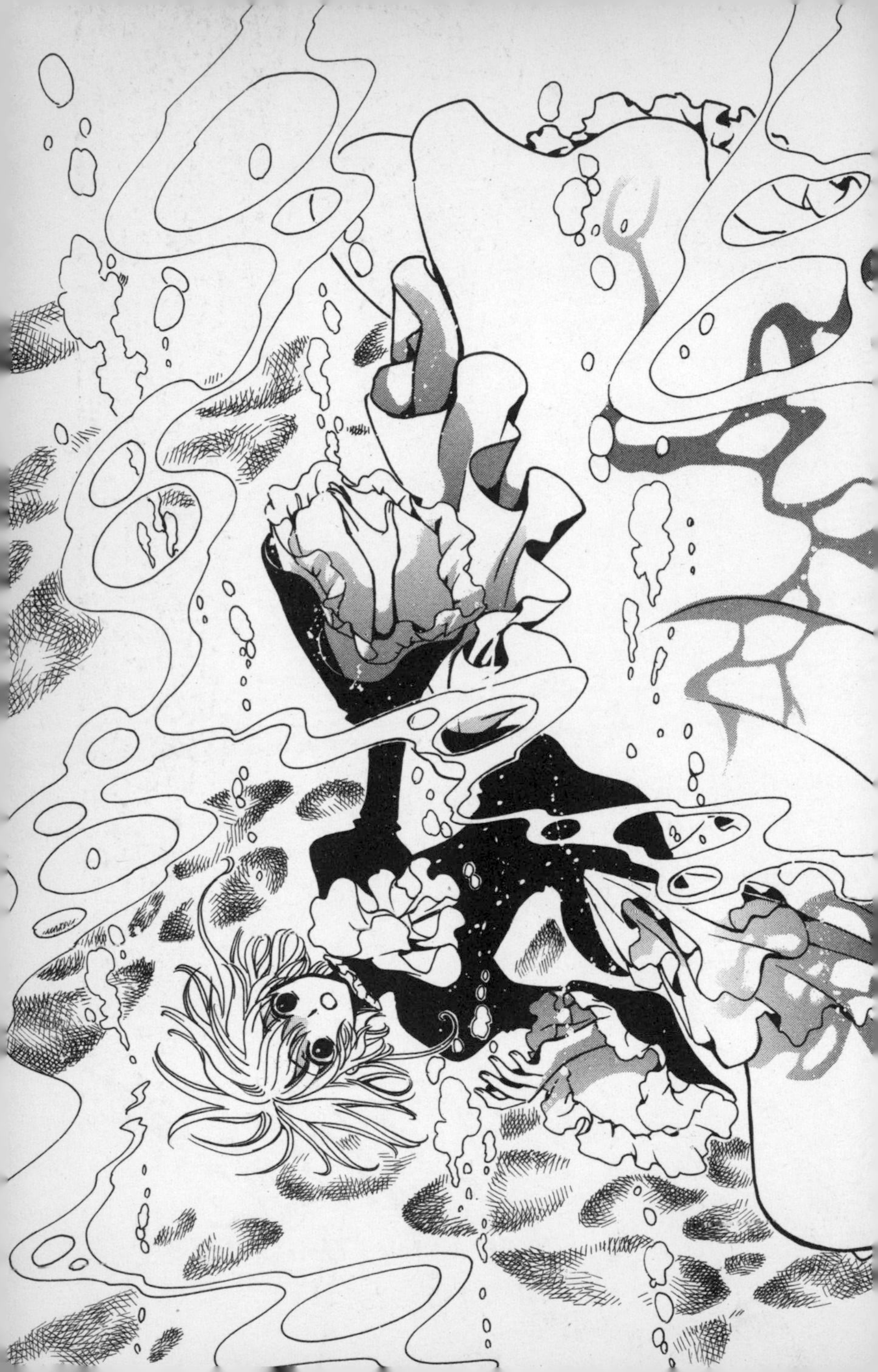

ツバサ

RESERVoir CHRoNiCLE

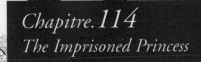

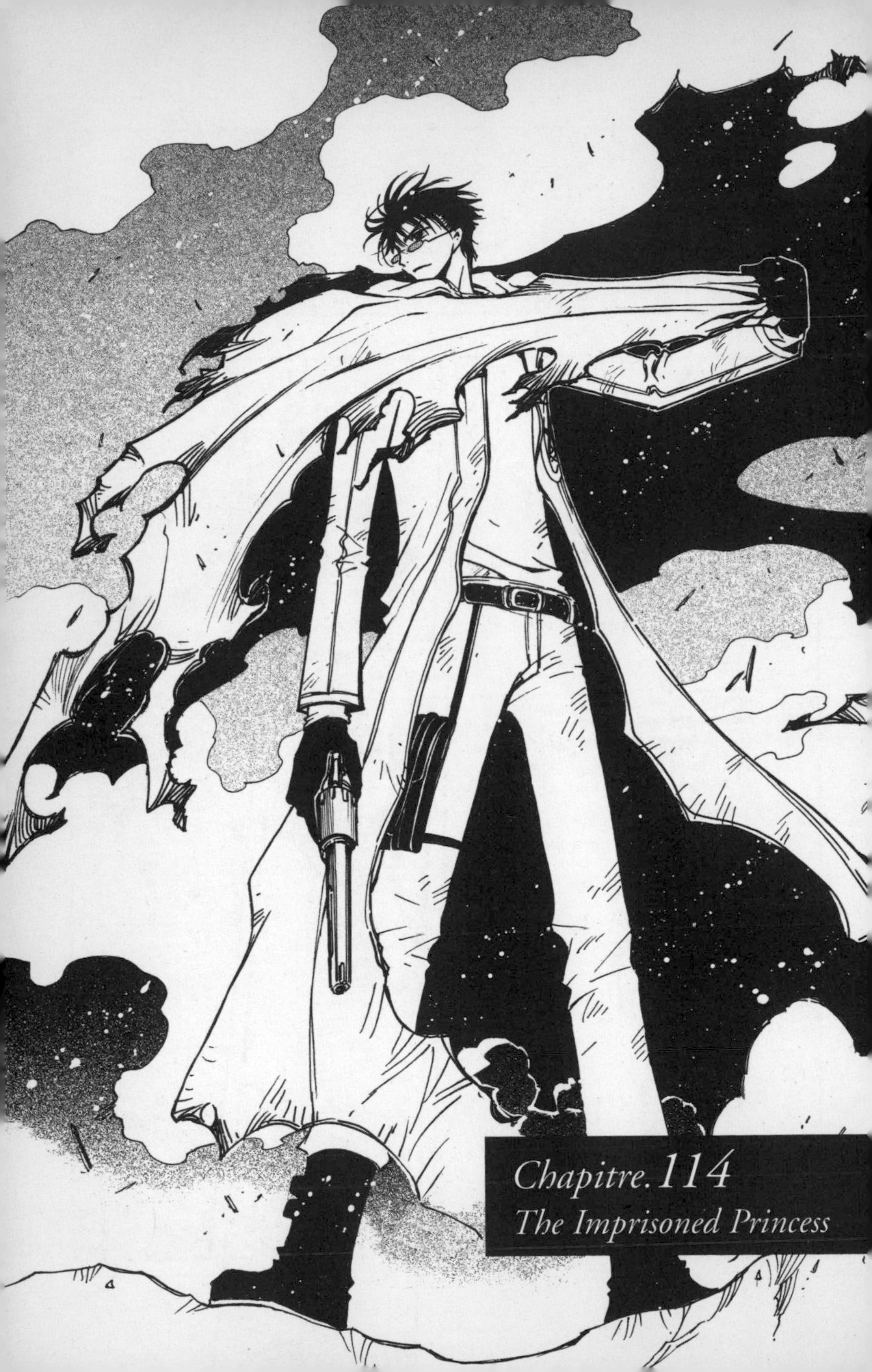

Chapitre.114
The Imprisoned Princess

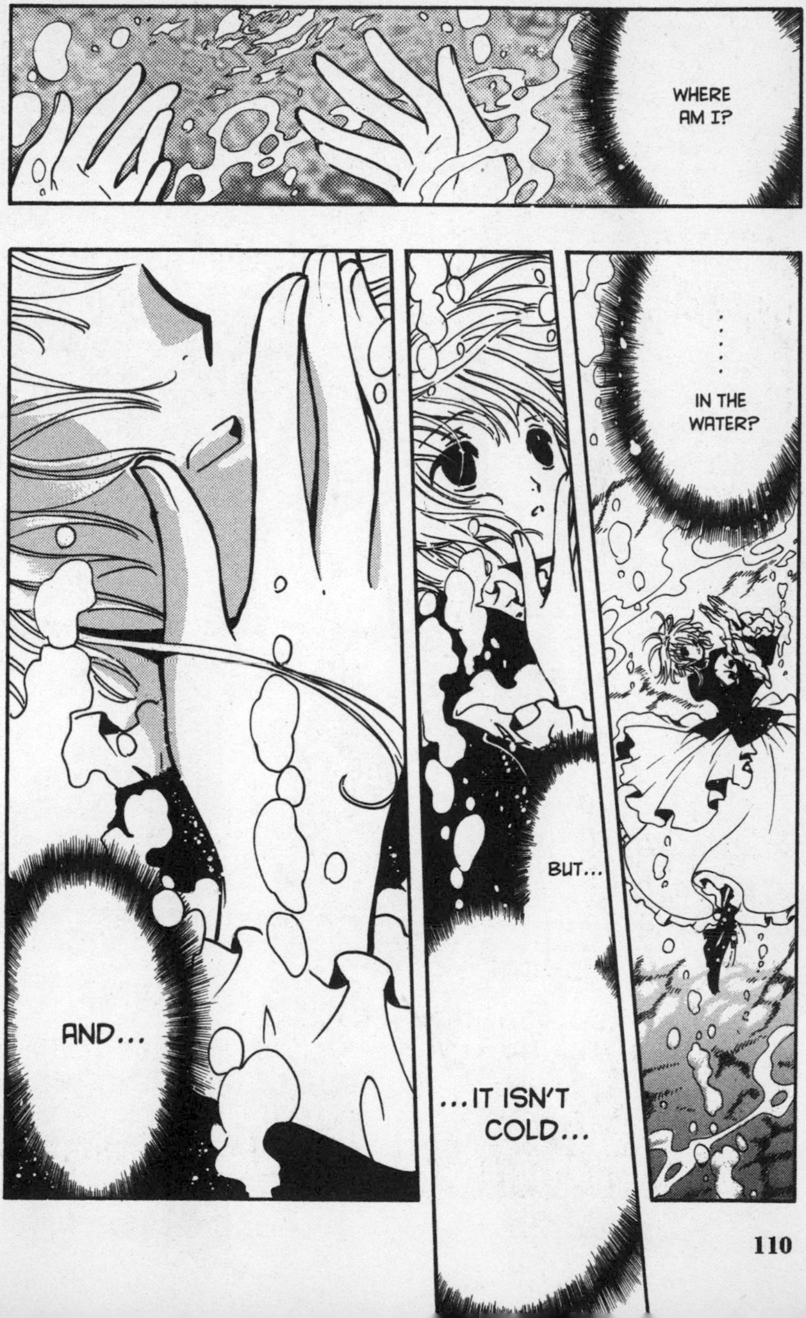
WHERE AM I?
....
IN THE WATER?
BUT...
...IT ISN'T COLD...
AND...

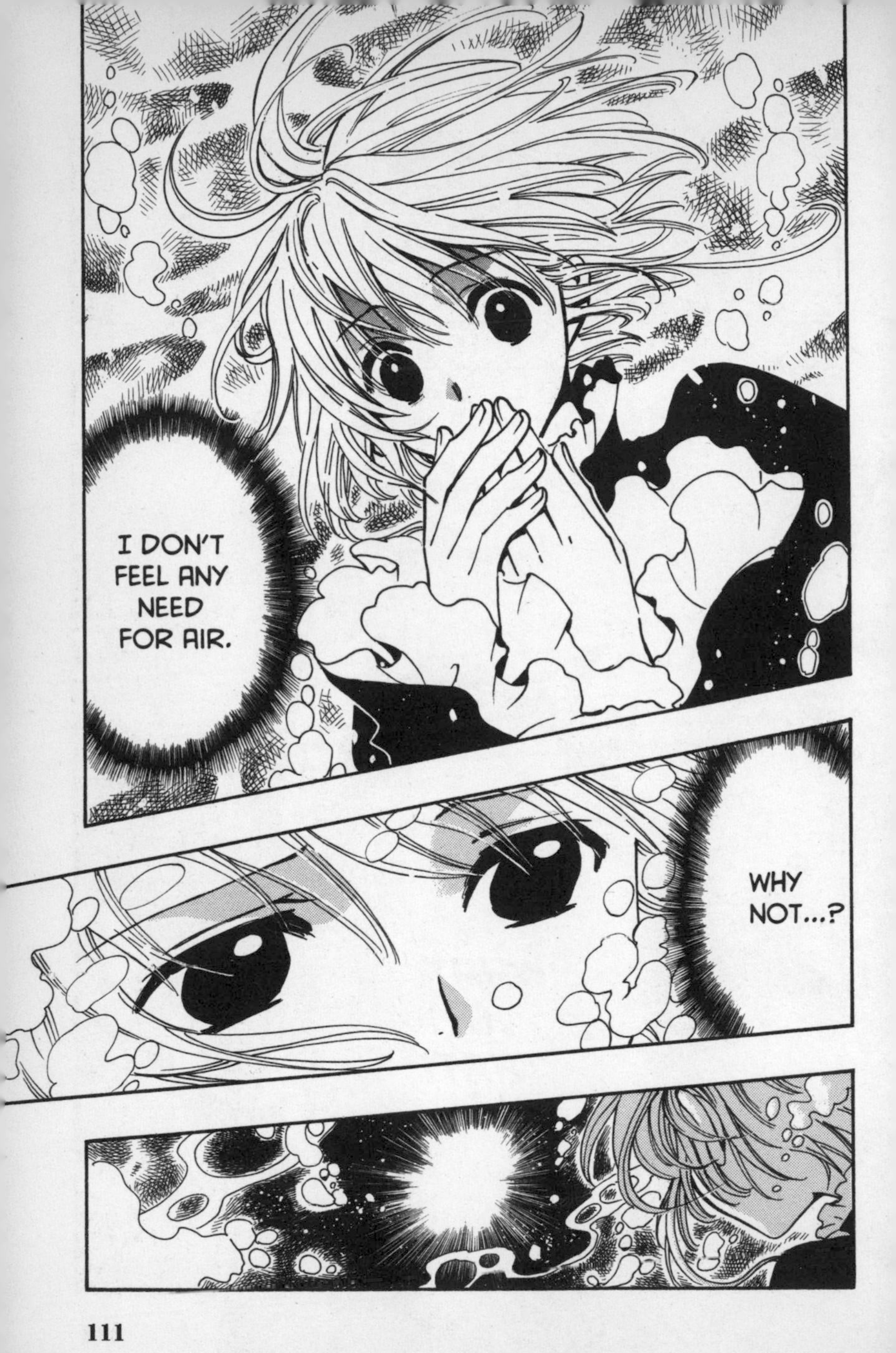
I DON'T FEEL ANY NEED FOR AIR.
WHY NOT...?

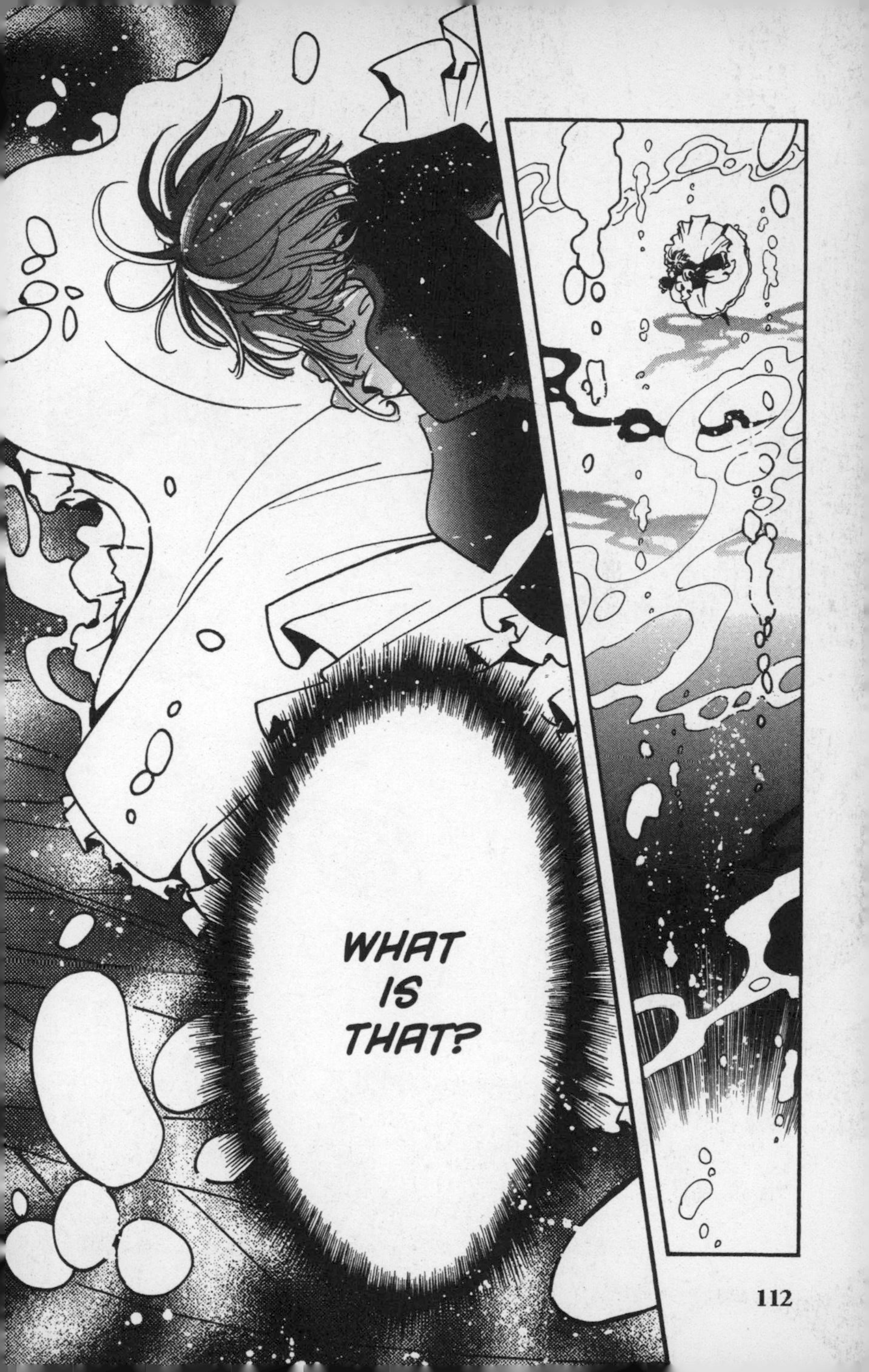
WHAT IS THAT?

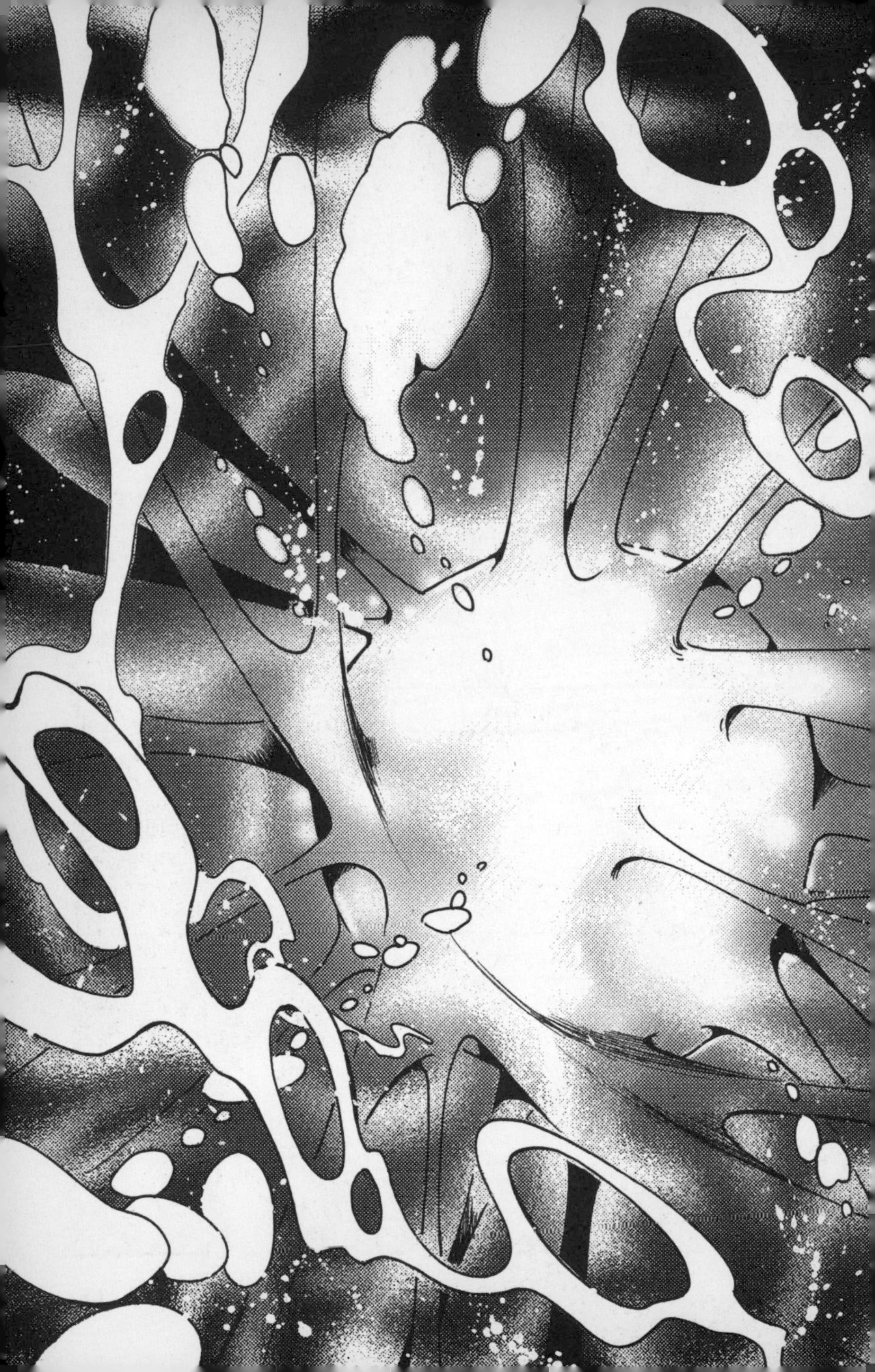

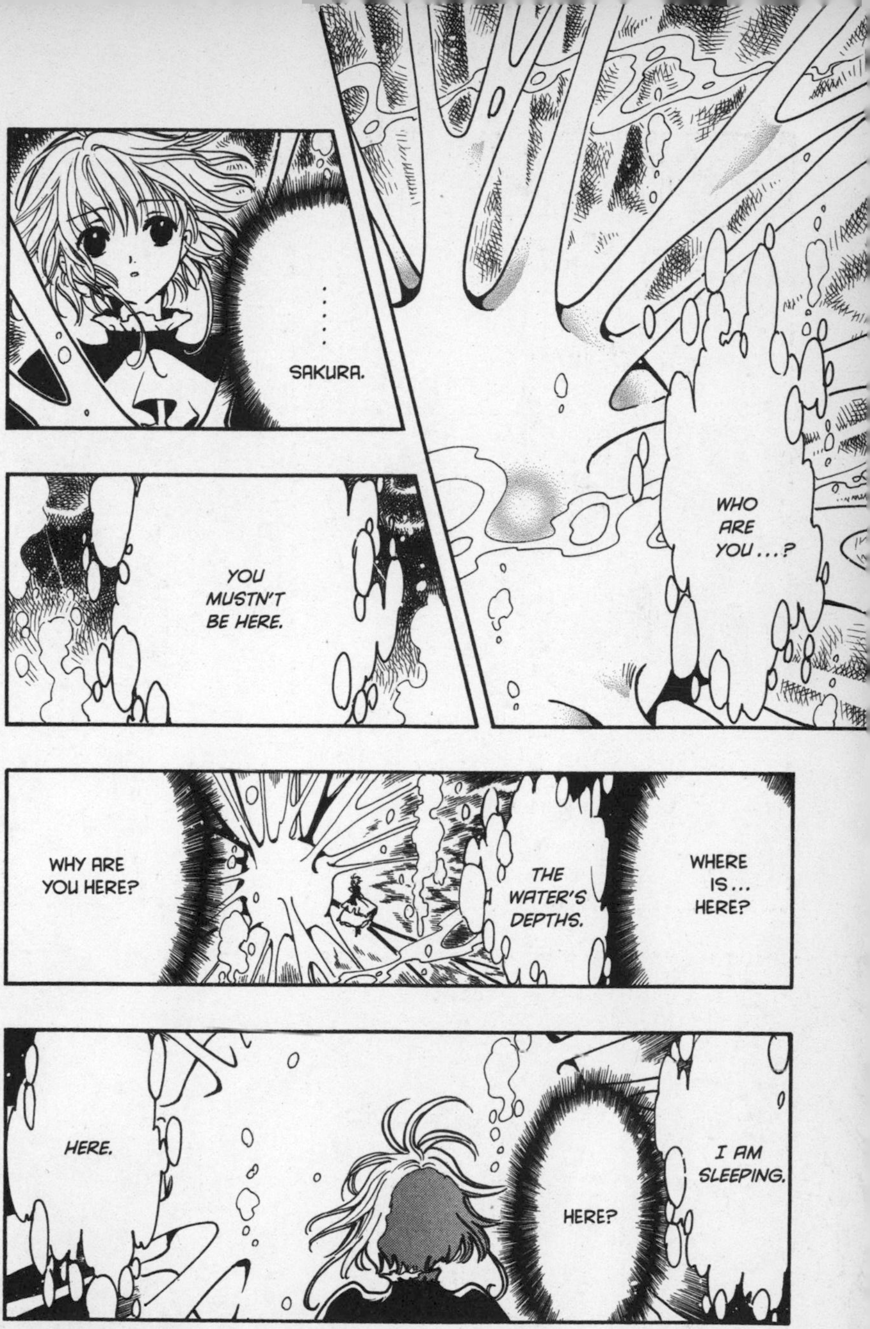
WHO ARE YOU...?
....
SAKURA.
YOU MUSTN'T BE HERE.
WHERE IS... HERE?
THE WATER'S DEPTHS.
WHY ARE YOU HERE?
I AM SLEEPING.
HERE?
HERE.

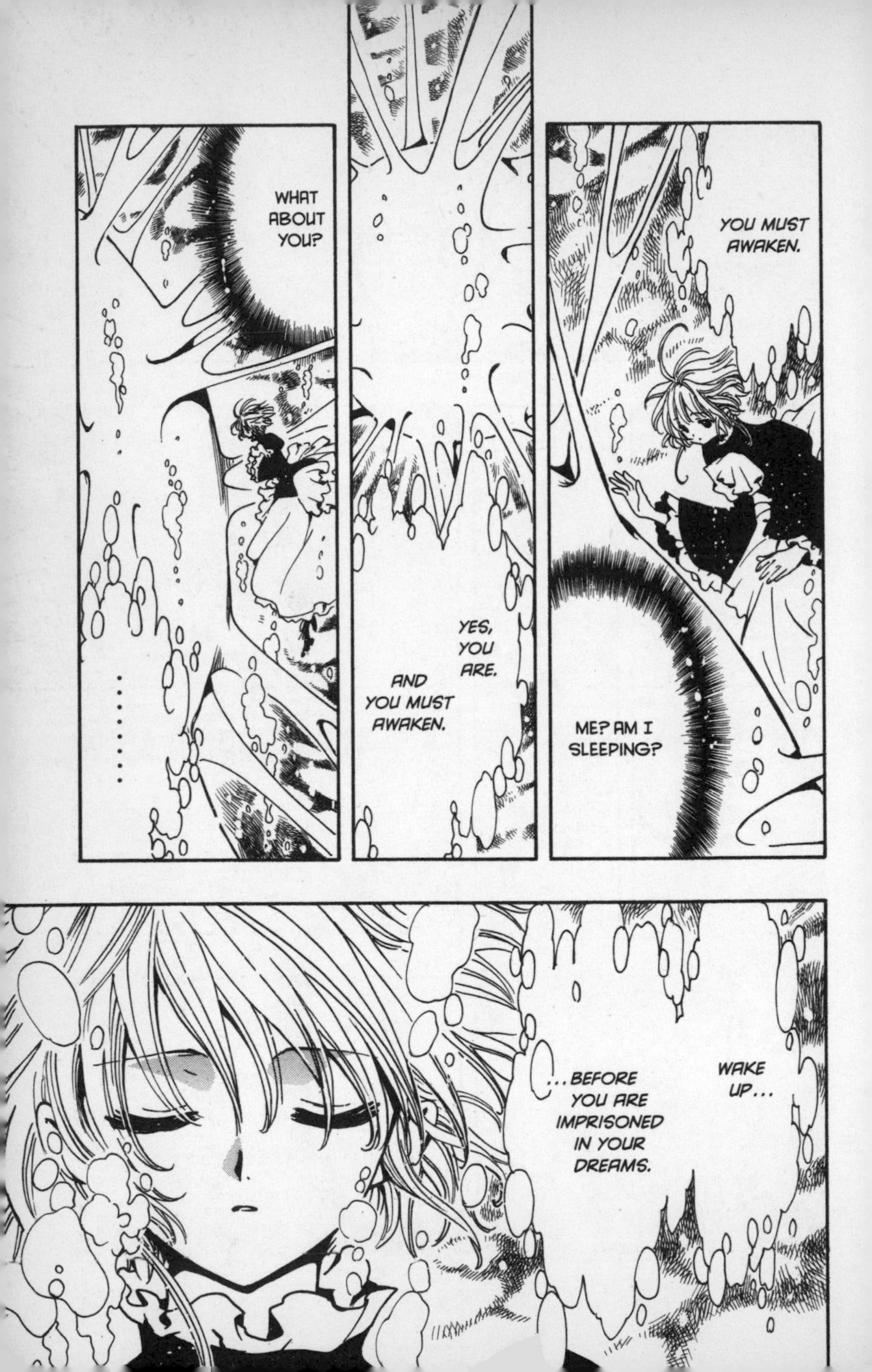
YOU MUST AWAKEN.
ME? AM I SLEEPING?
YES, YOU ARE.
AND YOU MUST AWAKEN.
WHAT ABOUT YOU?
......
WAKE UP...
...BEFORE YOU ARE IMPRISONED IN YOUR DREAMS.

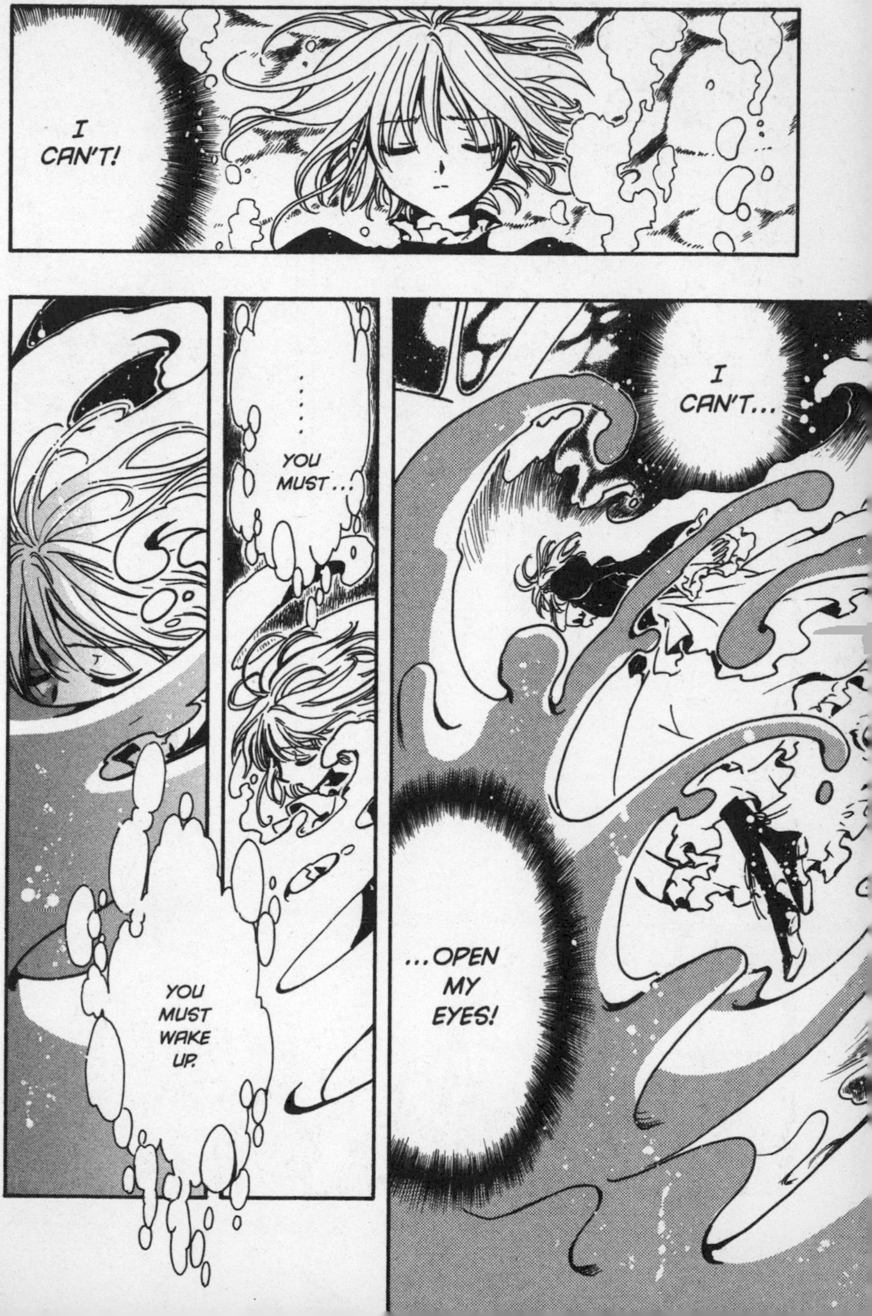
I CAN'T!
I CAN'T...
...OPEN MY EYES!
.....
YOU MUST...
YOU MUST WAKE UP.

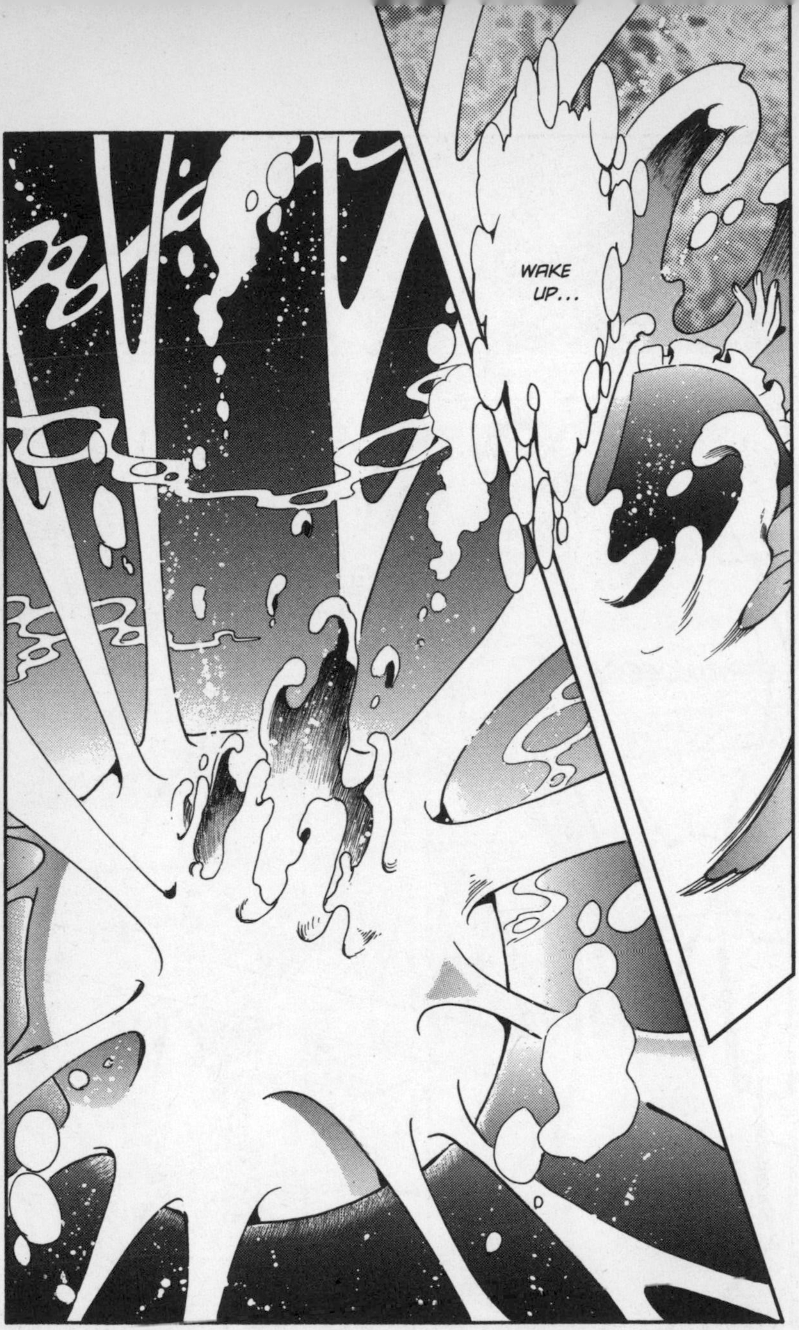
WAKE UP...

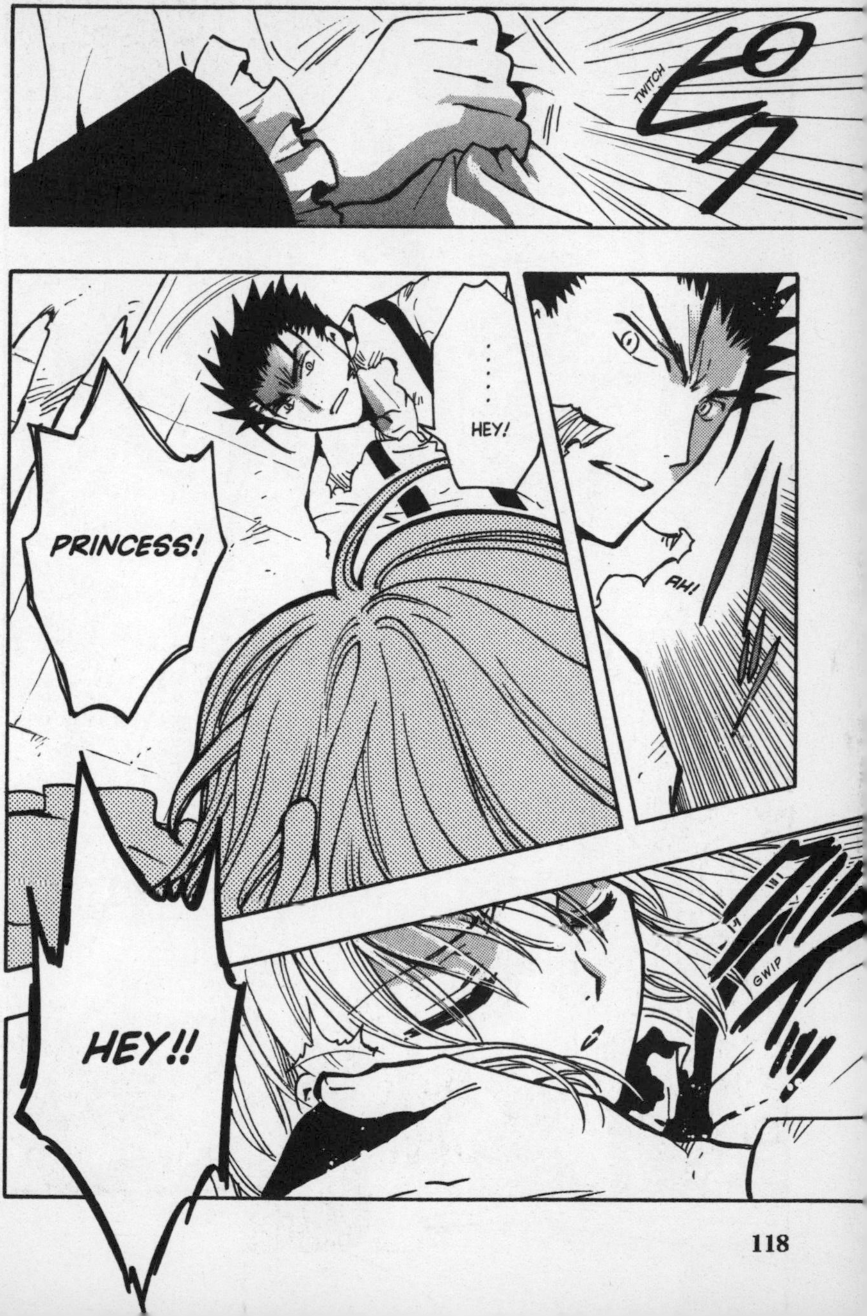
TWITCH
AH!
......
HEY!
PRINCESS!
GWIP
HEY!!

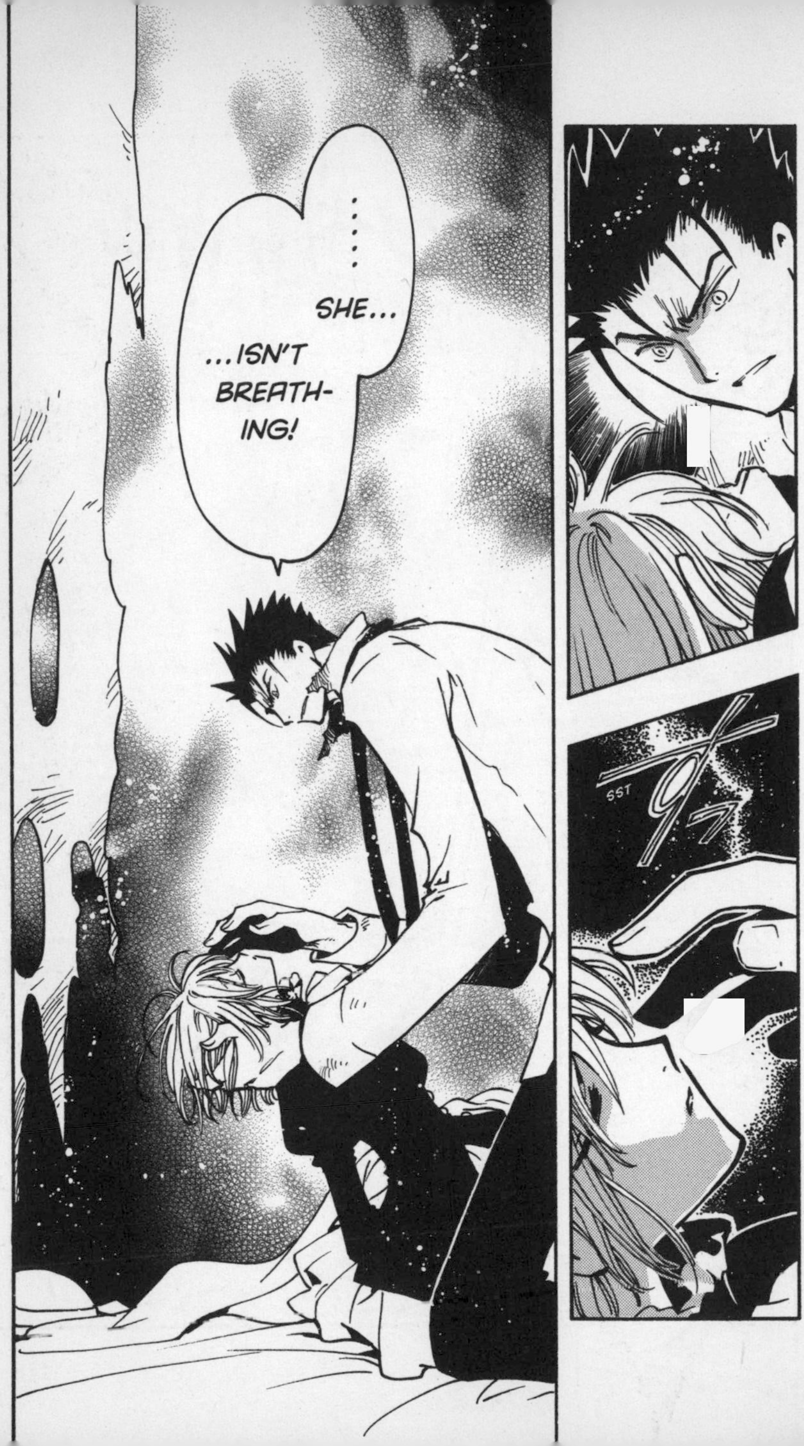
SST
.....
SHE...
...ISN'T BREATH-ING!

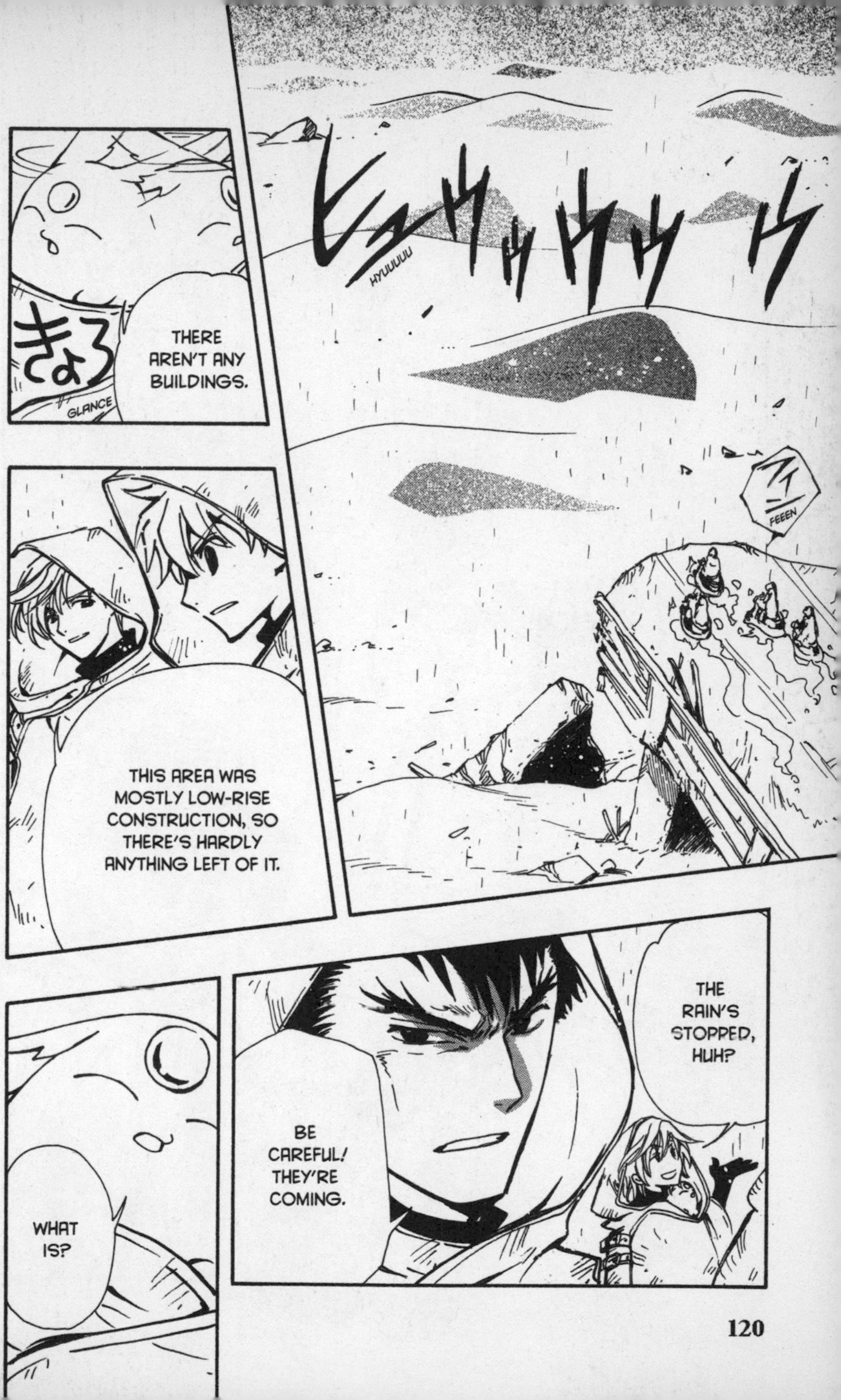
HYUUUUU
FEEEN
GLANCE
THERE AREN'T ANY BUILDINGS.
THIS AREA WAS MOSTLY LOW-RISE CONSTRUCTION, SO THERE'S HARDLY ANYTHING LEFT OF IT.
THE RAIN'S STOPPED, HUH?
BE CAREFUL! THEY'RE COMING.
WHAT IS?

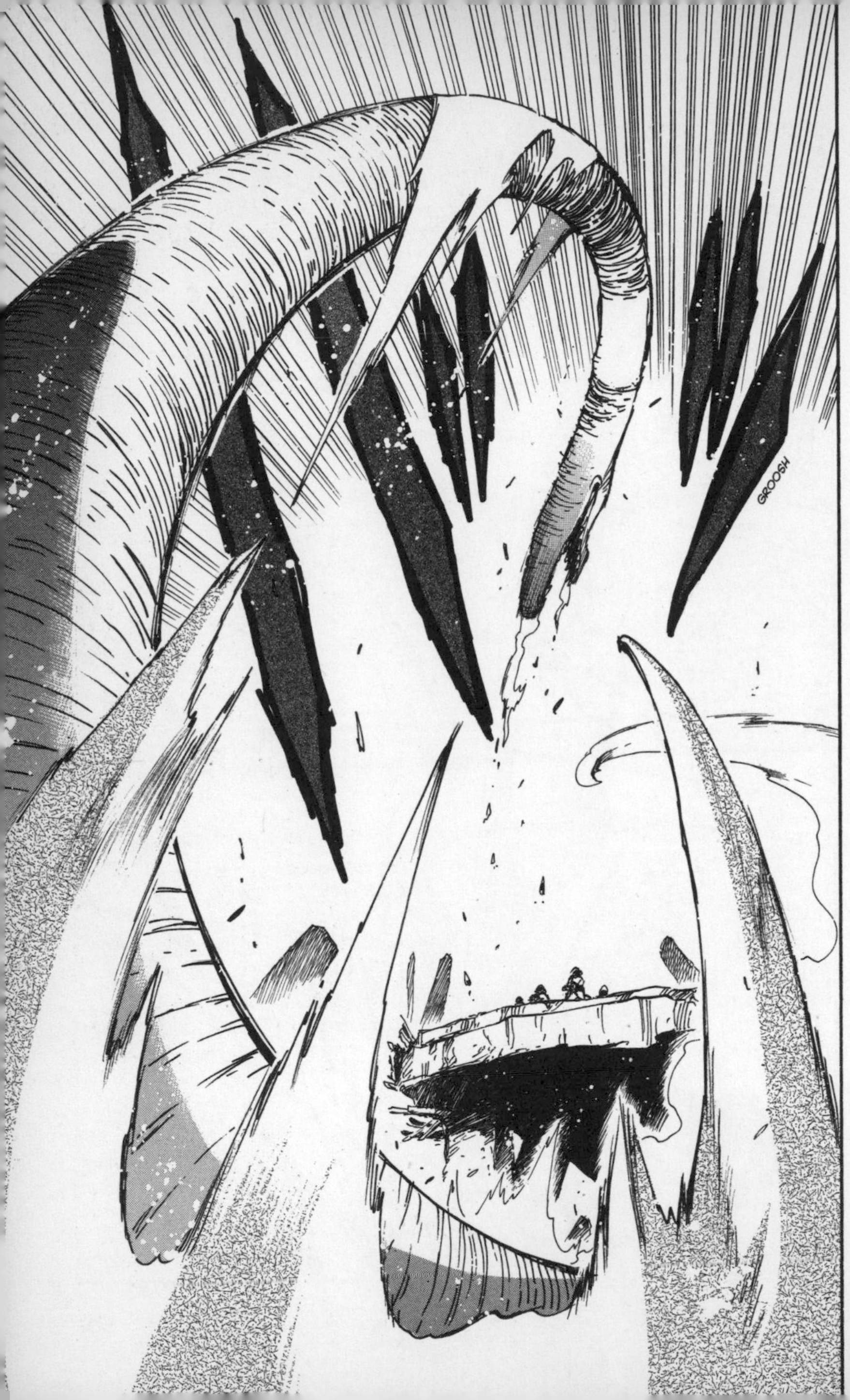
GROOSH

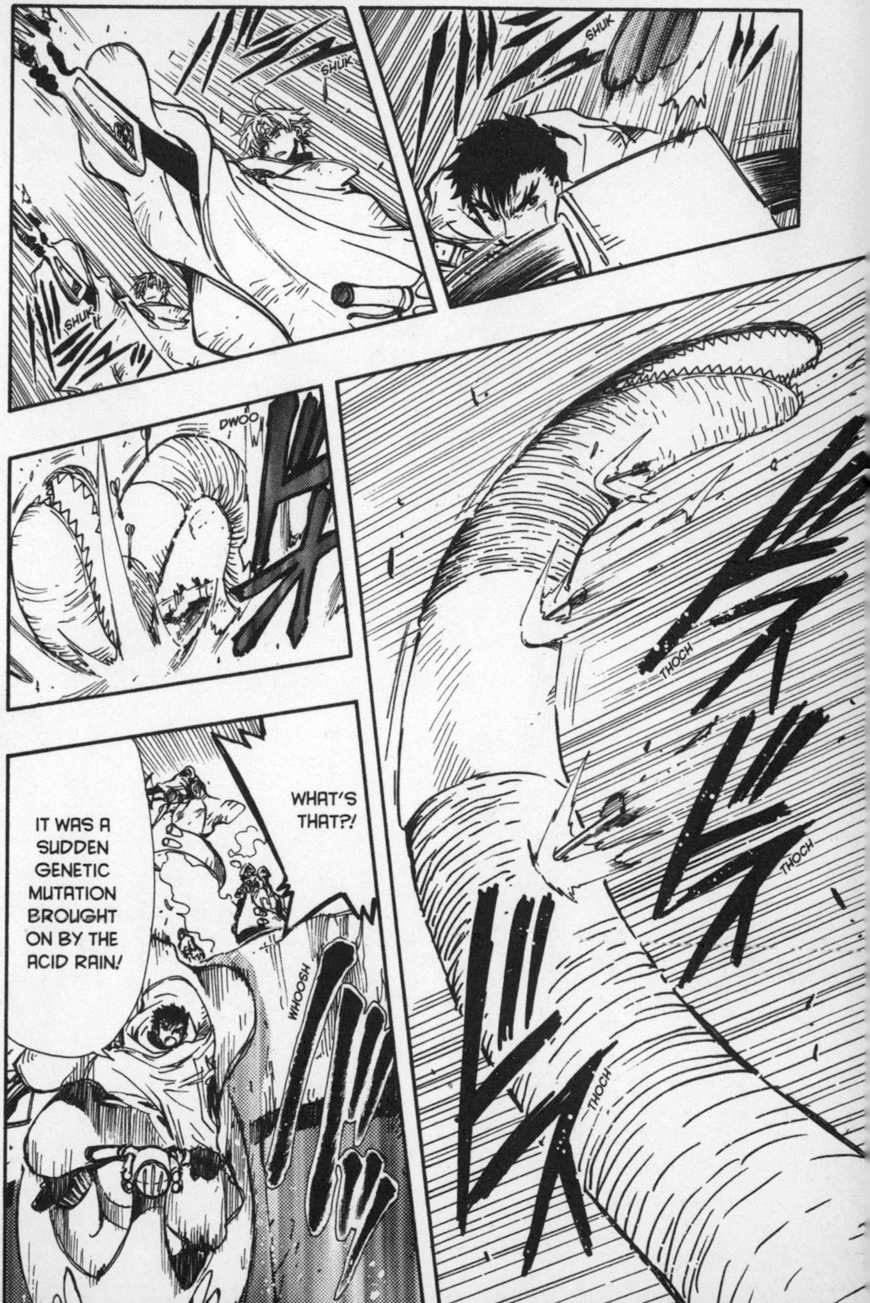
SHUK
SHUK
SHUK
THOCH
THOCH
THOCH
DWOO
WHAT'S THAT?!
IT WAS A SUDDEN GENETIC MUTATION BROUGHT ON BY THE ACID RAIN!
WHOOSH

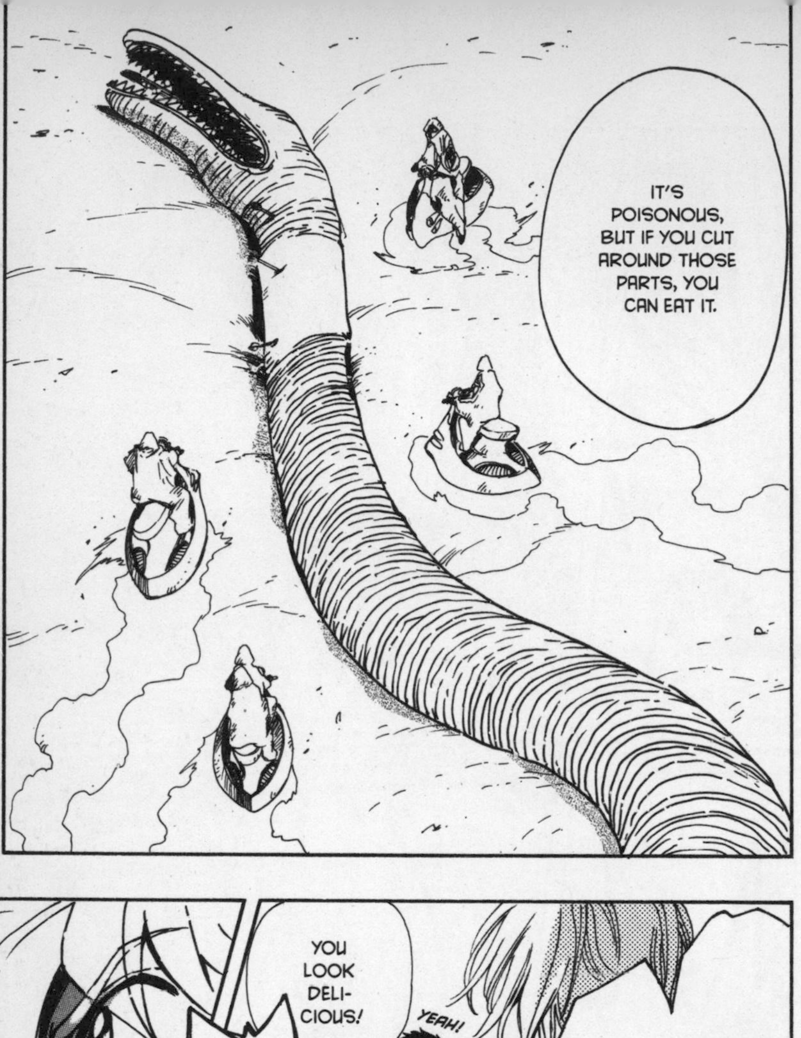
IT'S POISONOUS, BUT IF YOU CUT AROUND THOSE PARTS, YOU CAN EAT IT.
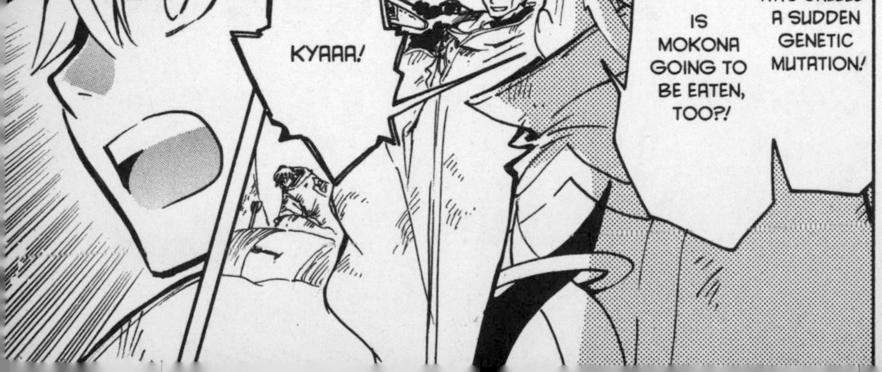
MOKONA WAS CALLED A SUDDEN GENETIC MUTATION!
IS MOKONA GOING TO BE EATEN, TOO?!
YEAH!
YOU LOOK DELI-CIOUS!
KYAAA!

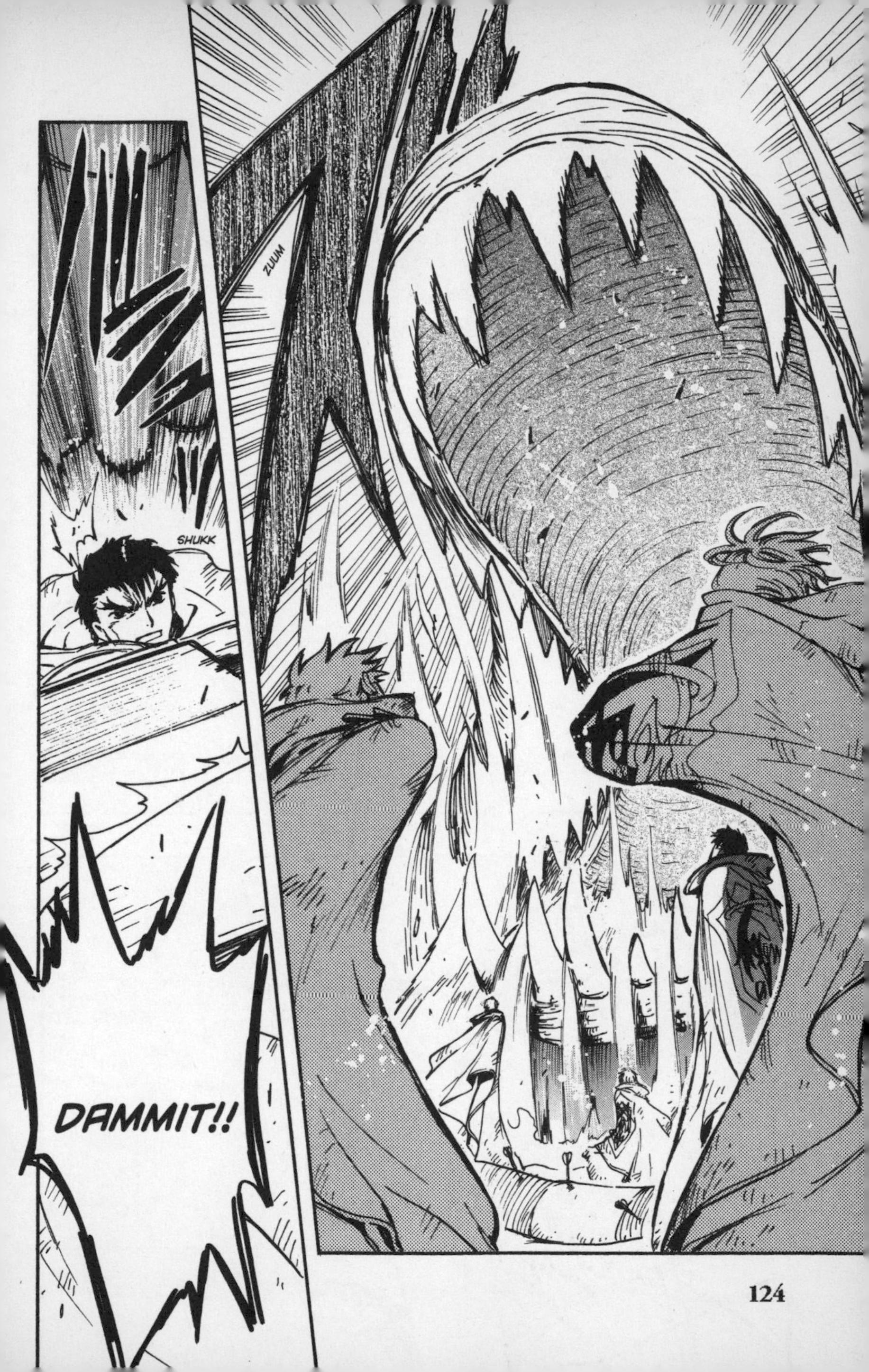
ZUUM
SHUKK
DAMMIT!!

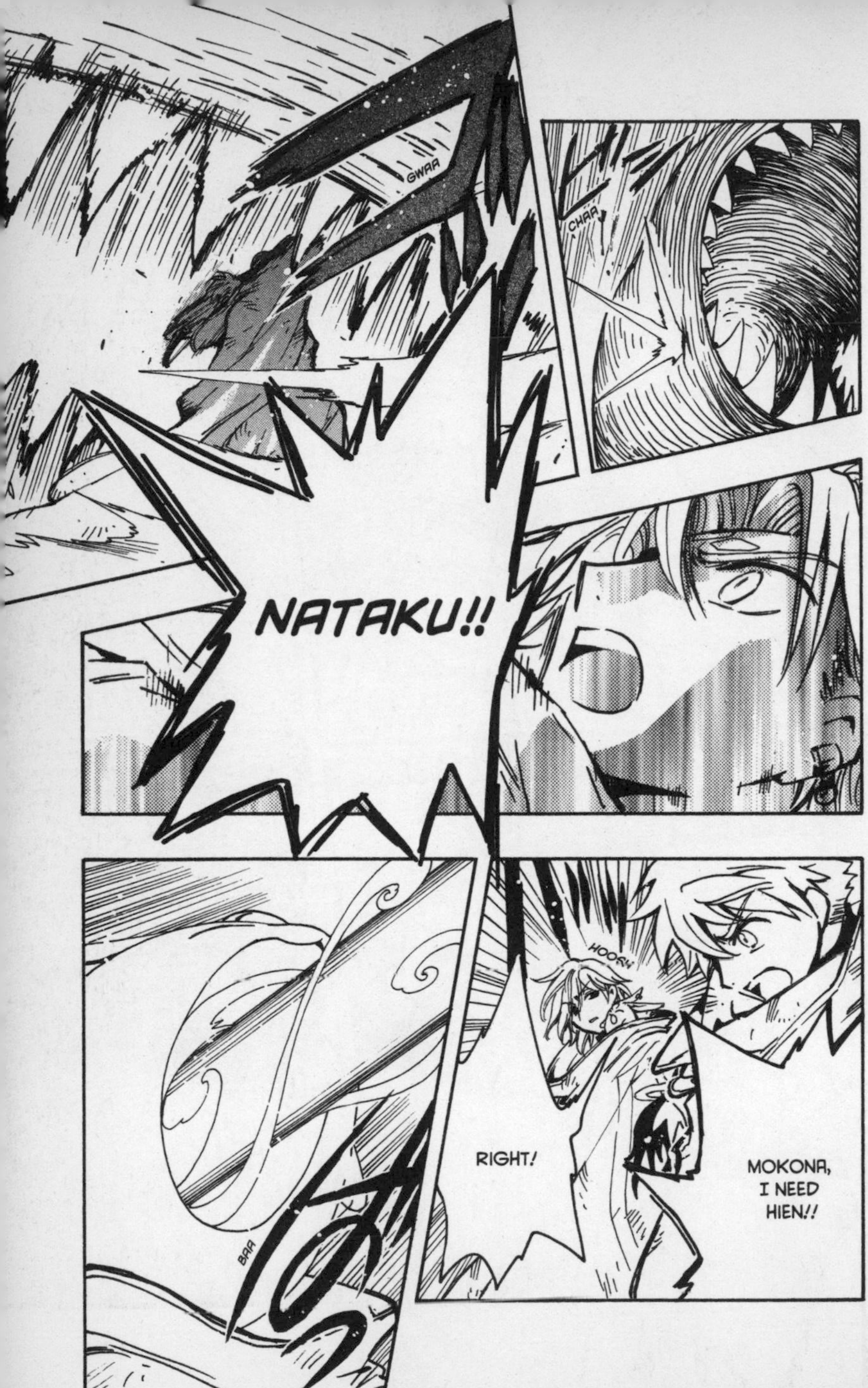
CHAA
GWAA
NATAKU!!
MOKONA, I NEED HIEN!!
HOOSH
RIGHT!
BAA

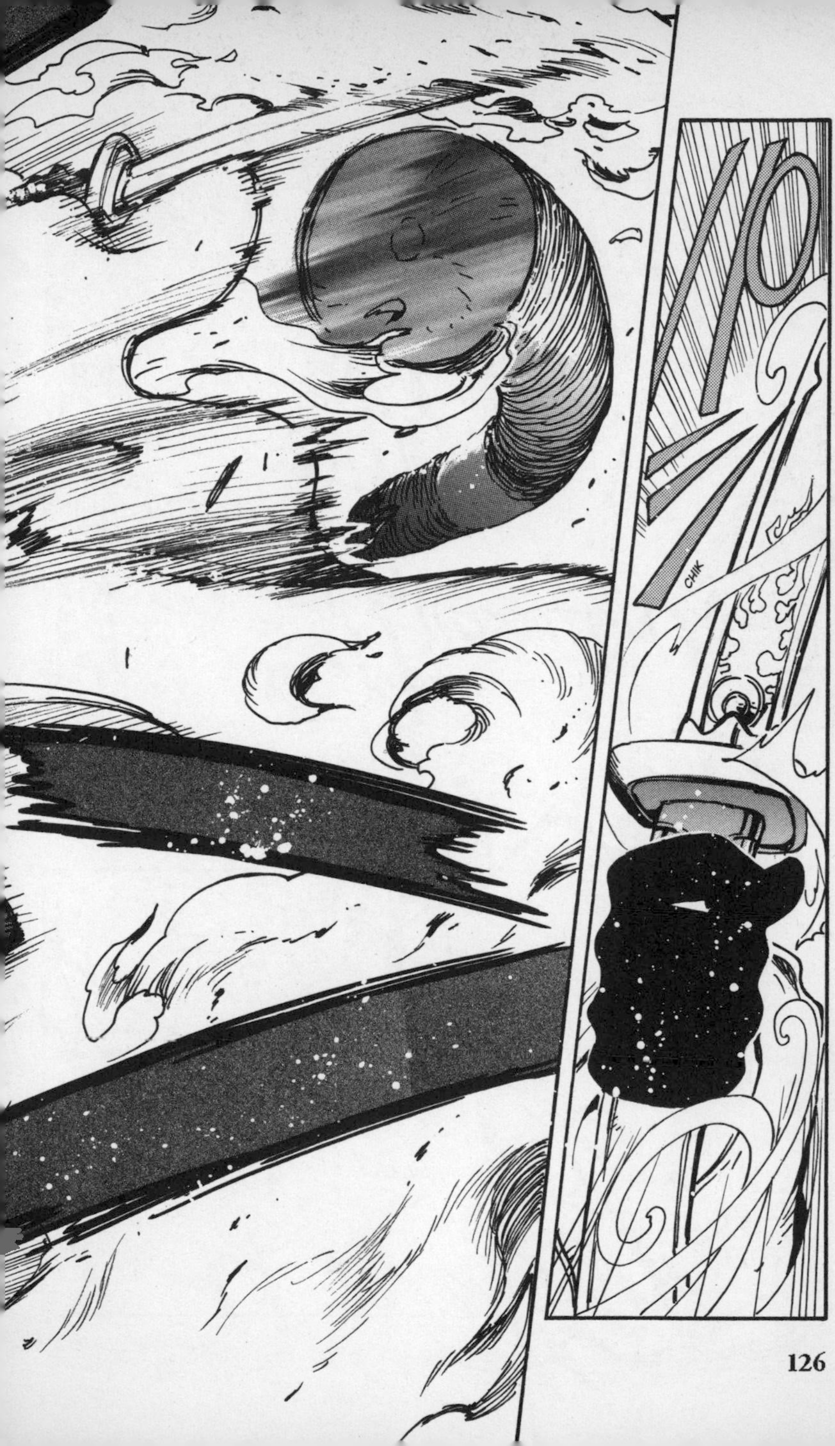
CHIK

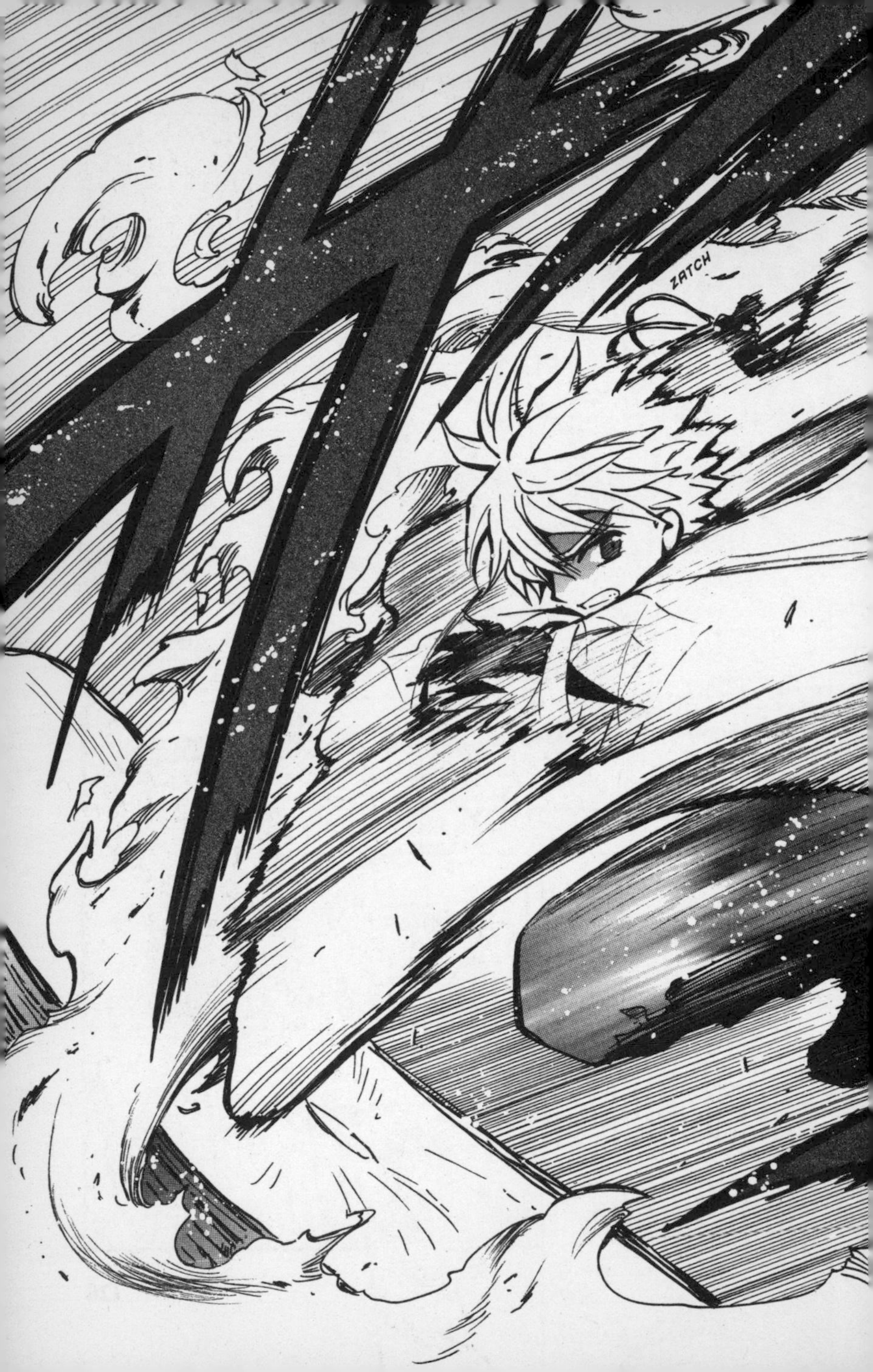
ZATCH

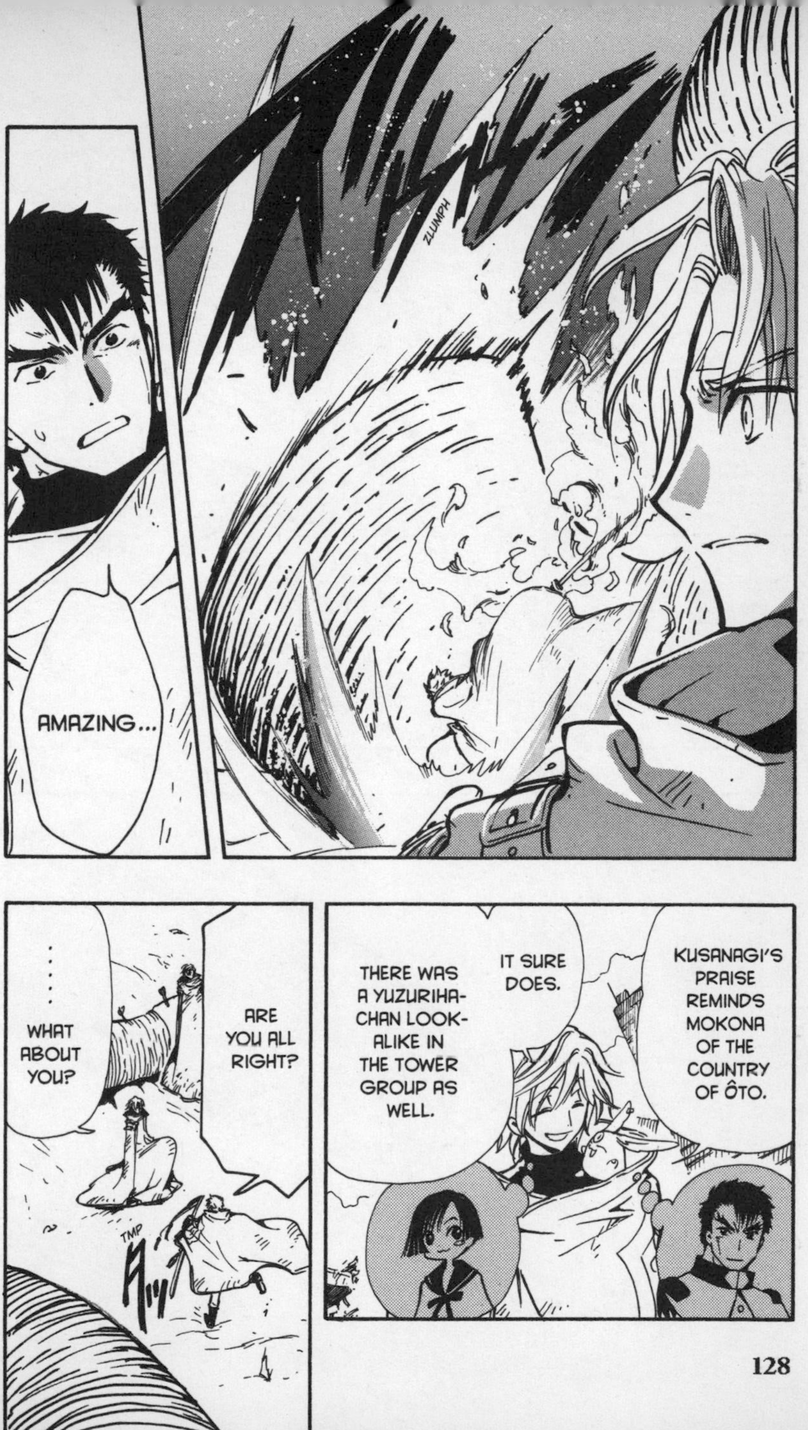
ZLUMPH
AMAZING...
KUSANAGI'S PRAISE REMINDS MOKONA OF THE COUNTRY OF ÔTO.
IT SURE DOES.
THERE WAS A YUZURIHA-CHAN LOOK-ALIKE IN THE TOWER GROUP AS WELL.
ARE YOU ALL RIGHT?
...... WHAT ABOUT YOU?
TMP

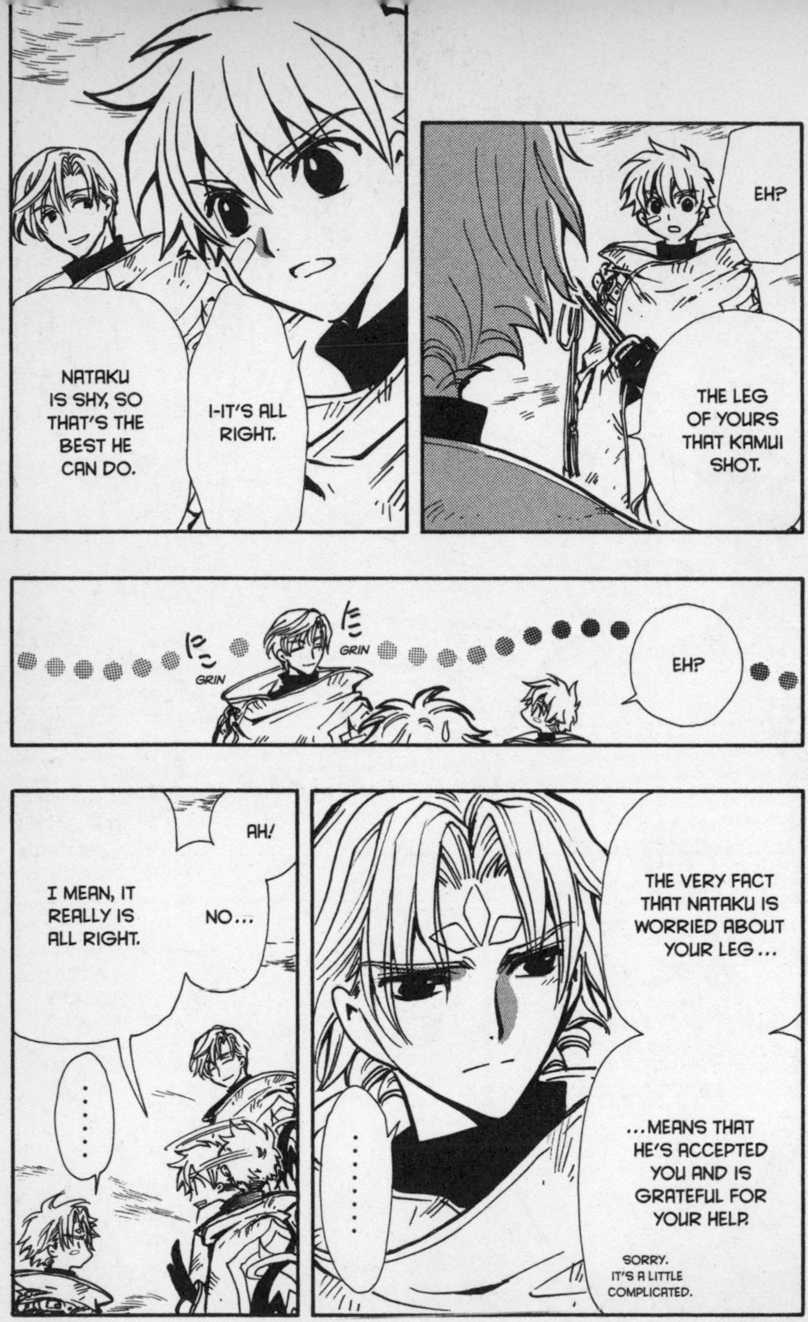
EH?
THE LEG OF YOURS THAT KAMUI SHOT.
I-IT'S ALL RIGHT.
NATAKU IS SHY, SO THAT'S THE BEST HE CAN DO.
EH?
GRIN
GRIN
THE VERY FACT THAT NATAKU IS WORRIED ABOUT YOUR LEG...
...MEANS THAT HE'S ACCEPTED YOU AND IS GRATEFUL FOR YOUR HELP.
......
SORRY. IT'S A LITTLE COMPLICATED.
AH!
NO...
I MEAN, IT REALLY IS ALL RIGHT.
......

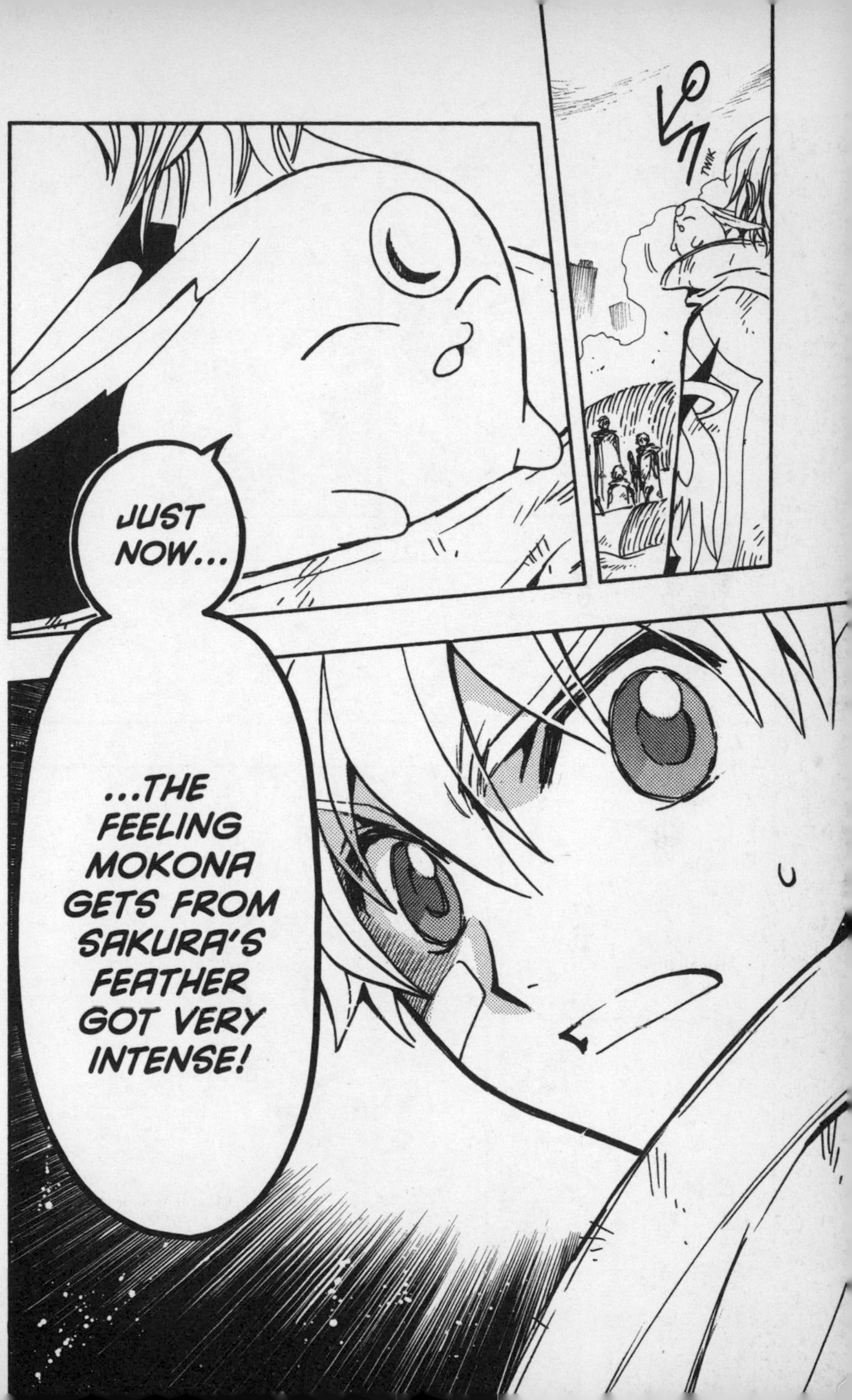
TWIK
JUST NOW...
...THE FEELING MOKONA GETS FROM SAKURA'S FEATHER GOT VERY INTENSE!

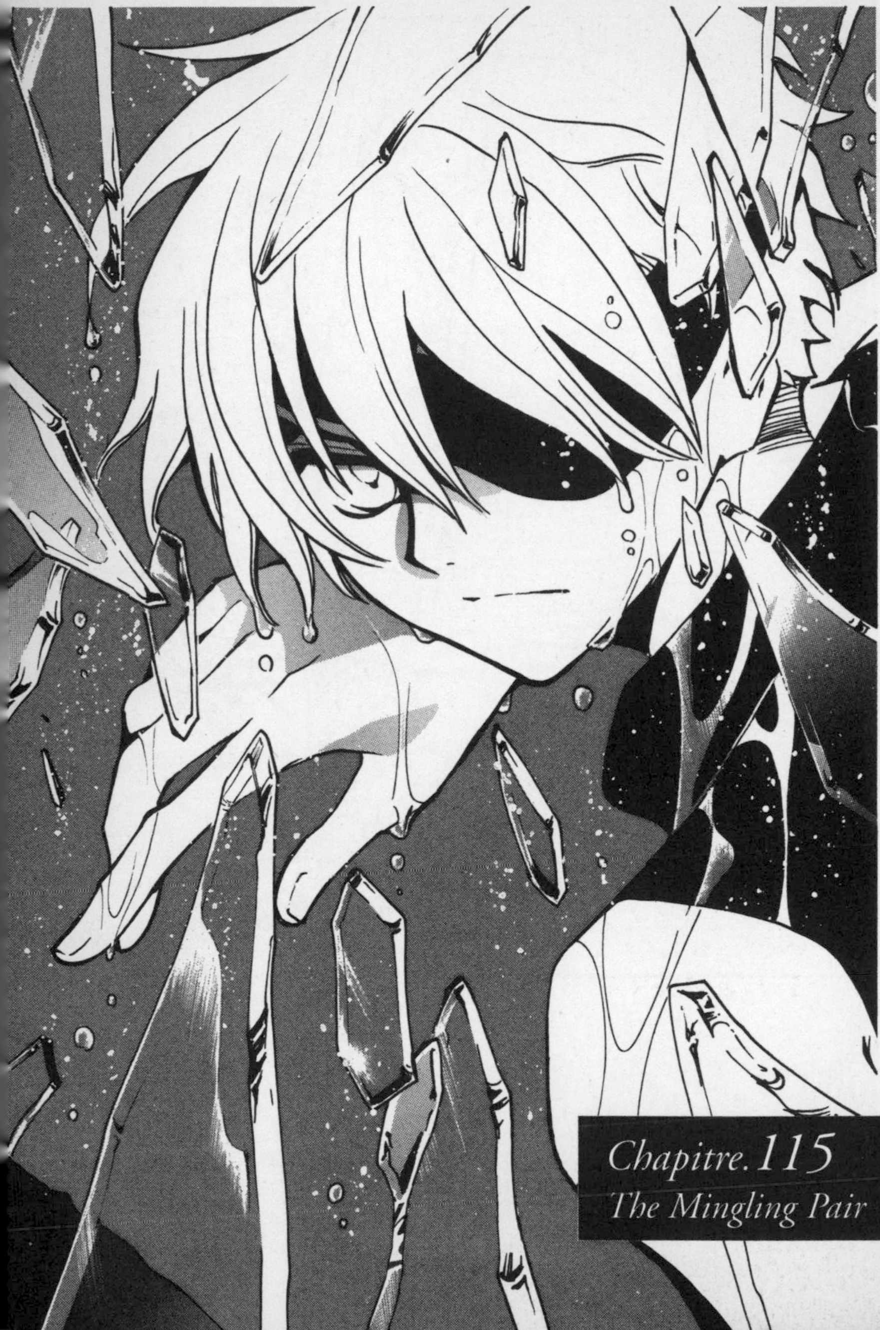
Chapitre. 115
The Mingling Pair

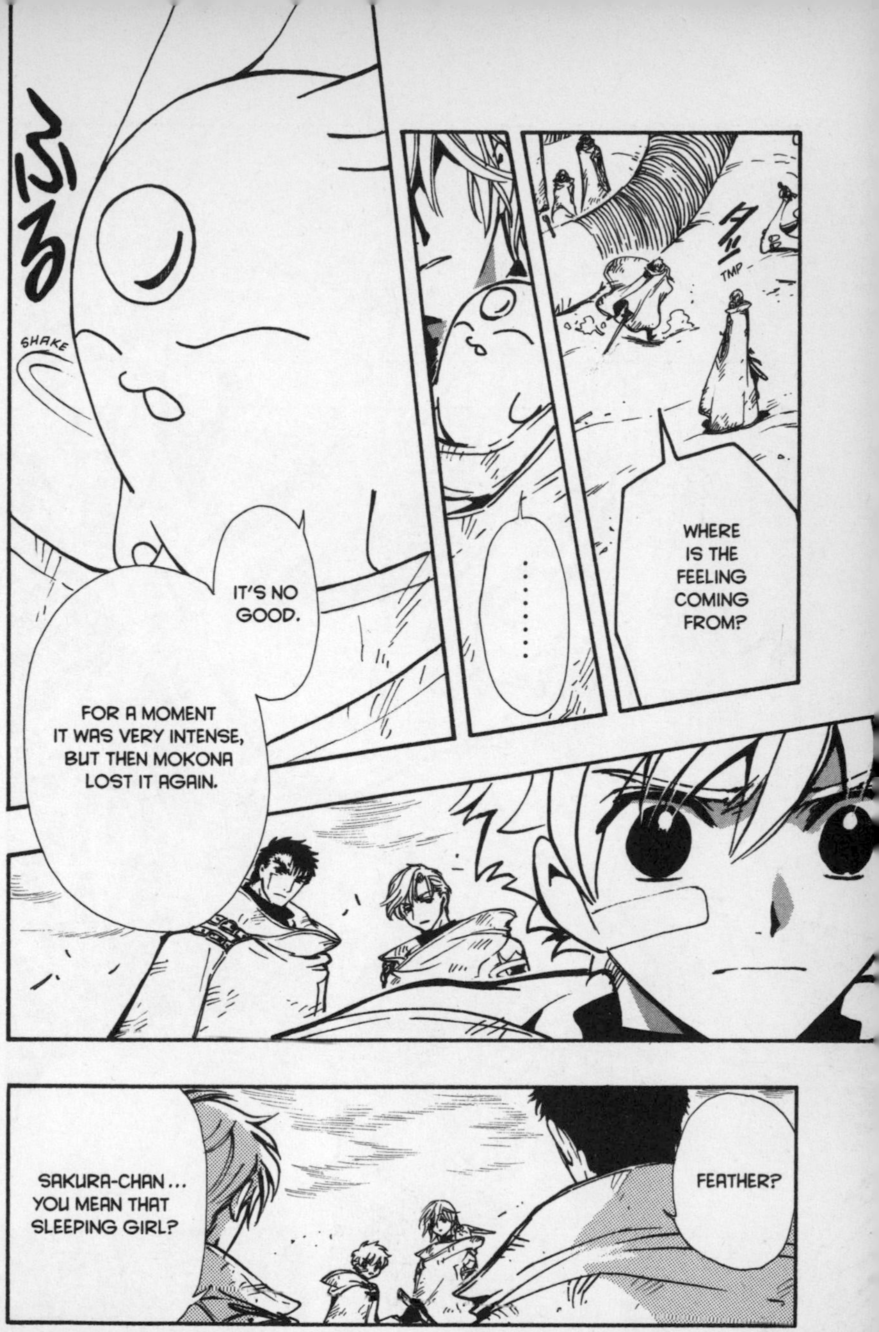
TMP
WHERE IS THE FEELING COMING FROM?
......
SHAKE
IT'S NO GOOD.
FOR A MOMENT IT WAS VERY INTENSE, BUT THEN MOKONA LOST IT AGAIN.
FEATHER?
SAKURA-CHAN... YOU MEAN THAT SLEEPING GIRL?

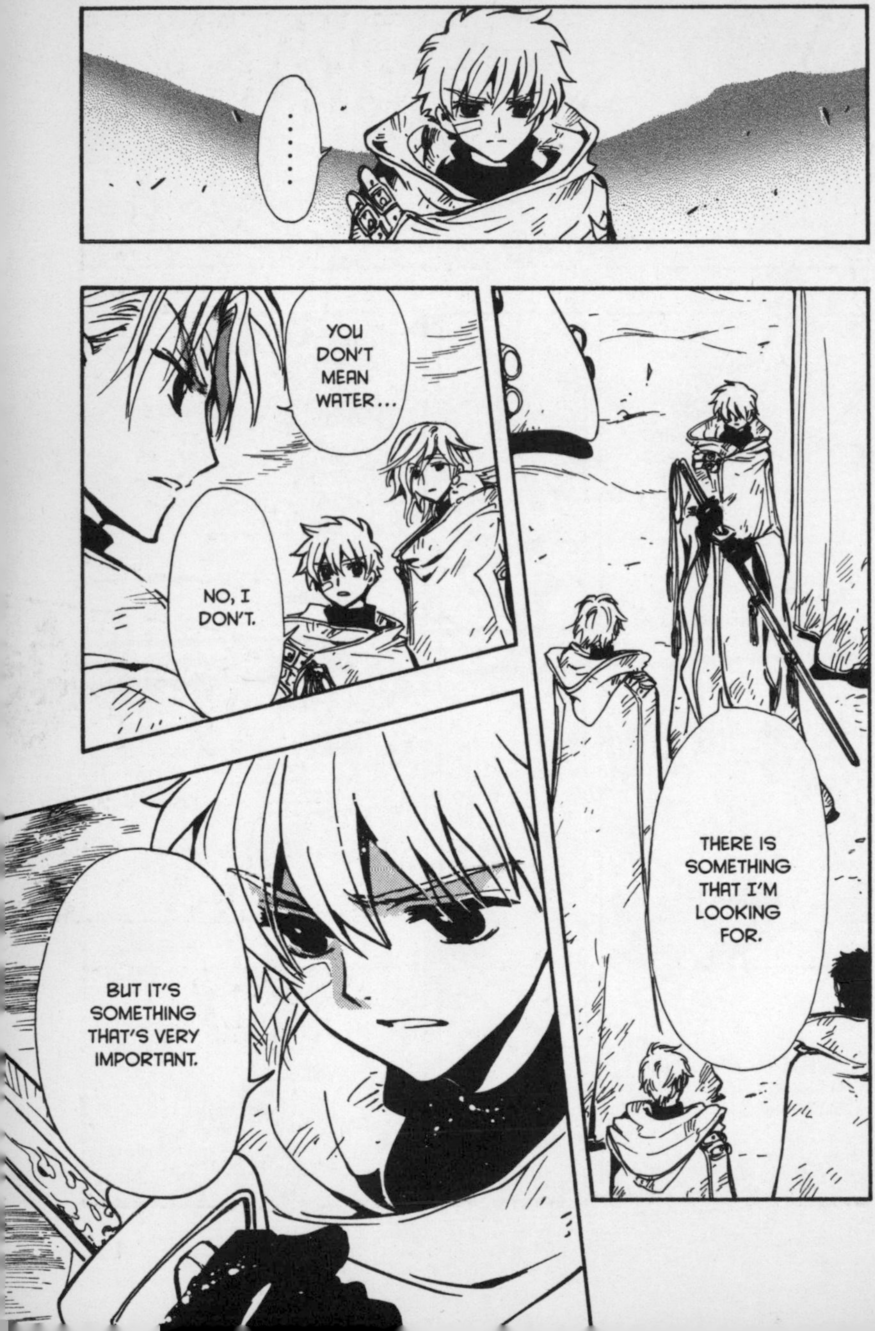
......
THERE IS SOMETHING THAT I'M LOOKING FOR.
YOU DON'T MEAN WATER...
NO, I DON'T.
BUT IT'S SOMETHING THAT'S VERY IMPORTANT.

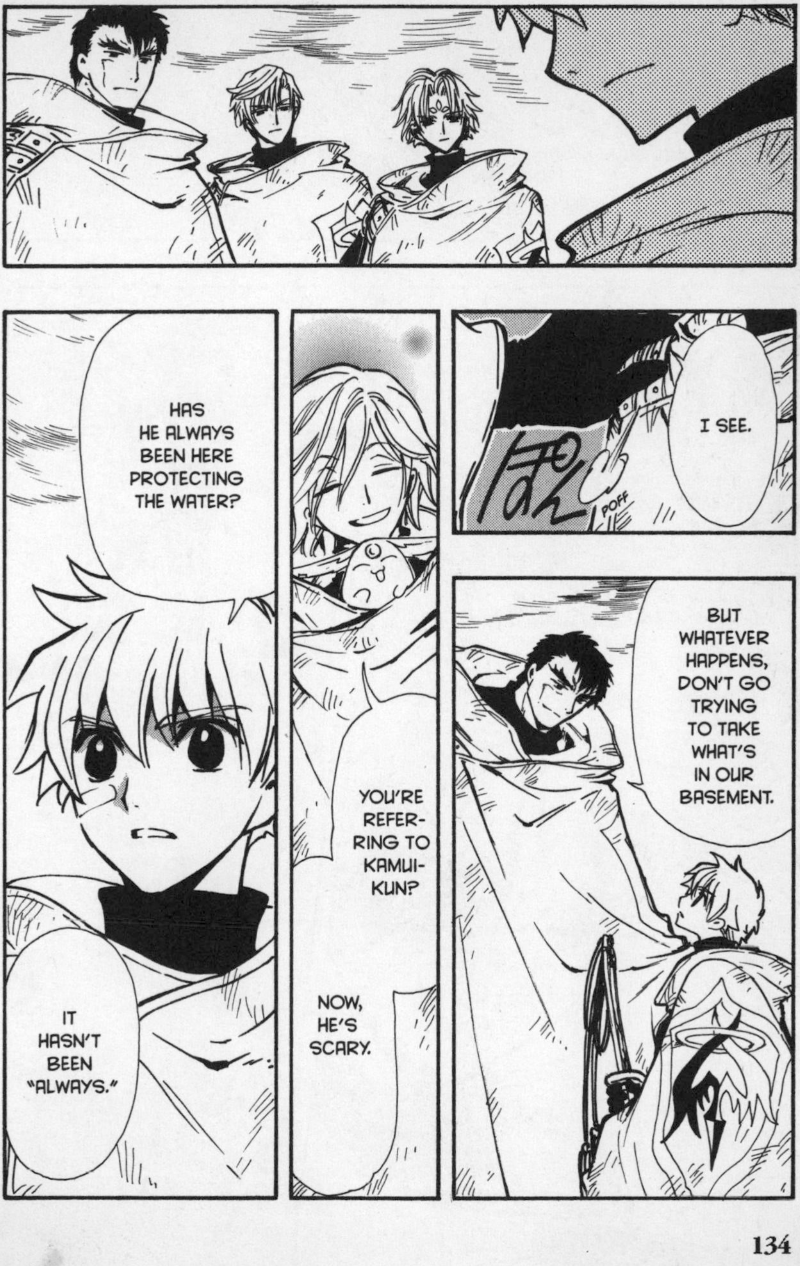
ぽん
POFF
I SEE.
BUT WHATEVER HAPPENS, DON'T GO TRYING TO TAKE WHAT'S IN OUR BASEMENT.
YOU'RE REFER-RING TO KAMUI-KUN?
NOW, HE'S SCARY.
HAS HE ALWAYS BEEN HERE PROTECTING THE WATER?
IT HASN'T BEEN "ALWAYS."

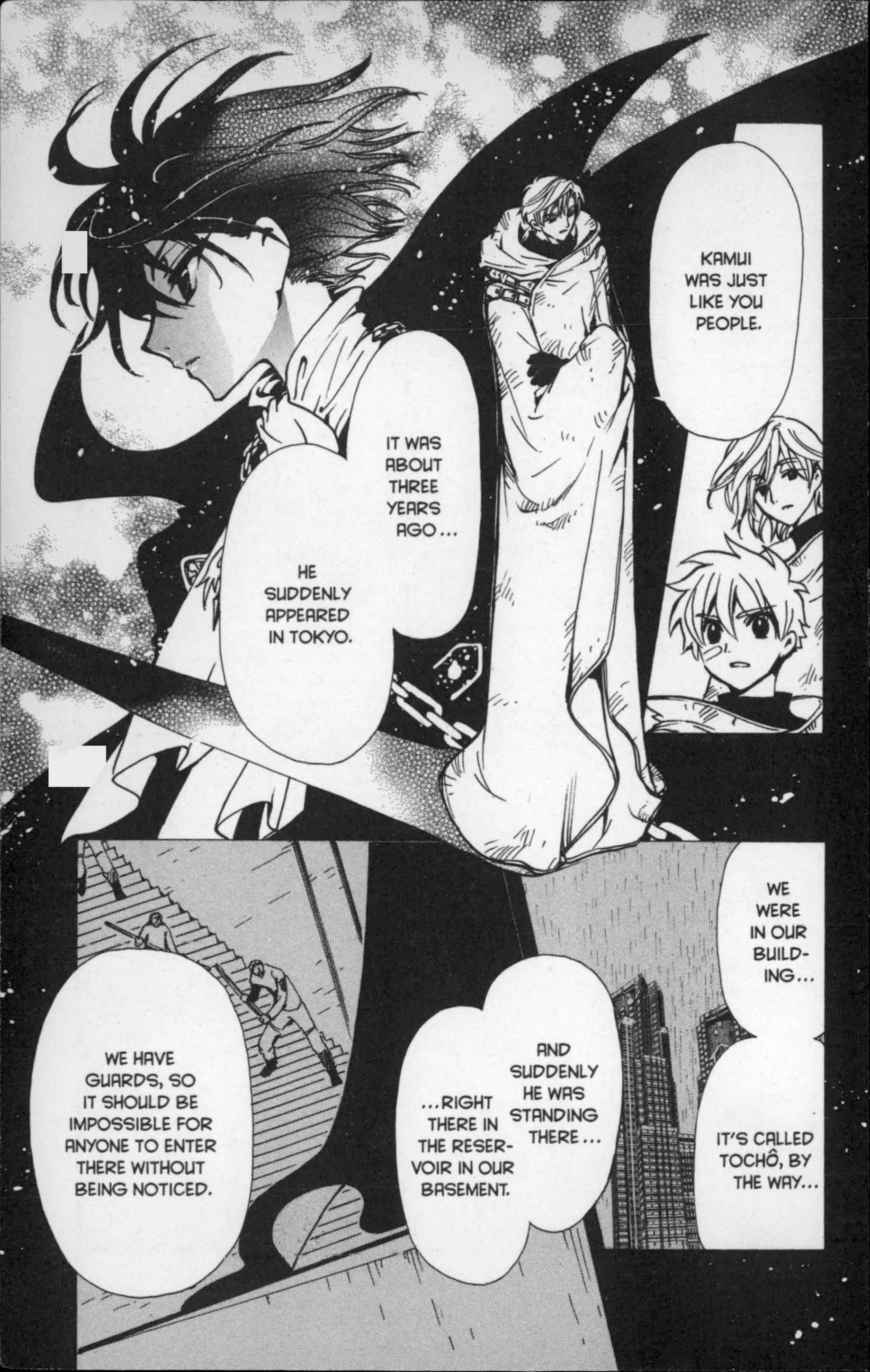
KAMUI WAS JUST LIKE YOU PEOPLE.
IT WAS ABOUT THREE YEARS AGO...
HE SUDDENLY APPEARED IN TOKYO.
WE WERE IN OUR BUILD-ING...
IT'S CALLED TOCHÔ, BY THE WAY...
AND SUDDENLY HE WAS STANDING THERE...
...RIGHT THERE IN THE RESER-VOIR IN OUR BASEMENT.
WE HAVE GUARDS, SO IT SHOULD BE IMPOSSIBLE FOR ANYONE TO ENTER THERE WITHOUT BEING NOTICED.

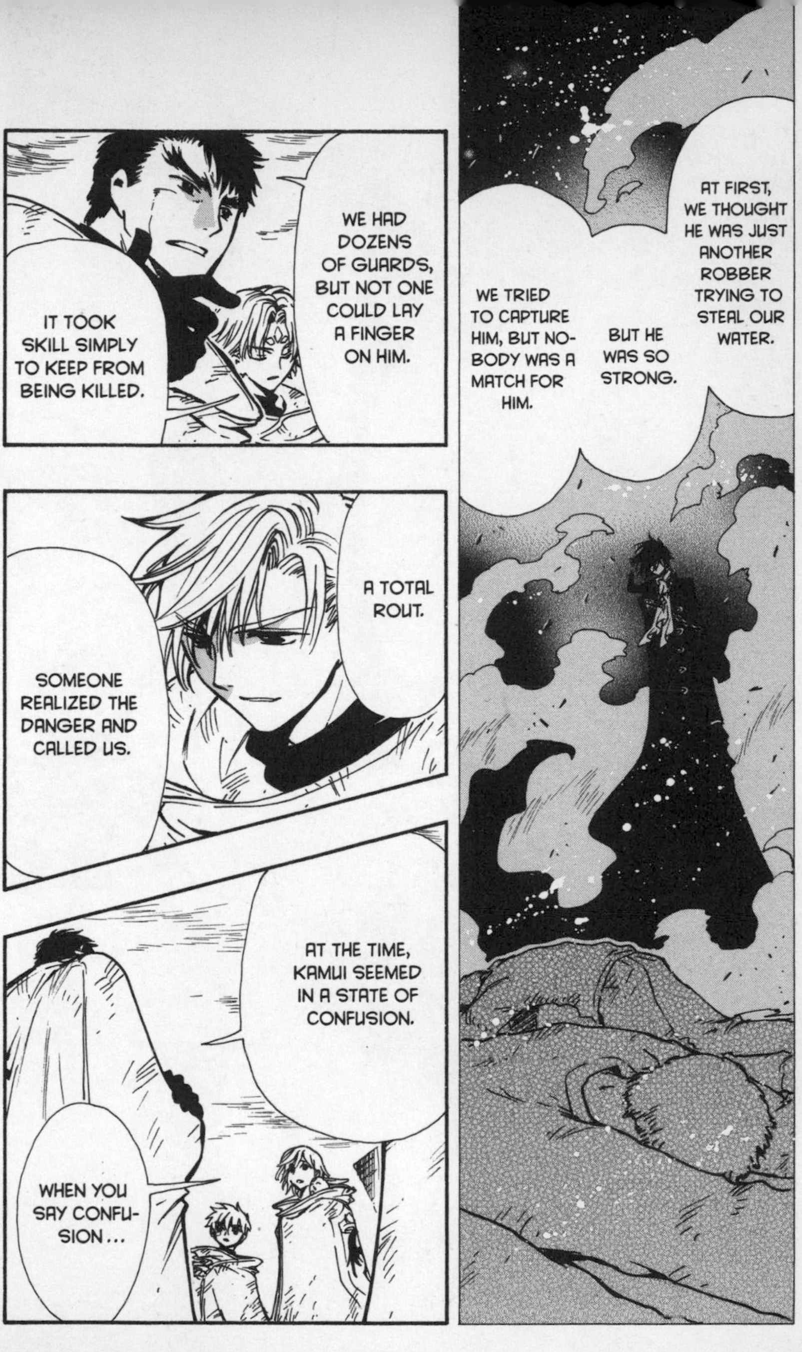
AT FIRST, WE THOUGHT HE WAS JUST ANOTHER ROBBER TRYING TO STEAL OUR WATER.
BUT HE WAS SO STRONG.
WE TRIED TO CAPTURE HIM, BUT NOBODY WAS A MATCH FOR HIM.
WE HAD DOZENS OF GUARDS, BUT NOT ONE COULD LAY A FINGER ON HIM.
IT TOOK SKILL SIMPLY TO KEEP FROM BEING KILLED.
A TOTAL ROUT.
SOMEONE REALIZED THE DANGER AND CALLED US.
AT THE TIME, KAMUI SEEMED IN A STATE OF CONFUSION.
WHEN YOU SAY CONFUSION…

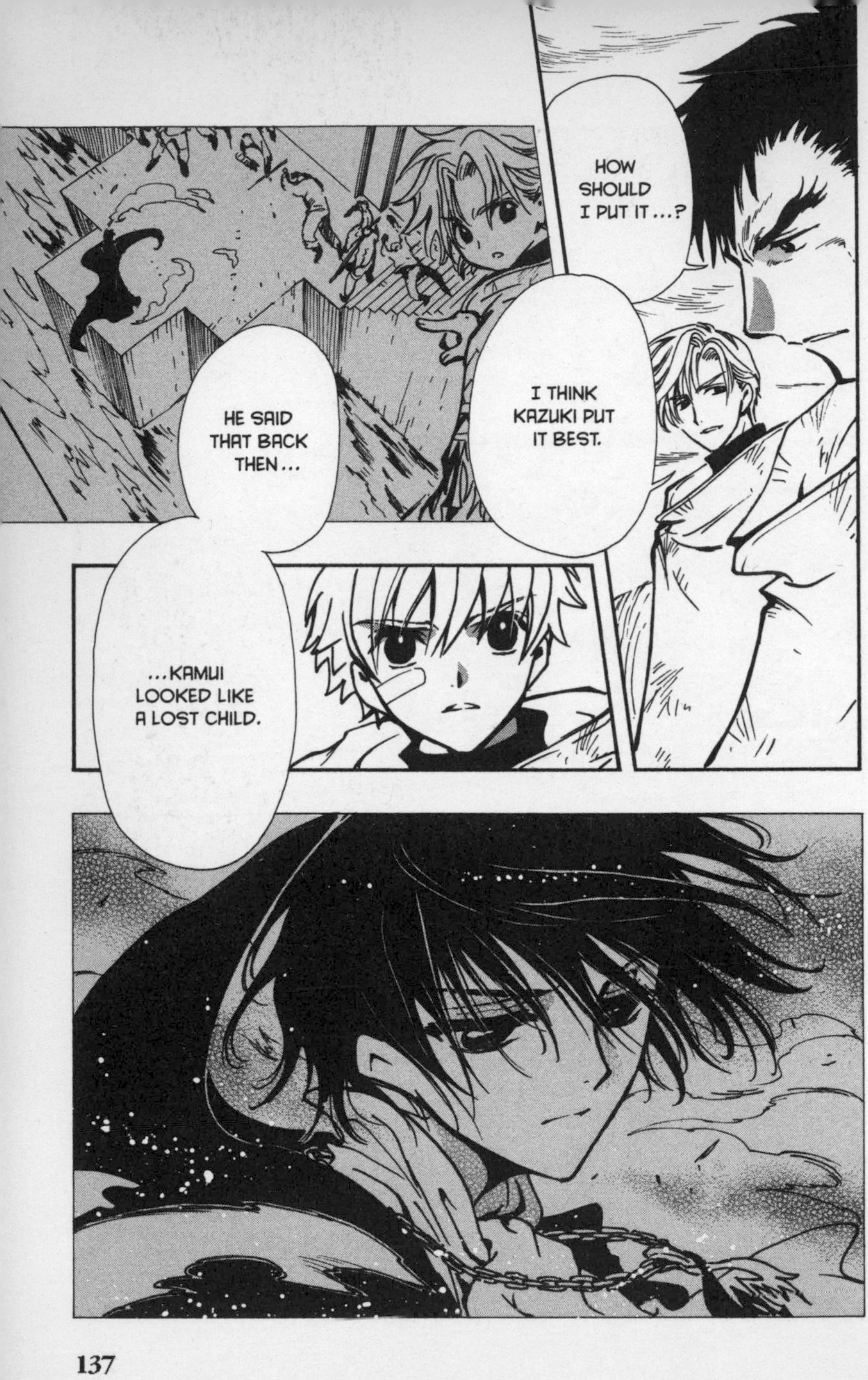
HOW SHOULD I PUT IT...?
I THINK KAZUKI PUT IT BEST.
HE SAID THAT BACK THEN...
...KAMUI LOOKED LIKE A LOST CHILD.

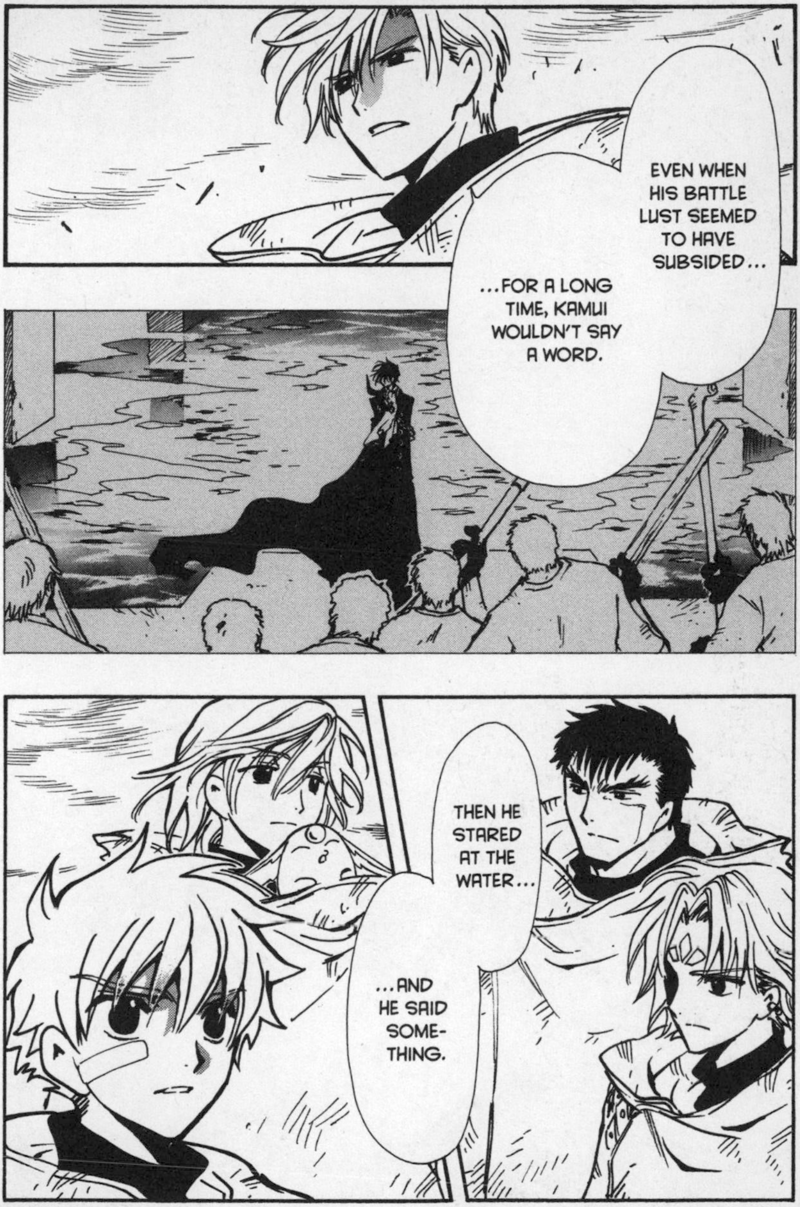
EVEN WHEN HIS BATTLE LUST SEEMED TO HAVE SUBSIDED...
...FOR A LONG TIME, KAMUI WOULDN'T SAY A WORD.
THEN HE STARED AT THE WATER...
...AND HE SAID SOME-THING.

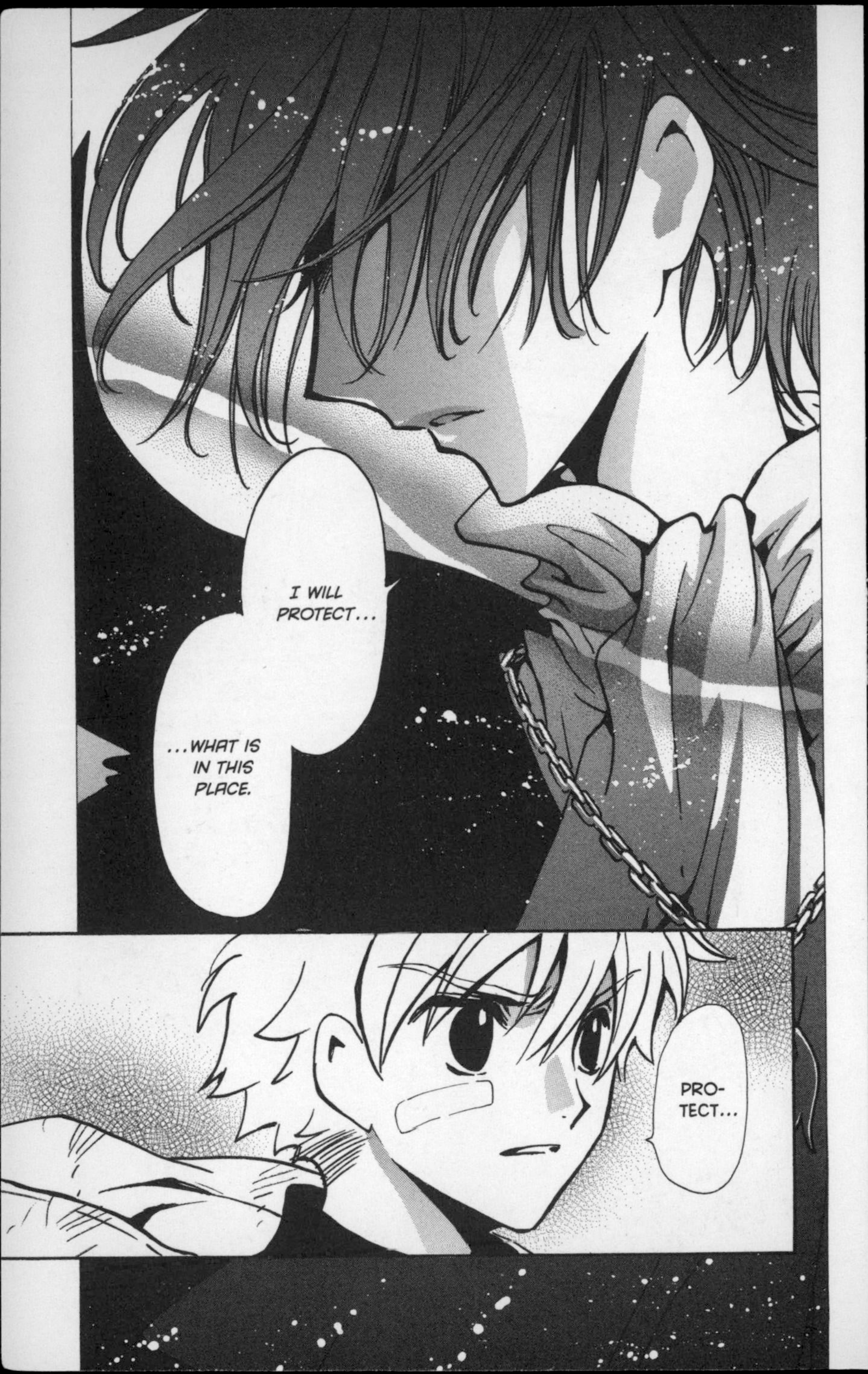
I WILL PROTECT...
...WHAT IS IN THIS PLACE.
PRO-TECT...

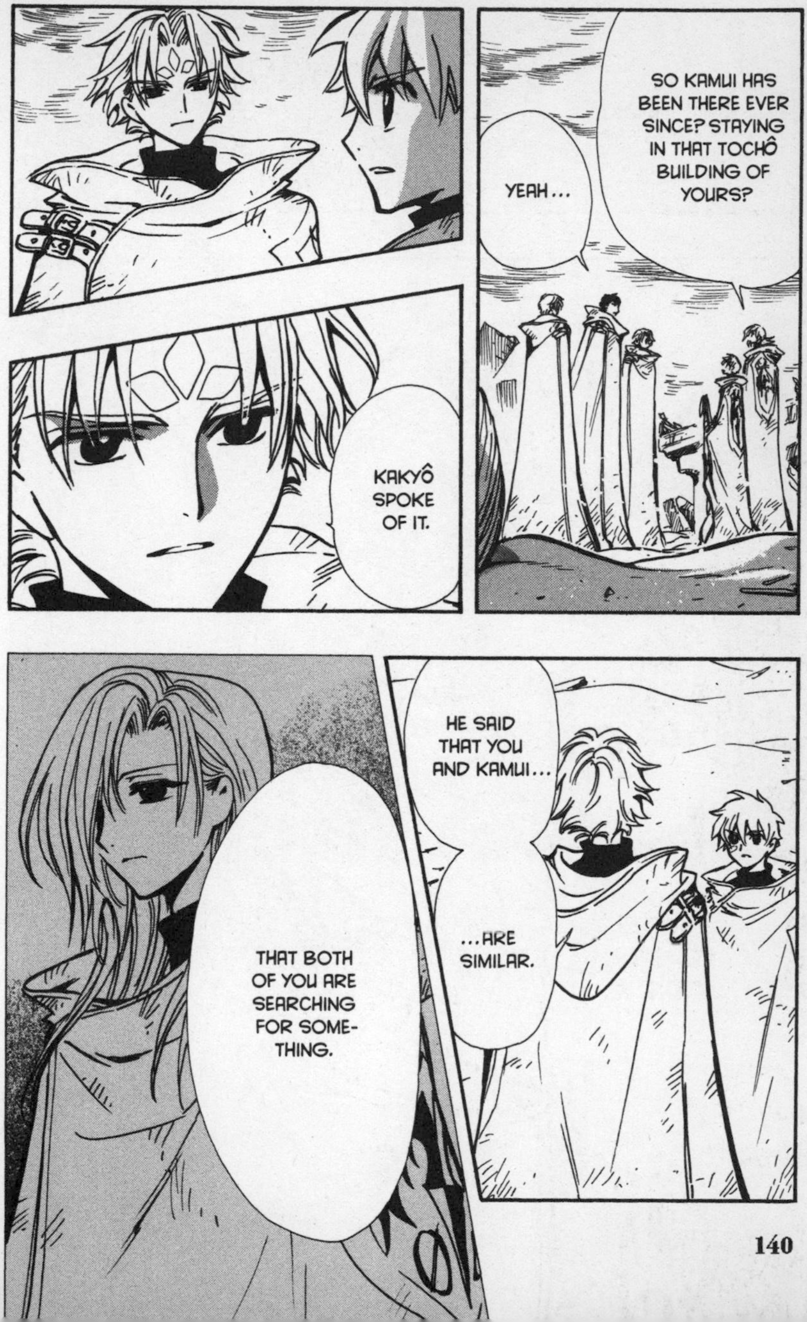
SO KAMUI HAS BEEN THERE EVER SINCE? STAYING IN THAT TOCHÔ BUILDING OF YOURS?
YEAH...
KAKYÔ SPOKE OF IT.
HE SAID THAT YOU AND KAMUI...
...ARE SIMILAR.
THAT BOTH OF YOU ARE SEARCHING FOR SOME-THING.

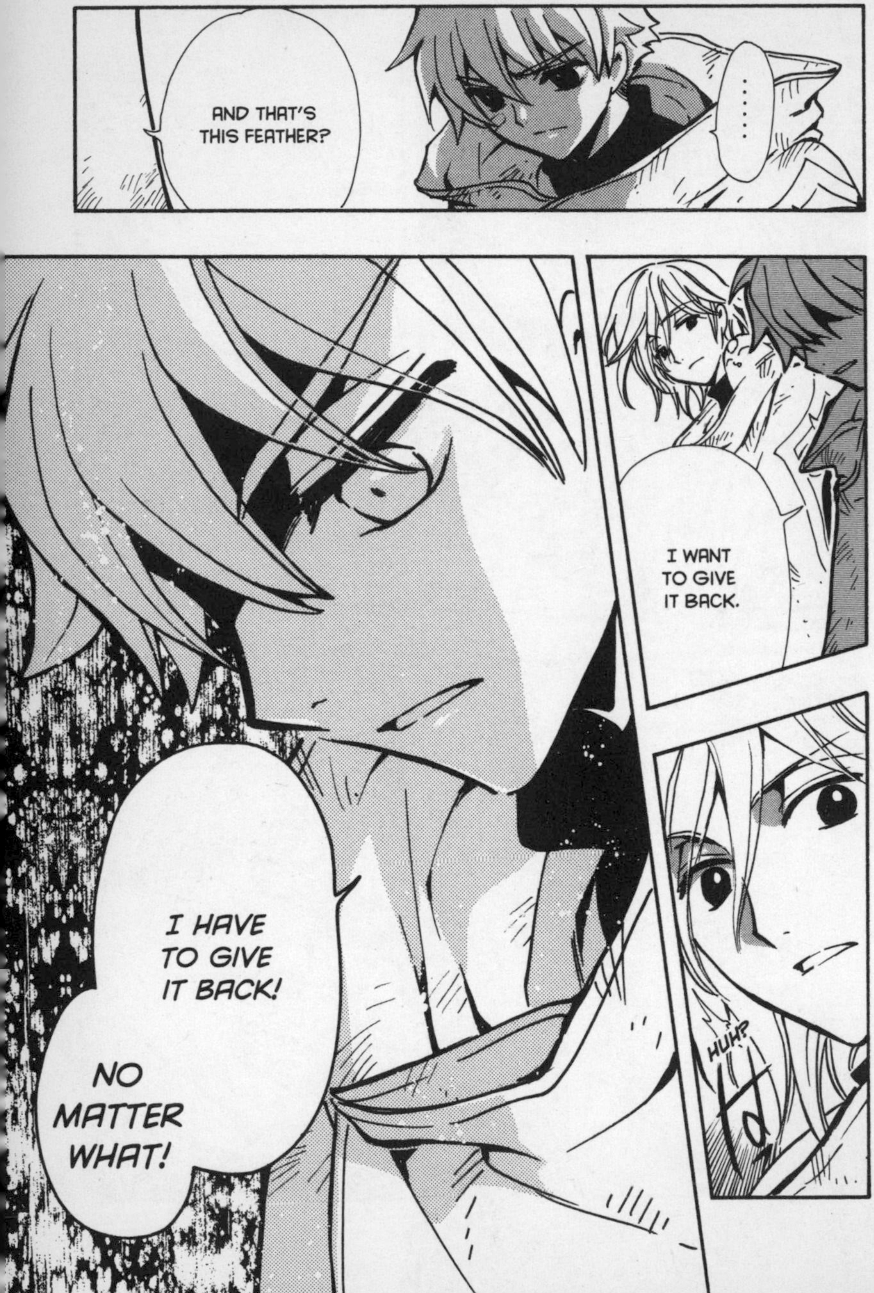
......
AND THAT'S THIS FEATHER?
I WANT TO GIVE IT BACK.
HUH?
I HAVE TO GIVE IT BACK!
NO MATTER WHAT!

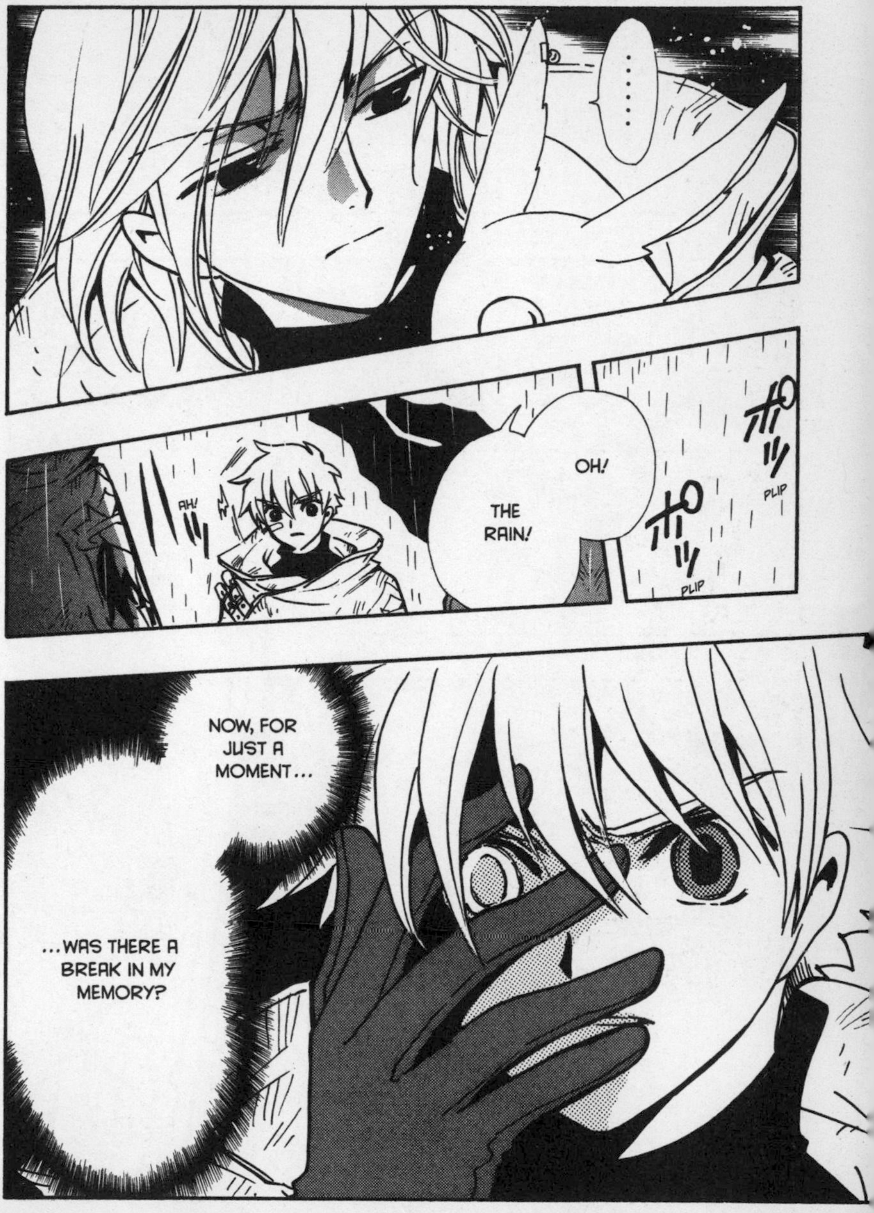
......
ポツ
PLIP
ポツ
PLIP
OH! THE RAIN!
AH!
NOW, FOR JUST A MOMENT...
...WAS THERE A BREAK IN MY MEMORY?

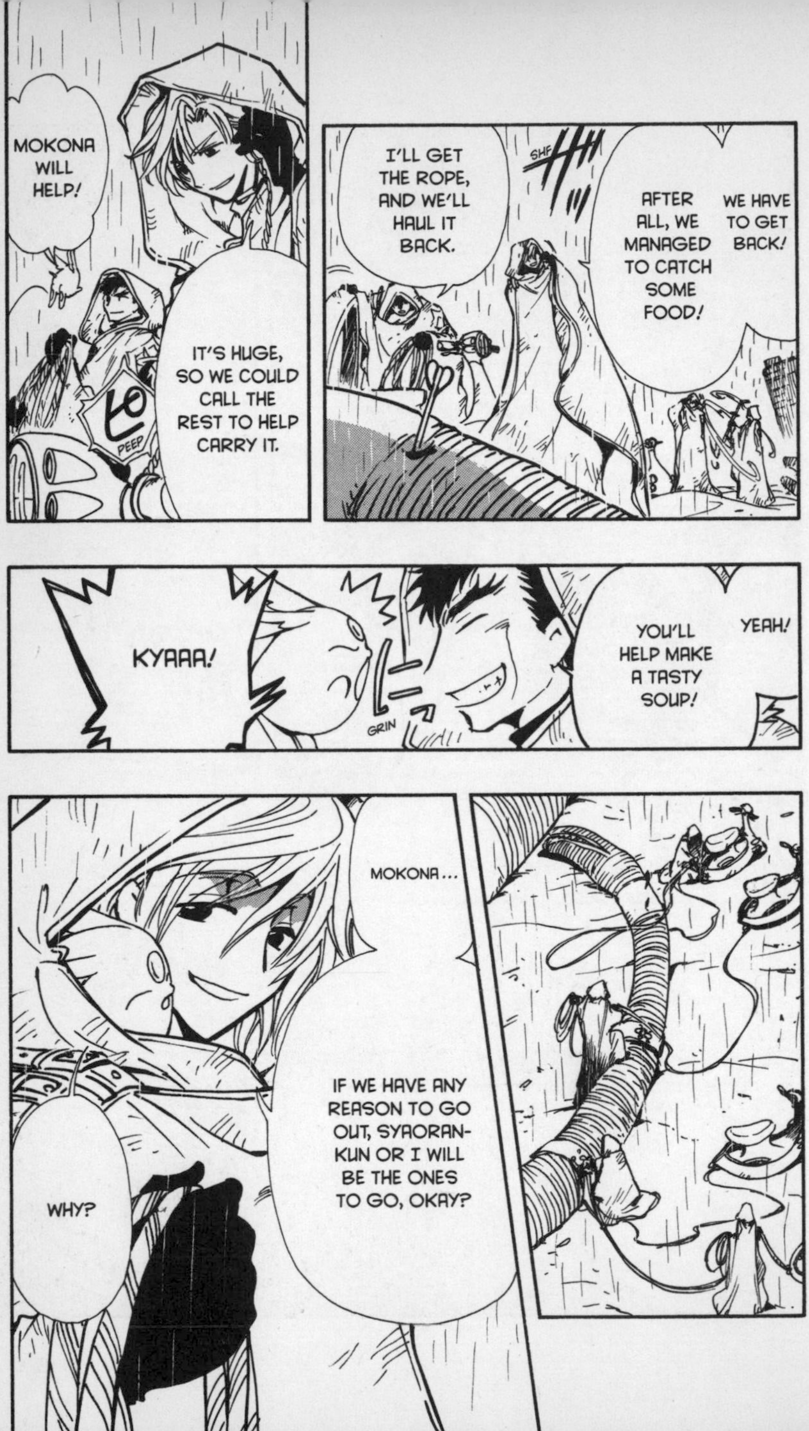
WE HAVE TO GET BACK!
AFTER ALL, WE MANAGED TO CATCH SOME FOOD!
SHF
I'LL GET THE ROPE, AND WE'LL HAUL IT BACK.
IT'S HUGE, SO WE COULD CALL THE REST TO HELP CARRY IT.
MOKONA WILL HELP!
PEEP
YEAH!
YOU'LL HELP MAKE A TASTY SOUP!
GRIN
KYAAA!
MOKONA...
IF WE HAVE ANY REASON TO GO OUT, SYAORAN-KUN OR I WILL BE THE ONES TO GO, OKAY?
WHY?

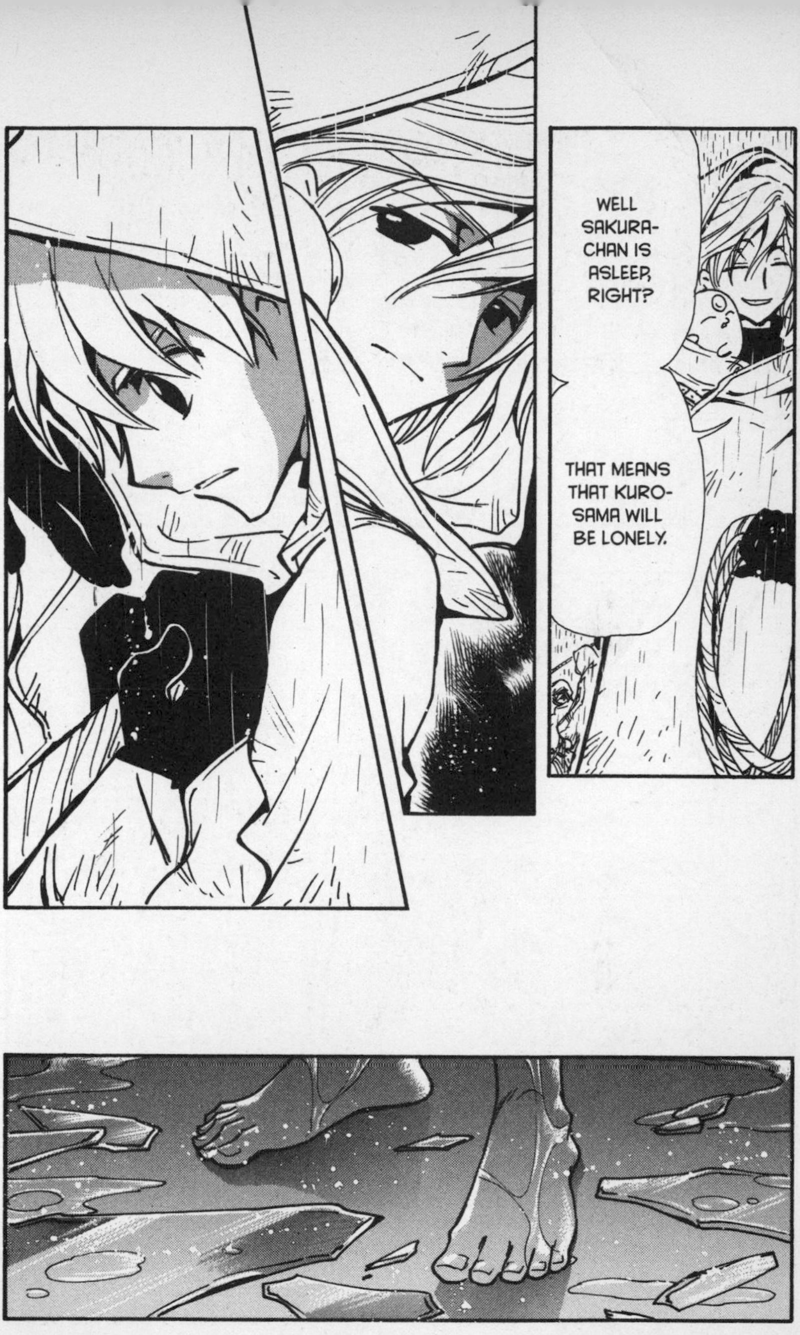
WELL SAKURA-CHAN IS ASLEEP, RIGHT?
THAT MEANS THAT KURO-SAMA WILL BE LONELY.

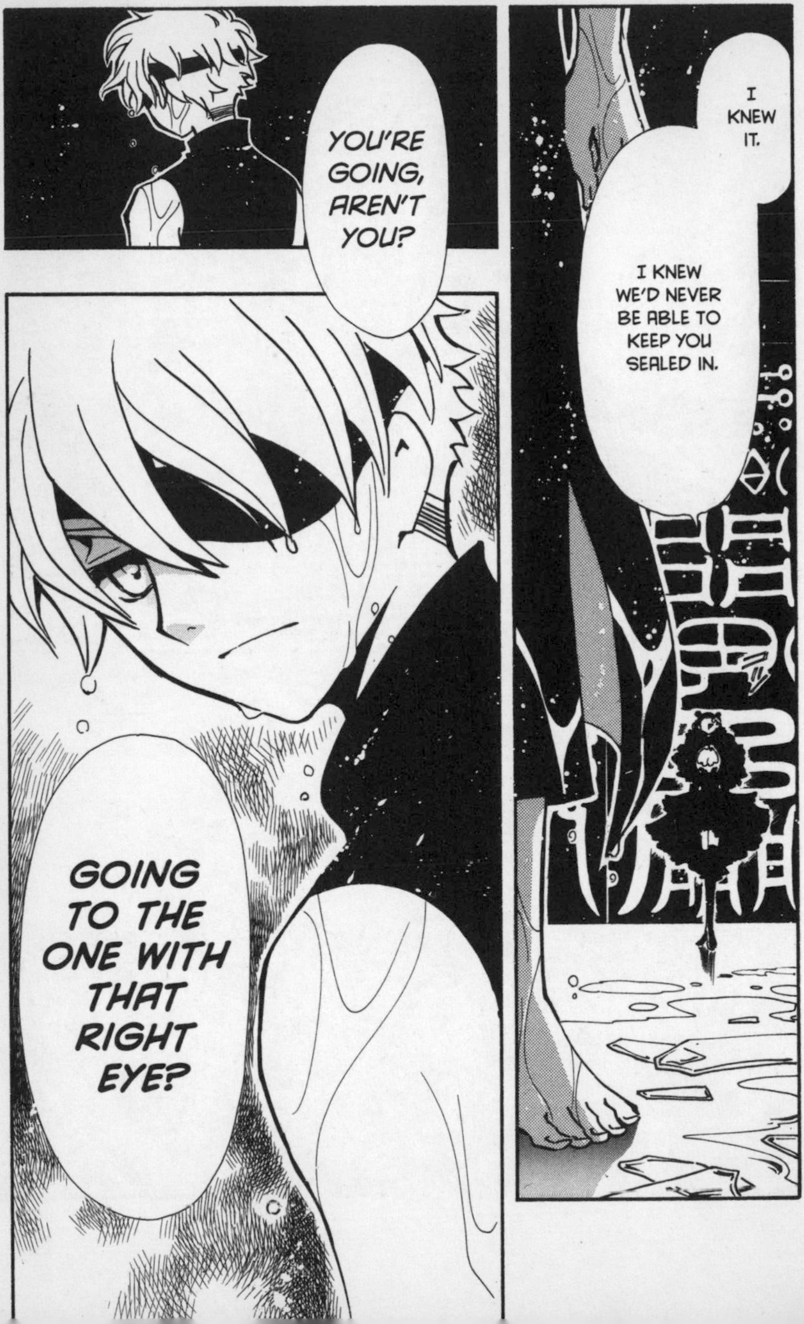
I KNEW IT.
I KNEW WE'D NEVER BE ABLE TO KEEP YOU SEALED IN.
YOU'RE GOING, AREN'T YOU?
GOING TO THE ONE WITH THAT RIGHT EYE?

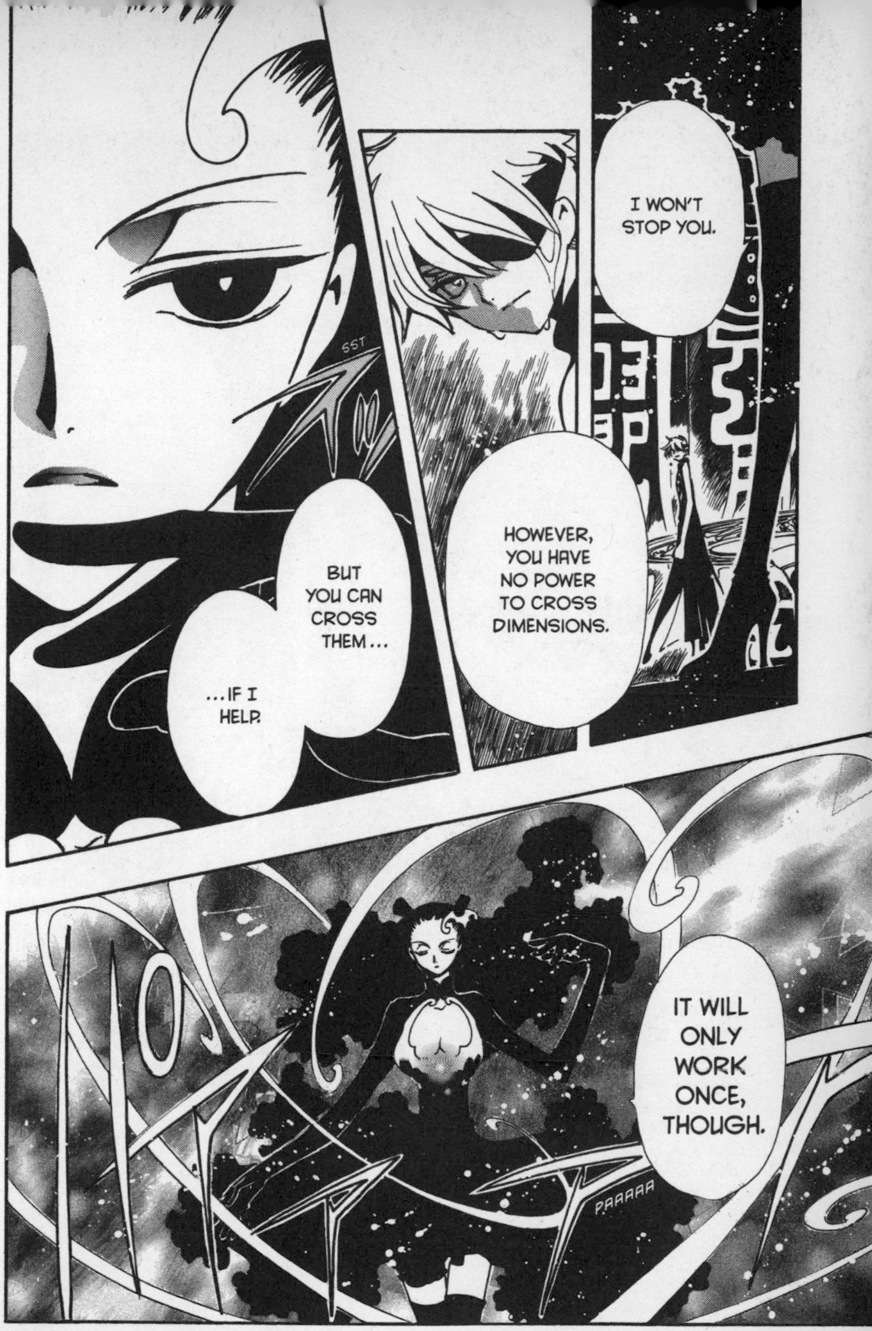
I WON'T STOP YOU.
HOWEVER, YOU HAVE NO POWER TO CROSS DIMENSIONS.
SST
BUT YOU CAN CROSS THEM...
...IF I HELP.
IT WILL ONLY WORK ONCE, THOUGH.
PAAAAA

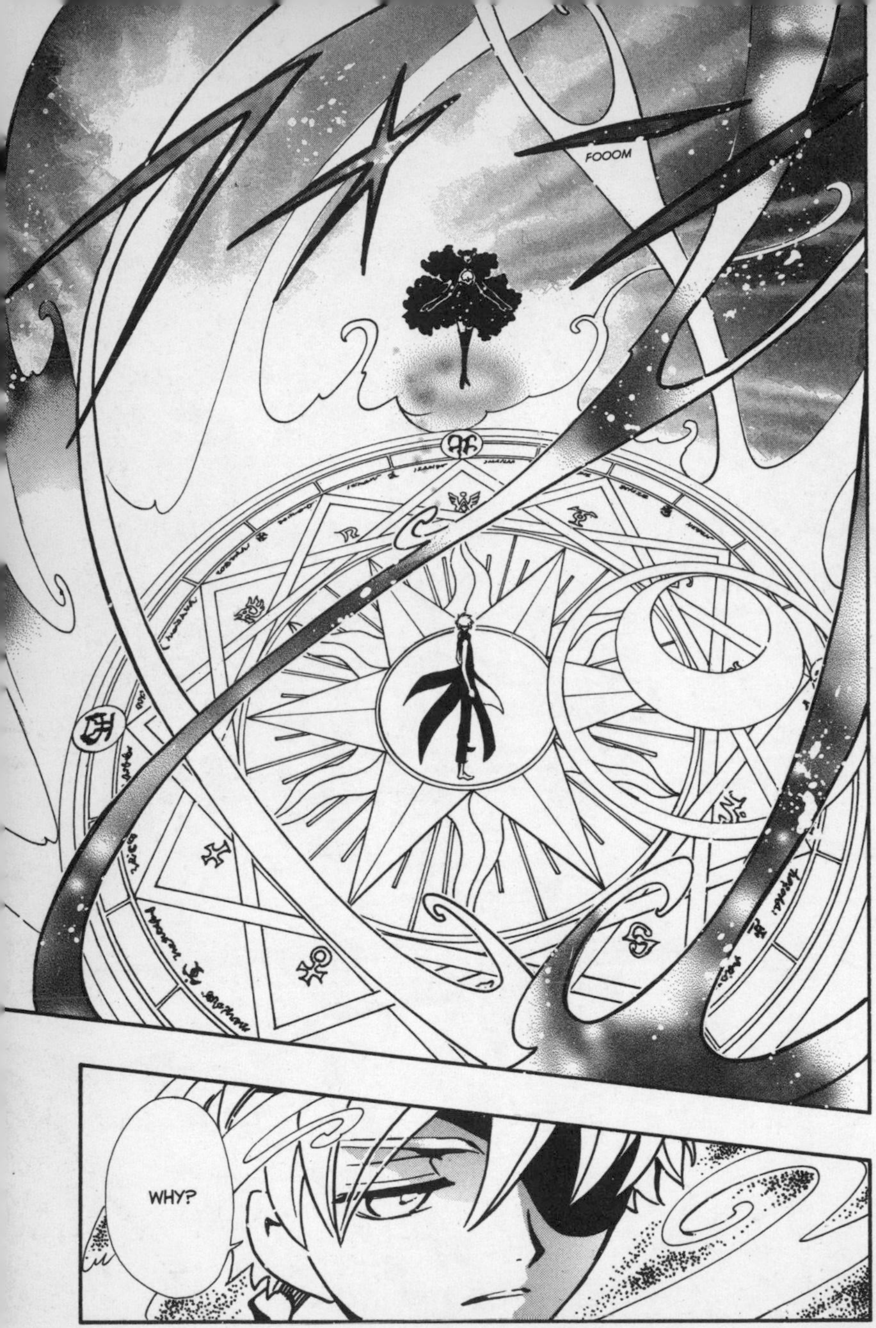
FOOOM
WHY?

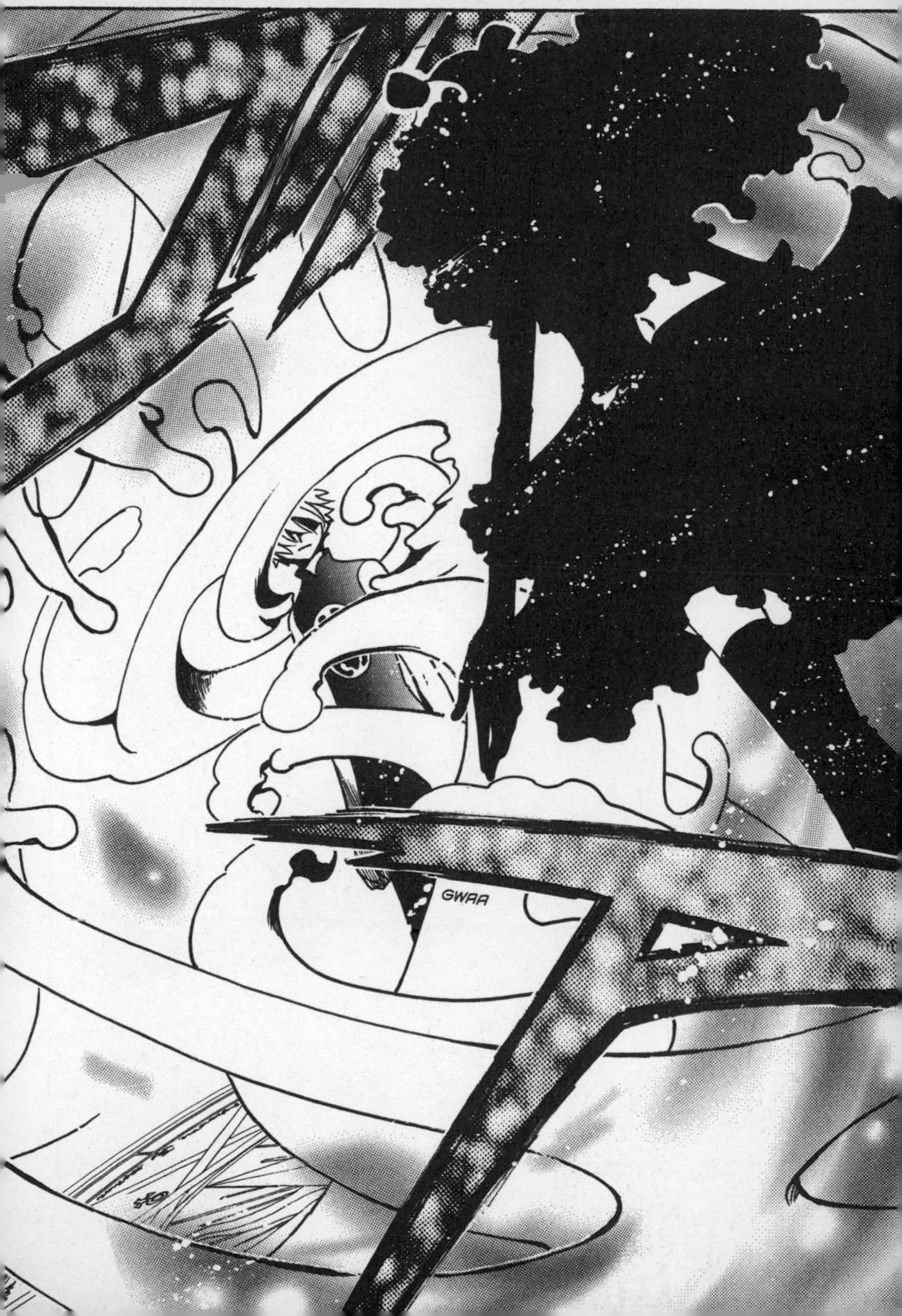
GWAA

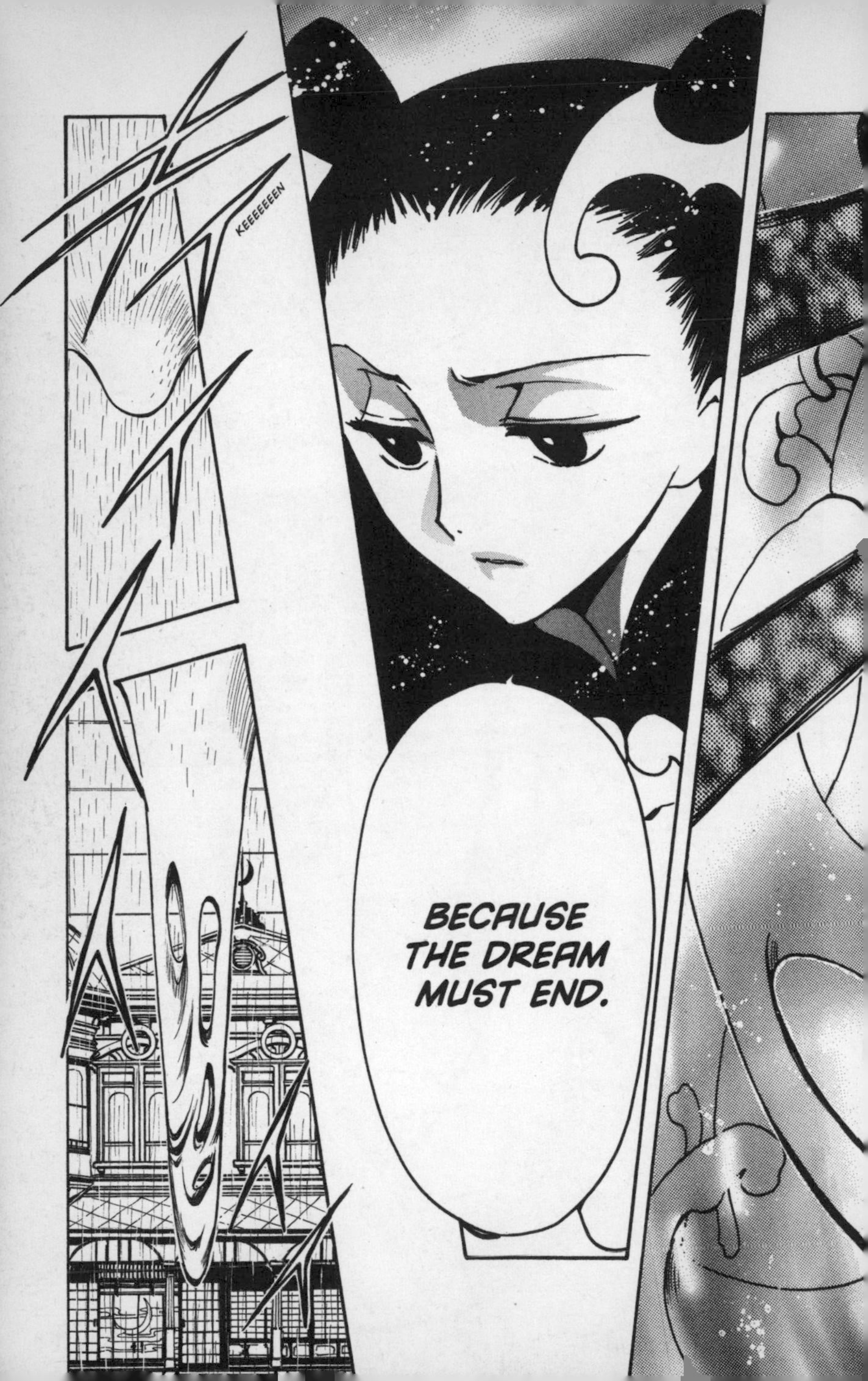
BECAUSE THE DREAM MUST END.
KEEEEEEEN

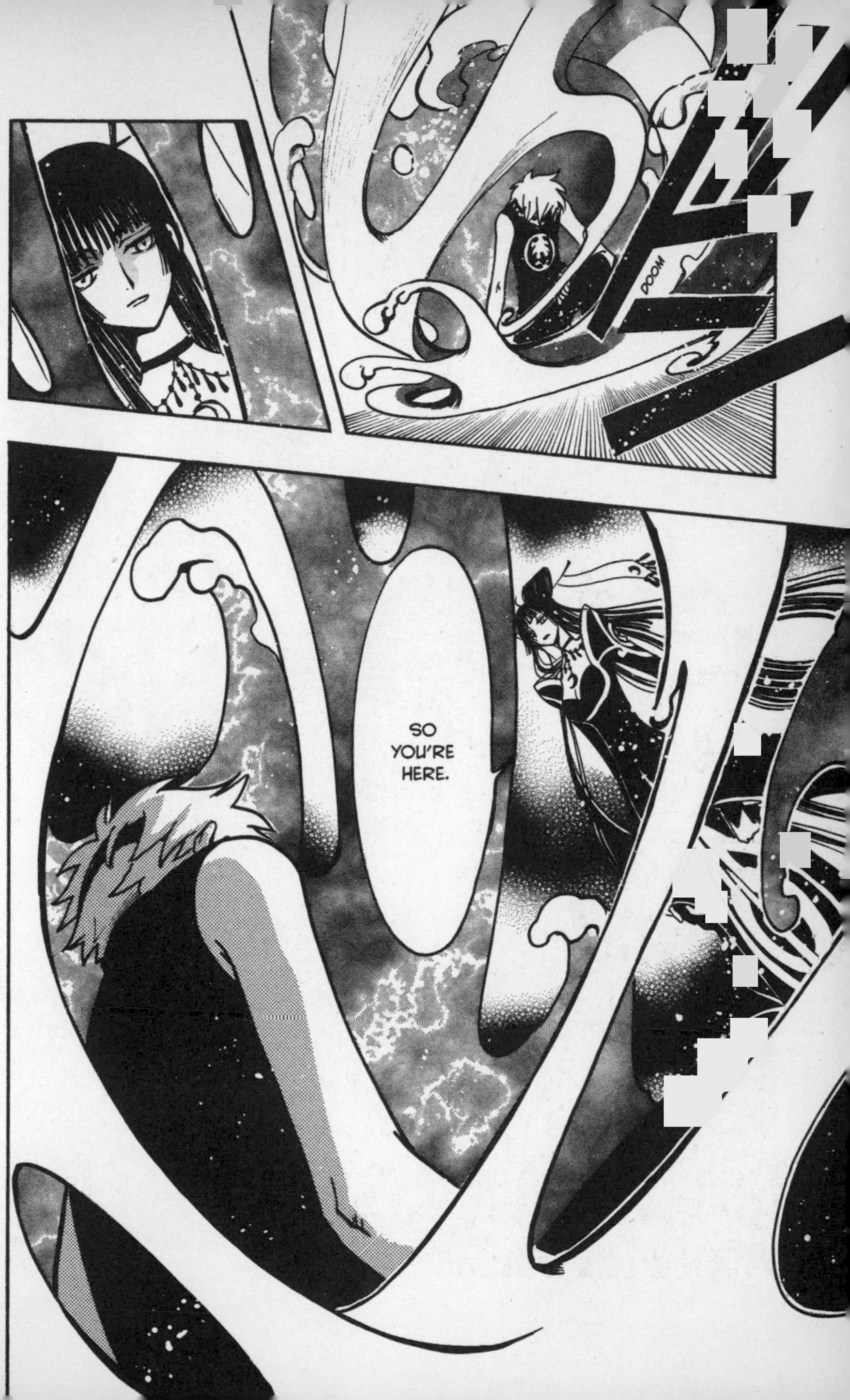
DOOM
SO YOU'RE HERE.

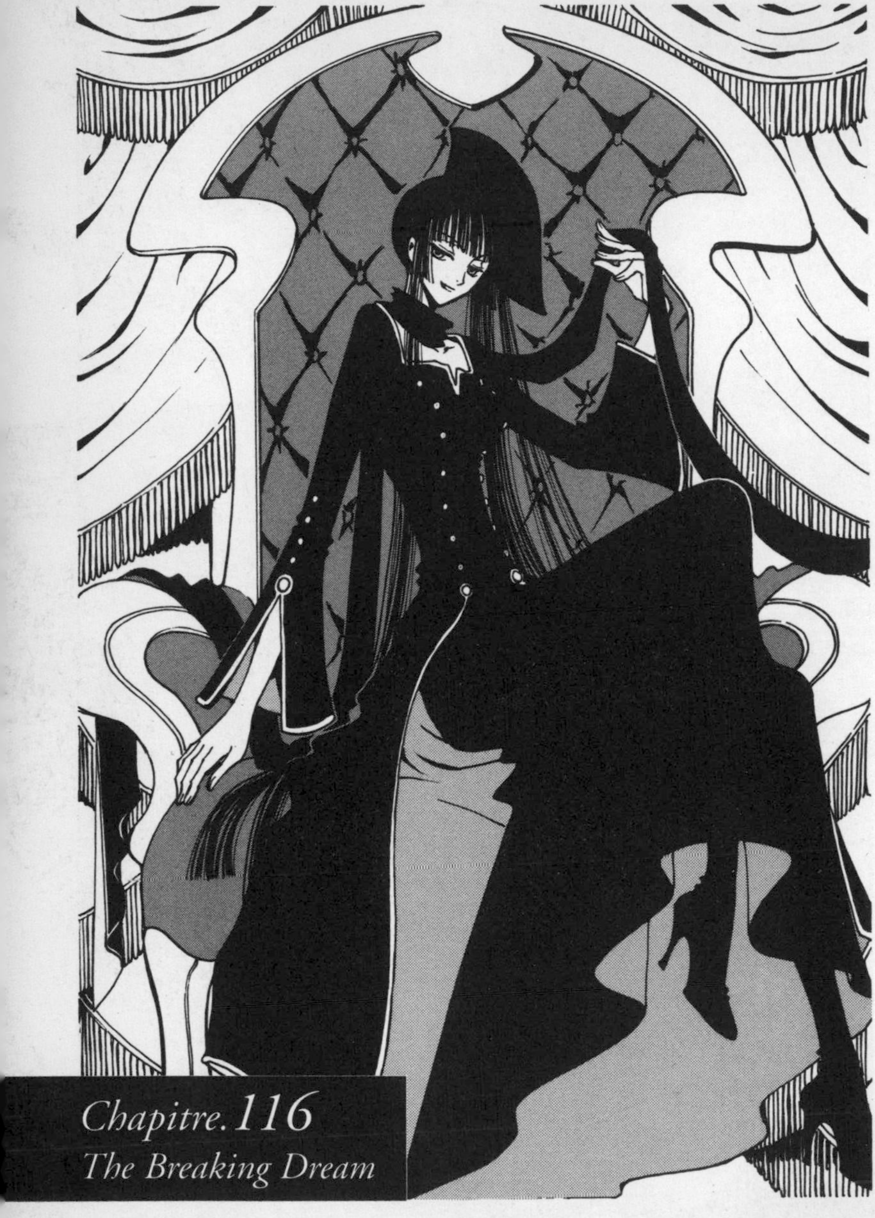
Chapitre. 116
The Breaking Dream

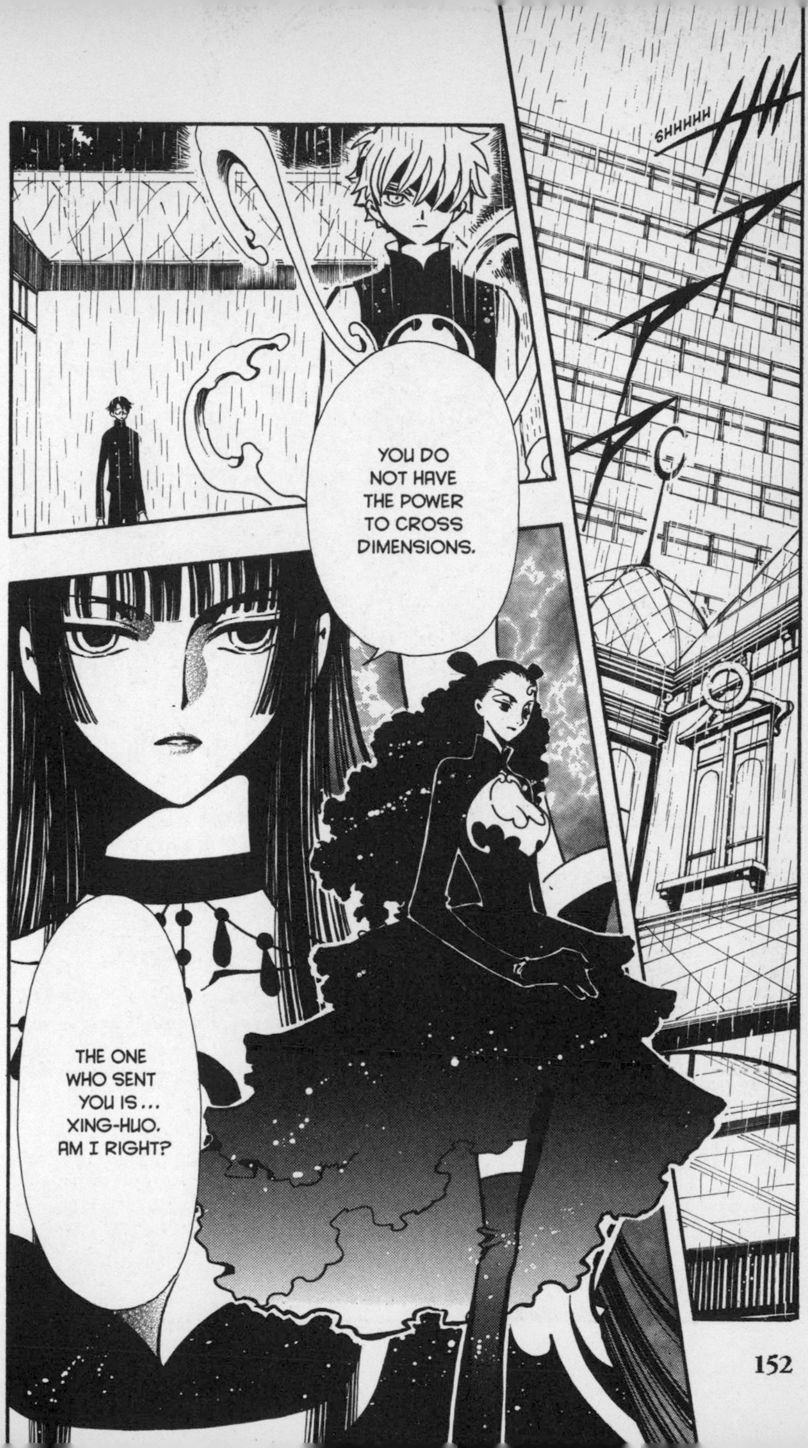
SHHHHH
YOU DO NOT HAVE THE POWER TO CROSS DIMENSIONS.
THE ONE WHO SENT YOU IS... XING-HUO. AM I RIGHT?

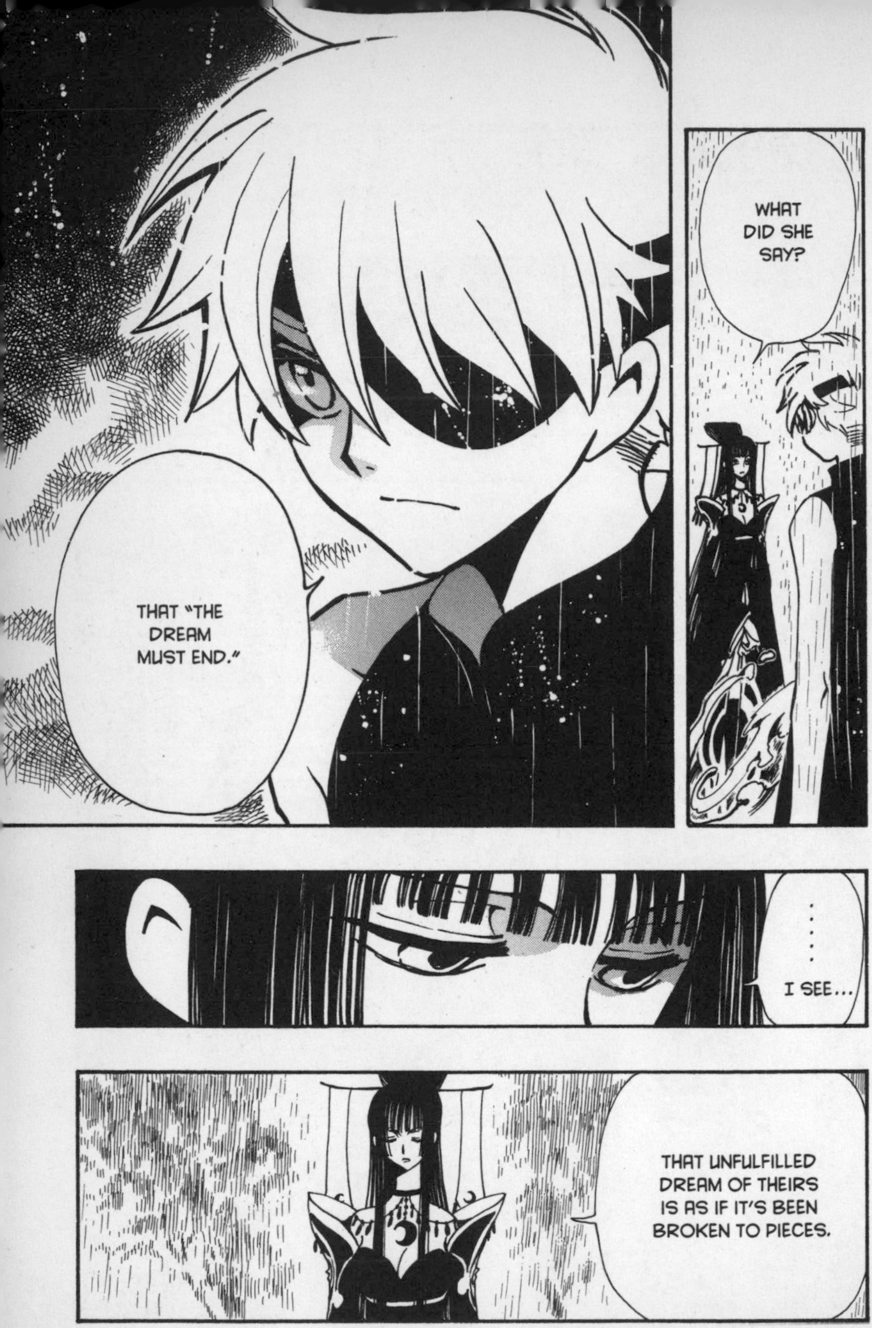
WHAT DID SHE SAY?
THAT "THE DREAM MUST END."
.....
I SEE...
THAT UNFULFILLED DREAM OF THEIRS IS AS IF IT'S BEEN BROKEN TO PIECES.

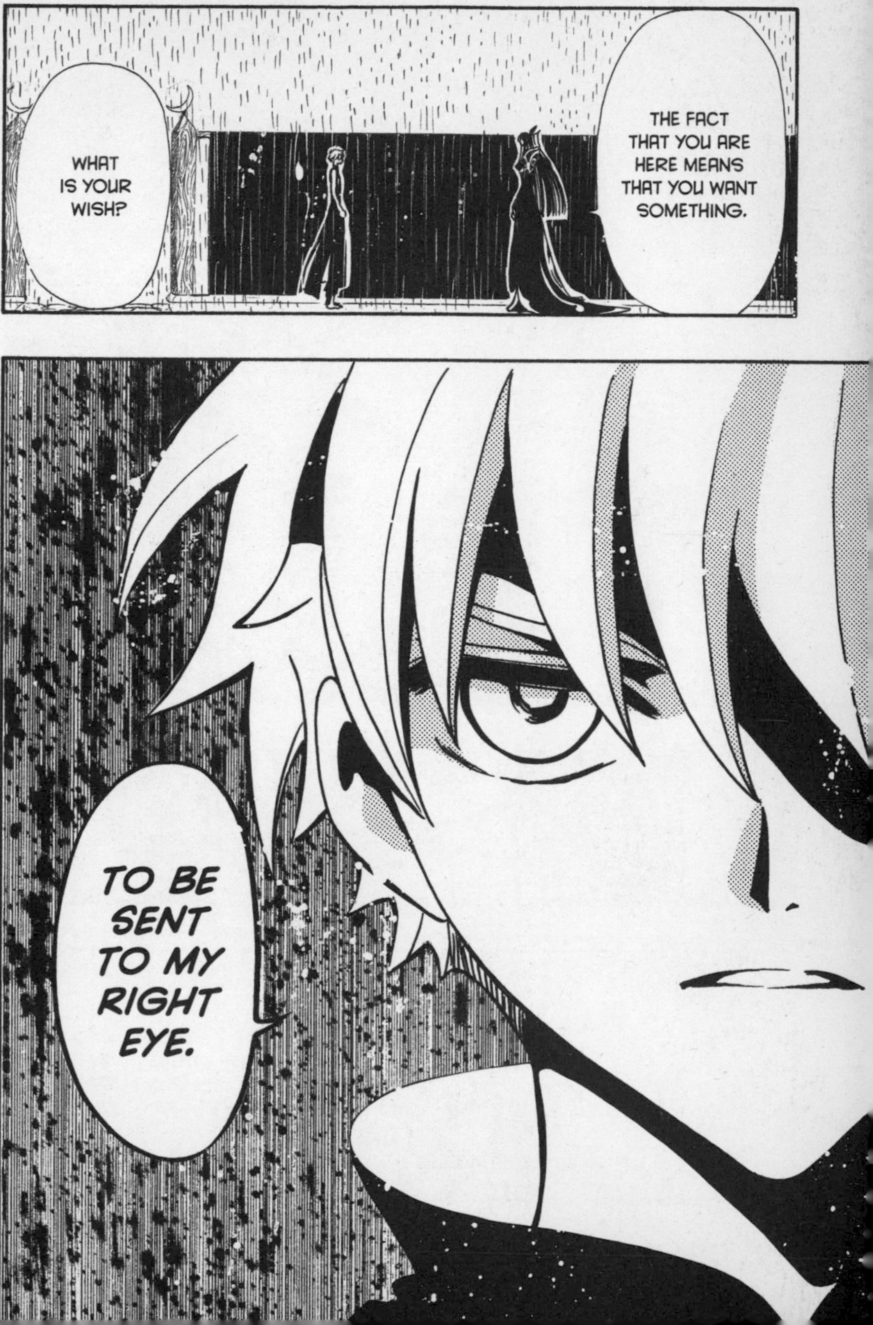
THE FACT THAT YOU ARE HERE MEANS THAT YOU WANT SOMETHING.
WHAT IS YOUR WISH?
TO BE SENT TO MY RIGHT EYE.

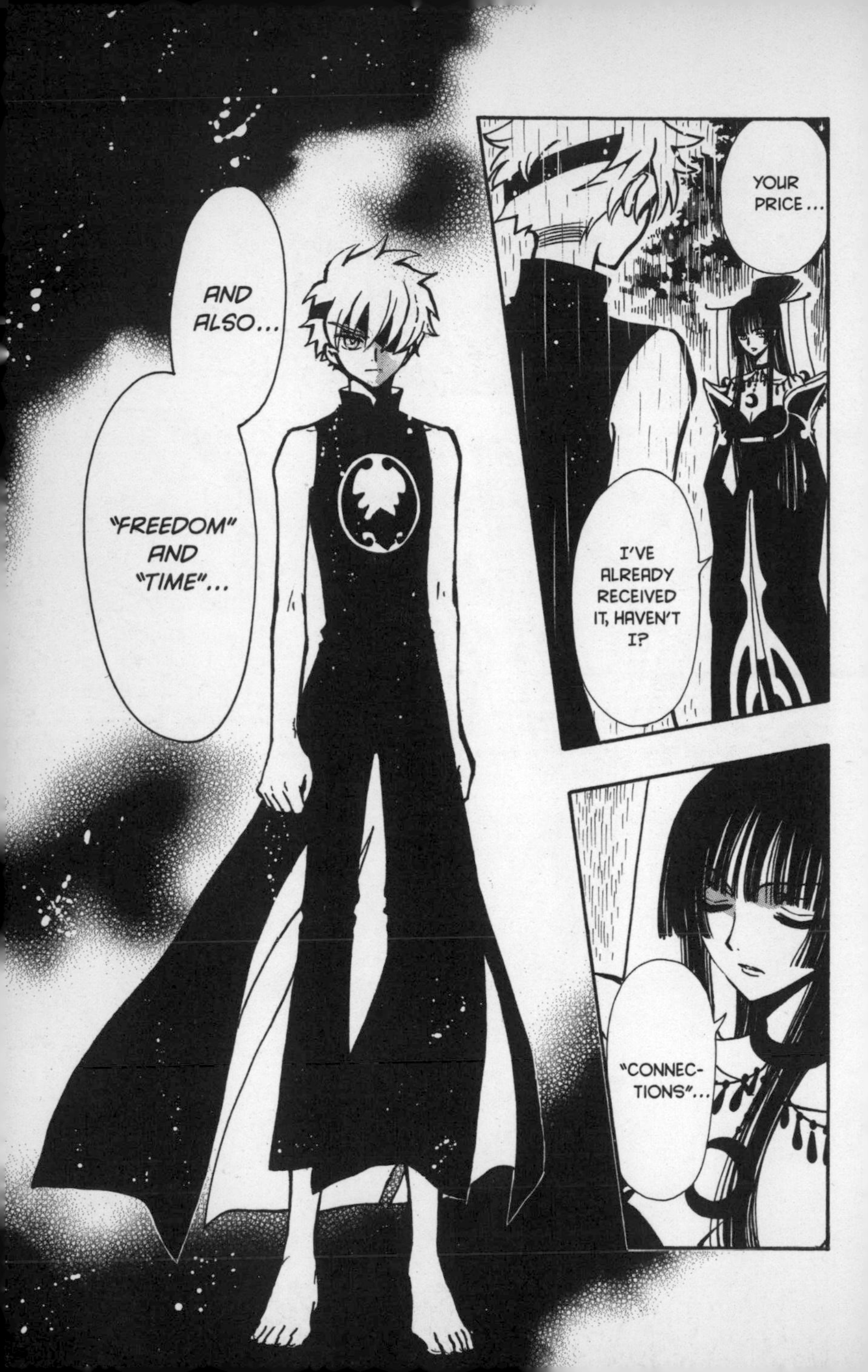
YOUR PRICE...
I'VE ALREADY RECEIVED IT, HAVEN'T I?
"CONNECTIONS"...
AND ALSO...
"FREEDOM" AND "TIME"...

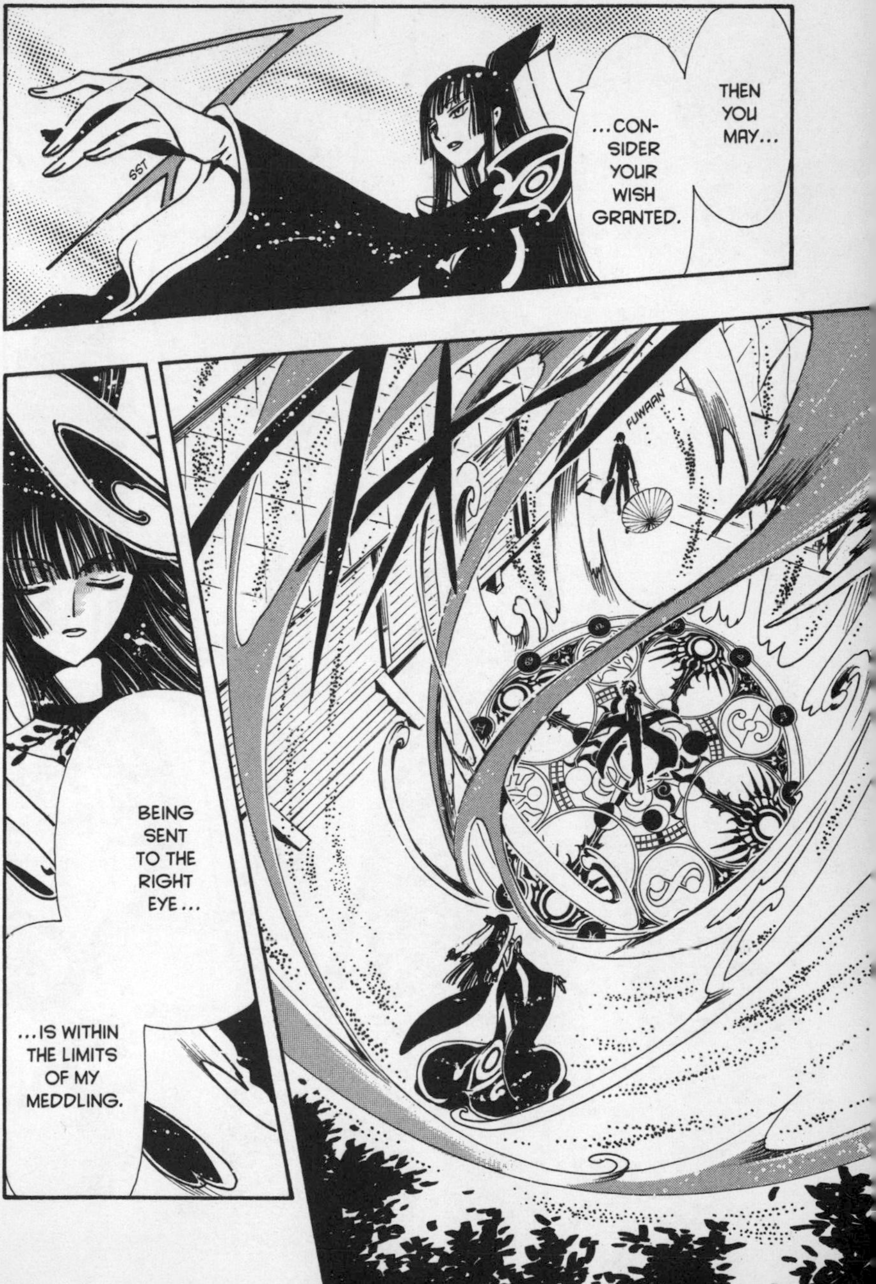
THEN YOU MAY...
...CON-SIDER YOUR WISH GRANTED.
SST
FUWAAN
BEING SENT TO THE RIGHT EYE...
...IS WITHIN THE LIMITS OF MY MEDDLING.

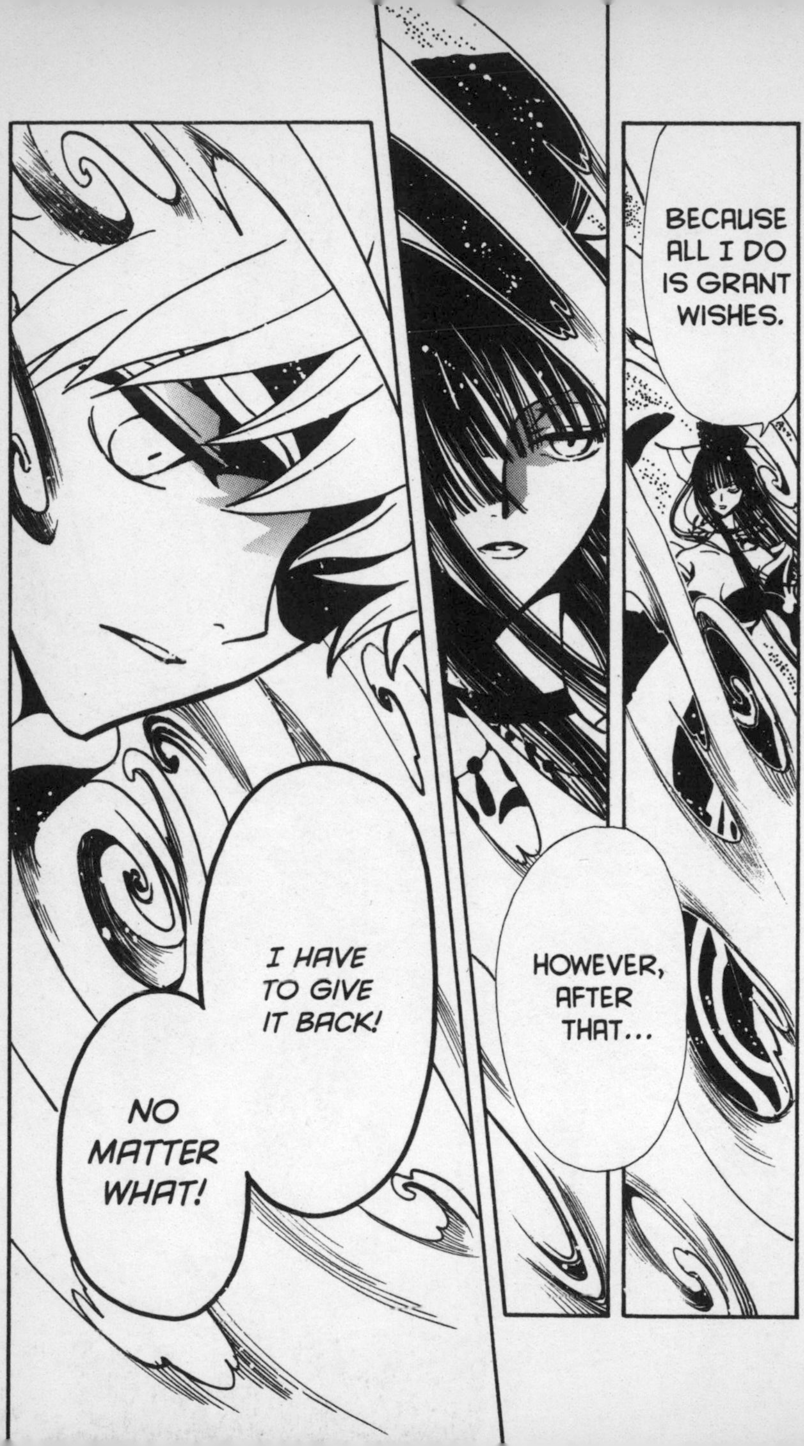
BECAUSE ALL I DO IS GRANT WISHES.
HOWEVER, AFTER THAT...
I HAVE TO GIVE IT BACK!
NO MATTER WHAT!

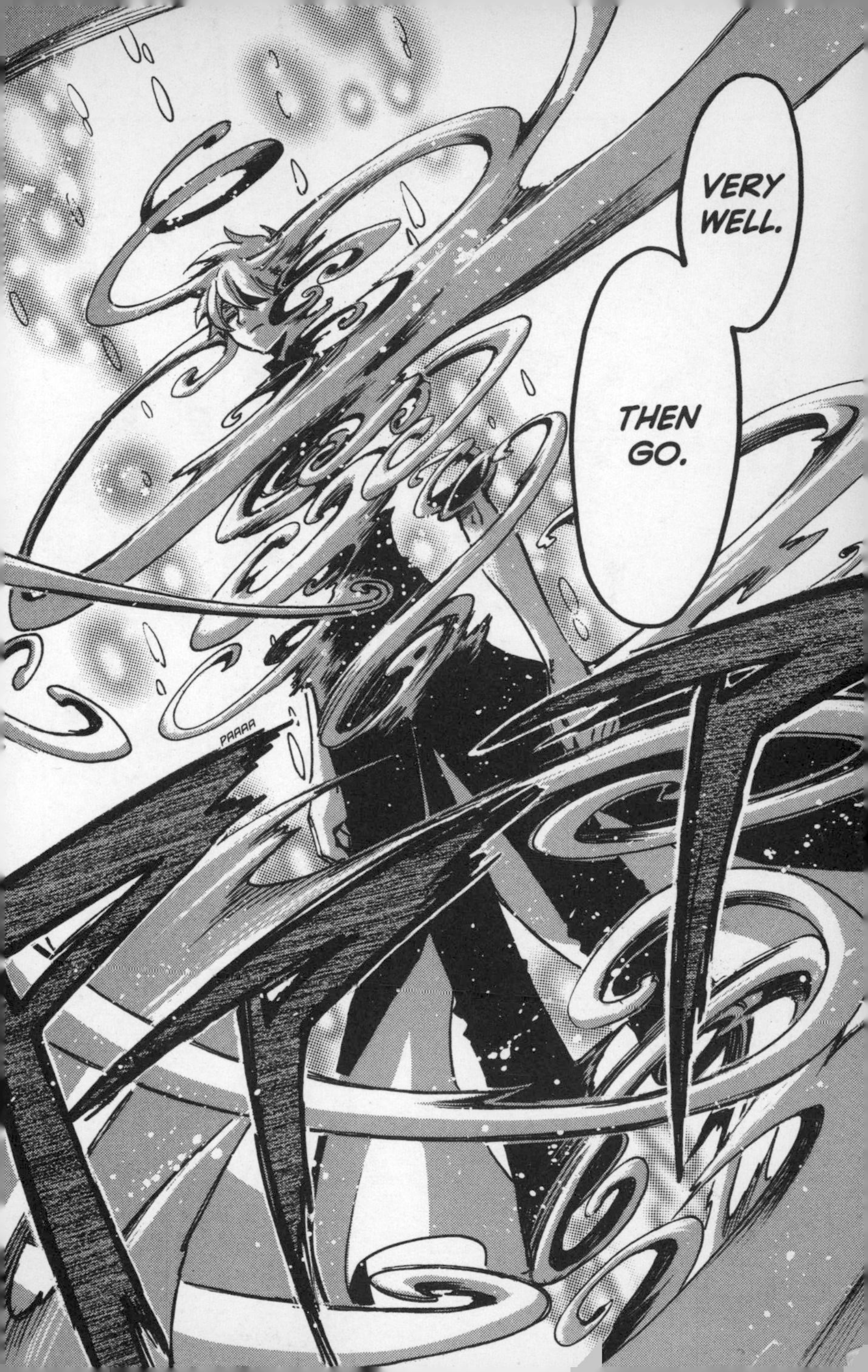
VERY WELL.
THEN GO.
PAAAA

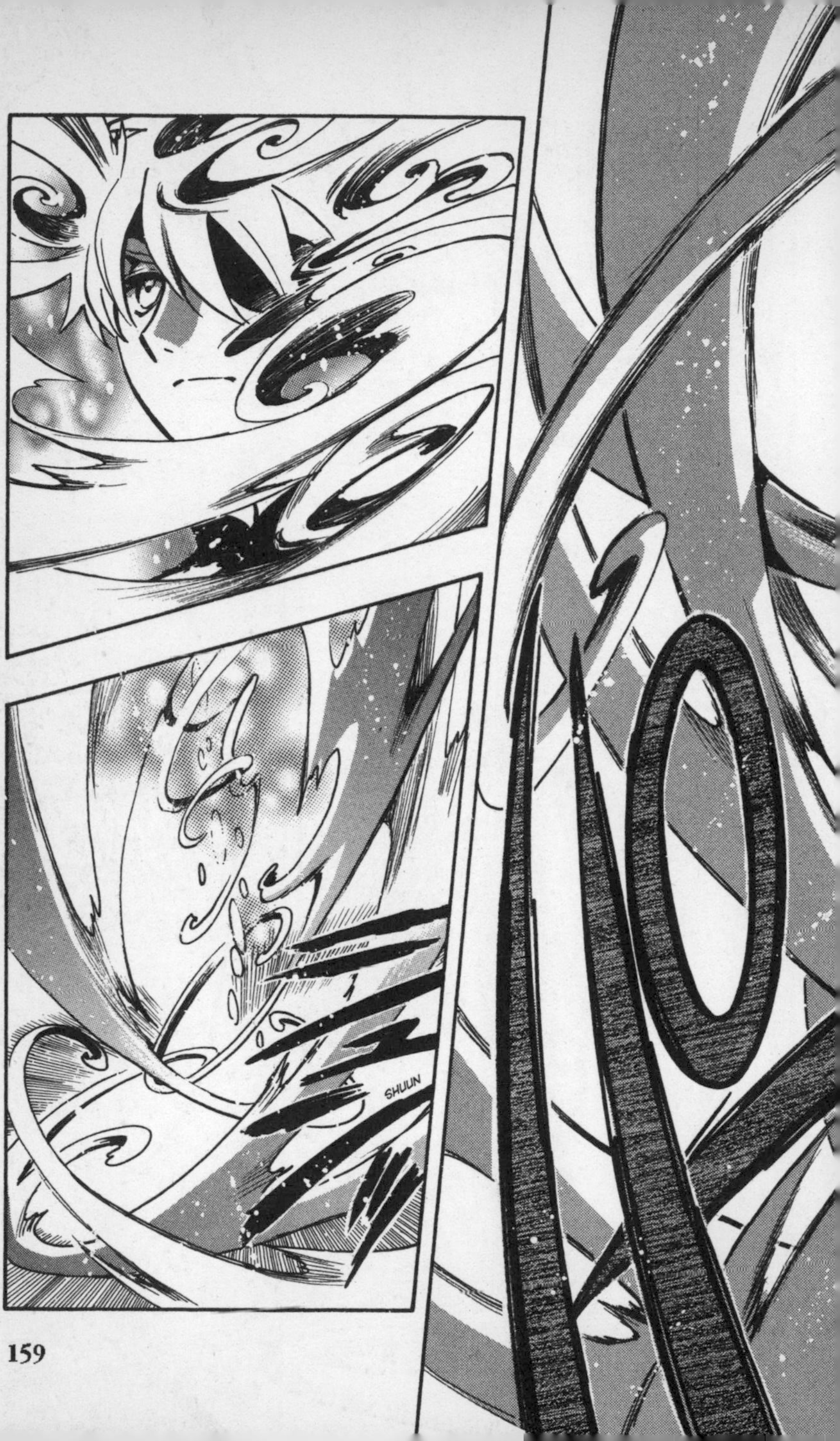
SHUUN

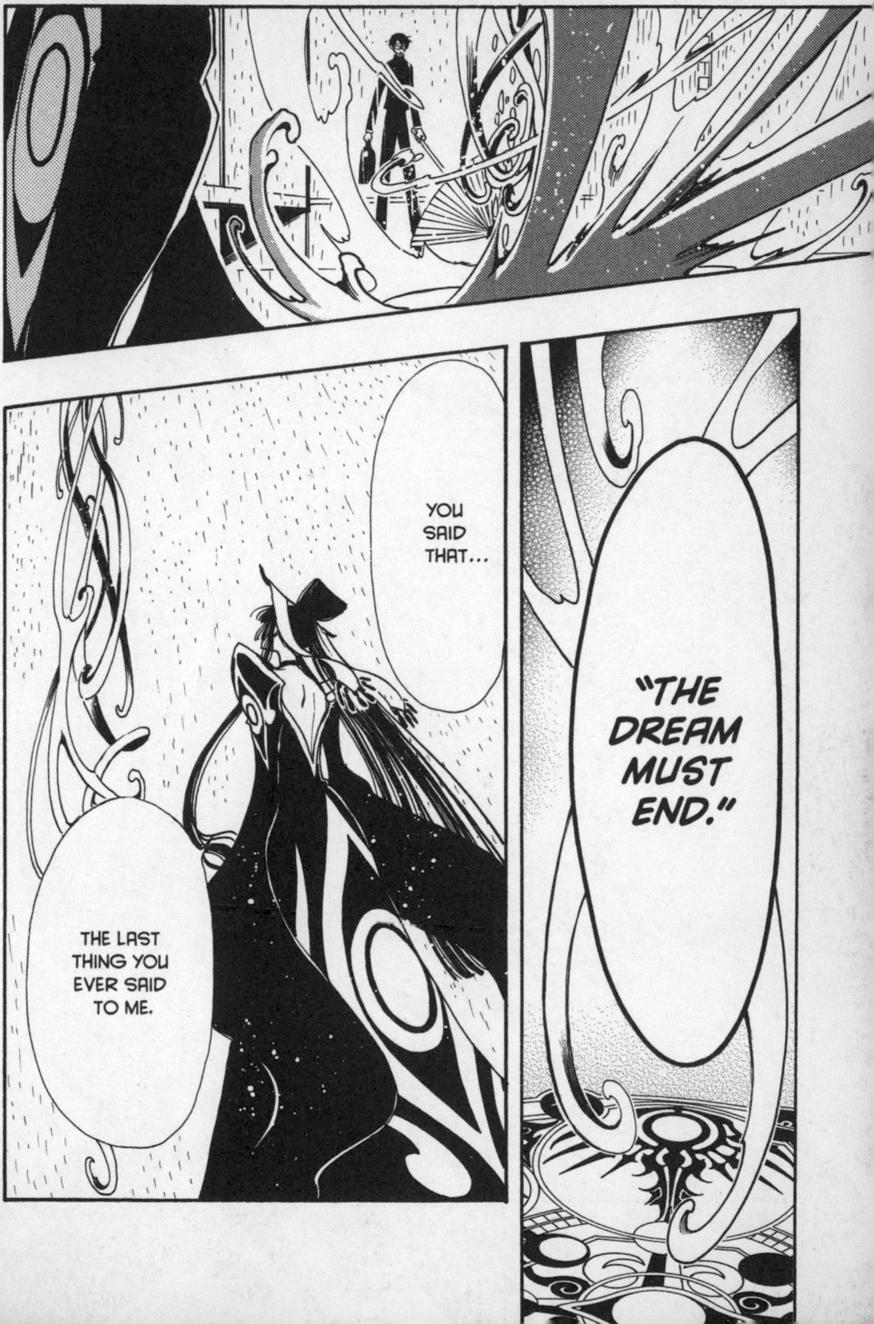
"THE DREAM MUST END."
YOU SAID THAT...
THE LAST THING YOU EVER SAID TO ME.

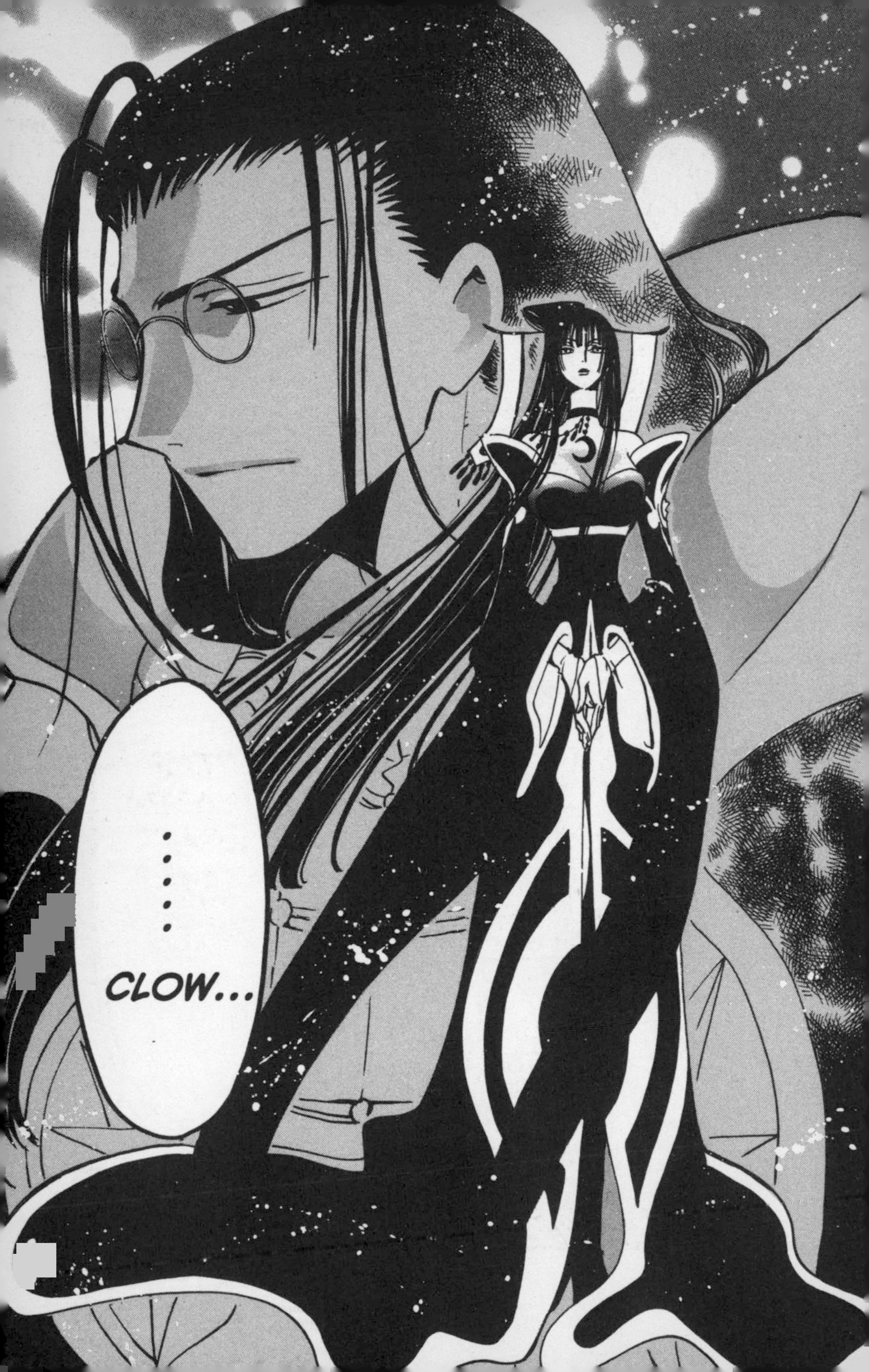
..... CLOW...

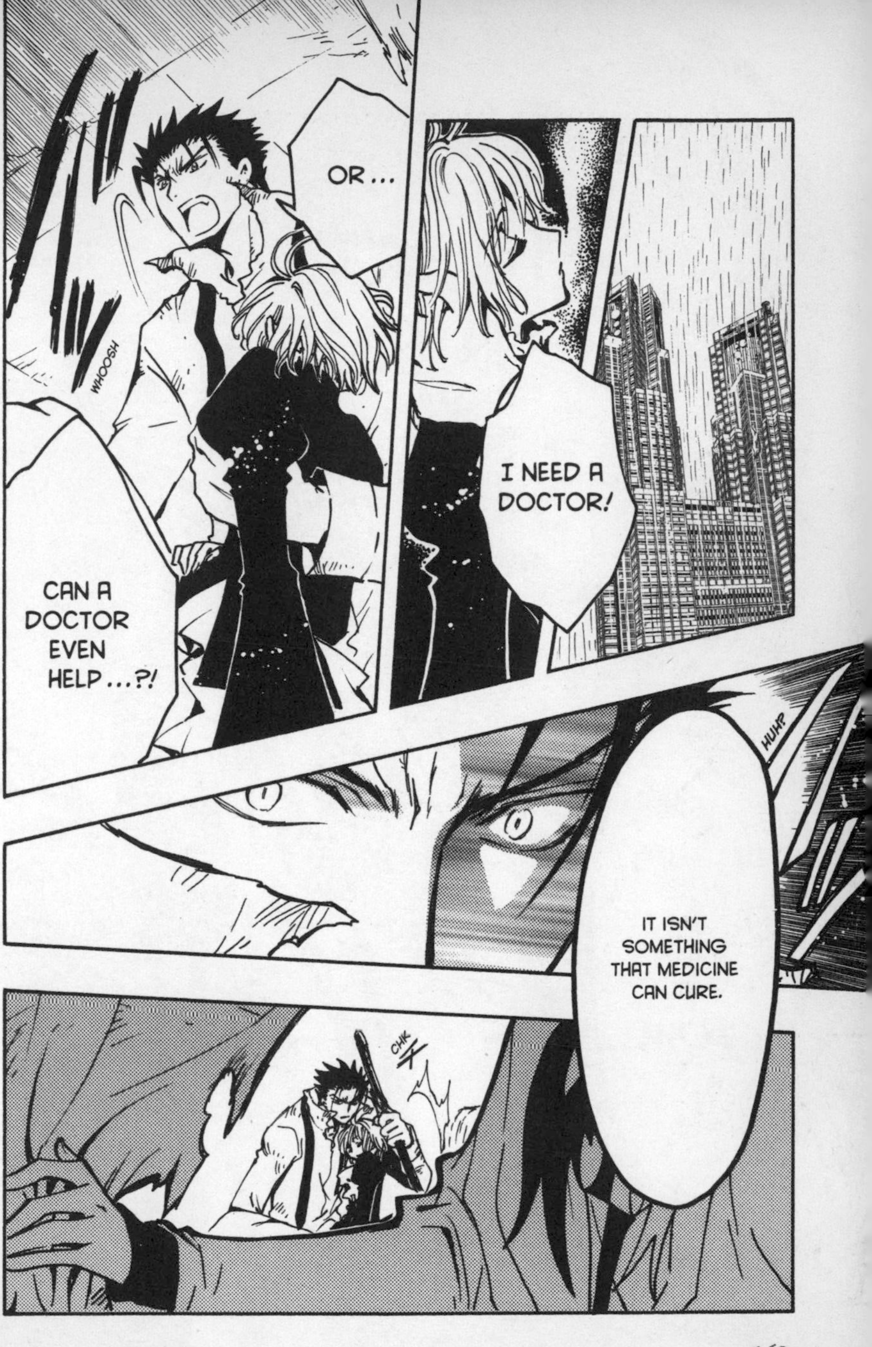
I NEED A DOCTOR!
OR...
WHOOSH
CAN A DOCTOR EVEN HELP...?!
HUH?
IT ISN'T SOMETHING THAT MEDICINE CAN CURE.
CHK

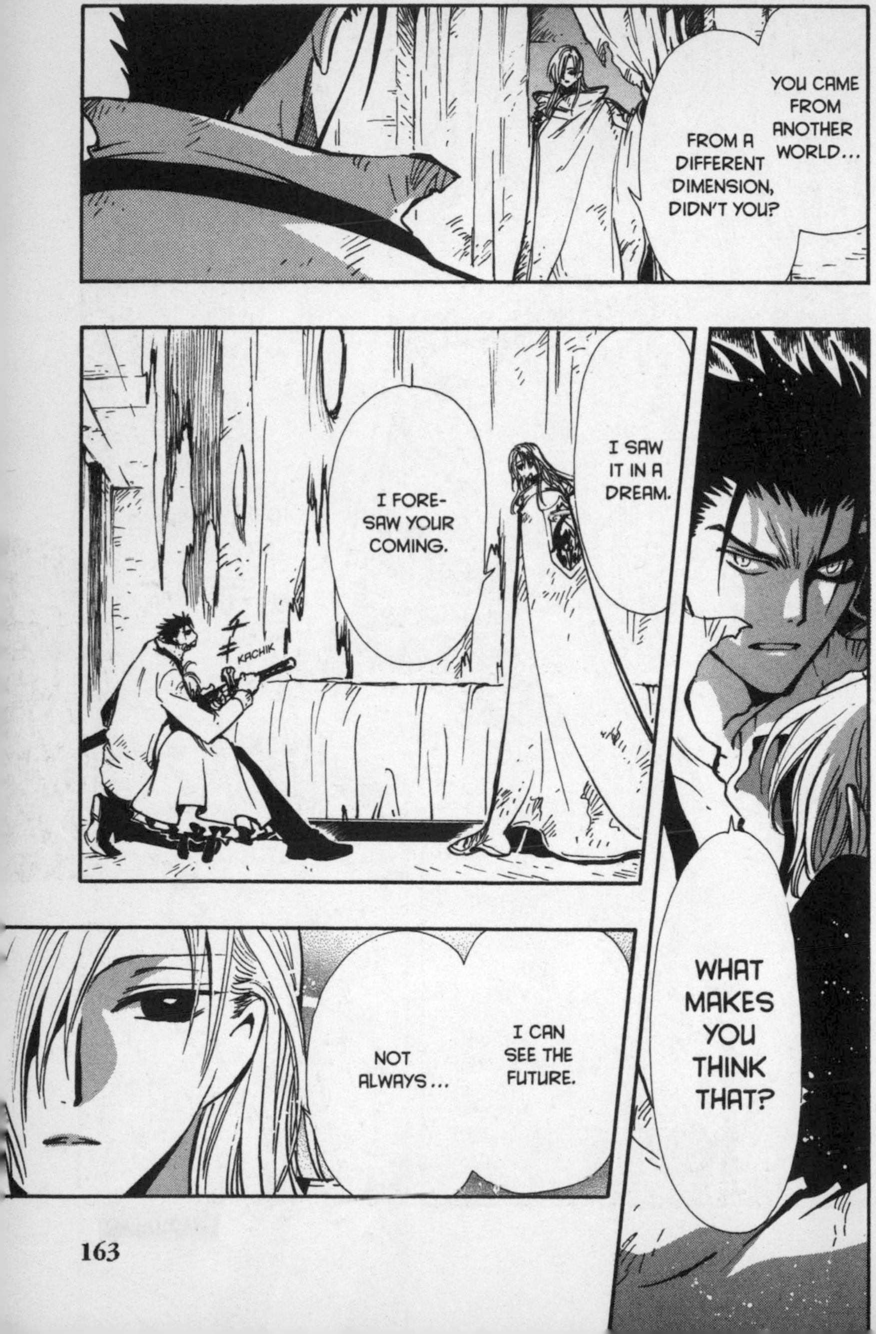
YOU CAME FROM ANOTHER WORLD...
FROM A DIFFERENT DIMENSION, DIDN'T YOU?
WHAT MAKES YOU THINK THAT?
I SAW IT IN A DREAM.
I FORE-SAW YOUR COMING.
KACHIK
I CAN SEE THE FUTURE.
NOT ALWAYS...

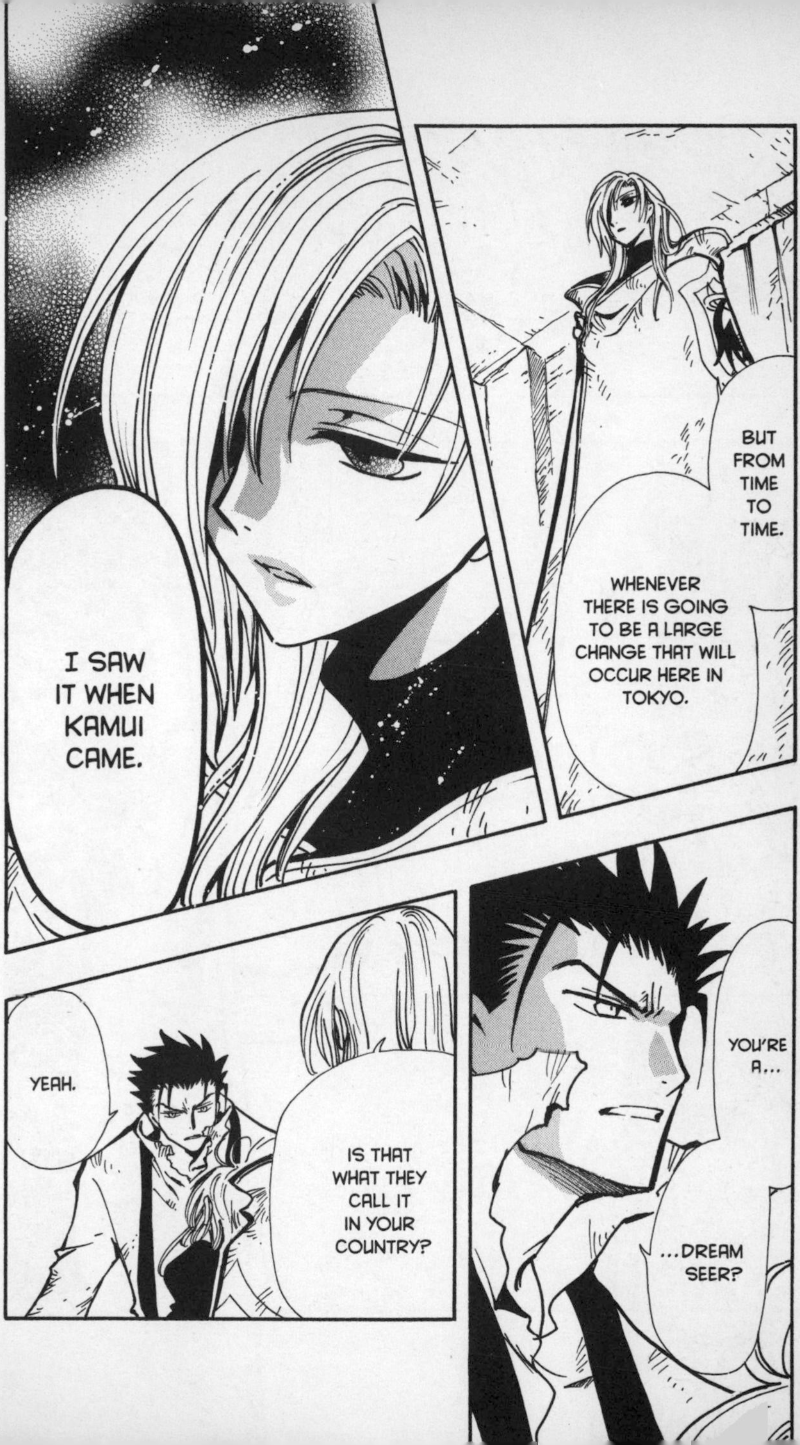
BUT FROM TIME TO TIME.
WHENEVER THERE IS GOING TO BE A LARGE CHANGE THAT WILL OCCUR HERE IN TOKYO.
I SAW IT WHEN KAMUI CAME.
YOU'RE A...
...DREAM SEER?
IS THAT WHAT THEY CALL IT IN YOUR COUNTRY?
YEAH.

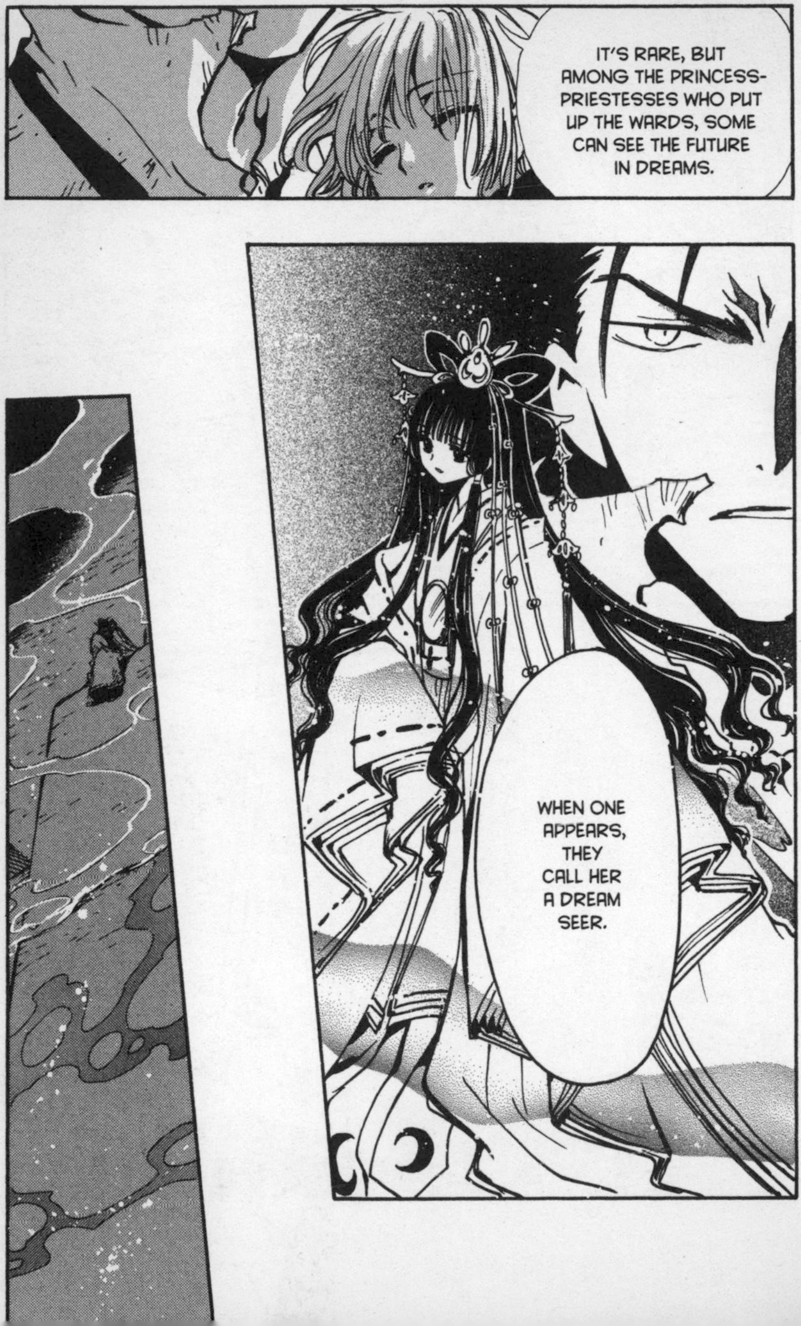
IT'S RARE, BUT AMONG THE PRINCESS-PRIESTESSES WHO PUT UP THE WARDS, SOME CAN SEE THE FUTURE IN DREAMS.
WHEN ONE APPEARS, THEY CALL HER A DREAM SEER.

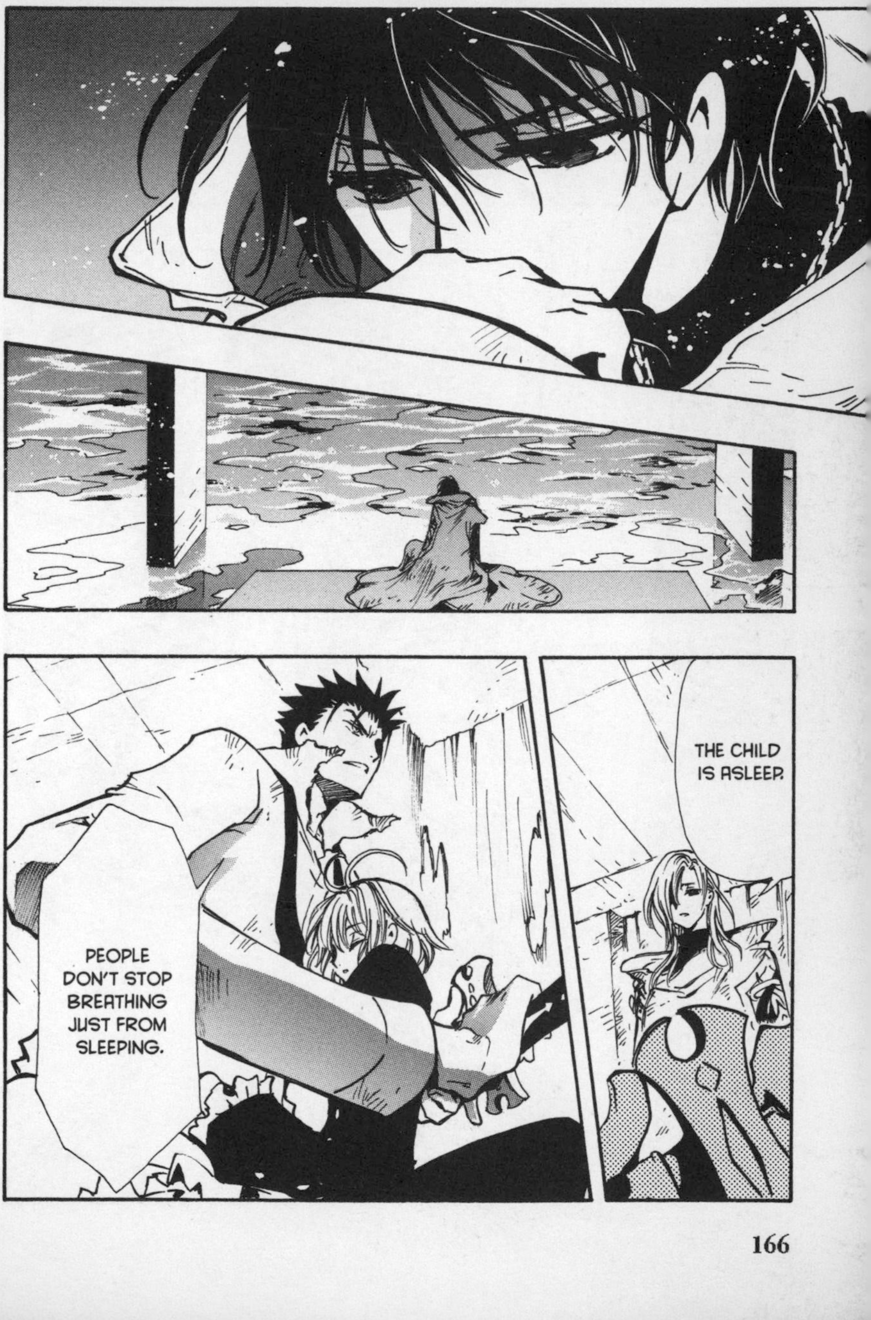
THE CHILD IS ASLEEP.
PEOPLE DON'T STOP BREATHING JUST FROM SLEEPING.

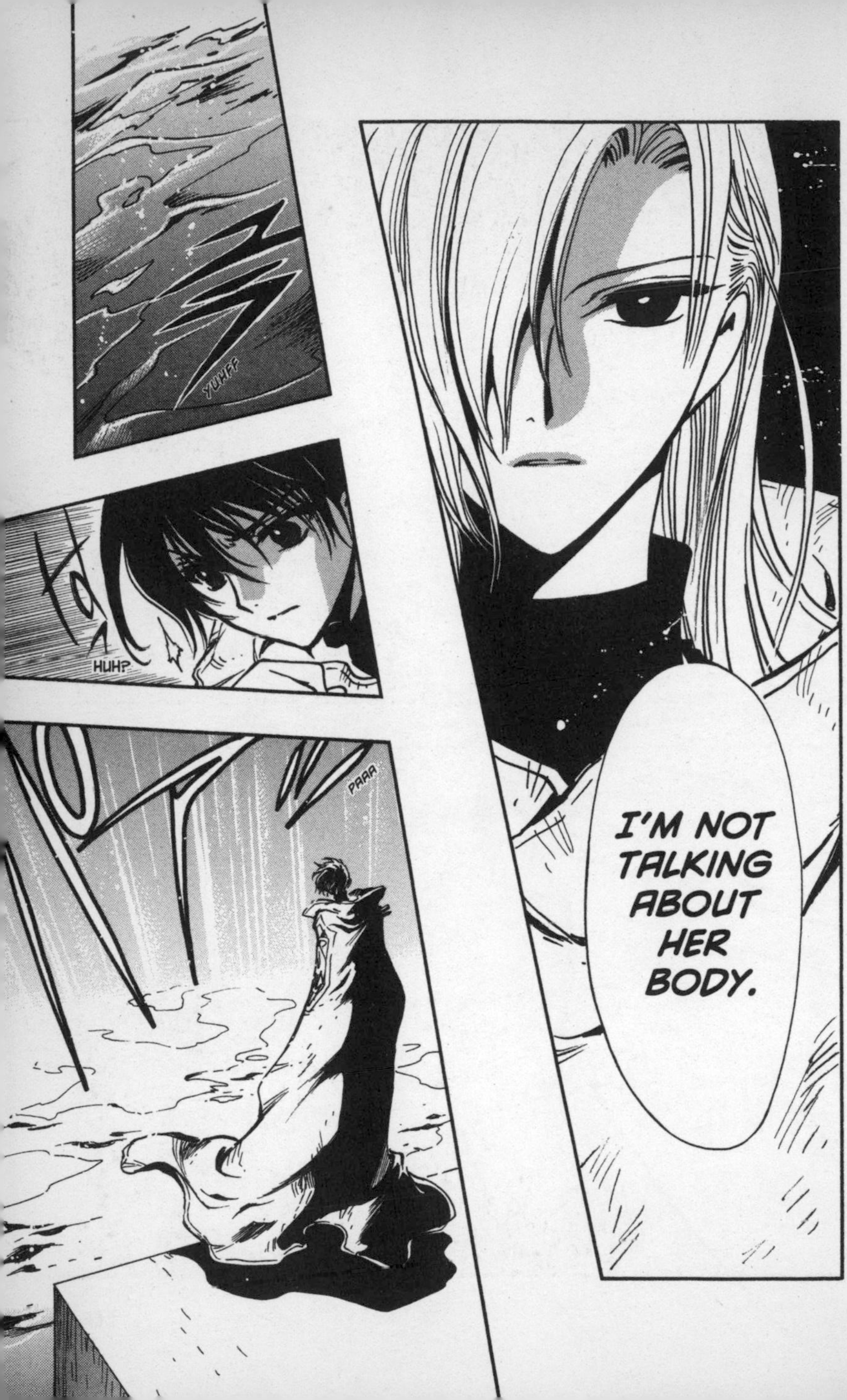
I'M NOT TALKING ABOUT HER BODY.
YUHFF
HUH?
PRAA

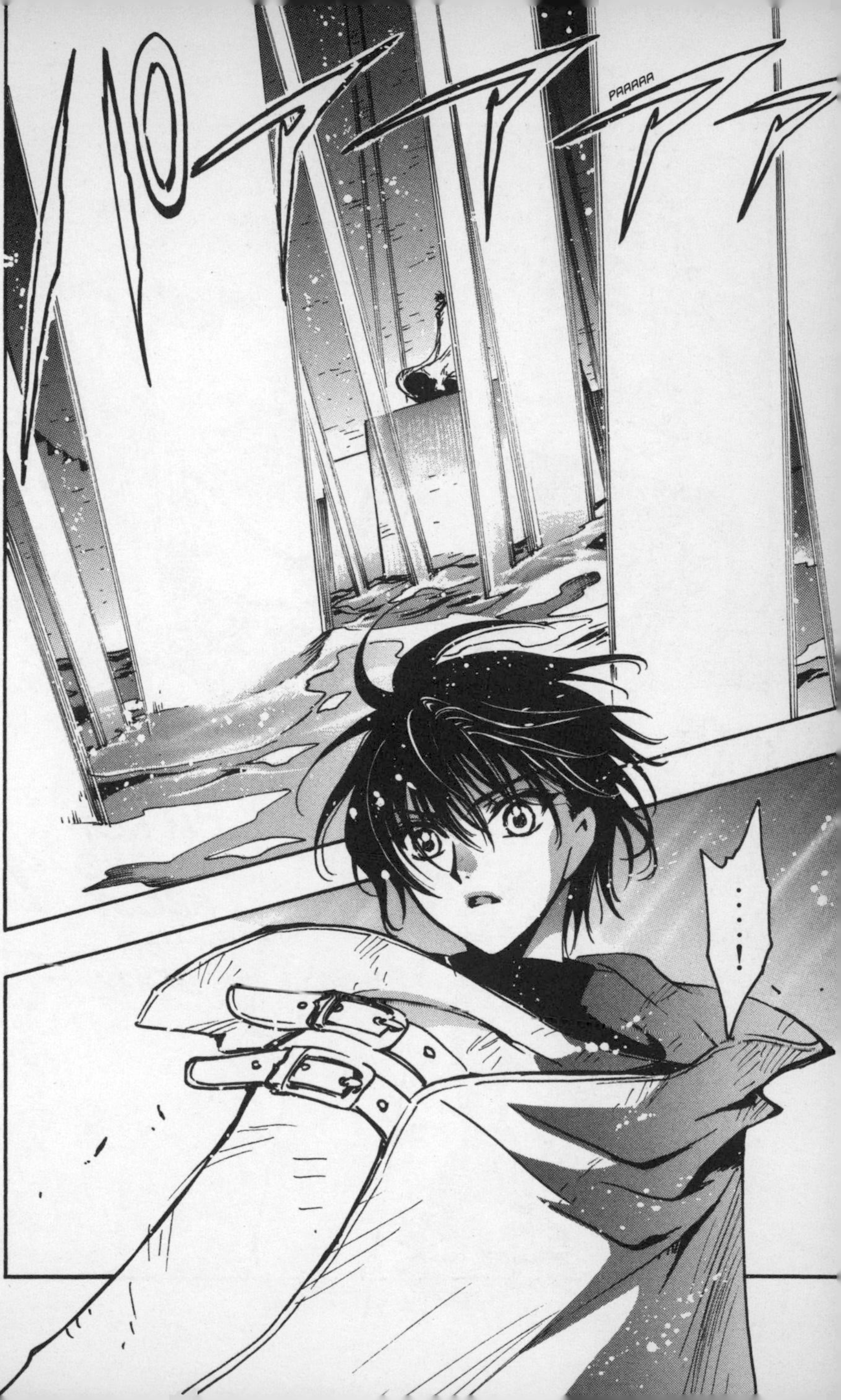
パァアアアア
PAAAAA
.....!

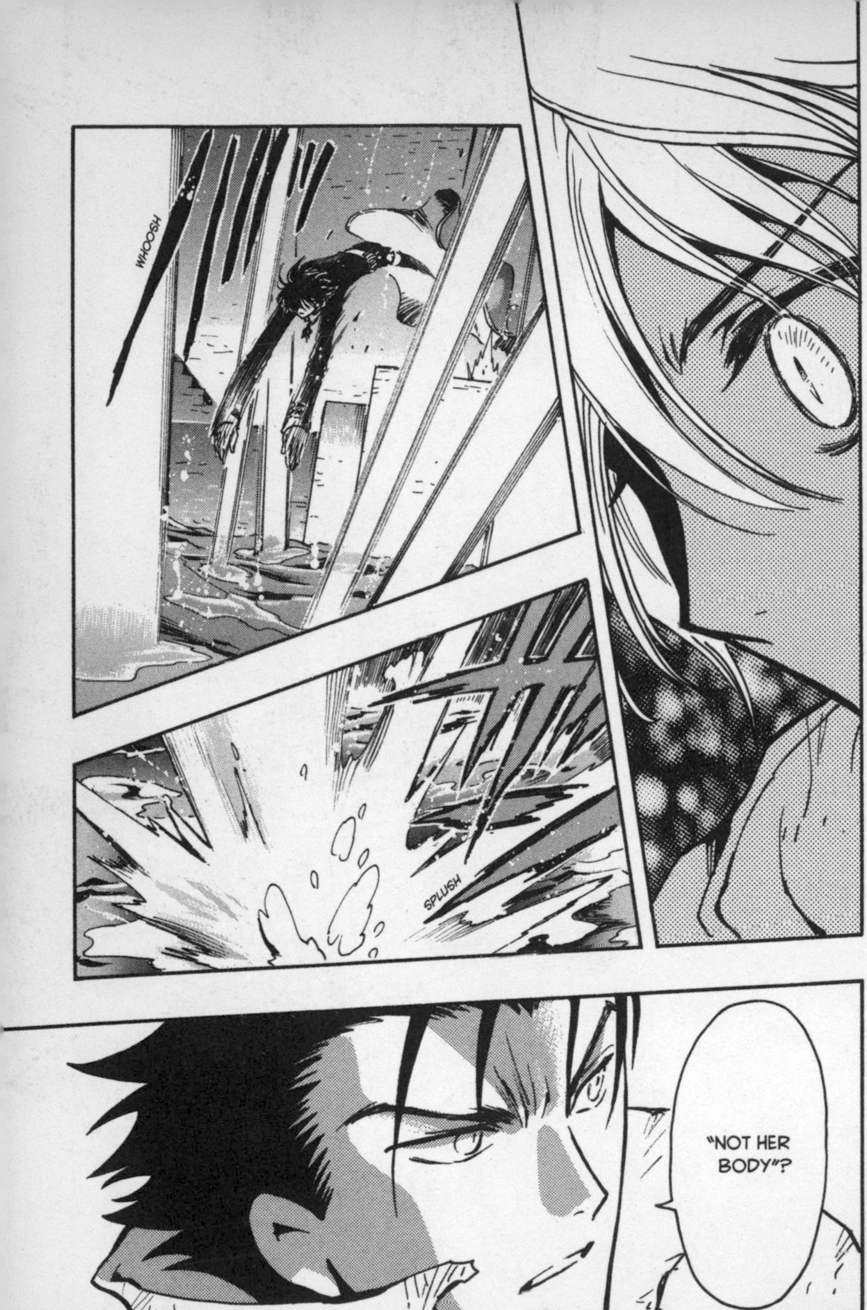
WHOOSH
SPLUSH
"NOT HER BODY"?

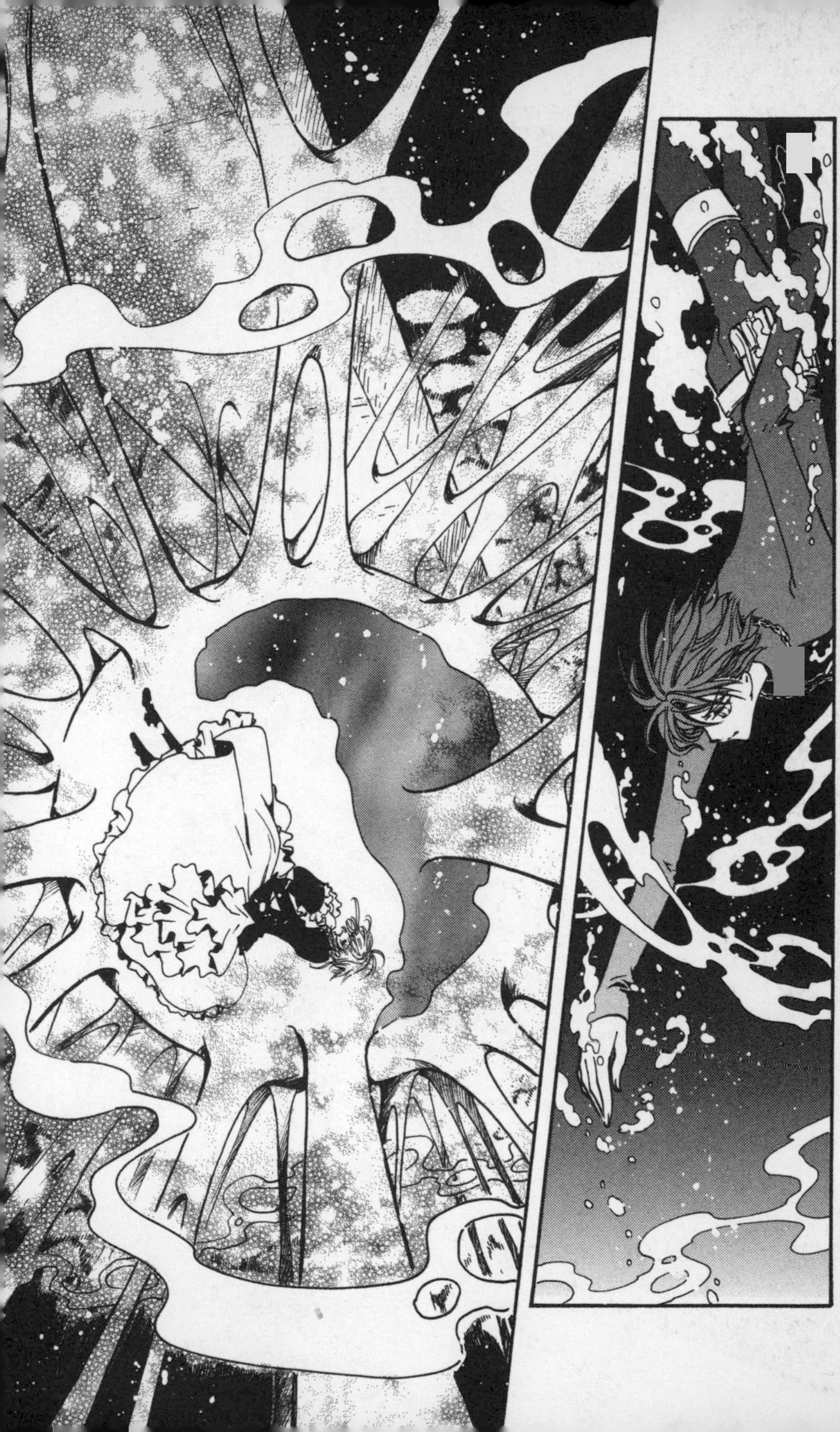

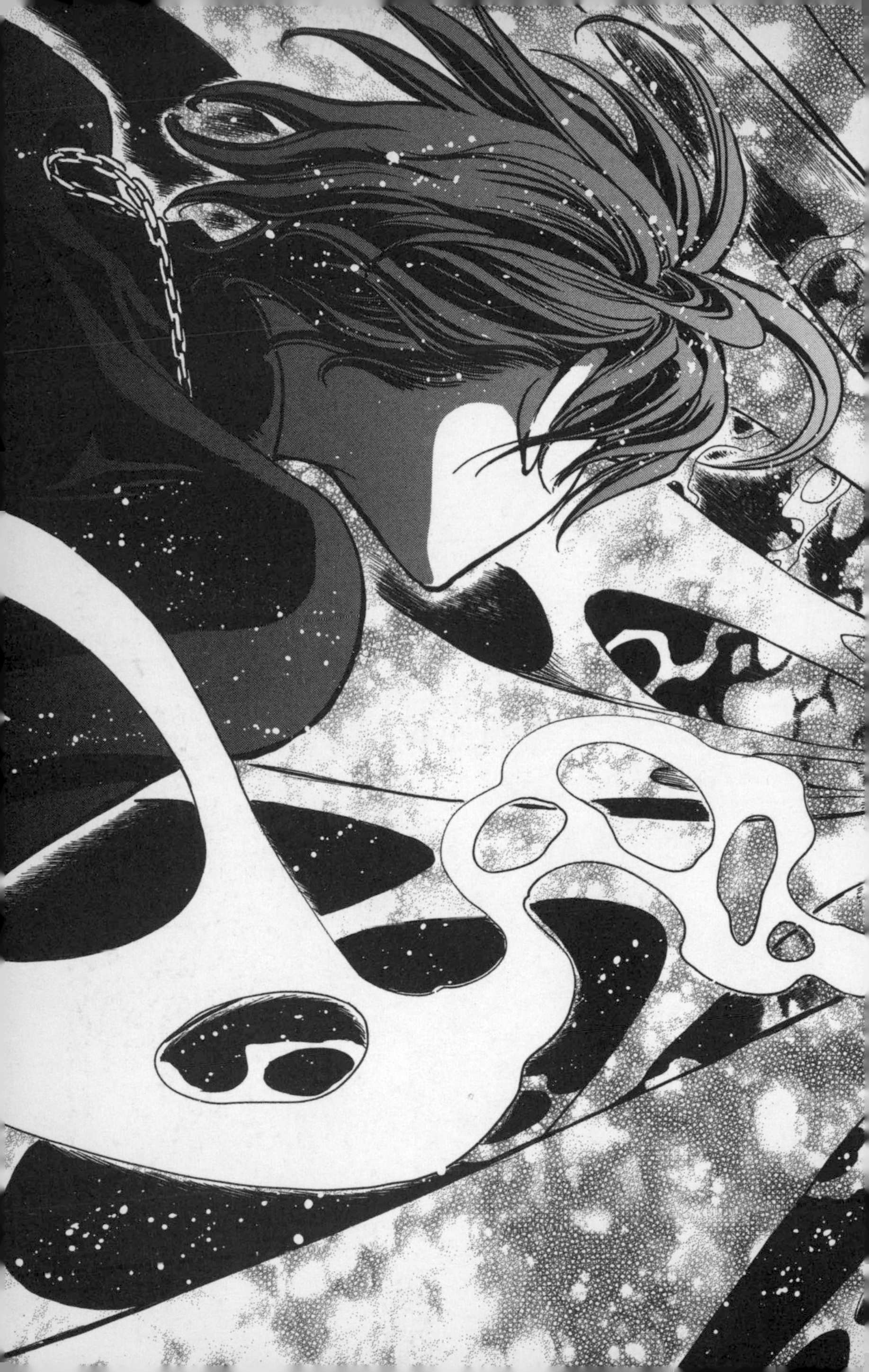

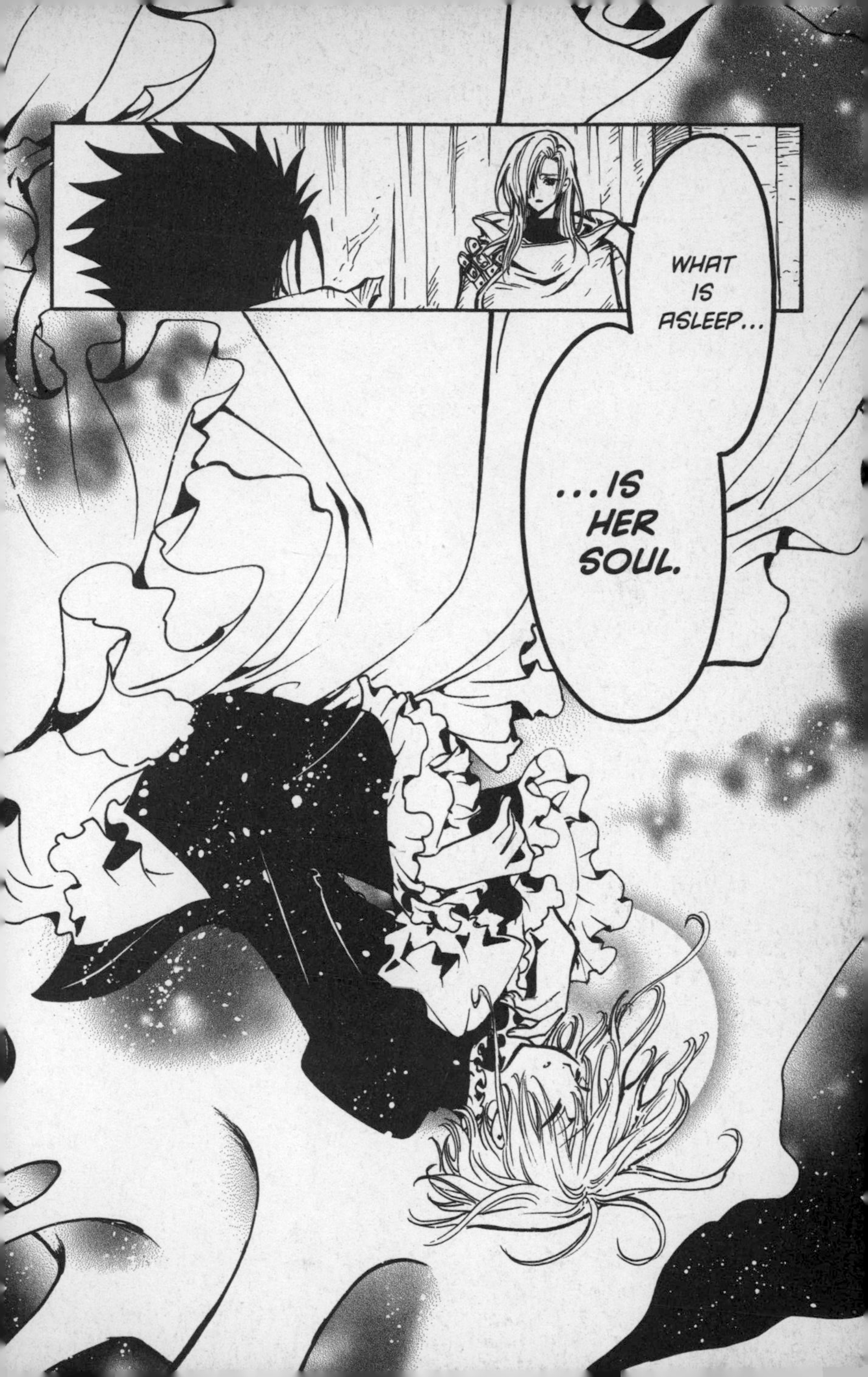
WHAT IS ASLEEP...
...IS HER SOUL.

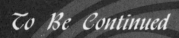

To Be Continued

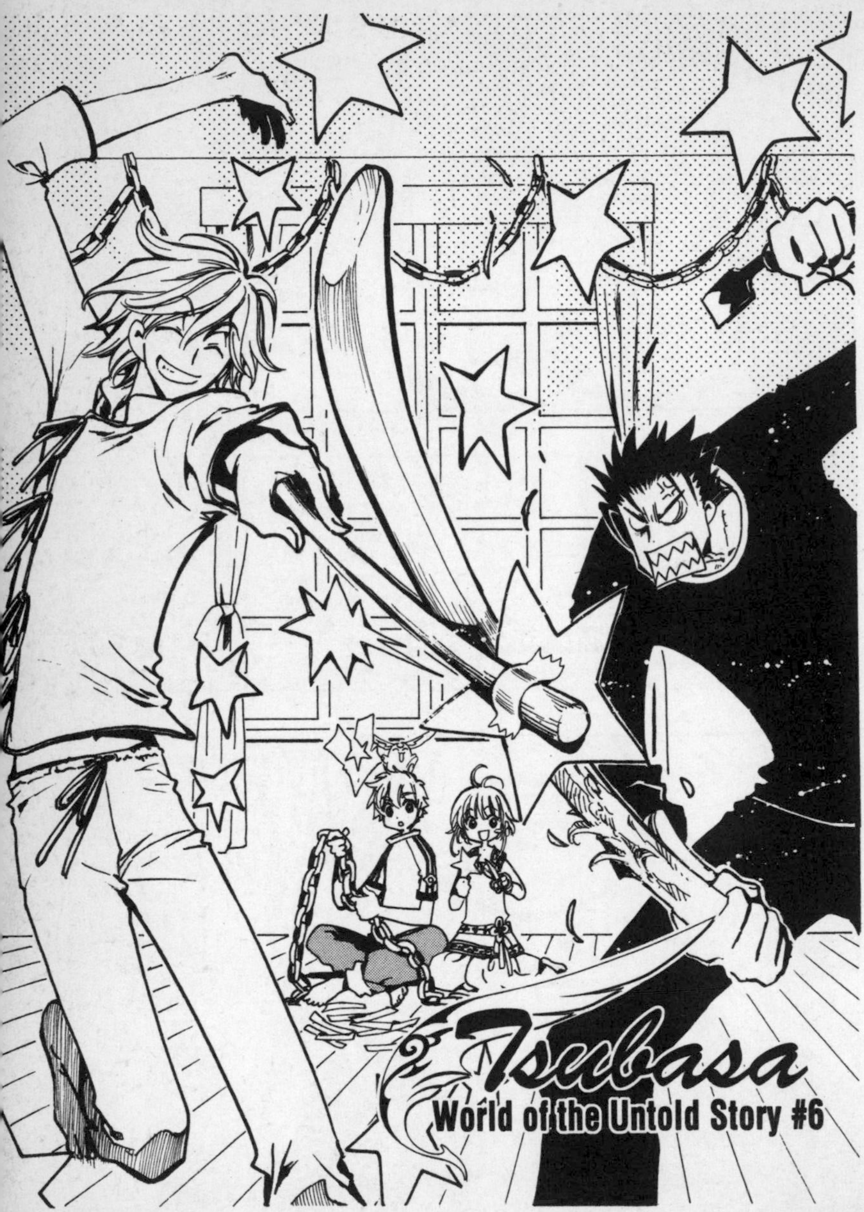
Tsubasa
World of the Untold Story #6

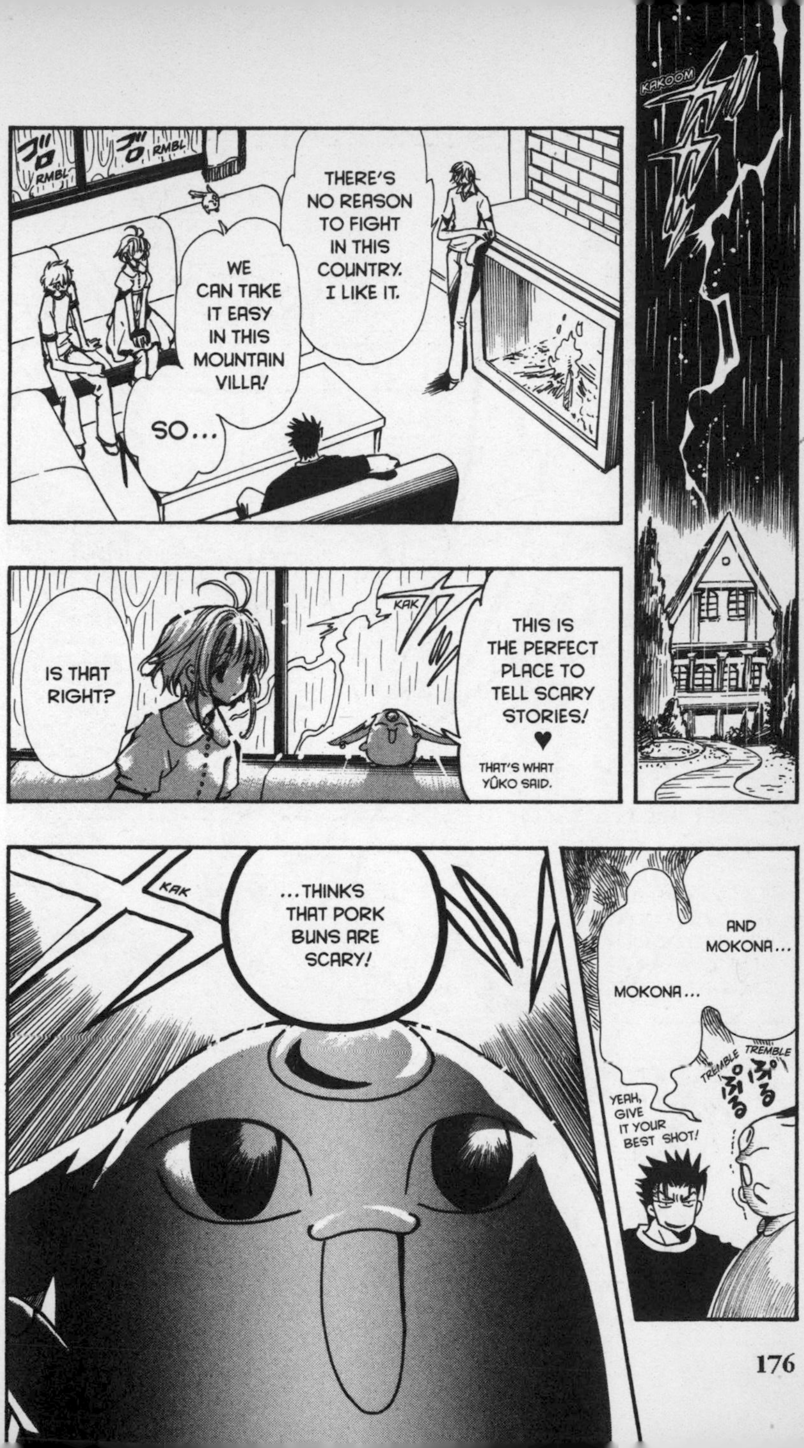
KAKOOM
RMBL
RMBL
SO...
WE CAN TAKE IT EASY IN THIS MOUNTAIN VILLA!
THERE'S NO REASON TO FIGHT IN THIS COUNTRY. I LIKE IT.
THIS IS THE PERFECT PLACE TO TELL SCARY STORIES! ♥
THAT'S WHAT YŪKO SAID.
KAK
IS THAT RIGHT?
AND MOKONA...
MOKONA...
TREMBLE TREMBLE
YEAH, GIVE IT YOUR BEST SHOT!
KAK
...THINKS THAT PORK BUNS ARE SCARY!

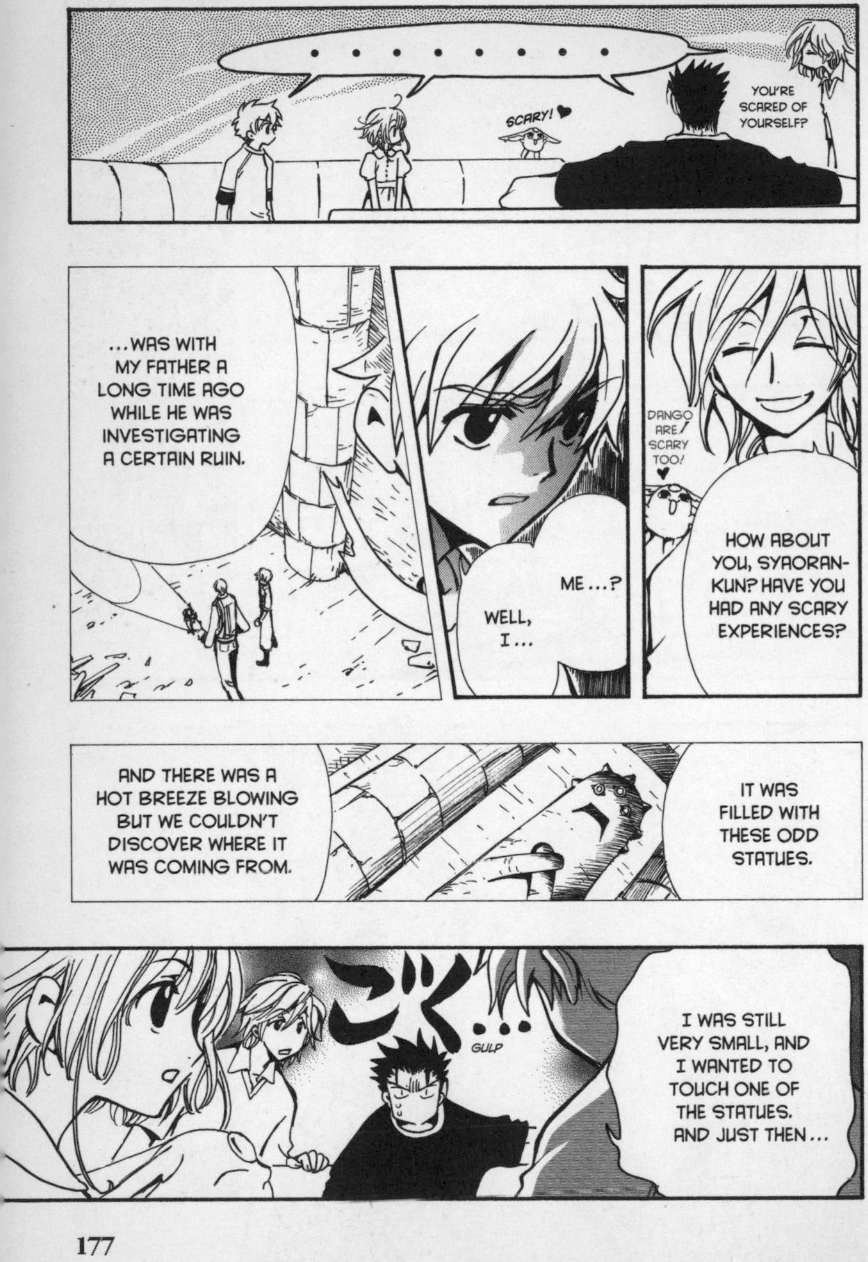
YOU'RE SCARED OF YOURSELF?
• • • • • • • •
SCARY! ♥
DANGO ARE SCARY TOO! ♥
HOW ABOUT YOU, SYAORAN-KUN? HAVE YOU HAD ANY SCARY EXPERIENCES?
ME...?
WELL, I...
...WAS WITH MY FATHER A LONG TIME AGO WHILE HE WAS INVESTIGATING A CERTAIN RUIN.
IT WAS FILLED WITH THESE ODD STATUES.
AND THERE WAS A HOT BREEZE BLOWING BUT WE COULDN'T DISCOVER WHERE IT WAS COMING FROM.
I WAS STILL VERY SMALL, AND I WANTED TO TOUCH ONE OF THE STATUES. AND JUST THEN...
ごく...
GULP

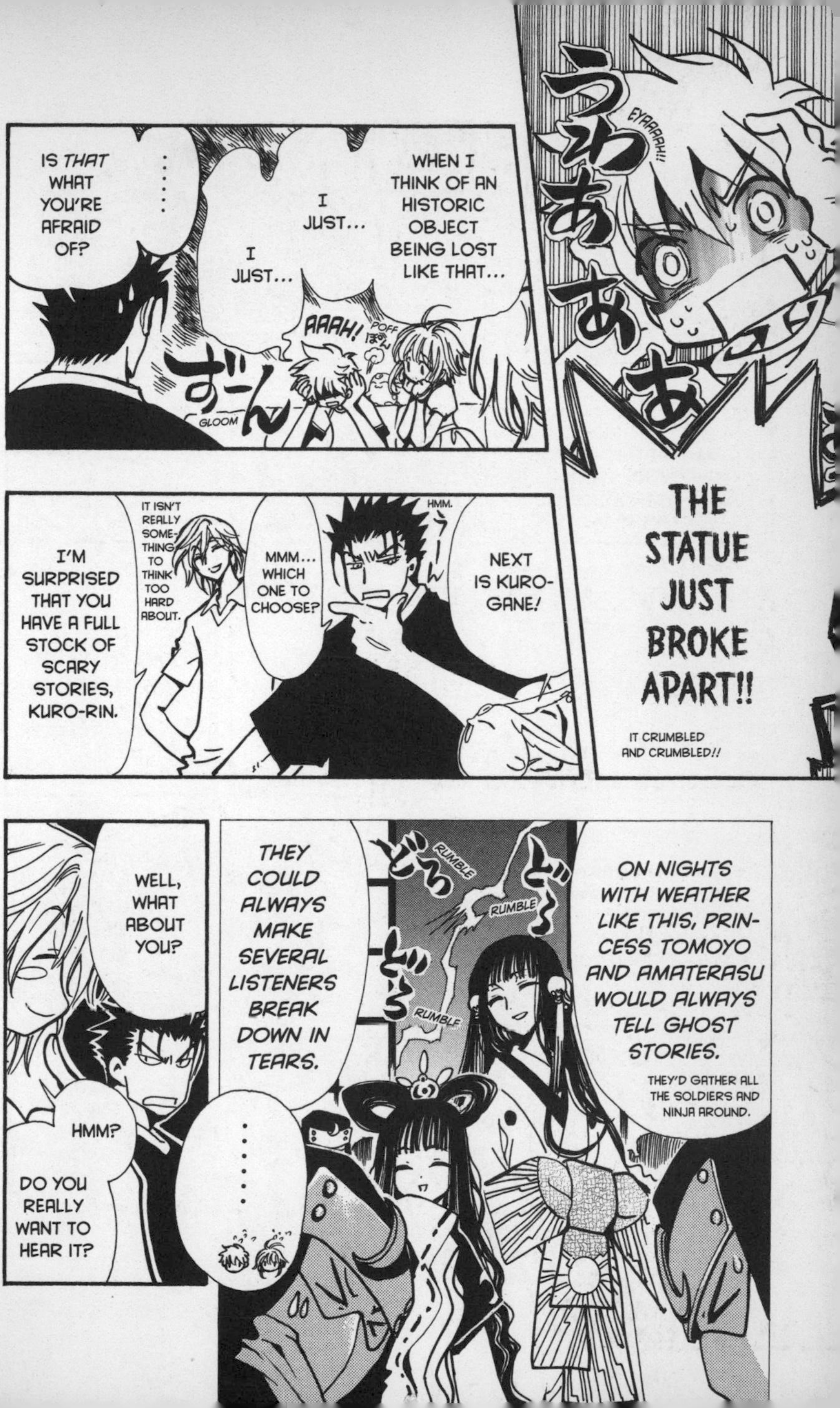
うわあああ
EYAAAAAH!!
THE STATUE JUST BROKE APART!!
IT CRUMBLED AND CRUMBLED!!
WHEN I THINK OF AN HISTORIC OBJECT BEING LOST LIKE THAT...
I JUST...
I JUST...
......
IS *THAT* WHAT YOU'RE AFRAID OF?
AAAH!
POFF
ずーん
GLOOM
NEXT IS KURO-GANE!
HMM.
MMM... WHICH ONE TO CHOOSE?
IT ISN'T REALLY SOMETHING TO THINK TOO HARD ABOUT.
I'M SURPRISED THAT YOU HAVE A FULL STOCK OF SCARY STORIES, KURO-RIN.
ON NIGHTS WITH WEATHER LIKE THIS, PRINCESS TOMOYO AND AMATERASU WOULD ALWAYS TELL GHOST STORIES.
THEY'D GATHER ALL THE SOLDIERS AND NINJA AROUND.
RUMBLE
RUMBLE
RUMBLE
THEY COULD ALWAYS MAKE SEVERAL LISTENERS BREAK DOWN IN TEARS.
......
WELL, WHAT ABOUT YOU?
HMM?
DO YOU REALLY WANT TO HEAR IT?

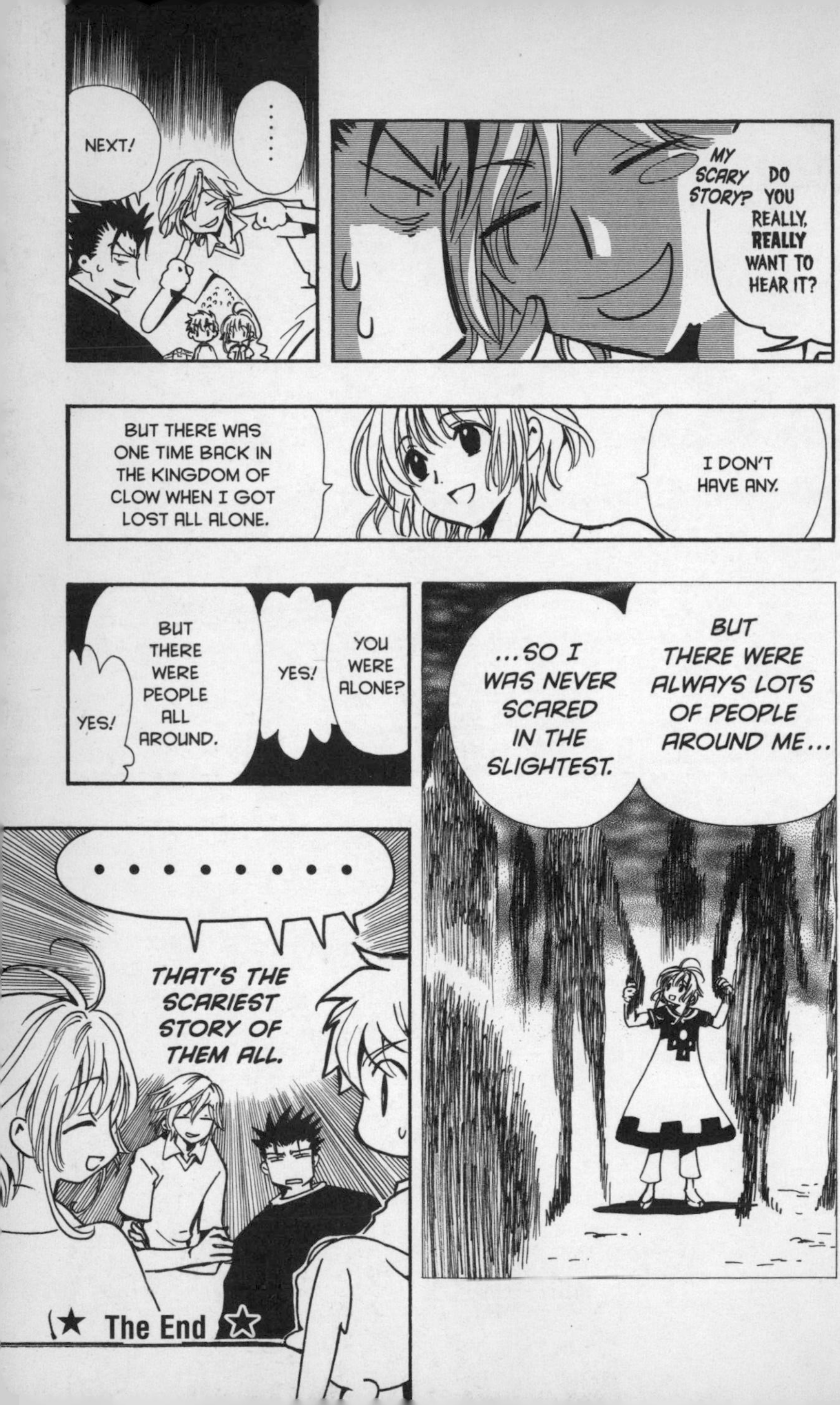
MY SCARY STORY? DO YOU REALLY, REALLY WANT TO HEAR IT?
......
NEXT!
I DON'T HAVE ANY.
BUT THERE WAS ONE TIME BACK IN THE KINGDOM OF CLOW WHEN I GOT LOST ALL ALONE.
BUT THERE WERE ALWAYS LOTS OF PEOPLE AROUND ME...
...SO I WAS NEVER SCARED IN THE SLIGHTEST.
YOU WERE ALONE?
YES!
BUT THERE WERE PEOPLE ALL AROUND.
YES!
....
THAT'S THE SCARIEST STORY OF THEM ALL.
★ The End ☆

About the Creators

CLAMP is a group of four women who have become the most popular manga artists in America—Ageha Ohkawa, Mokona, Satsuki Igarashi, and Tsubaki Nekoi. They started out as *doujinshi* (fan comics) creators, but their skill and craft brought them to the attention of publishers very quickly. Their first work from a major publisher was *RG Veda*, but their first mass success was with *Magic Knight Rayearth*. From there, they went on to write many series, including Cardcaptor Sakura and Chobits, two of the most popular manga in the United States. Like many Japanese manga artists, they prefer to avoid the spotlight, and little is known about them personally.

CLAMP is currently publishing three series in Japan: Tsubasa and xxxHOLiC with Kodansha and Gohou Drug with Kadokawa.

Translation Notes

Japanese is a tricky language for most Westerners, and translation is often more art than science. For your edification and reading pleasure, here are notes on some of the places where we could have gone in a different direction in our translation of the work, or where a Japanese cultural reference is used.

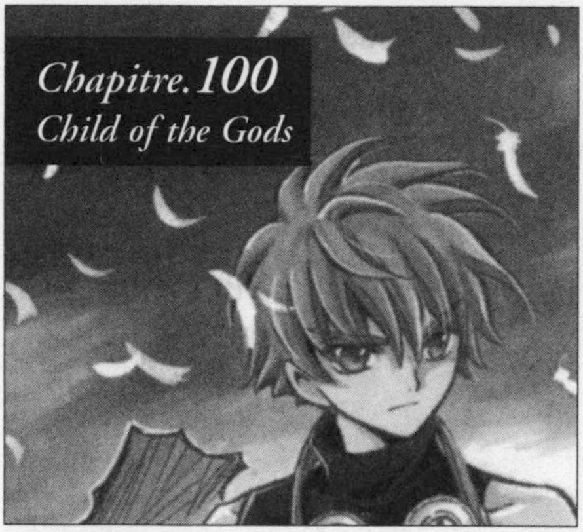
Chapitre.100
Child of the Gods

Child of the Gods, page 3
The kanji for god, *kami*, is the same kanji used for the first part of Kamui's name. The title of the chapter probably refers mainly to Kamui.

Game, page 6
What was used in Japanese was the *katakana* (the syllabary usually reserved for foreign words) symbol for "e" (pronounced eh). However readers of xxxHOLiC will recognize the same use of this symbol and the translation "game" from volume 5 of that series. If you don't follow xxxHOLiC, don't worry, it will be explained in future volumes of Tsubasa.

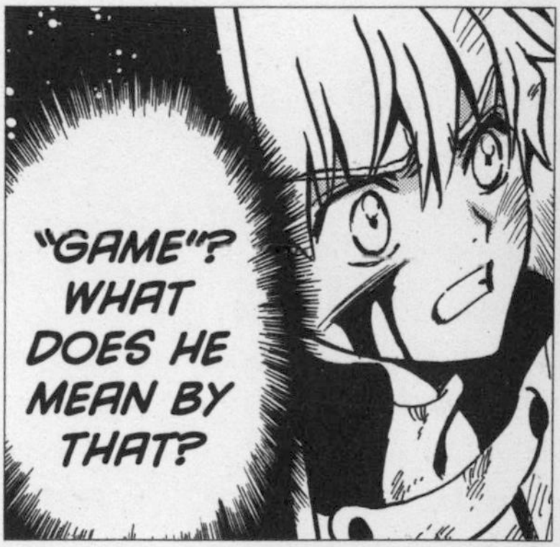
"GAME"? WHAT DOES HE MEAN BY THAT?

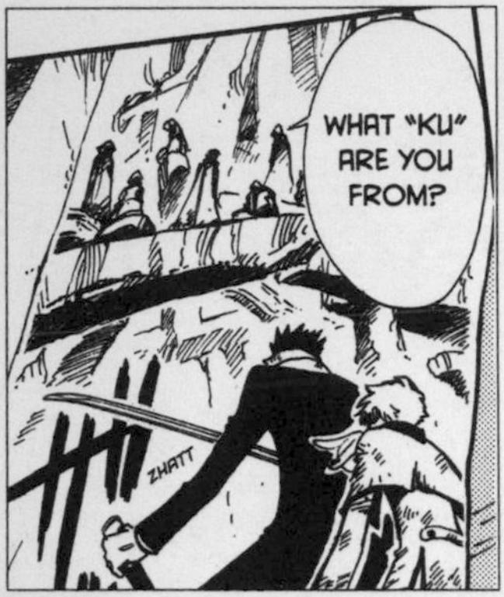
WHAT "KU" ARE YOU FROM?
ZHATT

Ku, page 9

Tokyo is divided into twenty-three wards or *ku* in Japanese. Examples include Shinjuku-ku, Shibuya-ku, Minato-ku, and Chiyoda-ku where the imperial palace stands. These should not be confused with downtown centers. Although the city centers of Shibuya and Shinjuku share the same name as their *ku*, other downtown centers such as Ueno (Taitô-ku) and the Ginza (Chûô-ku) reside in *ku* that are not named after them. The *ku* are much like the boroughs in New York City, and are used in addresses. Other big cities such as Osaka and Nagoya are also divided into *ku*.

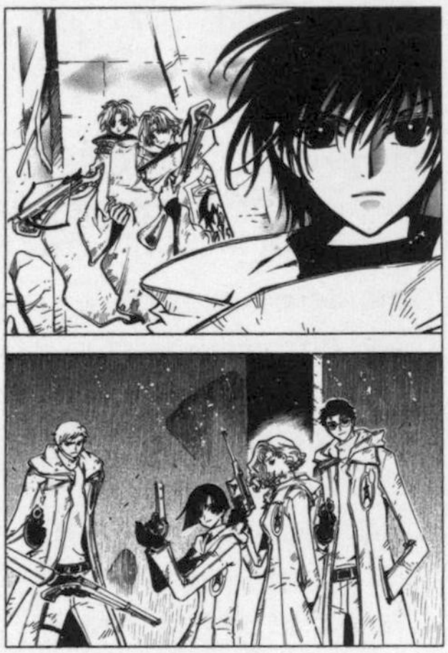

The two groups, page 32

CLAMP fans will recognize nearly all of the characters in these two panels. They are the Dragons of Heaven and Dragons of Earth from CLAMP's popular epic manga series X (X/1999). However fans will also notice that the teams that Kamui and Fûma are leading are reversed.

Tochô, page 64

Tochô is the Japanese name for the Tokyo Metropolitan Government Building (for more details, see the notes in Volume 14). The word is made up of the kanji *to* which means city, and *chô* which means government. This is where the nickname for the building, City Hall, comes from.

High-rise, Low-rise, page 120

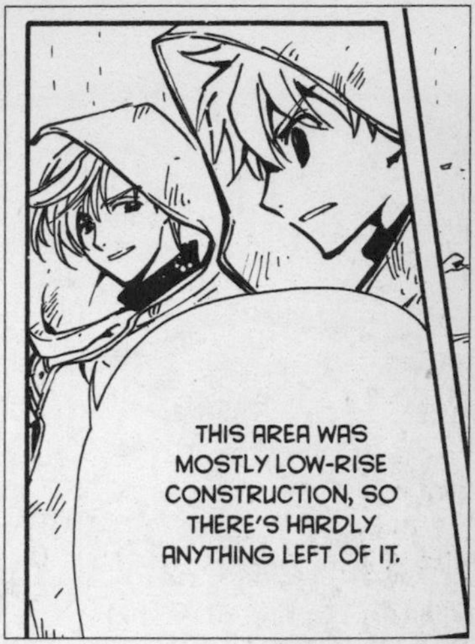
THIS AREA WAS MOSTLY LOW-RISE CONSTRUCTION, SO THERE'S HARDLY ANYTHING LEFT OF IT.

If one's opinion of Japan was formed only by central Tokyo, one might think that most of the buildings in Japan are around ten stories tall. But once one gets out of the city centers, the buildings return to a more normal two to four stories. The suburban landscape is peppered with taller apartment buildings and condos, but the rank and file are single-family homes that are usually two stories, and smaller apartment buildings that are usually two to four stories. (Buildings over four stories must install elevators.) These suburban areas are the low-rise districts that Yûto is referring to.

Xing-Huo, page 152

The pronunciation guide next to the kanji for Xing-Huo's name reads "shin-fo," but we know from the Tsubasa Character Guide that the alphabet spelling of Fei-Wang Reed's name follows the Pinyin system of spelling slightly modified to remove the diacritic marks (accents, etc.). The Pinyin system yields the spelling of this character's name (the kanji for star and fire) as Xing-Huo, and that pronunciation can lead to a Japanese pronunciation of "shin-fo." So until we see an official spelling that is different, we will use this spelling.

Ghost stories, page 176

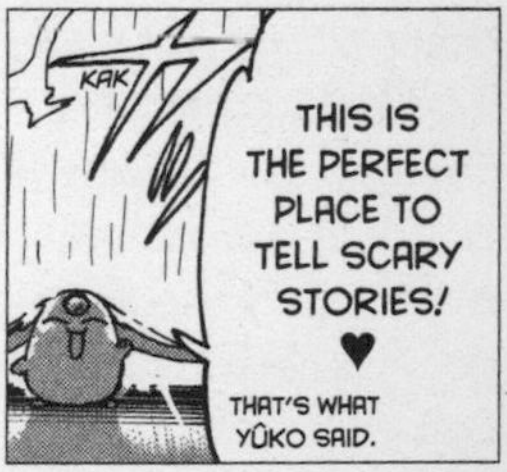
KAK
THIS IS THE PERFECT PLACE TO TELL SCARY STORIES! ♥
THAT'S WHAT YÛKO SAID.

In the Western tradition, sitting around a campfire and Halloween are the best times for ghost stories. In Japan, stormy nights spent indoors and the high-Summer festival of O-bon are the best time for ghost and other horror stories.

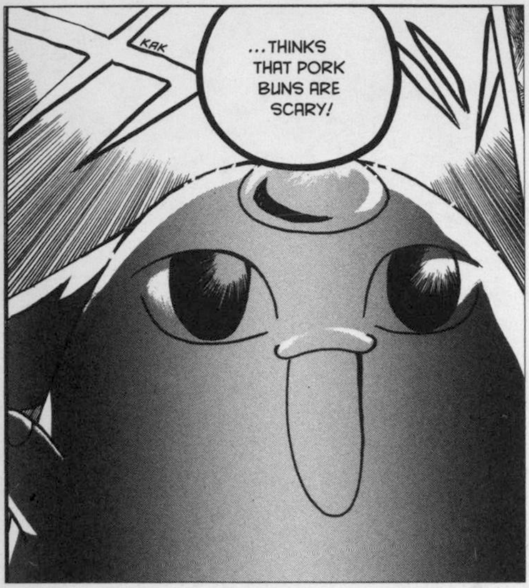
KAK
...THINKS THAT PORK BUNS ARE SCARY!

Pork buns, page 176

Fans of the Chinese dim sum menu are aware of the steamed white pork bun that Mokona resembles, but pork filling isn't the only thing that can fill the white buns. *Manjû*, as they are called in Japan, can have a variety of fillings from meat-based stuffing spiced with curry to very sweet red bean paste called *anko*. This translator has found none of them scary, but perhaps to a creature that looks like one . . .

Dango, page 177,

Dango are sticky dumplings made with rice flour that usually come in sets of three or four and are commonly sold on a wooden skewer. They can be flavored with sweet red beans (much like the anko-flavored *manju* in the note above), but there are plenty of variations including green-tea-flavored versions and the more tangy and spicy *dango*.

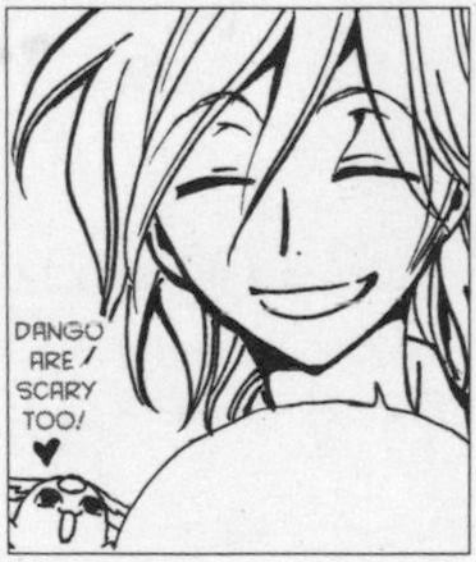
DANGO ARE SCARY TOO! ♥

TOMARE!

[STOP!]

You're going the wrong way!

Manga is a completely different type of reading experience.

To start at the *beginning*, go to the *end*!

That's right! Authentic manga is read the traditional Japanese way—from right to left. Exactly the *opposite* of how American books are read. It's easy to follow. Just go to the other end of the book, and read each page—and each panel—from right side to left side, starting at the top right. Now you're experiencing manga as it was meant to be.